MW00444194

The 50 Greatest Players in Indians History

Robert W. Cohen

BLUE RIVER PRESS

Indianapolis, Indiana

CONTENTS

ACKNOWLEDGMENTS

I would like to express my gratitude to the grandchildren of Leslie Jones, who, through the Trustees of the Boston Public Library, Print Department, supplied many of the photos included in this book.

I also wish to thank the Cleveland Indians, Troy R. Kinunen of MEARSonlineauctions.com, Kate of RMYauctions.com, Pristineauction. com, Clevelandmemory.org, George Kitrinos, Jerry Reuss, Keith Allison, and Alan Turkus, each of whom generously contributed to the photographic content of this work.

INTRODUCTION

The Indians Legacy

Originally founded in the state of Michigan in 1894, the team that eventually came to be known as the Cleveland Indians spent its formative years competing in the Western League as the Grand Rapids Rustlers. Retaining that moniker until 1900, when the franchise relocated to Cleveland and renamed itself the Lake Shores, the team continued to function as a minor league entity until 1901, when Ban Johnson changed the name of the Western League to the American League, which subsequently began competing against the more-established N.L. for major-league talent. Owned by wealthy tailor Jack Kilfoyl and coal magnate Charles Somers, who also owned a share of the Boston Americans, the franchise spent its first year in the big leagues competing as the Cleveland Bluebirds (in deference to the color of the players' uniforms), before adopting the nickname "Bronchos" prior to the start of the 1902 campaign. However, the moniker "Naps" soon became affixed to the team after Hall of Fame second baseman Napoleon Lajoie arrived in Cleveland midway through the 1902 season.

Spending their early years playing at League Park, located at the corner of East 66th Street and Lexington Avenue, Cleveland's A.L. entry experienced a moderate amount of success between 1901 and 1905, posting a winning record three times, but finishing higher than fourth in the eight-team junior circuit just once. After ranking among the league's stronger teams in both 1906 and 1907, the Naps nearly captured their first pennant in 1908, when, led by player-manager Lajoie and star hurler Addie Joss, they finished just one-half game behind the first-place Detroit Tigers. However, hard times followed, with Cleveland subsequently entering into a period of mediocrity that lasted nearly a decade. After Lajoie resigned as manager during the latter stages of the 1909 campaign, Joss died from tubercular meningitis a little over one year later. Lajoie continued to star in the field the next few seasons, during which time one of the game's truly great hitters, Shoeless Joe Jackson, joined him in the Cleveland lineup.

But, with little in the way of pitching, the Naps posted a winning record just twice between 1909 and 1915, as the club underwent numerous managerial changes, with Deacon McGuire, George Stovall, Harry Davis, and Joe Birmingham all serving as skipper at different times.

With the aging Lajoie dealt to the Philadelphia Athletics in January, 1915, Charles Somers, who assumed sole ownership of the club a few years earlier, asked the local baseball writers to come up with a new name for his team. Recalling a three-year period just prior to the turn of the century when the presence of a Native American named Louis Sockalexis on the roster of the Cleveland Spiders prompted that National League club to be dubbed the "Indians," the scribes ultimately chose the same moniker for Somers' team.

Unfortunately, changing names did little to improve the fortunes of the ball club, which, after finishing last in the league in 1914, advanced just one place in the standings the following year. With attendance falling off and Somers' business ventures failing, the Indians' owner found himself deep in debt, causing him to sell his best player, Joe Jackson, to the Chicago White Sox for the then-princely sum of $31,500 midway through the 1915 campaign. Shortly thereafter, Somers sold the team to a syndicate headed by Chicago railroad contractor James C. "Jack" Dunn.

The change in ownership proved to be extremely beneficial to the Indians, who acquired star center fielder Tris Speaker from the Boston Red Sox prior to the start of the 1916 season. That same year, the Indians obtained in separate deals a pair of minor league pitchers - Stan Coveleski and Jim Bagby - who helped fortify their starting rotation. Their roster strengthened, the Indians began in 1917 a successful seven-year run during which they posted a winning record each season, finishing second in the league three times, and capturing their first pennant in 1920, when, led by player-manager Speaker, they overcame the fatal beaning of star shortstop Ray Chapman by New York pitcher Carl Mays on August 16 to edge out the White Sox and Yankees for the A.L. flag. Cleveland then defeated the Brooklyn Robins 5-2 in a best-of-nine World Series that included three memorable "firsts", all of which occurred in Game 5. After Indians right-fielder Elmer Smith hit the first grand slam in Series history in the opening frame, 30-game winner Bagby increased Cleveland's lead with a fourth-inning homer that represented the first round-tripper by a pitcher in Series play. Then, in the top of the fifth inning, Indians second baseman Bill Wambsganss executed the first (and only) unassisted triple play in the history of the Fall Classic.

With Speaker continuing to serve as player-manager the next few seasons, the Indians remained in contention much of the time, earning close second-place finishes in both 1921 and 1926. During that period, Hall of Fame shortstop Joe Sewell, outfielder Charlie Jamieson, and first baseman George Burns, who captured league MVP honors in 1926, joined Speaker in the starting lineup. Meanwhile, right-handed hurler George Uhle emerged as the ace of the Cleveland pitching staff, twice leading the American League in victories. But, after Speaker joined the Washington Senators prior to the start of the 1927 campaign and a syndicate led by John Sherwin and Alva Bradley purchased the Indians from the Dunn estate later that year (Jack Dunn passed away in 1922), the team entered into another period of mediocrity, failing to contend for the A.L. flag in any of the next seven seasons, while posting a losing record on three separate occasions. Yet, in spite of the lack of success the Indians experienced during that time, center-fielder Earl Averill established himself as one of the league's finest all-around players, while Wes Ferrell and Mel Harder developed into two of the junior circuit's top hurlers.

Things began to look up shortly after Cleveland Municipal Stadium opened on July 31, 1932. Although the high costs of maintaining the enormous new stadium caused the Indians to avail themselves of League Park on a part-time basis for several more years, they eventually settled into their new home, adapting to the ball park's vast dimensions by building their team around strong pitching and outstanding defense. Flame-throwing right-hander Bob Feller arrived in Cleveland during the late 1930s and subsequently established himself as the league's dominant pitcher. Meanwhile, slugging first baseman Hal Trosky joined Earl Averill during the mid-1930s to give the Indians one of the most dynamic offensive tandems in all of baseball. And, over the course of the ensuing decade, shortstop Lou Boudreau, third baseman Ken Keltner, and outfielder Dale Mitchell all emerged as stars on offense, enabling the Indians to compile a winning record 10 times between 1934 and 1947, although they contended for the A.L. pennant just once during that time, finishing one game off the pace in 1940. Over the course of those 14 seasons, Hall of Fame pitcher Walter Johnson, former Tribe players Steve O'Neill and Roger Peckinpaugh, the acerbic Oscar Vitt, and star shortstop Lou Boudreau all took turns managing the team.

The colorful and innovative Bill Veeck ushered in perhaps the most successful period in Indians history when he led a syndicate that purchased the club on June 21, 1946. Moving the Indians into Municipal Stadium on a full-time basis in 1947, Veeck devised several innovative promotions that helped spark record attendance. An extremely astute baseball man who previously co-owned the American Association's Milwaukee Brewers, Veeck also improved the Indians on the playing field by signing some of the Negro Leagues' best players, including slugging outfielder Larry Doby, who became the first African-American player to perform for an American League team when he arrived in Cleveland in 1947. Bob Lemon joined Bob Feller in the starting rotation one year later, giving the Tribe the league's most formidable pitching duo, which combined with Doby, Ken Keltner, star second baseman Joe Gordon, and A.L. MVP Lou Boudreau to lead the Indians to their first pennant in 28 years - one they captured with a victory over the Boston Red Sox in a one-game playoff at Fenway Park. The Indians subsequently claimed their second world championship when they defeated the Boston Braves in six games in the 1948 World Series.

Although financial difficulties forced Veeck to sell the team to a syndicate headed by insurance magnate Ellis Ryan shortly thereafter, the Indians continued to perform at an elite level for eight more years, finishing second to the Yankees five times between 1949 and 1956, and winning the pennant again in 1954, when they posted a franchise-record 111 victories. The 1954 campaign ended on a sour note, though, with the Indians suffering an embarrassing four-game sweep at the hands of the underdog New York Giants in the Fall Classic. Standout performers during this period of excellence included Doby, slugging first baseman Luke Easter, second baseman Bobby Avila, third baseman and 1953 A.L. MVP Al Rosen, and pitchers Feller, Lemon, Mike Garcia, Early Wynn, and the ill-fated Herb Score, who appeared headed for greatness before being struck by a line drive off the bat of Yankee third baseman Gil McDougald early in 1957.

While ownership of the Indians passed from Bill Veeck to Ellis Ryan, to Myron Wilson, and, finally, to William Daley between 1949 and 1956, former Detroit Tigers great Hank Greenberg continued to serve as general manager - a position he maintained until 1957. While running the team, Greenberg replaced Lou Boudreau as manager with Al Lopez, who led the Tribe to one pennant and five second-place finishes in his six years at the helm, before surrendering his post following the conclusion of the 1956 campaign.

Unfortunately, the simultaneous departures of Greenberg and Lopez proved to be disastrous for the Indians, who subsequently entered into an extended period of mediocrity brought about by numerous changes in ownership, front office instability, and poor decision-making. The Tribe underwent six different ownership changes between 1956 and 1986, with some of the more notable individuals holding shares in the team during that time being longtime general manager Gabe Paul, Vernon Stouffer, of the Stouffer's frozen-food empire, Nick Meliti, who also owned the Cleveland Cavaliers and Cleveland Barons, trucking magnate Steve O'Neill, and real estate magnates Richard and David Jacobs, who purchased the ball club in 1986. Meanwhile, "Trader" Frank Lane, who served as the team's general manager from 1958 to 1961, made 60 separate deals over a two-year period at one point, trading away such young and talented players as Roger Maris and Rocky Colavito during his watch. More ill-advised moves followed after Lane left his post, with future stars Tommy John, Tommie Agee, Graig Nettles, Dennis Eckersley, Buddy Bell, and Chris Chambliss all being dealt away for lesser players during the 1960s and 1970s. To make matters worse, 16 different men managed the team between 1957 and 1986, with Birdie Tebbetts, Joe Adcock, Alvin Dark, Ken Aspromonte, Jeff Torborg, and Frank Robinson, who became the first black manager in Major League history when he assumed control of the club in 1975, being among those who called the signals from the Indians dugout. In the end, the instability surrounding the Indians caused them to compile a losing record in 21 of those 30 seasons, with only their 1959 and 1968 teams finishing higher than fourth in the standings. Yet, even in mediocrity, the Tribe remained competitive throughout much of the period, with outstanding players such as Rocky Colavito, Sam McDowell, Luis Tiant, Gaylord Perry, and Joe Carter gracing their roster at different times.

The Indians initially experienced very little success under new owners Richard and David Jacobs, finishing well below the .500-mark seven straight times between 1987 and 1993, including losing more than 100 games twice, en route to annually finishing at, or near, the bottom of the A.L. East. However, things began to turn around shortly after the Jacobs brothers hired former Tribe Farm Director Hank Peters to rebuild the organization. Peters, in turn, groomed John Hart to succeed him as General Manager and brought in Dan O'Dowd to run the farm system, which rapidly developed into one of the best in baseball. Cleveland's new management team also acquired top prospects Sandy Alomar Jr. and Carlos

Baerga from San Diego for outfielder Joe Carter prior to the start of the 1990 season and later fleeced the Houston Astros of speedy, young center-fielder Kenny Lofton.

With the aforementioned acquisitions and the additions of hard-hitting outfielder Albert Belle and pitcher Charles Nagy from their own minor league system, the Indians emerged as a force-to-be reckoned with by the time the majors adopted a new three-division alignment in each league in 1994 - the same year the Tribe moved into their new state-of-the-art ballpark, Jacobs Field (later re-named Progressive Field). Leaving anti-quated Municipal Stadium, which had served as their primary home for more than six decades, a young and exciting Indians team began drawing fans out to the stadium in droves, setting all kinds of attendance records as they established themselves as the dominant team in the newly-formed A.L. Central. After compiling a record of 66-47 under third-year manager Mike Hargrove in the strike-shortened 1994 campaign, the Indians cap-tured five consecutive division titles, posting 100 victories against only 44 losses in 1995, when they set a MLB record by winning their division by 30 games. They also claimed their first pennant in 41 years that season, sweeping Boston in the ALDS and disposing of Seattle in six games in the ALCS, before losing the World Series to Atlanta in six games. The Tribe returned to the Fall Classic two years later, only to suffer a heart-breaking seven-game defeat at the hands of the Florida Marlins. And, even though the Indians came up short in the 1999 playoffs, losing to the Red Sox in five games in the Division Series, they set a club record by scoring 1,009 runs during the regular season. Standout players for the Tribe during this period of excellence included Jim Thome, Manny Ramirez, David Justice, Omar Vizquel, Roberto Alomar, and Sandy Alomar Jr.

The Jacobs Era of Indians baseball came to an end in February 2000, when Lawrence J. Dolan and family trusts acquired all outstanding stock in the team. After Dolan replaced Hargrove as manager with hitting coach Charlie Manuel prior to the start of the 2000 campaign, the Indians re-mained contenders for two more years, barely missing the playoffs in Manuel's first year at the helm, before capturing their sixth division title in seven seasons in 2001. But, after Seattle defeated the Indians in five games in the ALDS, Dolan relieved John Hart of his duties as General Manager and replaced him with Mark Shapiro, who had spent the previous decade working his way up from player development director to assistant GM. When the Indians stumbled to a 74-88 record in 2002, Shapiro dismissed Manuel and hired Eric Wedge, who spent the previous five seasons managing in the Cleveland farm system. Although the Indians struggled their first two seasons under Wedge, they returned to the playoffs in 2007 with him calling the signals from the dugout, capturing their seventh division title, before eventually falling to the Boston Red Sox in seven games in the ALCS. However, the Tribe failed to post a winning record in any of the next five seasons, costing Wedge and his successor, Manny Acta, their jobs.

In an effort to return the Indians to prominence, Shapiro, who assumed the role of team president in 2011, and general manager Chris Antonetti replaced Acta with Terry Francona prior to the start of the 2013 campaign. The hiring of Francona, who previously won two World Series as manager of the Boston Red Sox, has since proven to be a stroke of genius. After leading the Indians into the playoffs as a wild card his first year at the helm, Francona guided them to within one victory of their first world championship in nearly 70 years in 2016, when they lost the World Series to Chicago in seven games after earlier taking a 3-1 series lead over the Cubs. The Indians once again proved to be one of the best teams in baseball in 2017, setting a new A.L. record at one point during the season by winning 22 consecutive games, en route to posting a league-best 102 victories over the course of the campaign. However, they subsequently suffered a five-game defeat at the hands of the New York Yankees in the ALDS, extending to 79 years their world championship drought.

Nevertheless, with an outstanding nucleus of players that includes young stars Francisco Lindor and Jose Ramirez, solid veterans Jason Kipnis, Michael Brantley, and Carlos Santana, ace relievers Cody Allen and Andrew Miller, and the American League's best pitcher, Corey Kluber, the Indians appear to have a bright future ahead of them. Their next World Series appearance will be their seventh, and their next A.L. Central title will be their 10th., which would place them well ahead of any other team in the division (the Minnesota Twins rank second, with six division championships).

Although the Indians have proven to be one of the American League's more enigmatic teams through the years, they have featured many exceptional players, several of whom have attained notable individual honors during their time in Cleveland. The franchise boasts three MVP winners and five Cy Young Award winners. The Indians have also featured seven home run champions, seven batting champions, and 12 RBI leaders. Tribe hurlers have also distinguished themselves, with a member of the Indians pitching staff leading the league in ERA 17 times and strikeouts 20 times. Meanwhile, 24 members of the Baseball Hall of Fame spent at least one full season playing for the Indians, 15 of whom had several of their finest seasons as a member of the team. And six Indians players have had their numbers retired, with Earl Averill (#3), Lou Boudreau (#5), Larry Doby (#14), Mel Harder (#18), Bob Feller (#19), and Bob Lemon (#21) being so honored.

FACTORS USED TO DETERMINE RANKINGS

It should come as no surprise that selecting the 50 greatest players ever to perform for a team with the rich history of the Indians presented a difficult and daunting task. Even after I narrowed the field down to a mere 50 men, I found myself faced with the challenge of ranking the elite players that remained. Certainly, the names of Bob Feller, Tris Speaker, Napoleon Lajoie, Earl Averill, Lou Boudreau, Bob Lemon, and Jim Thome would appear at, or near, the top of virtually everyone's list, although the order might vary somewhat from one person to the next. Several other outstanding performers have gained general recognition through the years as being among the greatest players ever to wear an Indians uniform. Mel Harder, Larry Doby, Kenny Lofton, and Omar Vizquel head the list of other Indians icons. But, how does one differentiate between the all-around brilliance of Tris Speaker and the pitching greatness of Bob Feller; or the exceptional slugging of Jim Thome and the outstanding defensive skills displayed by Omar Vizquel? After initially deciding who to include on my list, I then needed to determine what criteria to use when formulating my final rankings.

The first thing I decided to examine was the level of dominance a player attained during his time in Cleveland. How often did he lead the American League in some major offensive or pitching statistical category? How did he fare in the annual MVP and/or Cy Young voting? How many times did he make the All-Star Team?

I also needed to weigh the level of statistical compilation a player achieved while wearing an Indians uniform. Where does a batter rank in team annals in the major offensive categories? How high on the all-time list of Indian hurlers does a pitcher rank in wins, ERA, complete games, innings pitched, shutouts, and saves? Of course, I also needed to consider the era in which the player performed when evaluating his overall numbers. For example, modern-day starting pitchers such as C.C. Sabathia and Corey Kluber are not likely to throw nearly as many complete games or shutouts as either Addie Joss or Bob Feller, who anchored the Indians' starting rotation at different times during the first half of the twentieth century. Meanwhile, Hal Trosky had a distinct advantage over Andre Thornton in that he competed during an era far more conducive to posting huge offensive numbers. And *Dead Ball Era* stars such as Napoleon Lajoie and Shoeless Joe Jackson were not likely to hit nearly as many home runs as the players who performed for the team after the Major Leagues began using a livelier ball.

Other important factors I needed to consider were the overall contributions a player made to the success of the team, the degree to which he improved the fortunes of the ball club during his time in Cleveland, and the manner in which he impacted the team, both on and off the field. While the number of postseason appearances the Indians made during a particular player's years with the ball club certainly entered into the equation, I chose not to deny a top performer his rightful place on the list if his years in Cleveland happened to coincide with a lack of overall success by the team. As a result, the names of players such as Sam McDowell and Joe Carter will appear in these rankings.

One other thing I wish to mention is that I only considered a player's performance while playing for the Indians when formulating my rankings. That being the case, the names of Hall of Fame players such as Gaylord Perry and Roberto Alomar, both of whom had most of their finest seasons while playing for other teams, may appear lower on this list than one might expect.

Having established the guidelines to be used throughout this book, we are ready to take a look at the 50 greatest players in Indians history, starting with number one and working our way down to number 50.

The 50 Greatest Players in Indians History

Courtesy of the Leslie Jones Collection at the Boston Public Library

Despite missing almost four full seasons while serving his country during World War II, Bob Feller compiled more wins, strikeouts, innings pitched, and complete games than any other pitcher in franchise history

1

BOB FELLER
1936 – 1941, 1945 – 1956

Bob Feller received stiff competition from Tris Speaker and Napoleon Lajoie for the number one spot in these rankings, with Lajoie proving to be such a dominant figure during his time in Cleveland that the team actually renamed itself in his honor. Meanwhile, Speaker established himself as the finest all-around player in franchise history over the course of his 11 seasons with the Indians, making him an equally strong contender for the top spot. However, while both Lajoie and Speaker spent a significant amount of time playing for other teams, Feller spent his entire career with the Indians, tipping the scales ever so slightly in his favor. After joining the Tribe at only 17 years of age in 1936, Feller remained in Cleveland until 1956, compiling more wins and strikeouts, throwing more complete games, and tossing more innings during that time than anyone else in franchise history, despite missing almost four full seasons at the height of his career to join the war effort. Generally considered to be the greatest pitcher of his era, Feller used his blinding fastball and superb curveball to dominate American League hitters for more than a decade, tossing three no-hitters and a record 12 one-hitters over the course of 18 big-league seasons. In all, the flame-throwing right-hander posted at least 20 victories six times, recorded more than 300 strikeouts once, and threw more than 20 complete games six times, leading all AL hurlers in each of those categories on multiple occasions, with his fabulous pitching earning him eight All-Star selections, four top-five finishes in the AL MVP voting, one *Sporting News* MLB Player of the Year nomination, and a number 36 ranking on that same publication's 1999 list of Baseball's 100 Greatest Players.

Born in the small mid-western town of Van Meter, Iowa on November 3, 1918, Robert William Andrew Feller grew up on a farm, where he developed the arm strength for which he later became so well known by milking cows, picking corn, and baling hay. After being taught how to pitch by his father on a homemade ballfield, Feller starred on the mound for the Van Meter High School baseball team, prompting Cleveland Indians scout Cy Slapnicka to sign him to a contract for $1 and an autographed baseball. In discussing the impression Feller made on him at the time, Slapnicka later said, "This was a kid pitcher I had to get. I knew he was something special. His fastball was fast and fuzzy; it didn't go in a straight line; it would wiggle and shoot around. I didn't know then that he was smart and had the heart of a lion, but I knew that I was looking at an arm the likes of which you see only once in a lifetime."

Joining the Indians in the middle of the 1936 campaign without ever having spent a day in the minor leagues, the 17-year-old Feller struck out 15 St. Louis Browns in his first major-league start, before setting a new AL record three weeks later by fanning 17 Philadelphia batters during a 5-2 win over the Athletics. Finishing his rookie season with a record of 5-3, an ERA of 3.34, and 76 strikeouts in only 62 innings of work, Feller subsequently returned to Iowa for his senior year of high school, before rejoining the Indians the following spring.

After spending most of 1937 spring training attempting to refine his pitching fundamentals and working on his curveball and changeup, Feller gradually earned a regular spot in Cleveland's starting rotation, although he very much remained a work in progress. Even though his blazing fastball—which eventually became known as "the Van Meter heater"— helped Feller record 150 strikeouts in 148 2/3 innings, he struggled terribly with his control, issuing a total of 106 bases on balls. Nevertheless, Feller posted solid overall numbers, finishing his first full season with a record of 9-7 and an ERA of 3.39.

Still battling control problems in 1938, Feller led all AL hurlers with 208 walks. However, he also began a string of four straight seasons in which he topped the circuit in strikeouts, fanning a total of 240 batters. Feller also compiled a record of 17-11 and finished third in the league with 20 complete games and 277 2/3 innings pitched, earning in the process All-Star honors for the first of four consecutive times. Although Feller occasionally experienced lapses in control in subsequent seasons as well, leading all AL hurlers in bases on balls allowed in two of the next three seasons, he gradually gained better command of his pitches, enabling him to emerge as baseball's dominant pitcher. Here are the numbers he compiled from 1939 to 1941

1939: **24**-9, 2.85 ERA, 1.244 WHIP, **246** Strikeouts, 4 Shutouts, **24** CG, **296.2** IP*

1940: **27**-11, **2.61** ERA, **1.133** WHIP, **261** Strikeouts, **4** Shutouts, **31** CG, **320.1** IP

1941: **25**-13, 3.15 ERA, 1.394 WHIP, **260** Strikeouts, **6** Shutouts, 28 CG, **343.0** IP

* Please note that any numbers printed in bold throughout this book signify that the player led the American League in that particular statistical category that year.

In addition to leading the league in wins, strikeouts, and innings pitched all three years, Feller ranked among the league leaders in each of the other four categories each season, topping the circuit in complete games and shutouts twice, and in ERA and WHIP once. Particularly dominant in 1940, Feller won the pitcher's version of the Triple Crown, leading all AL hurlers in every major statistical category, en route to earning Major League Player of the Year honors and a runner-up finish to Detroit's Hank Greenberg in the league MVP voting. He also finished third in the balloting the other two years. Feller's dominance on the mound prompted Washington Senators manager Bucky Harris to tell his players to employ the following strategy when facing the six-foot, 185-pound flame-thrower: "Go on up there and hit what you see. If you can't see it, come on back."

Chicago White Sox Hall of Fame pitcher Ted Lyons said of his frequent foe, "It wasn't until you hit against him that you knew how fast he really was, until you saw with your own eyes that ball jumping at you."

Expressing his admiration for Feller during his epic season of 1941, when he hit safely in a record 56 consecutive games, Joe DiMaggio stated, "I don't think anyone is ever going to throw a ball faster than he does. And his curveball isn't human."

As DiMaggio suggested, even though "Rapid Robert" became known mostly for his blazing fastball, he also had an exceptional curve, with Ted Williams, who called Feller "the fastest and best pitcher I ever saw during my career" rating his curveball as a more difficult pitch to hit.

At the peak of his powers, Feller put aside his 3-C draft deferment status and became the first major league player to enlist in the armed forces, joining the United States Navy on December 8, 1941, one day after the Japanese attacked Pearl Harbor. He spent the next four years fighting the enemy overseas, serving as Gun Captain aboard the USS Alabama. Despite being decorated with five campaign ribbons and eight battle stars,

Feller later rejected the notion that those honors made him a hero, saying: "'I'm no hero. Heroes don't come back. Survivors return home. Heroes never come home. If anyone thinks I'm a hero, I'm not." And, even though Feller gave up nearly four full seasons of baseball in the prime of his career, he never expressed a single regret for doing so, stating, "I'm proud of that decision to enlist. It was important to serve your country. I didn't worry about losing my baseball career. We needed to win the war. I wanted to do my part."

Returning to the Indians during the latter stages of the 1945 campaign, Feller showed very little rust after his four-year layoff, compiling a record of 5-3 and an ERA of 2.50 in his nine starts, while tossing seven complete games and striking out 59 batters in 72 innings of work. He followed that up with arguably his greatest season in 1946, ranking among the league leaders with an ERA of 2.18 and a WHIP of 1.158, while topping the circuit with 26 wins, 10 shutouts, 348 strikeouts, 36 complete games, and 371⅓ innings pitched. Feller again performed extremely well in 1947, finishing the year with a record of 20-11, an ERA of 2.68, 20 complete games, and a league-leading five shutouts, 196 strikeouts, 299 innings pitched, and WHIP of 1.194, although he injured his back during a game against the Athletics, causing him to lose much of the velocity on his fastball for the remainder of his career.

Feller finally got an opportunity to pitch in the World Series in 1948 after he helped the Indians capture their first pennant in 28 years by posting 19 victories, throwing 18 complete games and 280⅓ innings, and leading the league with 164 strikeouts. Although he didn't fare particularly well in the Fall Classic, losing both his starts while compiling an ERA of 5.02, he turned in a strong outing in Game One, allowing just one run and two hits over eight innings, in dropping a 1-0 decision to Boston Braves ace right-hander Johnny Sain.

No longer in possession of his once-blazing fastball, Feller spent the next few seasons relying primarily on guile, improved control, and his superb breaking ball to remain one of the league's better pitchers. After posting 15 and 16 victories in 1949 and 1950, respectively, Feller had his last big year in 1951, when he compiled a record of 22-8 that gave him the most wins and highest winning percentage (.733) of any pitcher in the league. Although he struck out only 111 batters, the 32-year-old right-hander also posted a very respectable 3.50 earned run average and completed 16 of his 32 starts, en route to earning a fifth-place finish in the

AL MVP voting and recognition as *The Sporting News* American League Pitcher of the Year.

Feller never again came close to winning 20 games in his five remaining seasons, compiling an overall record of just 36-31 during that time. But, even though he took a backseat to fellow Indians starters Bob Lemon, Early Wynn, and Mike Garcia his last few years in Cleveland, Feller proved to be a key contributor to the Indians' 1954 pennant-winning ball club, posting a record of 13-3 and an ERA of 3.09, and completing nine of his 19 starts. After spending most of the 1956 season working out of the Tribe bullpen, Feller announced his retirement following the conclusion of the campaign, ending his career with a record of 266-162, an ERA of 3.25, a WHIP of 1.316, 44 shutouts, 22 saves, 279 complete games, and 2,581 strikeouts in 3,827 innings of work.

The Indians subsequently did not wait long to honor Feller, retiring his number 19 jersey in 1957, five years before the members of the BBWAA elected him to the Hall of Fame the first time his name appeared on the ballot. The Indians again paid tribute to Feller when they opened their downtown stadium in 1994, immortalizing the greatest pitcher in franchise history with a statue that depicts him in the middle of his patented windmill windup, rearing back to fire his blazing fastball.

Feller continued to live in Cleveland long after he retired, eventually returning to the Indians as a spring training instructor, while also serving in the team's public relations office. Remaining feisty and extremely opinionated well into his eighties, Feller frequently voiced his displeasure over the use of performance-enhancing drugs in baseball. He also spoke out against the possibility of Pete Rose ever being inducted into the Hall of Fame, as well as the growing inability of starting pitchers to last beyond the seventh inning.

Bob Feller, a true American institution, remained the oldest living member of the Baseball Hall of Fame until he succumbed to leukemia at 92 years of age on December 15, 2010. Following his passing, Indians President Mark Shapiro issued a statement that said, "Bob was that rare man whose legend and feats were matched by his intellect, strength and substance. He was inspirational as a competitor, and even more so as a man. I was privileged to have known him, and each time I visited with him, he reinforced my passion for baseball and my appreciation of the Indians' heritage."

Meanwhile, Indians broadcaster Mike Hegan, whose father, Jim, spent much of his career serving as Feller's primary catcher in Cleveland, suggested, "The Indians of the forties and fifties were the face of the city of Cleveland, and Bob was the face of the Indians. But, Bob transcended more than that era. In this day of free agency and switching teams, Bob Feller remained loyal to the city and the team for over seventy years. You will likely not see that kind of mutual loyalty and admiration ever again."

Career Highlights:

Best Season: Feller performed magnificently for the Indians from 1939 to 1941, compiling an overall record of 76-33 during that time, while leading the league in wins, strikeouts, and innings pitched all three years. Particularly effective in 1940, Feller led all AL hurlers in virtually every major statistical category, with his league-leading 27 victories, 2.61 ERA, and 261 strikeouts winning him the pitcher's Triple Crown and earning him *Sporting News* Major League Player of the Year honors. Nevertheless, the 1946 campaign would have to be considered the most dominant of Feller's career. Excelling on the mound in his first full season back after spending nearly four years in the military, Feller compiled an ERA of 2.18, posted a WHIP of 1.158, and led all AL hurlers with 26 wins, 348 strikeouts, 10 shutouts, 36 complete games, and 371⅓ innings pitched, with his 348 strikeouts nearly eclipsing Rube Waddell's then-league record of 349 strikeouts previously set in 1904. Feller's brilliant pitching earned him a sixth-place finish in the AL MVP voting and his fourth *Sporting News* All-Star selection.

Memorable Moments/Greatest Performances: Feller made his first major-league start a memorable one, allowing six hits and recording 15 strikeouts during a 4-1 win over the St. Louis Browns on August 23, 1936.

Although Feller walked nine batters during the contest, he proved to be equally dominant some three weeks later, when he surrendered just two hits and set a new AL record by striking out 17 Philadelphia batters during a 5-2 victory over the Athletics on September 13, 1936.

Feller nearly equaled his own mark on August 25, 1937, when he recorded 16 strikeouts and yielded only four hits during an 8-1 win over the Boston Red Sox.

Although he ended up losing the game by a score of 4-1, Feller established a new major-league record on October 2, 1938, when he struck out 18 Detroit batters, fanning Tigers center-fielder Chet Laabs five times.

Feller threw one of his 12 career one-hitters on May 25, 1939, when he yielded five walks and just a second-inning single to Hall of Fame second baseman Bobby Doerr, in shutting out the Red Sox by a score of 11-0. Feller also recorded 10 strikeouts during the game.

Feller tossed another one-hitter on July 12, 1940, when he struck out 13 batters, issued two walks, and surrendered only an eighth-inning lead-off single to first baseman Dick Siebert during a 1-0 win over the Philadelphia Athletics.

Feller recorded seven strikeouts and allowed only two men to reach base during a 5-0 shutout of the Athletics on September 15, 1940, yielding just an eighth-inning single to Dick Siebert and a ninth-inning single to catcher Frankie Hayes.

Feller surrendered just four walks and a fifth-inning single by third baseman Jimmy Outlaw during a 2-0, one-hit shutout of the Detroit Tigers on September 19, 1945.

Feller recorded 14 strikeouts and allowed just five hits during a 3-0 shutout of the Washington Senators on May 17, 1946.

Feller threw 35 consecutive scoreless innings from July 31 to August 13, 1946, with the highlight of his streak being a 5-0, one-hit shutout of the Chicago White Sox on August 8, during which he yielded just four walks and a seventh-inning single to catcher Frankie Hayes.

Feller tossed another one-hitter on April 22, 1947, surrendering just one walk and a seventh-inning single by right-fielder Al Zarilla during a 5-0 shutout of the St. Louis Browns. Feller also recorded 10 strikeouts during the contest.

Feller again dominated the St. Louis lineup on April 20, 1948, yielding just two hits and two walks during a 4-0 shutout of the Browns.

Feller turned in a similarly impressive performance against Philadelphia on June 18, 1950, allowing only two hits and two walks during a 7-0 shutout of the Athletics.

Feller surrendered just one walk and a pair of harmless singles during a 16-0 rout of the Washington Senators on May 24, 1951.

Feller allowed only two men to reach base during a 6-0 shutout of the Athletics on July 17, 1954, yielding just a pair of singles to Philadelphia first baseman Don Bollweg.

Feller turned in the last dominant pitching performance of his career on May 1, 1955, when he surrendered just one walk and a seventh-inning single to center field by Boston catcher Sammy White, in shutting out the Red Sox by a score of 2-0.

The author of three no-hitters, Feller accomplished the feat for the first time on April 16, 1940, when he recorded eight strikeouts and issued five walks during a 1-0 win over the White Sox on Opening Day.

Feller tossed his second no-hitter on April 30, 1946, when he struck out 11 batters and issued five bases on balls, in defeating the Yankees by a score of 1-0.

Feller threw his final no-hitter on July 1, 1951, when he recorded five strikeouts, walked three batters, and allowed one unearned run during a 2-1 victory over the Detroit Tigers.

Notable Achievements:

- Won at least 20 games six times, topping 25 victories on three occasions.
- Posted winning percentage in excess of .700 four times, topping the .800-mark once.
- Compiled ERA below 3.00 five times, posting mark under 2.50 once (2.18 in 1946).
- Struck out more than 200 batters five times, recording more than 300 strikeouts once (348 in 1946).
- Threw 10 shutouts in 1946.
- Threw more than 300 innings three times, tossing more than 250 innings four other times.
- Tossed more than 20 complete games six times, completing more than 30 of his starts twice.
- Led AL pitchers in: wins six times, winning percentage once, ERA once, WHIP twice, strikeouts seven times, shutouts four times, innings pitched five times, complete games three times, and starts five times.

- Finished second in AL in: winning percentage once, ERA once, shutouts three times, complete games once, and innings pitched once.
- Holds Indians single-season records for most: strikeouts (348 in 1946), shutouts (10 in 1946), complete games (36 in 1946), and innings pitched (371⅓ in 1946).
- Holds Indians career records for most: wins (266), strikeouts (2,581), complete games (279), innings pitched (3,827), and games started (484).
- Ranks among Indians career leaders in: winning percentage (10th), shutouts (2nd), and pitching appearances (2nd).
- Threw three no-hitters (vs. Chicago White Sox on April 16, 1940, vs. New York Yankees on April 30, 1946, vs. Detroit Tigers on July 1, 1951).
- Recorded 18 strikeouts vs. Detroit Tigers on October 2, 1938.
- Recorded 17 strikeouts vs. Philadelphia Athletics on September 13, 1936.
- 1940 AL Pitching Triple Crown winner.
- Finished in top five of AL MVP voting four times, placing second once and third twice.
- 1940 *Sporting News* Major League Player of the Year.
- 1951 *Sporting News* AL Pitcher of the Year.
- Five-time *Sporting News* All-Star selection (1939, 1940, 1941, 1946, and 1947).
- Eight-time AL All-Star (1938, 1939, 1940, 1941, 1946, 1947, 1948, and 1950).
- Two-time AL champion (1948 and 1954).
- 1948 world champion.
- Number 36 on *The Sporting News'* 1999 list of Baseball's 100 Greatest Players.
- Elected to Baseball Hall of Fame by members of BBWAA in 1962.

2

TRIS SPEAKER

1916 – 1926

Already an established star by the time he arrived in Cleveland in 1916, Tris Speaker spent the previous several seasons patrolling center field at Fenway Park, during which time he became known for his exceptional all-around play. En route to leading the Red Sox to two pennants and a pair of world championships in his seven full seasons in Boston, Speaker batted well over .300 each year, stole more than 30 bases five times, and led all AL outfielders in putouts five times, assists three times, and double plays on four separate occasions, earning in the process one league MVP award and two other top 10 finishes in the voting. Picking up right where he left off after joining the Indians, Speaker batted over .350 in seven of his 11 seasons with the Tribe, knocked in more than 100 runs twice, scored more than 100 runs four times, topped 200 hits three times, and led the American League in doubles on six separate occasions, en route to compiling more two-baggers than anyone else in Major League history. Meanwhile, Speaker continued to perform brilliantly in center field for the Indians, eventually gaining general recognition as arguably the finest defensive outfielder ever to play the game by setting the AL record for most career outfield putouts (6,706) and Major League marks for most career outfield assists (449) and double plays (143).

Born in Hubbard, Texas on April 4, 1888, Tristram E. Speaker suffered numerous setbacks as a youth that might have derailed the career of a less determined man. After fracturing his right arm in a fall from a horse, the right-handed Speaker taught himself to throw and bat left-handed, which he continued to do throughout his baseball career. A few years later, while playing his only year of college ball for Fort Worth Polytechnic Institute, the 17-year-old Speaker severely injured his left arm in a football accident. Choosing to ignore the advice of surgeons, who initially recommended amputation, Speaker eventually made a full recovery, enabling him to pursue his dream of playing Major League baseball.

Speaker got his start in professional ball one year later, spending the 1906 campaign with the Cleburne Railroaders of the Texas League, for whom he batted .318, prompting the Boston Red Sox to purchase his contract for $800. After spending most of the next two seasons in the minors, Speaker broke into Boston's starting lineup in 1909, batting .309, driving in 77 runs, scoring 73 times, stealing 35 bases, and leading all AL outfielders with 35 assists and 12 double plays. He subsequently increased his offensive production in each of the next two seasons, before emerging as one of the game's truly great players in 1912, when he earned league MVP honors by batting .383, knocking in 90 runs, scoring 136 times, accumulating 222 hits, stealing 52 bases, and topping the circuit with 10 homers, 53 doubles, and a .464 on-base percentage. Speaker followed that up with two more exceptional years, batting .363, scoring 94 runs, stealing 46 bases, and amassing a career-high 22 triples in 1913, before hitting .338 and leading the league with 193 hits, 46 doubles, and 287 total bases in 1914.

Yet, as well as Speaker performed at the plate and on the base paths, he developed an even greater reputation for his magnificent defensive work, playing his position in a bold and brazen manner unmatched by any other outfielder. Blessed with exceptional speed and an uncanny ability to track fly balls, Speaker played an extraordinarily shallow center field, typically positioning himself a mere 40 or 50 feet behind second base, which allowed him to frequently convert line drive singles into outs and throw out runners attempting to advance one base. He even occasionally served as the middle man on double plays. Speaker later gave much of the credit for his outstanding ability to judge fly balls to Cy Young, a member of Boston's pitching staff his first few years with the team, stating "When I was a rookie, Cy Young used to hit me flies to sharpen my abilities to judge in advance the direction and distance of an outfield-hit ball."

Still, in spite of Speaker's exceptional all-around play, Red Sox president J.J. Lannin elected to part ways with his team's best player when a war of words developed between the two men following an attempt by Lannin to reduce Speaker's salary from $15,000 to $9,000 after the latter batted "just" .322 for Boston's 1915 world championship team. Dealt to the Cleveland Indians for pitcher "Sad" Sam Jones, minor league infielder Fred Thomas, and $55,000 on April 9, 1916, Speaker immediately had his

Courtesy of MEARS Online Auctions

Tris Speaker proved to be the finest all-around player
in franchise history during his time in Cleveland

salary increased to $40,000 by his new employer, making him baseball's highest paid player.

Beginning his career anew in the city of Cleveland, Speaker had a huge year for the Indians in 1916, ranking among the league leaders with 79 RBIs, 102 runs scored, 274 total bases, 35 steals, and 82 walks, while topping the circuit in hits (211), doubles (41), batting average (.386), on-base percentage (.470), and slugging percentage (.502). Speaker's fabulous performance made an extremely favorable impression on Indians catcher (and future manager) Steve O'Neill, who suggested, "Tris Speaker is better at the hit-and-run play than either [Joe] Jackson or [Ty] Cobb, for he is like [Napoleon] Lajoie in that he can reach out and crack a pitch away on the other side of the plate if it will help the runner. He does not have to wait for a fast one, a floater, or a curve."

O'Neill added, "I would sum it up this way: Cobb is the fellow who is most apt to be safe on first on a ball hit anywhere; Jackson hits the ball more savagely, while Speaker is the best all-around player of the lot."

Nearly six feet tall and a sturdy 193 pounds, Speaker batted from a left-handed crouch and stood deep in the batter's box. He held his bat low, moving it up and down slowly, "like the lazy twitching of a cat's tail," according to an admirer, and took a full stride. "I don't find any particular ball easy to hit," he said. "I have no rule for batting. I keep my eye on the ball and, when it nears me, make ready to swing."

Plagued by injuries in each of the next three seasons, Speaker failed to perform at the same lofty level. Nevertheless, he remained one of the league's best players, batting .352 and scoring 90 runs in 1917, before hitting .318 and topping the circuit with 33 doubles the following year.

Continuing to play shallow in the outfield even though the center field fence at Cleveland's Dunn Field stood 460 feet from home plate (it was shortened to 420 feet in 1920), Speaker executed six career unassisted double plays at second base as a member of the Indians, catching low line drives on the run and then beating base runners to the bag. Commenting on Speaker's ability to go back on the ball, Smoky Joe Wood, who played with him in both Boston and Cleveland, stated, "At the crack of the bat, he'd be off with his back to the infield, and then he'd turn and glance over his shoulder at the last minute and catch the ball so easy it looked like there was nothing to it, nothing at all."

Explaining his strategy years later, Speaker commented, "I know it's easier, basically, to come in on a ball than go back. But so many more balls are hit in front of an outfielder, even now, that it's a matter of percentage to be able to play in close enough to cut off those low ones in front of him. I still see more games lost by singles that drop just over the infield than a triple over the outfielder's head. I learned early that I could save more games by cutting off some of those singles than I would lose by having an occasional extra-base hit go over my head."

Speaker's baseball acumen prompted Cleveland manager Lee Fohl to often seek his advice, until "The Grey Eagle," as he came to be known, replaced Fohl at the helm midway through the 1919 campaign. Assuming the role of player-manager his remaining time in Cleveland, Speaker began an exceptional six-year run in 1920, during which he posted the following numbers:

    1920: 8 HR, 107 RBI, 137 Runs Scored, 214 Hits, **50** 2B, .388 AVG, .483 OBP, .562 SLG
    1921: 3 HR, 75 RBI, 107 Runs Scored, 183 Hits, **52** 2B, .362 AVG, .439 OBP, .538 SLG
    1922: 11 HR, 71 RBI, 85 Runs Scored, 161 Hits, **48** 2B, .378 AVG, **.474** OBP, .606 SLG
    1923: 17 HR, **130** RBI, 133 Runs Scored, 218 Hits, **59** 2B, .380 AVG, .469 OBP, .610 SLG
    1924: 9 HR, 65 RBI, 94 Runs Scored, 167 Hits, 36 2B, .344 AVG, .432 OBP, .510 SLG
    1925: 12 HR, 87 RBI, 79 Runs Scored, 167 Hits, 35 2B, .389 AVG, **.479** OBP, .578 SLG

Speaker's outstanding play in 1920 helped lead the Indians to their first pennant and World Series championship. By topping the junior circuit in doubles each year from 1920 to 1923, Speaker became the only player in baseball history to lead his league in that category four straight times. He also placed in the league's top five in on-base percentage and OPS all six years, and he finished second in the league in runs scored twice, hits once, total bases once, and walks once. At the same time, Speaker continued to play a superb center field, annually placing near the top of the league rankings in outfield putouts and double plays recorded, while leading all AL center fielders in assists three times and fielding percentage twice.

Speaker spent one more year in Cleveland, batting .304, driving in 88 runs, scoring 96 times, and amassing 52 doubles in 1926, before resigning as Indians manager and being granted free agency following the conclusion of the campaign after being implicated in a gambling scandal involving himself and Ty Cobb. Eventually cleared of all charges by Commissioner Kenesaw Mountain Landis after the accuser, former pitcher Dutch Leonard, refused to appear at the January 5, 1927 hearing, Speaker signed with the Washington Senators, while Cobb joined the Philadelphia Athletics. Speaker left Cleveland having hit 73 homers, driven in 886 runs, scored 1,079 times, amassed 1,965 hits, 486 doubles, 108 triples, and 155 stolen bases, batted .354, compiled an on-base percentage of .444, and posted a slugging percentage of .520 as a member of the team. He continues to rank among the Indians' all-time leaders in most statistical categories, holding franchise records for most doubles and highest on-base percentage.

Speaker ended up playing one year in Washington, before spending his final season as a part-time player with Cobb on the Athletics. He retired following the conclusion of the 1928 campaign with 117 home runs, 1,531 RBIs, 1,882 runs scored, 436 stolen bases, a .345 career batting average, a .428 on-base percentage, a .500 slugging percentage, 3,514 hits, 222 triples, and an all-time record 792 doubles. In addition to amassing more doubles than any other player, Speaker ranks among Major League Baseball's all-time leaders in batting average, triples, hits, and runs scored.

Following his retirement, Speaker remained close to the game for several more years. Before serving as an adviser, coach and scout for the Indians from 1947 until his death, he briefly managed the Newark Bears of the International League. He also became a part owner of the Kansas City Blues and served for a time as chairman of Cleveland's Boxing Commission. Among his more philanthropic pursuits, Speaker helped found the Cleveland Society for Crippled Children and Camp Cheerful. Speaker gained induction into the Baseball Hall of Fame during the second year of balloting, in 1937, becoming just the seventh player to be so honored. He died of a heart attack on December 8, 1958, at the age of 70, collapsing as he and a friend pulled their boat into the dock at Lake Whitney following a fishing trip. Upon learning of his passing, a despondent Ty Cobb said, "I never let him know how much I admired him when we were playing against each other. . . . It was only after we finally became teammates and then retired that I could tell Tris Speaker of the underlying respect I had for him."

Some 60 years after his passing, Tris Speaker is still considered by many baseball historians to be the greatest defensive center fielder in baseball history. Pitcher Smoky Joe Wood, who roomed with him in Boston, said in *The Glory of Their Times*, "Speaker played a real shallow center field and had terrific instincts. . . . Nobody else was even in the same league with him."

Hall of Fame shortstop Joe Sewell, who played with Speaker in Cleveland, stated emphatically, "I played with Tris for seven years. I've seen Joe DiMaggio, and I've seen Willie Mays . . . and all the rest. Tris Speaker is the best center fielder I've seen."

Meanwhile, legendary sportswriter Grantland Rice wrote of Speaker, "You can write him down as one of the two models of ball-playing grace. The other was Napoleon Lajoie. Neither ever wasted a motion or gave you any sign of extra effort. . . . They had the same elements that made a Bobby Jones or the Four Horsemen of Notre Dame—the smoothness of a summer wind."

Indians Career Highlights:

Best Season: A strong argument could be made that Speaker had his finest all-around season for the Indians in 1916, when, in his first year as a member of the Tribe, he led the AL in six different offensive categories. In addition to ranking among the league leaders in RBIs (79), runs scored (102), total bases (274), and steals (35), Speaker topped the circuit with 211 hits, 41 doubles, a .386 batting average, a .470 on-base percentage, a .502 slugging percentage, and an OPS of .972. Nevertheless, even though the American League's use of a livelier ball aided Speaker's offensive production considerably during the early 1920s, he compiled the most prolific numbers of his career in 1923, when he finished in the league's top five in home runs (17), runs scored (133), batting average (.380), on-base percentage (.469), slugging percentage (.610), OPS (1.079), hits (218), total bases (350), and walks (93), while topping the circuit with 130 RBIs and 59 doubles. Furthermore, Speaker led all AL center-fielders with 26 assists and seven double plays. All things considered, Speaker had his best year for the Indians in 1923.

Memorable Moments/Greatest Performances: Speaker made perhaps his most memorable defensive play as a member of the Indians during the latter stages of the 1920 campaign, when he clinched a crucial 2-0 victory over the second-place White Sox by making a spectacular catch in deep right-center field. Moving swiftly in an effort to track down a line drive hit by Shoeless Joe Jackson, Speaker leaped into the air and, with both feet off the ground, snared the ball before crashing into a concrete wall. Despite being knocked unconscious, Speaker held onto the baseball, saving the game for the Indians.

Speaker compiled a pair of impressive hitting streaks during his time in Cleveland, with the first of those lasting from July 12 to August 13, 1916, when he hit safely in 27 straight games, going 44-for-98 (.449) during that time. He also hit safely in 23 consecutive games from August 26 to September 26, 1923, going 37-for-83 (.446), with four homers, one triple, eight doubles, 18 RBIs, and 25 runs scored during the streak.

Speaker hit two home runs in one game twice for the Indians, doing so for the first time during a 3-1 win over the Yankees at the Polo Grounds on July 8, 1922. He accomplished the feat again one month later, going deep twice during a 15-6 loss to the Red Sox in Cleveland on August 8.

Speaker had a big day at the plate against his former team on June 3, 1916, going 3-for-4, with a double, two triples, four RBIs, and three runs scored during an 11-2 rout of the Red Sox.

Exactly one week later, on June 10, Speaker went a perfect 5-for-5 during a lopsided 10-1 victory over the Philadelphia Athletics.

Speaker helped lead the Indians to a 15-9 win over the Yankees on August 11, 1919, by collecting three hits and scoring five times.

Speaker led a 9-3 mauling of the Detroit Tigers on May 1, 1920, by going 4-for-5, with a homer and seven RBIs.

In early July of 1920, Speaker set a record that went unsurpassed for 18 years when he hit safely in 11 consecutive trips to the plate. The highlight of the streak proved to be his performance against Washington on July 8, when he went 5-for-5 and knocked in three runs during a 9-6 win over the Senators.

Speaker contributed to a 17-2 pasting of the St. Louis Browns on April 18, 1922, by going 4-for-6, with a pair of doubles, four RBIs, and two runs scored.

Speaker helped lead the Indians to a lopsided 10-0 victory over Detroit on July 5, 1923, by going 4-for-4, with a walk, a pair of doubles, three RBIs, and three runs scored.

Although the Indians lost their July 28, 1923 meeting with the Boston Red Sox by a score of 10-5, Speaker went a perfect 5-for-5 during the contest.

Speaker again starred in defeat a little over two weeks later, going 5-for-5, with a homer, a pair of doubles, and two RBIs during an 8-6 loss to the Red Sox on August 15.

Speaker hit safely in all five of his trips to the plate for the third time in 1923 on October 4, when he led the Indians to a 9-1 rout of the St. Louis Browns by going 5-for-5, with a homer, a double, two RBIs, and four runs scored.

Speaker had the final 5-for-5 day of his career on August 8, 1924, when he doubled three times and singled twice during a 10-8 win over the Yankees.

Speaker had an extremely productive day at the plate against Washington on September 12, 1926, leading the Indians to a 14-4 victory over the Senators by going 4-for-4, with a triple, two doubles, four RBIs, and four runs scored.

Speaker became just the fifth member of the exclusive 3,000-hit club on May 17, 1925, when he singled off Washington pitcher Tom Zachary during a 2-1 loss to the Senators.

Notable Achievements:

- Batted over .300 ten times, topping the .340-mark eight times and surpassing .380 on four occasions.
- Knocked in more than 100 runs twice, driving in as many as 130 runs once (1923).
- Scored more than 100 runs four times, topping 130 runs scored twice.
- Surpassed 200 hits three times.
- Finished in double digits in triples six times.
- Surpassed 30 doubles 11 times, topping 40 two-baggers seven times and 50 two-baggers on four occasions.
- Stole more than 30 bases twice.
- Compiled on-base percentage in excess of .400 ten times.
- Posted slugging percentage in excess of .500 seven times, topping the .600-mark twice.

- Posted OPS in excess of 1.000 four times.
- Led AL in: batting average once, RBIs once, hits once, doubles six times, on-base percentage three times, slugging percentage once, OPS once, and at-bat-to-strikeout ratio twice.
- Finished second in AL in: batting average twice, runs scored twice, hits once, doubles twice, total bases twice, bases on balls once, on-base percentage twice, slugging percentage once, and OPS three times
- Led AL outfielders in: putouts twice, fielding percentage twice, and double plays twice.
- Led AL center-fielders in: putouts twice, assists four times, fielding percentage four times, and double plays six times.
- Holds MLB record for most career doubles (792).
- Ranks among MLB career leaders in: hits (5th), batting average (6th), triples (6th), on-base percentage (11th), runs scored (13th), and total bases (17th).
- Hold MLB records for most assists (449) and double plays (143) by an outfielder.
- Ranks second all-time among MLB outfielders in putouts (6,788).
- Holds Indians single-season record for highest on-base percentage (.483 in 1920).
- Holds Indians career records for most doubles (486) and highest on-base percentage (.444).
- Ranks among Indians career leaders in: batting average (2nd), RBIs (5th), runs scored (2nd), hits (2nd), extra-base hits (2nd), triples (2nd), total bases (2nd), bases on balls (2nd), stolen bases (10th), slugging percentage (8th), OPS (4th), games played (5th), plate appearances (4th), and at-bats (9th).
- 1920 AL champion.
- 1920 world champion.
- Member of Major League Baseball All-Century Team.
- Number 27 on *The Sporting News'* 1999 list of Baseball's 100 Greatest Players.
- Elected to Baseball Hall of Fame by members of BBWAA in 1937.

3

NAPOLEON LAJOIE

1902 – 1914

The American League's first true superstar, Napoleon Lajoie combined powerful hitting with graceful, effortless fielding to establish himself as one of the greatest all-around players of the *Dead Ball Era* and one of the finest second basemen of all time. Rivaling Pittsburgh's Honus Wagner as the best position player in the game for much of the first decade of the 20th century, Lajoie proved to be easily the junior circuit's top offensive performer prior to the arrival of Ty Cobb. After earlier starring in the National League, Lajoie lead the AL in major statistical categories a total of 28 times between 1901 and 1910, en route to winning five batting titles and one Triple Crown. An outstanding defender as well, Lajoie led all AL second basemen in putouts four times, assists three times, double plays turned five times, and fielding percentage five times, with his brilliant all-around play making him so popular with the fans of Cleveland that they chose to re-name their baseball team in his honor.

Born to French-Canadian parents in Woonsocket, Rhode Island on September 5, 1874, Napoleon Lajoie lost his father at the age of five, prompting him to take a job in the local cotton mills just a few short years later. Developing an interest in the national pastime by the time he turned 10, Lajoie grew up idolizing baseball pioneers Mike "King" Kelly, "Old Hoss" Radbourn, John Montgomery Ward, and John Clarkson.

Choosing to pursue a career on the diamond himself, Lajoie began playing semi-pro ball in Rhode Island in 1895, before turning pro the following year, when he joined the Fall River team in the New England League. Playing mostly in the outfield, Lajoie performed so well during his three-month minor-league stint that the Philadelphia Phillies purchased him from Fall River on August 8, 1896. Appearing in 39 games with the Phillies over the final seven weeks of the campaign, Lajoie batted .326 and accumulated 57 hits. After claiming Philadelphia's starting first base job the following year, Lajoie went on to have a sensational season, placing among the NL leaders in home runs (9), RBIs (127), runs scored (107), triples (23), doubles (40), and batting average (.361), while topping the circuit with 310 total bases and a .569 slugging percentage. Moved to second base in 1898, Lajoie struggled somewhat in the field, committing a total of 46 errors. However, he continued his onslaught on National League pitching, batting .324, scoring 113 runs, and leading the league with 127 runs batted in and 43 doubles.

Although injuries cut into Lajoie's playing time significantly in each of the next two seasons, he still managed to compile batting averages of .378 and .337, making him a much sought-after commodity when the newly-formed American League began raiding the more established NL for top talent prior to the start of the 1901 campaign. Choosing to jump to the crosstown Philadelphia Athletics after team owner and manager Connie Mack offered him a contract that nearly tripled the annual salary he received from the Phillies, Lajoie ended up topping the junior circuit in nine different offensive categories, including home runs (14), RBIs (125), runs scored (145), hits (232), doubles (48), and batting average (.426), with the last figure remaining the highest single-season mark attained by any player since 1900.

With the Phillies subsequently obtaining a court injunction that prohibited Lajoie from playing for any other team in the city of Philadelphia, Mack released his star second baseman in order to allow him to sign with the struggling Cleveland Bronchos. Although the legal wrangling that ensued limited Lajoie to just 87 games and 352 official at-bats in 1902, he finished the season with 65 RBIs, 81 runs scored, and a league-leading .378 batting average. Lajoie's exceptional play, which helped resuscitate the moribund Cleveland franchise, endeared him to the local fans to such an extent that a readers' poll released by the Cleveland Press at season's end resulted in the team name being changed to the Napoleons ("Naps" for short) prior to the start of the ensuing campaign.

His legal troubles behind him, Lajoie won his third and fourth consecutive batting titles in 1903 and 1904, posting averages of .344 and .376, respectively. Particularly effective in the second of those campaigns, during which he received a brief suspension for spitting tobacco juice in an umpire's eye, Lajoie also led the league with 102 RBIs, 208 hits, 49 doubles, 302 total bases, a .413 on-base percentage, and a .546 slugging percentage.

Napoleon Lajoie proved to be such a dominant figure
during his time in Cleveland that the team
re-named itself the Naps in his honor

Named Cleveland's player-manager prior to the start of the 1905 season, Lajoie subsequently suffered through an injury-marred campaign during which he appeared in only 65 games. After suffering a spike wound that caused him to develop blood poisoning and nearly cost him his leg, Lajoie had to attend games in a wheelchair before he finally returned to action some two months later. Shortly thereafter, he sustained an injury to his ankle from a foul tip, forcing him to miss the remainder of the season. Yet, in spite of his bad luck, Lajoie once again batted well over .300, finishing the year with a mark of .329. Healthy again by the start of the ensuing campaign, Lajoie returned to top form in 1906, driving in 91 runs, finishing second in the league with a batting average of .355, and topping the circuit with 214 hits and 48 doubles.

Much of Lajoie's success as a hitter could be attributed to the specially designed bat he used that featured two knobs, one of which sat partway up the handle. The uniquely constructed lumber, which allowed Lajoie to employ a split-handed grip, offered him superior bat control, enabling him to place the ball basically where he wanted. An expert bunter as well,

Lajoie often used that technique to reach base, even though he possessed only average running speed.

Yet, Lajoie's slugging ability must not be overlooked. Although playing during the Dead Ball Era prevented him from ever hitting more than 14 home runs in any single season, Lajoie reputedly hit the ball as hard as anyone in the game during his playing days, with Cy Young stating, "Lajoie was one of the most rugged hitters I ever faced. He'd take your leg off with a line drive, turn the third baseman around like a swinging door and powder the hand of the left fielder." Meanwhile, 19th-century star Hugh Duffy once observed, "Good Old Ed Delahanty could clout the horsehide some, but Lajoie seemed to be just as powerful, if not more so." Indeed, Lajoie swung so hard and met the ball with such force that, on three separate occasions in 1899, he literally tore the cover off the ball. Still, it should be noted that Lajoie proved to be totally undisciplined at the plate, regularly swinging at pitches well out of the strike zone. As a result, he drew more than 40 bases on balls in a season just twice his entire career.

In discussing his approach to hitting, Lajoie offered, "Position at the bat is a big thing in hitting. A batter should be firmly on his feet, with the balls of his feet holding the ground tightly, and he should not shift position while striking. . . . I do not try to hit the ball as hard as possible, but, rather, to meet it squarely, and, in this, I think a quick and steady eye helps."

Always seeking to gain an advantage at the plate, Lajoie continued:

> "It [hitting] is a guessing match between the pitcher and the batter at the best, and experience ought to show a batter just what a pitcher is likely to throw him on any given ball. When runners are on base, batting becomes more of an art. . . . .I think my position at the bat and long, steady, sweeping stroke helps me very much in the hit-and-run game, for I am able to hit balls that other batters would miss entirely. Even if I am certain of missing the ball, I swing at it hard so as to cause the catcher to lose a step, or a foot or two of ground, in making his throw."

Although opposing pitchers often attempted to upset Lajoie's timing by throwing him off-speed pitches, he maintained that this approach had little effect on him, claiming, "As far as I am concerned, I win games by hitting. It seems to me I always could hit, and, in spite of the fact that some pitchers think otherwise, I hit almost any kind of ball equally hard. I have often wondered why this was. Perhaps it was natural. I never want to know what a pitcher is going to pitch and would much rather figure out for myself what ball is coming than have a coach or anyone else tell me."

More than just a great hitter, the 6'1", 200-pound Lajoie proved to be an exceptional fielder and surprisingly good base-runner as well, stealing 380 bases over the course of his career even though he lacked outstanding running speed. Extremely quick on his feet in the field, the New York Press noted that Lajoie "glides toward the ball and gathers it in nonchalantly, as if picking fruit." Connie Mack elaborated, "He plays so naturally and so easily that it looks like lack of effort. Larry's [Lajoie's nickname] reach is so long, and he's fast as lightning." Meanwhile, in discussing Lajoie's defense, fellow infielder Tommy Leach gushed, "What a ballplayer that man was. Every play he made he executed so gracefully that it looked like it was the easiest thing in the world."

Leach added, "He was a pleasure to play against, too; always laughing and joking. Even when the son of a gun was blocking you off the base, he was smiling and kidding with you. You just had to like the guy."

Although Lajoie remained baseball's top second baseman from 1907 to 1909, the pressure of managing the Naps caused his on-field performance to suffer somewhat, preventing him from batting any higher than .324 or knocking in more than 74 runs in any of those three seasons. However, after relinquishing his managerial duties prior to the start of the 1910 campaign, Lajoie regained his batting eye, battling Ty Cobb right down to the wire in what proved to be a memorable and highly-controversial race for the AL batting title.

With baseball fan Hugh Chalmers, who served as President and General Manager of the Chalmers Motor Company, having announced earlier in 1910 that he intended to present one of his company's automobiles to the major league player who compiled the highest batting average, Cobb and Lajoie entered the season's final few days as the only two players with a legitimate chance of winning the title. Believing that his .383 to .376 edge over Lajoie virtually guaranteed him the batting championship, the unpopular Cobb elected to sit out Detroit's final two games, leaving Lajoie the almost impossible task of raising his average seven points during Cleveland's season-ending doubleheader against the St. Louis Browns. However, St. Louis manager Jack O'Connor instructed his third baseman to play Lajoie unusually deep, enabling the popular Cleveland second baseman to bunt safely seven times and finish the season a fraction of a point ahead of Cobb in the batting race. O'Connor ended up losing his job due to his role in the alleged fix, and American League President Ban Johnson subsequently announced that a "discrepancy" had been found in the official records, and that Cobb had actually won the batting crown after all. Nevertheless, both Cobb and Lajoie received automobiles from Chalmers, with uncertainty still existing to this day as to the true winner of the batting title.

Despite being plagued by injuries in each of the next three seasons, Lajoie continued to perform well for the Naps, posting batting averages of .365, .368, and .335 from 1911 to 1913. However, after clashing with manager Joe Birmingham and batting just .258 in 1914, the 40-year-old second baseman asked to be traded to another team. Granting Lajoie's request, Cleveland owner Charles Somers sold him back to the Philadelphia Athletics, with whom he ended his big-league career two years later. Over parts of 21 seasons in the majors, Lajoie hit 82 homers, knocked in 1,599 runs, scored 1,504 others, amassed 3,243 hits, 657 doubles, 163 triples, and 380 stolen bases, batted .338, compiled an on-base percentage of .380, and posted a slugging percentage of .466. At the time of his retirement, Lajoie ranked second only to Honus Wagner (3,420) in career hits. During his time in Cleveland, Lajoie hit 33 homers, drove in 919 runs, scored 865 times, collected 2,047 hits, 424 doubles, 78 triples, and 240 stolen bases, batted .339, compiled a .389 on-base percentage, and posted a .452 slugging percentage. He continues to hold franchise records for most hits and most at-bats (6,034).

After announcing his retirement following the conclusion of the 1916 campaign, Lajoie managed in the minor leagues for two years, before leaving the game for good in 1918. The members of the BBWAA voted him into the Baseball Hall of Fame in 1937 as part of the second group of inductees that also included Tris Speaker and Cy Young. He entered Cooperstown two years later, taking part in the festivities when the Hall officially opened in 1939. Lajoie lived another 20 years, passing away from complications associated with pneumonia on February 7, 1959, at the age of 84.

Indians (Naps) Career Highlights:

Best Season: Lajoie had a big year for the Naps in 1910, finishing second in the American League with 94 runs scored, a .445 on-base percentage, and a .514 slugging percentage, while leading the majors with a .384

batting average, 227 hits, 51 doubles, and 304 total bases. Nevertheless, Lajoie compiled slightly better overall numbers in 1904, when he stole a career-high 29 bases, ranked among the league leaders with 15 triples and 92 runs scored, and topped the circuit with 102 RBIs, 208 hits, 49 doubles, 302 total bases, a .376 batting average, a .413 on-base percentage, and a .546 slugging percentage.

Memorable Moments/Greatest Performances: Since box scores for games played prior to 1911 are incomplete, it became impossible to identify Lajoie's top performances from his first several years in Cleveland. However, he put together an impressive hitting streak for the Naps from July 16 to August 8, 1913, hitting safely in 23 consecutive games, during which time he went a combined 37-for-81, for a batting average of .457.

Lajoie helped lead the Naps to an 8-3 victory over Smoky Joe Wood and the Boston Red Sox on August 7, 1911 by going 4-for-5, with a homer, three doubles, and two runs batted in.

Lajoie starred at the plate and on the base paths during a 9-2 win over the St. Louis Browns on September 9, 1911, collecting three hits and stealing three bases.

Lajoie led the Naps to a lopsided 10-2 victory over the Philadelphia Athletics on September 13, 1912 by going 4-for-4, with a pair of doubles, two RBIs, and two runs scored.

Lajoie turned in a similarly impressive performance against Detroit two weeks later, pacing the Naps to a 16-5 win over the Tigers on September 27 by going 4-for-4, with a double, four RBIs, and two runs scored.

Lajoie had a big day at the plate on October 6, 1912, when he went 5-for-5, with a triple, three RBIs, and one run scored during an 8-3 victory over the St. Louis Browns.

Lajoie proved to be a one-man wrecking crew during a 5-0 win over the Athletics on August 5, 1913, going 3-for-4, with a homer, double, three RBIs, and two runs scored.

Lajoie reached a notable milestone on September 27, 1914, when his double off New York Yankees pitcher Marty McHale enabled him to join Cap Anson and Honus Wagner as the only players in at that time in Major League history to reach the 3,000-hit plateau.

Notable Achievements:

- Batted over .300 11 times, topping the .340-mark on seven occasions.
- Knocked in more than 100 runs once (102 in 1904).
- Topped 200 hits three times.
- Finished in double digits in triples twice.
- Surpassed 30 doubles nine times, topping 40 two-baggers on four occasions, and 50 two-baggers once (51 in 1910).
- Stole more than 20 bases five times.
- Compiled on-base percentage in excess of .400 five times.
- Posted slugging percentage in excess of .500 four times.
- Led AL in: batting average four times, hits three times, doubles three times, RBIs once, total bases twice, on-base percentage once, slugging percentage twice, and OPS twice.
- Finished second in AL in: batting average once, RBIs once, runs scored once, doubles twice, total bases once, on-base percentage three times, slugging percentage three times, and OPS three times.
- Led AL second basemen in: assists three times, putouts three times, fielding percentage four times, and double plays turned five times.
- Member of 3,000-hit club.
- Ranks seventh in MLB history with 657 career doubles.
- Ranks fifth all-time among MLB second basemen with 5,496 career putouts.
- Holds Indians career records for most hits (2,047) and most at-bats (6,034).
- Ranks among Indians career leaders in: batting average (3rd), RBIs (3rd), runs scored (7th), doubles (2nd), triples (8th), total bases (3rd), stolen bases (4th), games played (2nd), and plate appearances (3rd).
- Number 29 on The Sporting News' 1999 list of Baseball's 100 Greatest Players.
- Elected to Baseball Hall of Fame by members of BBWAA in 1937.

4

BOB LEMON

1941 – 1942, 1946 – 1958

The only 20th-century player in the Hall of Fame who became a pitcher after beginning his major-league career as a position player, Bob Lemon spent all of his 13 big-league seasons with the Indians, establishing himself during his time in Cleveland as one of the top hurlers in the game. Experiencing most of his success between 1948 and 1956, Lemon compiled an overall record of 186-106 over the course of those nine seasons, en route to becoming the last American League pitcher to surpass 20 victories in a season as many as seven times. In addition to annually placing at, or near, the top of the league rankings in wins, Lemon typically finished among the AL pitching leaders in most other statistical categories, topping the circuit in WHIP once, strikeouts once, shutouts once, innings pitched four times, and complete games five times, with his superb pitching earning him seven All-Star selections, three top-five finishes in the AL MVP voting, and Sporting News AL Pitcher of the Year honors on three separate occasions. Meanwhile, Lemon's previous experience as a third baseman helped make him one of the top-fielding and best-hitting pitchers ever, with his 35 career home runs as a pitcher (he also hit two as a pinch-hitter) representing the second-highest total in MLB history.

Born in San Bernardino, California on September 22, 1920, Robert Granville Lemon grew up in Long Beach, where he attended Woodrow Wilson Classical High School, earning recognition as the California Inter-scholastic Federation and State Baseball Player of the Year as a senior in 1938, while playing both shortstop and pitcher. Subsequently signed as an amateur free agent by the Indians, the right-handed throwing, left-handed hitting Lemon spent the next five years advancing through Cleveland's farm system, making brief appearances with the parent club in both 1941 and 1942, before having his career interrupted by three years of military service during World War II. After playing shortstop, third base, and the outfield in the minor leagues, Lemon spent most of his time in the service pitching for the Navy's baseball team, making a lasting impression on fellow big leaguers—such as Birdie Tebbetts, Johnny Pesky, and Bill Dickey—who competed with and against him.

His defensive skills at third base having eroded during his time in the Navy, Lemon moved to center field when he joined the Indians following his discharge early in 1946. However, after struggling terribly at the plate during the early stages of the campaign, Lemon spent the next few months serving the Tribe primarily as a pinch-hitter, before player-manager Lou Boudreau decided to convert him into a pitcher after hearing positive reports from the aforementioned major league players who faced him in the service. Reflecting back on his reasoning at the time, Boudreau later wrote, "I knew Lemon had a strong arm, and, once I realized he was not going to hit with consistency as an outfielder, I thought it would be worthwhile to look at him as a pitcher."

After initially balking at the idea of switching positions again, Lemon became convinced to make the move when he learned that starting pitchers typically earned more money than position players. Lemon subsequently spent the rest of the year working out of the Tribe bullpen, although he also made five starts, finishing the season with a record of 4-5, an ERA of 2.49, one save, 39 strikeouts, and 68 bases on balls, in only 94 innings of work. Meanwhile, he compiled a batting average of just .180 in a total of 98 plate appearances, although he also hit the first home run of his major league career.

Lemon remained in the Indians bullpen at the start of the 1947 season, before gradually working his way into the starting rotation over the course of the campaign. Aided by coach Bill McKechnie, who he later credited with helping him adjust to his new position, and pitching coach Mel Harder, who taught him how to throw a slider and helped him develop a devastating curveball and a "sidearm crossfire fastball," Lemon reeled off 10 consecutive victories during the season's second half, enabling him to finish the year with a record of 11-5. Impressed with Lemon's performance, Indians owner Bill Veeck predicted that the 27-year-old right-hander "will someday become the best pitcher in the American League."

Proving Veeck to be prophetic, Lemon subsequently began an extremely successful nine-year run during which he established himself as arguably the junior circuit's top hurler, winning at least 20 games in seven of those seasons. These are the numbers he compiled in each of his 20-win campaigns:

1948: 20-14, 2.82 ERA, **1.226** WHIP, 147 Strikeouts, **10** Shutouts, **20** CG, **293.2** IP

1949: 22-10, 2.99 ERA, 1.244 WHIP, 138 Strikeouts, 2 Shutouts, 22 CG, 279.2 IP

1950: **23**-11, 3.84 ERA, 1.483 WHIP, **170** Strikeouts, 3 Shutouts, **22** CG, **288.0** IP

1952: 22-11, 2.50 ERA, 1.101 WHIP, 131 Strikeouts, 5 Shutouts, **28** CG, **309.2** IP

1953: 21-15, 3.36 ERA, 1.371 WHIP, 98 Strikeouts, 5 Shutouts, 23 CG, **286.2** IP

1954: **23**-7, 2.72 ERA, 1.239 WHIP, 110 Strikeouts, 2 Shutouts, **21** CG, 258.1 IP

1956: 20-14, 3.03 ERA, 1.249 WHIP, 94 Strikeouts, 2 Shutouts, **21** CG, 255.1 IP

Lemon finished either first or second in the AL in complete games in each of those seven seasons, topping the circuit on five separate occasions. He also ranked among the league leaders in each of the other six categories virtually every year, finishing first in innings pitched four times, wins twice, and WHIP, strikeouts, and shutouts once each. Lemon also posted 17 victories in 1951 and a league-leading 18 wins in 1955, with his fabulous pitching earning him All-Star honors each year from 1948 to 1954, six top-10 finishes in the AL MVP balloting, and Sporting News AL Pitcher of the Year honors in 1948, 1950, and 1954. The Indians won the pennant in 1948 and 1954, with Lemon leading them to victory over Boston in the 1948 World Series by defeating the Braves twice.

Having developed an outstanding changeup to go with his sinking fastball, exceptional curve, and baffling slider, Lemon gradually emerged as the ace of an outstanding Indians starting rotation that also included Early Wynn, Mike Garcia, and an aging Bob Feller, who later said of his teammate, "Bob had a good curve, a good slider, and a vicious sinker. He wasn't overly fast, but he always stayed ahead of the hitters, and he didn't walk many batters, which is the key to success in the majors."

In discussing his repertoire of pitches during the pennant-winning campaign of 1954, Lemon stated, "I suppose that the slider is the pitch I've relied on most during these last few years. I didn't have to work to develop it, as I did to develop a good curve. I don't try to throw a sinker. My fastball sinks naturally. I've always assumed my short fingers do it."

Lemon also proved to be a threat at the plate, compiling a lifetime batting average of .232, driving in a total of 147 runs, and hitting 37 homers over the course of his career, including seven in 1949 alone. Meanwhile, his earlier days as an infielder enabled him to establish himself as the finest fielding pitcher of his time—one that led all AL hurlers in putouts five times and assists six times. In fact, Lemon set a major-league record in 1953 that still stands by participating in 15 double plays as a mounds-man. A fierce competitor as well, Lemon drew praise from sportswriter Bob Broeg, who wrote, "No statistic, though, could capture the man's competitive fire and bulldog nature that made him the Indians' most feared pitcher."

Unfortunately, age and injuries ended up bringing Lemon's days as a dominant pitcher to an end in 1957, with bone chips in his elbow limiting him to only 17 starts. After compiling a dismal record of 6-11 and an inordinately high ERA of 4.60 in easily his worst season, Lemon failed to make it all the way back the following year, when, working primarily out of the bullpen, he lost his only decision before the Indians placed him on waivers in July. Unable to mount a comeback during 1959 spring training, the 38-year-old Lemon decided to announce his retirement, ending his career with a record of 207-128, an ERA of 3.23, a WHIP of 1.337, 188 complete games, 31 shutouts, 22 saves, and 1,277 strikeouts in 2,850 innings pitched.

Following his playing days, Lemon worked for a number of years as a scout and a pitching coach, serving on the staffs of the Indians, Philadelphia Phillies, California Angels, and Kansas City Royals. He also later managed the Royals, Chicago White Sox, and New York Yankees, leading the Yankees to the 1978 world championship after replacing Billy Martin as skipper midway through the campaign. Relieved of his duties in New York following a second stint as manager of the Yankees in 1982, Lemon retired from baseball for good, returning to his home in Long Beach, California, where he spent the remainder of his life. Inducted into the Baseball Hall of Fame by the members of the BBWAA in 1976, Lemon received the additional distinction of having his jersey #21 retired by the Indians in 1998, two years before he passed away at the age of 79, on January 11, 2000, after spending his final years suffering from the effects of a stroke.

Bob Lemon won more than 20 games
seven times for the Indians

Courtesy of Mears Online Auctions

Career Highlights:

Best Season: Lemon had a huge year for the Indians in 1948, when, in addition to finishing in the league's top three in wins (20) and ERA (2.82), he topped the circuit with 20 complete games, 293 2/3 innings pitched, a WHIP of 1.226, and a career-best 10 shutouts. He also performed exceptionally well during the pennant-winning campaign of 1954, going 23-7, with a 2.72 ERA, a WHIP of 1.239, 258⅓ innings pitched, and a league-leading 21 complete games. Nevertheless, Lemon pitched his best ball for the Indians in 1952, when he ranked among the league leaders with 22 victories, a 2.50 ERA, five shutouts, and a WHIP of 1.101, and topped the circuit with 28 complete games and 309 2/3 innings pitched, establishing career-best marks in each of the last three categories.

Memorable Moments/Greatest Performances: One of the best hitting pitchers in the history of the game, Lemon had a number of memorable days at the plate, with the first of those coming on September 15, 1946, when he went 3-for-5, with a double and two runs scored, during a complete-game 8-1 victory over the Philadelphia Athletics.

Lemon again touched up Philadelphia pitching for three hits on September 15, 1947, going 3-for-4 at the plate during a 2-1 victory over the Athletics that took 11 innings to complete.

Lemon turned in a tremendous all-around effort against Washington on May 7, 1948, allowing just four hits and two walks, while collecting three hits himself, during an 8-0 shutout of the Senators.

Lemon led the Indians to a 12-2 win over the Red Sox on August 1, 1948, by surrendering just six hits and going 3-for-4 at the plate, with a homer, three RBIs, and two runs scored.

Although Lemon pitched less effectively against Washington on July 24, 1949, he hit two home runs for the only time in his career and scored three times during a 7-5 win over the Senators.

Lemon homered, singled twice, and scored a pair of runs during a convincing 9-2 victory over the Red Sox on June 20, 1952.

Lemon turned in one of his first dominant pitching performances for the Indians on May 25, 1948, when he recorded a career-high 11 strikeouts and yielded just four hits and three walks during a 4-0 shutout of the Washington Senators.

Lemon nearly matched that strikeout total less than one month later, when he fanned 10 batters, surrendered only four hits, and homered during a 10-0 win over Philadelphia on June 20, 1948.

Lemon hurled a gem against St. Louis on July 11, 1948, allowing just three hits and two walks during a 5-0 shutout of the Browns.

Lemon performed equally well on August 29, 1948, pitching the Indians to a 6-0 win over Washington by once again yielding only three hits and two walks to the opposition.

Lemon came up big for the Indians in the 1948 World Series, leading them to a six-game victory over the Boston Braves by winning both his starts, including the Game Six clincher. He finished the Series with a record of 2-0 and an ERA of 1.65.

Lemon out-dueled Hall of Fame left-hander Hal Newhouser on April 17, 1951, surrendering just two hits and one walk during a 2-1 victory over Newhouser and the Tigers.

Lemon again dominated Detroit's lineup on May 29, 1951, allowing just one base-runner during a 2-1 win over the Tigers, who recorded their only safety of the game when Vic Wertz led off the bottom of the eighth inning with a home run.

Lemon won a 1-0 pitcher's duel with the Browns' Ned Garver on May 11, 1952, surrendering only two hits and four walks to St. Louis during the contest.

Lemon made history on April 14, 1953, when, during a 6-0 win over the White Sox in which he allowed just one hit, he became the last pitcher to throw a complete-game shutout and hit a home run on Opening Day until Clayton Kershaw accomplished the feat for the Dodgers 60 years later.

Yet, Lemon experienced the most memorable moment of his career on June 30, 1948, when he threw a no-hitter against Detroit, allowing just three bases on balls during a 2-0 victory.

Notable Achievements:

- Won at least 20 games seven times, surpassing 17 victories on two other occasions.
- Posted winning percentage in excess of .600 six times, topping .700-mark once (.767 in 1954).
- Compiled ERA under 3.00 five times.
- Tossed 10 shutouts in 1948.
- Threw more than 250 innings eight times, topping 300 innings pitched once (309 ⅔ in 1952).
- Threw more than 20 complete games seven times.
- Led AL pitchers in: wins three times, WHIP once, strikeouts once, shutouts once, innings pitched four times, complete games five times, starts three times, putouts five times, and assists six times.
- Finished second in AL in: wins three times, WHIP once, strikeouts once, shutouts once, innings pitched once, and complete games twice.

- Ranks among Indians career leaders in: wins (3rd), strikeouts (tied-3rd), shutouts (tied-3rd), innings pitched (3rd), complete games (4th), pitching appearances (4th), and games started (3rd).
- Holds major league record for most double plays in one season by a pitcher (15 in 1953).
- Threw no-hitter vs. Detroit Tigers on June 30, 1948.
- Finished in top 10 of AL MVP voting six times, placing fifth in balloting on three occasions.
- Three-time Sporting News AL Pitcher of the Year (1948, 1950, and 1954).
- Three-time Sporting News All-Star selection (1948, 1950, and 1954).
- Seven-time AL All-Star (1948, 1949, 1950, 1951, 1952, 1953, and 1954).
- Two-time AL champion (1948 and 1954).
- 1948 world champion.
- Elected to Baseball Hall of Fame by members of BBWAA in 1976.

5

EARL AVERILL
1929 – 1939

Bridging the gap between Tris Speaker and Joe DiMaggio as Major League Baseball's preeminent center fielder, Earl Averill patrolled that spacious region of League Park for the Indians from 1929 to 1938, during which time he batted over .300 eight times, topping the .330-mark on five separate occasions. The left-handed hitting Averill also surpassed 30 home runs three times, 100 RBIs five times, 100 runs scored nine times, and 200 hits twice, setting numerous franchise batting records along the way. Averill's exceptional play earned him four top-10 finishes in the AL MVP voting, four Sporting News All-Star selections, and six trips to the All-Star Game, making him one of the most decorated outfielders of his time. Averill accomplished all he did as a member of the Indians even though he did not arrive in Cleveland until shortly before he celebrated his 27th birthday, having previously spent several years starring at the semi-pro and minor-league levels.

Born in Snohomish, Washington, a small town situated some 30 miles northeast of Seattle, on May 21, 1902, Howard Earl Averill attended Snohomish High School, where he made a name for himself as a promising young outfielder before suffering a severe arm injury that temporarily caused him to give up his dream of pursuing a career in baseball. However, after making a full recovery in 1920, Averill returned to the diamond, joining a local semi-pro team called the Pilchuckers, with whom he spent the next four seasons. Leaving Snohomish in 1925 to play for another semi-pro team in Bellingham, Averill performed so well that the minor-league San Francisco Seals of the Pacific Coast League signed him to a contract at season's end.

Beginning his professional career in 1926, at the rather advanced age of 24, Averill still had a lot to learn about the fundamentals of the game.

Nevertheless, his offensive prowess soon became apparent to all, prompting San Francisco to retain his rights until late in 1928, when Billy Evans, business manager of the Cleveland Indians, finally pried him away from the Seals by offering them the princely sum of $50,000 for his services.

Finally making his major league debut with the Indians on April 16, 1929, less than five weeks before he celebrated his 27th birthday, Averill made an immediate impact, becoming the first player in American League history to hit a home run in his first big-league at-bat. From there, Averill went on to bat .332, hit 18 homers, drive in 96 runs, score 110 times, amass 198 hits, 43 doubles, and 13 triples, post an on-base percentage of .398 and a slugging percentage of .538, and lead all AL outfielders with 383 putouts, compiling in the process one of the most outstanding rookie campaigns in franchise history. He followed that up with a similarly impressive performance in 1930, finishing the season with 19 home runs, 119 RBIs, 102 runs scored, 181 hits, 33 doubles, eight triples, a .339 batting average, a .404 on-base percentage, and a .537 slugging percentage. Averill continued to play at an extremely high level in each of the next eight seasons, performing particularly well in 1931, 1932, 1934, and 1936, when he compiled the following numbers:

> 1931: 32 HR, 143 RBI, 140 Runs Scored, 209 Hits, 36 2B, .333 AVG, .404 OBP, .576 SLG
>
> 1932: 32 HR, 124 RBI, 116 Runs Scored, 198 Hits, 37 2B, .314 AVG, .392 OBP, .569 SLG
>
> 1934: 31 HR, 113 RBI, 128 Runs Scored, 187 Hits, 48 2B, .313 AVG, .414 OBP, .569 SLG
>
> 1936: 28 HR, 126 RBI, 136 Runs Scored, **232** Hits, 39 2B, .378 AVG, .438 OBP, .627 SLG

In addition to leading the American League with 232 hits in 1936, Averill topped the circuit with 15 triples, finished second in batting average, and placed near the top of the league rankings in runs scored, total bases (385), on-base percentage, slugging percentage, and OPS (1.065). He also ranked among the league leaders in home runs, RBIs, runs scored, hits, total bases, slugging percentage, and OPS in each of the other three seasons, earning in the process three top-five finishes in the AL MVP voting and Sporting News All-Star honors all four years.

While not a big man, the 5′9″, 172-pound Averill generated a good deal of power from his muscular frame, which earned him the nickname "Rock." He also learned to take advantage of the short right field porch at

League Park, compiling a lifetime batting average of .360 and an OPS of 1.064 at home while playing for the Indians. Employing an unorthodox swing in which he held the bat low as he awaited the opposing pitcher's offering, Averill used his shoulders and arms much more than his wrists to drive the ball with power to all parts of the ball park and, quite often, beyond the right field wall at League Park, which stood 60 feet high.

Expressing his admiration for Averill's hitting prowess, New York Yankees Hall of Fame pitcher Lefty Gomez stated, "No other left-hander gave me so much trouble. When I think about how many points in Earl Averill's lifetime batting average [.318] came off Gomez deliveries, I thank the good Lord he wasn't twins. One more like him would probably have kept me out of the Hall of Fame."

Indians pitcher Mel Harder also praised Averill, describing his long-time teammate in three words: "Great, great, great!" In addition to extolling Averill's virtues as a hitter, Harder discussed his defensive skills, claiming, "He was a fine defensive center fielder and saved many games for me. He is a true Hall of Famer."

Although Averill continued his string of six consecutive All-Star selections in 1937, concluding the campaign with 21 homers, 92 RBIs, 121 runs scored, and a .299 batting average, he began to experience back problems that adversely affected his performance for the remainder of his career. Diagnosed at midseason with a congenital malformation of the lower spine after momentarily losing all feeling in his legs while attempting to leave the Cleveland clubhouse for a pre-game workout, Averill subsequently had to alter his hitting style to continue playing. Transitioning into more of a spray hitter the following year, Averill hit only 14 homers, although he still managed to knock in 93 runs, score 101 times, collect 15 triples, and compile a batting average of .330, earning in the process his final All-Star selection and an eighth-place finish in the league MVP balloting. Looking back years later on how his malady impacted the rest of his career, Averill stated, "I could have been as good as [Pete] Rose. I was having a hell of a year in 1937 until my back went haywire in Philadelphia." His batting average stood at a lofty .394 when his back gave out on June 26.

With Averill's condition worsening and his production continuing to decline in 1939, the Indians decided to trade the 37-year-old outfielder to the Detroit Tigers for pitcher Harry Eisenstat and cash on June 14, bringing to an end his 11-year stay in Cleveland. Averill left the Indians with career totals of 226 home runs, 1,084 RBIs, 1,154 runs scored, 1,903 hits, 377 doubles, 121 triples, 66 stolen bases, a batting average of .322, an on-base percentage of .399, and a slugging percentage of .542. Nearly 80 years after he played his last game for the Tribe, Averill continues to hold franchise records for most RBIs (1,164), runs scored (1,224), triples (128), extra-base hits (724), total bases (3,200), and plate appearances (6,712).

Averill subsequently spent most of the next two seasons serving the Tigers as a part-time player, compiling an overall batting average of .267, hitting 12 homers, and knocking in 78 runs, in a total of 151 games and 427 official at-bats, before appearing in eight games with the Boston Braves, who released him during the early stages of the 1941 campaign. Announcing his retirement after being released by Boston, Averill ended his career with 238 home runs, 1,164 RBIs, 1,224 runs scored, 2,019 hits, 401 doubles, 128 triples, 70 stolen bases, a lifetime batting average of .318, an on-base percentage of .395, and a slugging percentage of .534.

Following his playing days, Averill returned to Snohomish, where he ran the family greenhouse and, later, opened the Earl Averill Motel, which remained in business until 1969. During that time, he saw his son, Earl Jr., spend parts of seven seasons playing in the Major Leagues, including two brief tours of duty with the Indians in 1956 and 1958.

Elected to the Hall of Fame by the members of the Veteran's Committee in 1975, Averill, who felt strongly that he deserved to be admitted to Cooperstown, later admitted, "Had I been elected after my death, I had made arrangements that my name never be placed in the Hall of Fame." Upon learning of his election, the 73-year-old Averill said, "I could have gotten in sooner. But it's sure better late than never." That same year, Averill received the additional distinction of having his uniform number 3 retired by the Indians. In addressing that honor, Averill stated, "They told me I was the greatest player ever to wear their uniform. I thanked them, but I didn't believe it."

Indians Career Highlights:

Best Season: Averill had a tremendous year for the Indians in 1931, earning a fourth-place finish in the AL MVP voting by establishing career-high marks in home runs (32), RBIs (143), and runs scored (140), while also amassing 209 hits, 36 doubles, 10 triples, and 361 total bases, batting .333, compiling a .404 on-base percentage, and posting a .576 slugging percentage. However, he compiled slightly better overall numbers in 1936, when, in addition to topping the circuit with 232 hits and 15 triples, he knocked in 126 runs and placed in the league's top five in homers (28), runs scored (136), total bases (385), batting average (.378), on-base percentage (.438), slugging percentage (.627), and OPS (1.065), reaching career-best marks in each of the last five categories en route to earning a third-place finish in the MVP balloting.

Memorable Moments/Greatest Performances: Averill made his major league debut a memorable one, homering off Detroit starter Earl Whitehill in his first big league at-bat during a 5-4, 11-inning victory over the Tigers on April 16, 1929.

Although the Indians lost their May 17, 1929 meeting with the St. Louis Browns by a score of 7-6, Averill had a big day at the plate, going 3-for-5, with two homers, a double, four RBIs, and three runs scored.

Averill led the Indians to a 10-8 win over the Yankees on July 22, 1930, by going 4-for-5, with a pair of homers and five RBIs, with his two-run blast in the bottom of the eighth inning providing the margin of victory.

Averill helped pace the Indians to a 10-5 win over the Chicago White Sox on May 23, 1931, by going a perfect 4-for-4, with a walk, a homer, three doubles, four RBIs, and three runs scored.

Averill again proved to be a thorn in the side of Chicago pitchers on July 11, 1931, when he homered twice and knocked in four runs during a 7-4, extra-inning victory over the White Sox highlighted by his game-winning three-run homer in the top of the 11th inning.

Averill had a huge game against St. Louis on April 24, 1932, leading the Tribe to a lopsided 14-3 victory over the Browns by collecting two homers and a double, driving in seven runs, and scoring three times.

Averill turned in another outstanding performance later in the year, going 4-for-5, with a pair of homers, five RBIs, and three runs scored during a 12-7 win over the Philadelphia Athletics.

Averill again feasted off of Philadelphia pitching on August 17, 1933, when he became just the second player in franchise history to hit for the cycle during a 15-4 thrashing of the Athletics, finishing the game a perfect 4-for-4, with three RBIs and four runs scored.

Courtesy of the Leslie Jones Collection at the Boston Public Library

Earl Averill knocked in more runs and scored more times
than any other player in franchise history

Just four days after homering twice and driving in five runs during a 9-5 victory over the Yankees, Averill collected five hits, including a homer and two doubles, knocked in another five runs, and scored three times, in leading the Indians to an 18-3 mauling of the Boston Red Sox on May 25, 1934.

Averill had the first 5-for-5 day of his career on August 18, 1934, collecting a triple, three doubles, and a single during a 10-0 shutout of the Philadelphia Athletics.

Once again belaboring Philadelphia pitchers on July 24, 1936, Averill led the Indians to a 16-3 romp over the Athletics by going 4-for-5, with a homer, two triples, five RBIs, and a career-high five runs scored.

Averill proved to be the difference in a 6-3 victory over the Washington Senators on July 28, 1936, driving in four runs with two singles and a pair of solo homers.

Averill led the Indians to a 9-5 win over the Yankees on May 24, 1938, by driving in six runs with a three-run homer and a bases-loaded triple off New York starter Lefty Gomez.

Averill had the greatest day of his career on September 17, 1930, when he became the first player in Major League history to hit four home runs in a doubleheader. Before homering once and driving in another three runs in the nightcap, Averill reached the seats three times and knocked in a career-high eight runs during Cleveland's 13-7 win over Washington in the opener. Commenting on his performance years later, Averill noted, "When I played, they [umpires] went by where you could last see the ball. I hit two or three more that went out [fair] over the screen, before hooking foul. A couple could have been called fair."

Yet, Averill is remembered as much as anything else for the line drive he hit off Dizzy Dean's left foot during the 1937 All-Star Game. Dean, who suffered a fractured big toe as a result, subsequently tried to return to action too soon, injuring his arm in the process, which brought his days as a dominant pitcher to an end.

Notable Achievements:

- Hit more than 20 home runs five times, topping 30 homers on three occasions.
- Knocked in more than 100 runs five times, topping 120 RBIs on three occasions.
- Scored more than 100 runs nine times, scoring more than 120 runs on four occasions.
- Batted over .300 eight times, topping the .330-mark five times.
- Surpassed 200 hits twice.
- Finished in double digits in triples eight times.
- Surpassed 30 doubles nine times, topping 40 two-baggers twice.
- Compiled on-base percentage in excess of .400 five times.
- Posted slugging percentage in excess of .500 seven times, topping the .600-mark once (.627 in 1936).
- Posted OPS in excess of 1.000 once (1.065 in 1936).
- Led AL in: hits once, triples once, games played once, and at-bats once.
- Finished second in AL in: batting average once, hits once, and triples twice.
- Led AL outfielders in putouts twice and double plays once.

- Led AL center-fielders in: putouts twice, assists once, and double plays twice.
- Holds Indians single-season record for most runs scored (140 in 1931).
- Holds Indians career records for most: RBIs (1,084), runs scored (1,154), triples (121), extra-base hits (724), total bases (3,200), and plate appearances (6,712)
- Ranks among Indians career leaders in: home runs (4th), batting average (8th), hits (3rd), doubles (3rd), bases on balls (4th), on-base percentage (7th), slugging percentage (tied-5th), OPS (6th), games played (8th), and at-bats (2nd).
- Hit three home runs in one game vs. Washington Senators on September 17, 1930.
- Hit for cycle vs. Philadelphia Athletics on August 17, 1933.
- Finished in top five of AL MVP voting three times.
- Four-time Sporting News All-Star selection (1931, 1932, 1934, and 1936).
- Six-time AL All-Star (1933, 1934, 1935, 1936, 1937, and 1938).
- Elected to Baseball Hall of Fame by members of Veteran's Committee in 1975.

6

ADDIE JOSS

1902 – 1910

His career tragically cut short by a bacterial infection that claimed his life all too soon, Addie Joss spent just eight full seasons in the Major Leagues. Nevertheless, the right-handed hurler accomplished enough during his time in Cleveland to eventually gain induction into the Baseball Hall of Fame. Over the course of his relatively brief big-league career, Joss compiled an overall record of 160-97, winning at least 20 games four times. He also tossed 45 shutouts, two no-hitters (one of them a perfect game), and five one-hitters. He led the league in WHIP twice, and captured two ERA titles, with his career mark of 1.89 placing him second among hurlers with more than 1,000 innings pitched behind long-time rival Ed Walsh. The level of dominance Joss displayed, albeit for just a few short seasons, proved to be so great that the members of the Veteran's Committee elected him to the Hall of Fame in 1978, 68 years after he threw his last pitch for the Cleveland Naps.

Born in Woodland, Wisconsin on April 12, 1880, Adrian Joss grew up the only child of Jacob and Theresa Joss, Swiss immigrants who originally came to the United States to learn the cheese-making trade. After losing his father to liver disease caused by alcoholism at the age of 10, young Addie developed into a tall, skinny boy with noticeably long arms. Yet, even though he possessed the ideal physique for a pitcher, Joss spent his earliest days on the diamond playing second base for the Wayland Academy baseball team while attending high school in Beaver Dam, Wisconsin. Graduating from Wayland at the tender age of 16, Joss briefly entered the teaching profession, before being offered a scholarship to attend St. Mary's College in Watertown, where he pitched for the school's baseball team. Joss later enrolled at the University of Wisconsin, where he studied engineering, while also playing ball at the semipro level. Offered a contract by Toledo of the Inter-State League prior to the start of the 1900 season, Joss began his professional career by posting 19 victories for the Mud Hens, before winning another 25 games for them the following year. Taking note of Joss's strong performance at Toledo, the Cleveland Bronchos invited him to spring training in 1902, with the lanky 6'3", 185-pound right-hander making enough of an impression on them to earn a regular spot in the starting rotation as a 22-year-old rookie.

Joss had a solid first year in Cleveland, compiling a record of 17-13 for the newly-named Naps, completing 28 of his 29 starts, throwing 269⅓ innings, ranking among the league leaders with a 2.77 ERA and a WHIP of 1.114, and topping the circuit with five shutouts. Improving upon his performance the following year, Joss went 18-13, with a 2.19 ERA, 31 complete games, 283 2/3 innings pitched, and a league-leading WHIP of 0.948. Although illness limited him to just 24 starts and 14 wins in 1904, Joss remained one of the American League's most effective pitchers, tossing five shutouts, compiling a WHIP of 0.988, and leading the league with a 1.59 ERA. Joss subsequently established himself as one of the game's most dominant pitchers in 1905, beginning an exceptional four-year run during which he posted the following numbers:

    1905: 20-12, 2.01 ERA, 132 Strikeouts, 1.021 WHIP, 3 Shutouts, 31 CG, 286.0 IP
    1906: 21-9,   1.72 ERA, 106 Strikeouts, 0.933 WHIP, 9 Shutouts, 28 CG, 282.0 IP
    1907: **27**-11, 1.83 ERA, 127 Strikeouts, 0.983 WHIP, 6 Shutouts, 34 CG, 338.2 IP
    1908: 24-11, **1.16** ERA, 130 Strikeouts, **0.806** WHIP, 9 Shutouts, 29 CG, 325.0 IP

In addition to leading all AL pitchers in wins, ERA, and WHIP once each during that period, Joss finished either second or third in the league in wins once, ERA twice, WHIP twice, shutouts three times, complete games twice, and innings pitched once. Meanwhile, his brilliant performance in 1908, in which he compiled career-best marks in ERA, WHIP, and shutouts, nearly led the Naps to their first league championship, with Cleveland finishing just one-half game behind first-place Detroit in the pennant race.

Blessed with exceptional control, Joss relied primarily on a good fastball, an excellent changeup, and an extremely effective curve to thwart the opposition, with former player-turned-umpire George Moriarty explaining that the tall right-hander employed only one curveball because "he believed that, with a few well-mastered deliveries, he could acquire great control and success with less strain on his arm." Choosing not to throw the spitter, as so many other pitchers of his era did, Joss achieved his success without ever altering the baseball. Instead, he deceived the batter with his unusual pitching motion, one in which he turned his back entirely to the hitter before coming at him with an exaggerated sidearm delivery. In describing Joss's windup, Cleveland infielder Roger Peckinpaugh commented, "He would turn his back toward the batter as he wound up, hiding the ball all the while, and then whip around and fire it in." Meanwhile, an article in a 1911 issue of *Baseball Magazine* suggested, "Joss not only had great speed and a fast-breaking curve, but also a very effective pitching motion, bringing the ball behind him with a complete body swing and having it on the batter almost before the latter got sight of it." And, despite turning his body toward second base and employing a high leg kick, Joss did not fall off the mound on his follow-through, completing his motion in an upright position that left him in excellent fielding position. As a result, he annually placed near the top of the league rankings in putouts and assists for pitchers.

After spending the 1908-09 off-season using his engineering background to design an electric scoreboard that Cleveland management subsequently installed at League Park, Joss returned to the pitching mound for his eighth big-league season. However, even though he performed well for the Naps in 1909, winning 14 games, tossing four shutouts, completing 24 of his 28 starts, and ranking among the league leaders with a 1.71 ERA and a WHIP of 0.944, Joss spent most of the year suffering from fatigue, forcing him to the bench for much of September.

Feeling stronger by the start of the 1910 campaign, Joss began the season well, tossing the second no-hitter of his career against the Chicago White Sox on April 20, before tearing a ligament in his right elbow a few weeks later. Limited to just 12 starts on the year, Joss made his final mound appearance on July 25, 1910, working five innings against the Philadelphia Athletics, before being forced to the sidelines by his ailing elbow. Although Joss continued to experience discomfort in his arm the following spring, he planned to return to the Naps at some point during the season. However, while conversing with a friend prior to the start of an April 3 exhibition game in Chattanooga, Tennessee, Joss fainted on the field. After his condition continued to worsen, he returned to Toledo, where his personal physician, Dr. George Chapman, diagnosed him as suffering from pleurisy. Just a few days later, in the early morning hours of April 14, two days after he turned 31 years of age, Joss died suddenly of tubercular meningitis. Learning of his teammate's passing later that day, Cleveland first baseman George Stovall said sadly, "No better man ever lived than Addie." Napoleon Lajoie added, "In Joss's death, baseball loses one of the best pitchers and men that has ever been identified with the game."

Addie Joss died having compiled a record of 160-97, an ERA of 1.89, and a WHIP of 0.968 over parts of nine big-league seasons, with the last figure representing an all-time MLB record. He also recorded 920 strikeouts and threw 45 shutouts, 234 complete games, and 2,327 innings.

Joss's funeral was held three days after his passing, on April 17, in Toledo, with all of his former teammates in attendance, even though American League President Ban Johnson earlier ordered them to play their scheduled game against Detroit. However, Johnson finally relented, postponing the contest after Naps captain George Stovall declared his team on strike, proclaiming, "I may be captain, but I'm still a ballplayer." Former ballplayer-turned-evangelist Billy Sunday delivered the eulogy, stating, "Joss tried hard to strike out death, and it seemed for a time as though he would win. The bases were full. The score was a tie, with two outs. Thousands, yes, millions in a nation's grandstands and bleachers sat breathless watching the conflict. The great twirler stood erect in the box. Death walked to the plate."

Joss's passing prompted players from all eight American League teams to gather together on July 24, 1911 for what amounted to the first "All-Star" game, with all the proceeds from the contest going to Joss's family. Among those in attendance were future Hall of Famers Ty Cobb, Tris Speaker, Eddie Collins, Sam Crawford, and Walter Johnson, who said, "I'll do anything they want for Addie Joss's family." Washington Senators manager Jimmy McAleer, who volunteered to manage one of the squads, suggested, "The memory of Addie Joss is sacred to everyone with whom he ever came into contact. The man never wore a uniform who was a greater credit to the sport than he."

In 1978, the Veteran's Committee made a special exception for Joss and waived the minimum 10-year requirement, electing him to the Hall of Fame, 67 years after his untimely death.

Career Highlights:

Best Season: Joss performed brilliantly for the Naps in 1907, leading all AL hurlers with a career-high 27 victories, while also ranking among the league leaders in ERA (1.83), winning percentage (.711), WHIP (0.983), shutouts (6), complete games (34), and innings pitched (338 2/3), establishing career-best marks in each of the last two categories as well. However, he pitched even more effectively the following year, nearly leading the Naps to the pennant by finishing second in the league with 24 wins, nine shutouts, and 325 innings pitched, tossing 29 complete games, and ranking first in the AL with an ERA of 1.16 and a WHIP of 0.806. In the process of compiling the ninth-lowest single-season ERA in MLB history, Joss walked only 30 batters in 325 innings of work.

Memorable Moments/Greatest Performances: Joss made his major league debut a memorable one, allowing just one hit and driving in a run with an RBI double, in defeating the St. Louis Browns by a score of 3-0 on April 26, 1902. The Browns got their only hit of the game when Jesse Burkett led off the sixth inning with a short fly ball to right field that home plate umpire Bob Caruthers ruled a base hit after outfielder Zaza Harvey failed to make a sliding catch.

Joss, who threw five one-hitters over the course of his career, tossed two of those within a span of three weeks in September 1907, allowing just one safety during a 3-0 victory over the Detroit Tigers on the fifth of the month, before duplicating that effort during a 3-1 win over the New York Highlanders on the 25th.

Joss turned in the greatest performance of his career on October 2, 1908, when he out-dueled Chicago White Sox Hall of Fame right-hander Ed Walsh by a score of 1-0, tossing just the second perfect game in American League history in the process. Chicago came closest to putting a man on base with two men out in the top of the ninth inning, when pinch-hitter John Anderson smashed a would-be double down the third base line that barely went foul. Anderson then grounded harmlessly to third baseman Bill Bradley, who nearly spoiled the perfecto by bobbling the ball and throwing low to first base. However, Cleveland first sacker George Stovall dug the throw out of the dirt to preserve the 1-0 gem.

Joss threw the second no-hitter of his career on April 20, 1910, once again victimizing the White Sox. Allowing only three men to reach base,

Courtesy of Mears Online Auctions

Addie Joss compiled the second lowest career ERA
of any pitcher in MLB history

one on an infield error and two on walks, Joss aided his own cause by flaw-
lessly fielding 10 ground balls hit back to the mound.

Notable Achievements:

- Won at least 20 games four straight times, topping 25 victories
  once (27 in 1907).

- Posted winning percentage in excess of .600 four times, finishing
  with mark above .700 twice.

- Compiled ERA under 2.00 five times, finishing with mark under 2.50 three other times.
- Threw more than 300 innings twice, topping 280 innings pitched three other times.
- Threw at least 20 complete games eight times, completing more than 30 of his starts on three occasions.
- Tossed nine shutouts twice.
- Posted WHIP under 1.000 six times.
- Led AL pitchers in: wins once, ERA twice, shutouts once, and WHIP twice.
- Finished second in AL in: wins once, innings pitched once, shutouts twice, and WHIP twice.
- Holds MLB record for lowest career WHIP (0.968).
- Ranks second all-time among MLB pitchers in career ERA (1.89).
- Holds Indians single-season records for lowest ERA (1.16) and lowest WHIP (0.806), both in 1908.
- Holds Indians career records for: lowest ERA (1.89), lowest WHIP (0.968), and most shutouts (45).
- Ranks among Indians career leaders in: wins (6th), winning percentage (8th), innings pitched (6th), complete games (2nd), and strikeouts-to-walks ratio (10th).
- Threw perfect game vs. Chicago on October 2, 1908.
- Threw no-hitter vs. Chicago on April 20, 1910.
- Elected to Baseball Hall of Fame by members of Veteran's Committee in 1978.

7

LOU BOUDREAU
1938 – 1950

The American League's preeminent shortstop for much of the 1940s, Lou Boudreau excelled both at the bat and in the field for the Indians throughout the decade. An outstanding hitter, Boudreau batted over .300 on four separate occasions, winning one batting title and finishing second in the league another time. Boudreau also knocked in more than 100 runs twice and led the AL in doubles three times. An adept fielder as well, Boudreau led all league shortstops in putouts four times, assists twice, double plays five times, and fielding percentage eight times, finishing first among players at his position in the last category in eight out of nine seasons at one point. Boudreau's consistently outstanding play earned him eight All-Star selections, eight top-10 finishes in the league MVP voting, and one MVP trophy, which he claimed in 1948, when, as Cleveland's player-manager, he led the team to its first world championship in 28 years.

Born to a French father and a Jewish mother in the Chicago suburb of Harvey, Illinois on July 17, 1917, Louis Boudreau, Jr. attended local Thornton Township High School, where he made a name for himself as a standout basketball player (the school did not have a baseball team). Offered an athletic scholarship to attend the University of Illinois at Urbana-Champaign, Boudreau subsequently starred in both basketball and baseball in college, displaying the leadership skills for which he later became well known by serving as captain of his team in both sports. In addition to earning All-American honors for his outstanding play on the hardwood in 1938, Boudreau drew raves for his fielding ability at third base, prompting the Cleveland Indians to sign him to a contract in which he agreed to join them once he graduated from college. However, once Big Ten officials learned of the agreement made between the two parties, they ruled Boudreau ineligible to compete at the amateur level for the remainder of his college career. With his amateur status rescinded, Boudreau turned pro, playing basketball with the Hammond All-Americans of the National Basketball League during his junior and senior years at Illinois, while also making his major-league debut late in 1938 in a one-game appearance as a pinch-hitter for the Indians.

Moved to shortstop after he joined the Buffalo Bisons of the International League at the start of the 1939 campaign, Boudreau had no qualms about making the switch since he knew that Ken Keltner held down the starting third base job in Cleveland. Called up by the Indians during the season's second half, Boudreau appeared in 53 games at shortstop, batting .258, driving in 19 runs, and scoring 42 times.

After claiming the starting job at short the following year, Boudreau performed exceptionally well in his first full season, earning All-Star honors for the first of six straight times and a fifth-place finish in the AL MVP voting by hitting nine homers, knocking in 101 runs, scoring 97 times, collecting 185 hits, and finishing second in the league with 46 doubles, while also leading all players at his position in double plays and fielding percentage. Although Boudreau scored 95 runs and led the American League with 45 doubles in 1941, he batted just .257, with both he and the Indians failing to repeat their strong performances from the previous year. As a result, team owner Alva Bradley decided to move manager Roger Peckinpaugh into the front office and assign Boudreau the task of serving as the team's player-manager, making him, at only 24 years of age, the youngest man ever to manage a major-league ball club from the outset of a season.

Proving himself capable of handling the additional responsibilities, Boudreau posted solid numbers for the Indians in each of the next two seasons, compiling batting averages of .283 and .286 in 1942 and 1943, respectively, with the shortstop remaining available to the Tribe in the second of those campaigns since the arthritis he developed in his ankles from playing basketball caused him to be declared unfit for military duty. Boudreau then earned a sixth-place finish in the MVP balloting in 1944 by topping the circuit with 45 doubles and a .327 batting average, while also scoring 91 runs and finishing second in the league with 191 hits and a .406 on-base percentage. Although limited by a broken ankle to just 97 games the following year, Boudreau still managed to earn an eighth-place finish in the MVP voting by batting .307 and compiling a career-high .983 fielding percentage at shortstop.

Extremely consistent at the plate, the right-handed hitting Boudreau held his hands high, with his bat pointed at a 45-degree angle towards the stands. Although he did not hit a lot of home runs, finishing in double digits in that category just twice his entire career, he had good gap-to-gap power and a keen batting eye, annually ranking among the league leaders in doubles and walks, while posting the best at-bat-to-strikeout ratio in the circuit on three separate occasions.

Equally proficient in the field, the 5'11", 185-pound Boudreau compensated for his average arm, small hands, limited range, and lack of foot speed by positioning himself wisely and making good use of his exceptional baseball acumen, stating on one occasion, "Playing shortstop is seventy-five to eighty percent anticipation, knowing the hitter and the pitch being thrown."

Speaking of Boudreau in an article that appeared in the June 29, 1948 edition of *The Sporting News*, H.S. Salsinger wrote, "He discounts his lack of speed by getting an uncanny jump on the ball and playing hitters with rare judgment and instinct. His hands are 'too small,' but there is not a surer pair on any infield. He has an 'impossible stance,' but he won the American League batting championship. As a competitor, he has few equals and no superiors."

Meanwhile, in discussing the qualities that made his longtime teammate such an outstanding defender, Bob Feller offered, "He had terrific instincts and was a great competitor. As a player-manager, he became so good that he went as far as calling pitches from shortstop. He was always thinking, always in the game."

Boudreau also possessed an extremely innovative managerial mind. The creator of the "Williams Shift," Boudreau came up with the idea of defending against Ted Williams by placing six men on the right side of the diamond. He also oversaw the transformation of Bob Lemon from an infielder into a Hall of Fame pitcher.

Yet, in spite of the creativity Boudreau demonstrated during his first few years as Cleveland manager, Bill Veeck wanted to replace "The Boy Wonder" at the helm when he purchased the team in 1946. However, when Veeck's plans leaked out, a public outcry arose, causing Boudreau to be retained as skipper.

With most of the game's best players returning from the military following the end of World War II, Boudreau continued to perform at a high level in 1946, batting .293 and leading all AL shortstops in fielding percentage for the sixth time. He followed that up by batting .307, driving in 67 runs, scoring 79 others, and topping the circuit with 45 doubles in 1947, earning in the process his seventh All-Star nomination and a third-place finish in the league MVP voting. Boudreau then put together the finest season of his career in 1948, leading the Indians to the AL pennant by hitting 18 homers, driving in 106 runs, finishing second in the league with a .355 batting average and a .453 on-base percentage, and also ranking among the leaders with 116 runs scored, 199 hits, 299 total bases, 98 walks, a .534 slugging percentage, and an OPS of .987, with his fabulous performance earning him AL MVP and *Sporting News* Major League Player of the Year honors. Boudreau solidified his MVP credentials by going four-for-four with two home runs in Cleveland's pennant-clinching victory over Boston in a one-game playoff. He then drove in three runs and batted .273 during the Tribe's six-game World Series victory over the Boston Braves. Commenting years later on the magical season turned in by Boudreau and the Indians, former manager Bill McKechnie, who had been hired as a Cleveland coach at Bill Veeck's suggestion prior to the start of the campaign, stated, "I have never known another year like the one we had in Cleveland in '48. Every day was like a final game of the World Series. And, that year, Lou Boudreau was the greatest shortstop and leader I have ever seen."

Boudreau had one more good year left in him, compiling a batting average of .284 in 1949, before Father Time began to rear his ugly head. After serving the Indians as a part-time player in 1950, Boudreau left Cleveland when the team traded him to the Boston Red Sox following the conclusion of the campaign, bringing to an end his 13-year association with the Tribe and nine-year managerial reign. During his time with the Indians, Boudreau hit 63 homers, knocked in 740 runs, scored 823 others, amassed 1,706 hits, 367 doubles, and 65 triples, batted .296, compiled a .382 on-base percentage, and posted a .416 slugging percentage.

After joining the Red Sox, Boudreau appeared in 82 games in 1951, before assuming the role of player-manager the following year, which proved to be his last as an active player (he appeared in only four games). Announcing his retirement at season's end, Boudreau finished his career with 68 home runs, 789 RBIs, 861 runs scored, 1,779 hits, 385 doubles, 66 triples, a .295 batting average, .380 on-base percentage, .415 slugging percentage, and only 309 strikeouts in 7,024 total plate appearances.

Boudreau continued to manage the Red Sox through the 1954 season, before spending the next three years piloting the Kansas City Athletics. After leaving Kansas City, he became a WGN radio and television announcer for Chicago Cubs games for two years, before switching roles with manager Charlie Grimm in 1960. After one season as Cubs manager, Boudreau returned to the radio booth, where he remained until 1987, 17 years after the members of the BBWAA elected him to the Baseball Hall of Fame. Boudreau passed away on August 10, 2001, a little less than one month after he turned 84, after suffering from cardiac arrest following a long bout with circulatory problems.

In paying tribute to his former teammate and close friend, Bob Feller said, "Boudreau was one of the most talented players in baseball in his time, in addition to being one of the classiest human beings you'd ever want to meet. Even before he was manager, as a twenty-one-year-old shortstop, he was our on-field leader."

Indians Career Highlights:

Best Season: Although Boudreau also performed extremely well for the Indians in 1940 and 1944, batting .295, driving in 101 runs, and scoring 97 times in the first of those campaigns, before leading the league with 45 doubles and a .327 batting average in the second, he had easily his finest season in 1948. En route to leading the Indians to the AL pennant and capturing league MVP honors, Boudreau established career-high marks in 10 different offensive categories, including home runs (18), RBIs (106), runs scored (116), hits (199), batting average (.355), on-base percentage (.453), and slugging percentage (.534), placing in the league's top five in seven of those. He also struck out only nine times in 676 total plate appearances and led all AL shortstops in double plays and fielding percentage.

Memorable Moments/Greatest Performances: Boudreau hit two home runs in one game for the first of five times in his career on April 27, 1940, when he reached the seats twice and drove in three runs during a 4-2 victory over the Detroit Tigers.

Boudreau had a big day at the plate against Washington on July 26, 1940, going a perfect 4-for-4, with a double, triple, two RBIs, and three runs scored, during a 13-2 romp over the Senators.

Boudreau helped lead the Indians to a 9-3 win over the Chicago White Sox on August 7, 1940, by going 3-for-5, with a pair of homers, three runs scored, and a career-high six runs batted in.

Boudreau proved to be the difference in a 3-1 victory over the White Sox on June 30, 1942, going 4-for-4, with a homer and a double, and scoring all three Cleveland runs.

Continuing to be a thorn in the side of Chicago pitchers, Boudreau paced the Indians to a lopsided 10-0 victory over the White Sox on September 8, 1942, by going 4-for-5, with a pair of doubles and four runs scored.

Although the Indians lost their July 14, 1946 matchup with the Boston Red Sox by a score of 11-10, Boudreau starred in defeat, going 5-for-5, with a homer, four RBIs, and three runs scored, and setting a major-league record by smashing four consecutive doubles.

Boudreau had another big day at the plate exactly one month later, when he went 4-for-5, with two RBIs, during a 12-inning, 6-5 victory over the Detroit Tigers on August 14, 1946, that ended when he delivered the game's winning run with an opposite field double in the bottom of the 12th.

Boudreau came up a home run short of hitting for the cycle on April 26, 1948, when he went 5-for-6, with a triple, double, three singles, and four RBIs, during a 14-inning, 12-11 victory over the Chicago White Sox that the Indians won with a solo homer by first baseman Eddie Robinson in the top of the 14th.

Boudreau led the Indians to a 5-2 win over the St. Louis Browns on April 29, 1948, by going 4-for-5, with a homer, double, three RBIs, and two runs scored.

Boudreau defeated Philadelphia almost singlehandedly on September 19, 1948, when his two solo homers gave the Indians a 2-0 victory over the Athletics.

However, there is little doubt that Boudreau experienced the finest moment of his career on October 4, 1948, when he led the Indians to an 8-3 victory over the Boston Red Sox in a one-game playoff to determine the American League champion by going 4-for-4, with a pair of solo homers and three runs scored. After homering over Fenway Park's "Green Monster" in the top of the first inning, Boudreau singled in the fourth to

Courtesy of RMY Auctions

Lou Boudreau earned AL MVP honors in 1948 when
he led the Indians to their first pennant in 28 years

begin a four-run rally, homered again in the fifth inning, and singled again
in the top of the ninth.

Notable Achievements:

- Batted over .300 four times, topping the .320-mark twice.
- Knocked in more than 100 runs twice.
- Scored more than 100 runs once (116 in 1948).
- Finished in double digits in triples twice.
- Surpassed 30 doubles seven times, topping 40 two-baggers on four occasions.
- Compiled on-base percentage in excess of .400 twice.

- Posted slugging percentage in excess of .500 once (.534 in 1948).
- Led AL in: batting average once, doubles three times, sacrifice hits twice, at-bat-to-strikeout ratio three times, and games played once.
- Finished second in AL in: batting average once, hits once, doubles once, and on-base percentage twice.
- Led AL shortstops in: putouts four times, assists twice, fielding percentage eight times, and double plays five times.
- Ranks among Indians career leaders in: runs scored (9th), hits (6th), extra-base hits (7th), doubles (5th), total bases (7th), bases on balls (3rd), games played (3rd), plate appearances (2nd), and at-bats (4th).
- 1948 AL MVP.
- Finished in top 10 of AL MVP voting seven other times, making it into top five on two other occasions.
- 1948 Sporting News Major League Player of the Year.
- Two-time Sporting News All-Star selection (1947 and 1948).
- Eight-time AL All-Star (1940, 1941, 1942, 1943, 1944, 1945, 1947, and 1948).
- 1948 AL champion.
- 1948 world champion.
- Elected to Baseball Hall of Fame by members of BBWAA in 1970.

8

JIM THOME
1991 – 2002, 2011

One of only nine players in MLB history to hit as many as 600 home runs over the course of his career, Jim Thome slugged a franchise-record 337 homers over parts of 12 seasons with the Indians. Averaging 40 round-trippers a year his final seven seasons in Cleveland, Thome established another franchise mark in 2002, when he reached the seats 52 times. More than just a home-run hitter, Thome also batted over .300 three times, compiled an on-base percentage in excess of .400 seven times, and knocked in more than 100 runs on six separate occasions as a member of the Indians, en route to earning three top-10 finishes in the AL MVP voting, three trips to the All-Star Game, and three *Sporting News* All-Star selections. Meanwhile, Thome's powerful bat helped lead the Tribe to six division titles and two American League pennants.

Born in Peoria, Illinois on August 27, 1970, James Howard Thome learned how to play baseball from his father, who recalled, "The only thing the kid ever wanted to do was play baseball. He used to have a hard time getting kids to spend as much time on the field as he wanted to. Rain or shine, he'd take a bucket of rubber baseballs and hit them for hours."

Following in the footsteps of his two older brothers, both of whom starred on the diamond at Limestone Community High School in nearby Bartonville, Jim attended that same institution, where he earned All-State honors as a guard in basketball and a shortstop in baseball. After enrolling at Illinois Central College following his graduation in 1988, Thome continued to compete in both sports, performing well enough in his one year of college ball to draw interest from the Cleveland Indians, who selected him in the 13th round of the 1989 MLB Draft. Thome then spent most of the next five seasons in the minor leagues, although he also appeared in a total of 114 games for the Indians from 1991 to 1993, hitting 10 homers and driving in 43 runs for the Tribe during that time.

Thome's lengthy stint in the minors could be attributed primarily to his subpar defense. Manning the hot corner while advancing through Cleveland's farm system, Thome later recalled, "There were times when I really needed to work, especially defensively. I had to put in a lot of extra work and hard times defensively to make myself an even adequate defensive player. Early on, I had a hard time defensively."

The left-handed swinging Thome also struggled at the plate during the early stages of his pro career, displaying a lack of patience as a hitter, and often waving at curveballs and splitters in the dirt, particularly against southpaw pitching. However, things finally started to come together for Thome at Triple-A Scranton in 1993, when, with the help of future Major League manager Charlie Manuel, he earned International League MVP honors by hitting 25 home runs and batting .332. Crediting Manuel with his development as a hitter, Thome claims, "He was everything to me. Hands down. From confidence, to what he taught me, to the mental side of hitting. We didn't talk about mechanics a whole lot, but he got me in position when he put me on home plate with my back foot and opened me up. I really saw my power keep progressing."

Thome also revealed that he first began using the technique of pointing his bat toward the pitcher while awaiting his delivery at Manuel's behest, stating, "I did that in Scranton when Charlie Manuel had seen a clip of Roy Hobbs [the protagonist in the movie, The Natural]. Roy Hobbs would point his bat, and, when I got in the box, I was really tense. I was tight, and he wanted to create that relaxing feeling in the box, and it got my trigger ready to hit."

Thome's stellar 1993 performance earned him a promotion to the Indians the following year, when, after laying claim to the starting third base job, he batted .268, hit 20 homers, and knocked in 52 runs, even though a player's strike shortened the season to just 113 games. Thome followed that up with a solid 1995 campaign in which he hit 25 homers, knocked in 73 runs, scored 92 times, drew 97 bases on balls, batted .314, and finished third in the league with a .438 on-base percentage.

Emerging as a true offensive force in 1996, Thome hit 38 homers, knocked in 116 runs, scored 122 others, batted .311, finished second in the league with 123 walks, and placed third in the circuit with an OPS of

1.062. Continuing to excel at the plate after moving across the diamond to play first base in order to make room at third for Matt Williams in 1997, Thome helped the Indians capture their second pennant in three seasons by hitting 40 homers, driving in 102 runs, scoring 104 times, batting .286, and leading the league with 120 bases on balls, earning in the process a sixth-place finish in the AL MVP voting and All-Star honors for the first of three straight times.

Thome, who stood 6'4" tall and weighed close to 250 pounds, proved to be a slugger in the truest sense of the word, intimidating opposing pitchers with his size, brute strength, and potent swing. Possessing tremendous power to all fields, Thome had the ability to drive the ball out of any part of the park, hitting many of his home runs to center and left-center. Thome also gradually developed a keen batting eye and superior knowledge of the strike zone, enabling him to draw more than 100 bases on balls in nine different seasons. However, he also struck out frequently, fanning more than any other AL hitter on three separate occasions, en route to whiffing more times than anyone else in franchise history.

In discussing his greatest flaw as a hitter, Thome stated, "The strikeouts were a part of my game that I didn't like, but I wasn't going to take away the aggressiveness. I think the biggest help to my game was the fact that I walked. I was a hitter that did strike out, but also went through periods of good contact. I had the ability to take the ball the other way, I had power, but the strikeouts were a part of my game that I always tried to improve on, but it was just a part of my game. It was the way that I was constructed."

As Thome continued his rise to stardom, he grew increasingly popular with the hometown fans, writers, and broadcasters, who very much appreciated his strong work ethic, old-fashioned values, and friendly demeanor. Extremely approachable, Thome never rejected autograph requests, once stating, "I sign every autograph I can for kids because I remember myself at that age. I think it's ridiculous that some guys won't sign for a kid."

Commenting on Thome's likeable personality, Indians GM John Hart suggested, "He's got that 'aw gee, aw shucks' air about him. Jim is Huck Finn personified, and he really likes to play baseball."

Identifying former Indians first baseman Eddie Murray as his role model, Thome credited his calm demeanor to his onetime teammate, noting, "Eddie taught me to play the game exactly the same when you fail and when you succeed. Hit a home run, hey, enjoy the moment, but then let it go. If you strike out with the bases loaded, same thing, let it go. I don't smash helmets when I strike out, because it's not the helmet's fault, it's my fault."

Yet, in spite of his gentle nature, Thome possessed a fierce competitive spirit, with Richie Sexson saying of his former teammate, "He's an emotional player who likes to play for something. Every team has a guy who refuses to lose, a big-time player who pushes and pulls the rest of the team."

Although Thome posted outstanding numbers his first few seasons in Cleveland, he often found himself being overlooked in favor of some of his more colorful teammates, as former Indians outfielder Jeromy Burnitz suggested when he said, "You can't really say he's underrated because everybody considers him one of the top hitters in the American League, but he's surrounded by so many good players, it's hard to stand out on that team."

Thome continued to put up excellent numbers for the Indians from 1998 to 2000, averaging 33 home runs, 100 RBIs, and 99 runs scored over the course of those three seasons, while walking more than 100 times twice and compiling batting averages of .293, .277, and .269. However, after shedding some weight and improving his agility, Thome reached the apex of his career the next two seasons, earning a pair of top-10 finishes in the AL MVP balloting by driving in 124 runs, scoring 101 others, batting .291, and finishing second in the league with 49 homers and an OPS of 1.040 in 2001, before hitting a franchise-record 52 homers, knocking in 118 runs, scoring 101 times, batting .304, and topping the circuit with 122 walks, a .677 slugging percentage, and an OPS of 1.122 the following year.

A free agent heading into the 2003 campaign, Thome hoped to remain in Cleveland. But, with the Indians offering him $60 million over five years, Thome elected to sign with the Philadelphia Phillies when they came calling with a six-year, $85 million offer.

Thome performed extremely well his first two seasons in Philadelphia, earning a fourth-place finish in the 2003 NL MVP voting by topping the circuit with 47 homers, driving in 131 runs, scoring 111 others, and batting .266, before hitting 42 homers, knocking in 105 runs, scoring 97 times, and batting .274 the following year. But, when back problems he first began experiencing his last few seasons in Cleveland limited him to only 59 games in 2005, Thome hit just seven homers, knocked in only 30 runs, and batted just .207.

Dealt to the Chicago White Sox during the subsequent off-season, Thome spent most of the next four years serving the Sox as a designated hitter, totaling 134 home runs and 369 RBIs during that time. Playing his best ball for Chicago in 2006, Thome earned the last of his five All-Star nominations by hitting 42 homers, knocking in 109 runs, scoring 108 times, and batting .288. After being traded to the Dodgers during the latter stages of the 2009 campaign, Thome spent the remainder of his career serving as a backup on four different teams, splitting his final three seasons between the Twins, Indians, Phillies, and Orioles, before announcing his retirement following the conclusion of the 2012 campaign. Prior to officially announcing his retirement, though, Thome signed a one-day contract with the Indians, enabling him to end his career as a member of the team with which he made his major-league debut 22 years earlier. Thome retired with career totals of 612 home runs, 1,699 RBIs, 1,583 runs scored, 2,328 hits, 451 doubles, and 26 triples, a .276 batting average, a .402 on-base percentage, and a .554 slugging percentage. As a member of the Indians, he hit a franchise-record 337 homers, knocked in 937 runs, scored 928 times, amassed 1,353 hits, 263 doubles, and 20 triples, established franchise marks for most bases on balls (1,008) and strikeouts (1,400), batted .287, compiled a .414 on-base percentage, and posted a .566 slugging percentage.

Some two years after Thome concluded his playing career, the Indians erected a statue of him behind the center field wall at Progressive Field. Upon viewing the depiction of himself for the first time, Thome commented, "It's pretty awesome. How could you ever imagine, when you play this game, getting the opportunity to have an organization put up a statue of you? I am a little lost for words. I can't even say that, as a player, you dream of that. When it happens, it's humbling."

After retiring as an active player, Thome joined the White Sox organization as a special assistant to the GM. He later accepted a part-time studio analyst position with MLB Network, with whom he currently works, while still fulfilling his role with the White Sox. Yet, Thome, who a 2003 *Cleveland Plain Dealer* fan poll named the most popular athlete in Cleveland sports history, still considers his years with the Indians to be his happiest in baseball, stating, "I would say my most fun time was from the strike until 1997. We were dominant. We had dominant teams, and we were ready to win. Then. Right there. We had an aura about ourselves—a confidence that you couldn't teach. We all wanted to be great, and we fed off of each other."

Indians Career Highlights:

Best Season: Thome performed exceptionally well for the Indians in 1996, earning his lone Silver Slugger by hitting 38 homers, driving in 116 runs, establishing career-high marks in runs scored (122), batting average (.311), and on-base percentage (.450), and placing near the top of the league rankings with 123 bases on balls and an OPS of 1.062. Nevertheless, Thome's final season with the Indians would have to be considered his finest as a member of the team. In addition to finishing second in the American League with 52 homers and a .445 on-base percentage in 2002, Thome knocked in 118 runs, scored 101 times, batted .304, and topped the circuit with 122 bases on balls, a .677 slugging percentage, and an OPS of 1.122, establishing in the process career-high marks in the last two categories.

Memorable Moments/Greatest Performances: Thome led the Indians to a lopsided 11-3 victory over Detroit on August 18, 1996, by going 4-for-5, with a pair of homers, six RBIs, and three runs scored, with his eighth-inning grand slam putting the game out of reach.

Thome had another huge game on May 19, 1998, going 4-for-5, with a homer, four RBIs, and three runs scored, during a 16-3 thrashing of the Kansas City Royals.

Although the Indians ended up losing the 1998 ALCS to the Yankees in six games, Thome performed magnificently, hitting four homers, driving in eight runs, and batting .304.

Thome turned in another brilliant postseason performance the following year, hitting four homers, knocking in 10 runs, and batting .353 during the Tribe's five-game loss to Boston in the 1999 ALDS.

Thome set a club record by hitting home runs in seven consecutive games during a hot streak that lasted from June 25 to July 3, 2002.

Thome gave the Indians a 2-1 win over the Tigers on August 28, 2002, by hitting a pair of solo homers off Detroit starter Brian Powell.

Courtesy of MEARS Online Auctions

Jim Thome's 337 home runs as a member
of the Indians represent a franchise record

Thome hit a number of memorable home runs during his time in Cleveland, with one of those coming on August 3, 1999, when, after homering off Pedro Martinez earlier in the contest, he tied the score with Boston at 4-4 with a two-out, two-run blast off Tim Wakefield in the top of the eighth inning. The Indians subsequently scored the game-winning run in the ensuing frame on an RBI single by Omar Vizquel.

Thome came up big in the clutch again on July 28, 2002, when his grand slam homer in the bottom of the ninth inning gave the Indians a 9-6 victory over the Detroit Tigers.

Thome provided further heroics on September 28, 2002, when his three-run homer in the bottom of the eighth inning drew the Indians even with Kansas City at 5-5 in a game they ended up winning two frames later on an unearned run.

Thome also hit three home runs in one game twice as a member of the Indians, doing so for the first time on July 22, 1994, when he hit three solo blasts during a 9-8 win over the White Sox.

Thome accomplished the feat again on July 6, 2001, when he reached the seats three times and knocked in six runs during a convincing 14-2 victory over the St. Louis Cardinals.

Notable Achievements:

- Hit more than 30 home runs seven times, topping 40 homers three times and 50 homers once.
- Knocked in more than 100 runs six times, surpassing 120 RBIs once (124 in 2001).
- Scored more than 100 runs six times, topping 120 runs scored once (122 in 1996).
- Batted over .300 three times.
- Surpassed 30 doubles twice.
- Drew more than 100 bases on balls six times, topping 120 walks on four occasions.
- Compiled on-base percentage in excess of .400 seven times.
- Posted slugging percentage in excess of .500 nine times, topping the .600-mark three times.
- Posted OPS in excess of 1.000 four times.
- Led AL in: bases on balls three times, slugging percentage once, and OPS once.
- Finished second in AL in: home runs twice, bases on balls twice, on-base percentage once, slugging percentage once, and OPS twice.
- Finished third in AL in: bases on balls once, on-base percentage four times, and OPS once.

- Holds Indians single-season records for most home runs (52 in 2002) and walks (127 in 1999).
- Holds Indians career records for most home runs (337) and walks (1,008).
- Ranks among Indians career leaders in: RBIs (2nd), runs scored (5th), doubles (10th), extra-base hits (3rd), total bases (4th), on-base percentage (3rd), slugging percentage (3rd), OPS (3rd), and sacrifice flies (7th).
- Ranks among MLB all-time leaders with 612 home runs (7th) and 1,747 walks (7th).
- Hit three home runs in one game twice (vs. Chicago White Sox on July 22, 1994, and vs. St. Louis Cardinals on July 6, 2001).
- July 2001 AL Player of the Month.
- 1996 Silver Slugger winner.
- 2002 Roberto Clemente Award winner.
- Finished in top 10 of AL MVP voting three times.
- Three-time Sporting News All-Star selection (1995, 1996, and 2001).
- Three-time AL All-Star (1997, 1998, and 1999).
- Two-time AL champion (1995 and 1997).

9

JOE SEWELL

1920 – 1930

The holder of every major career and single-season record for fewest strikeouts by a batter, Joe Sewell established himself as one of the greatest contact hitters in baseball history over the course of his career. Fanning only 114 times in 14 big-league seasons, 8,333 total plate appearances, and 7,132 official at-bats, Sewell averaged just one whiff for every 63 trips to the plate, giving him the second-best ratio in the history of the game, behind only 19th-century star "Wee" Willie Keeler. More than just an extremely difficult man to strike out, Sewell batted over .300 a total of 10 times, doing so on nine separate occasions as a member of the Indians. Having most of his finest seasons in Cleveland, Sewell also topped 200 hits once and surpassed 90 RBIs, 90 runs scored, and 40 doubles five times each while playing for the Tribe, en route to earning four top-10 finishes in the AL MVP voting. An excellent fielder as well, Sewell led all American League shortstops in fielding percentage three times and assists and putouts four times each, with his stellar all-around play eventually landing him in Cooperstown.

Born in Titus, Alabama on October 9, 1898, Joseph Wheeler Sewell starred in multiple sports while attending Wetumpka High School, excelling in baseball, football, and basketball. Although Sewell originally intended to follow in his father's footsteps and pursue a career in medicine when he enrolled at the University of Alabama in 1916, he later chose to sign with the minor-league New Orleans Pelicans of the Southern Association in 1920 after spending the previous three years lettering in football and baseball for the Crimson Tide.

Adapting well to the pro game, Sewell remained in New Orleans for only a few short months, before the Cleveland Indians purchased his contract during the latter stages of the 1920 campaign after they lost their starting shortstop, Ray Chapman, to a fatal beaning in Mid-August. Joining the Tribe in early September, Sewell spent the final three weeks of the 1920 season manning shortstop for the Indians, batting .329 and driving in 12 runs in only 22 games, although he struggled somewhat defensively, committing 15 errors in the field.

After returning to the University of Alabama to continue his pre-med studies during the subsequent off-season, Sewell rejoined the Indians prior to the start of the 1921 campaign. Appearing in every game for the Tribe for the first of eight times, Sewell had an outstanding rookie season, batting .318, knocking in 93 runs, scoring 101 times, and finishing fourth in the league with 80 bases on balls, although he continued to perform erratically in the field, committing 47 defensive miscues. Sewell then batted .299, drove in 83 runs, and scored 80 times in 1922, before having the finest offensive season of his career the following year, when he earned a fourth-place finish in the AL MVP voting by ranking among the league leaders in several statistical categories, including batting average (.353), RBIs (109), and on-base percentage (.456).

The left-handed hitting Sewell established himself as a solid RBI-man his first few seasons in Cleveland even though, at just 5'6" tall and 155 pounds, he had very little home run power, reaching the seats as many as 10 times in a season just twice his entire career. Yet, he drove the ball well to the outfield gaps, surpassing 30 doubles in a season eight times. And, whatever Sewell lacked in physical strength, he made up for with an incredible ability to make solid contact with the ball, enabling him to use the same 40-ounce black bat that he named "Black Betsy" throughout his entire career. After striking out a total of 62 times over the course of his first four full seasons, Sewell never again fanned more than nine times in any single campaign, twice whiffing as few as three times in a season. The diminutive infielder's ability to spoil a pitcher's best offering prompted Hall of Fame southpaw Lefty Grove, who never struck out Sewell in 96 career at-bats, to call him the toughest batter he ever faced.

In explaining the secret to his success, Sewell noted years later, "I followed the ball all the way. I could even see it hit the bat. Anyone can—if he concentrates on picking up the ball and not watching the pitcher's motion. . . . .Ted [Williams] said he could see the ball leave his bat, and I could too. I did that from the first day until I finished, and that's the reason why I didn't strike out much."

Sewell then added, "There's no excuse for a major league player striking out a hundred times a season. Unless, of course, he's blind."

Meanwhile, after leading all American League players in errors in two of his first three seasons, committing as many as 59 defensive miscues in 1923, Sewell gradually evolved into an extremely reliable defender, leading all AL shortstops in fielding percentage three times, while also finishing first among players at his position in assists five times, putouts four times, and double plays once.

Sewell followed up his exceptional 1923 campaign with another outstanding season in 1924, batting .316, driving in 106 runs, scoring 99 times, and leading the league with 45 doubles. He then earned a third-place finish in the AL MVP voting in 1925 by batting .336, knocking in 98 runs, amassing a career-high 204 hits, and leading all players at his position in putouts, assists, and fielding percentage. Sewell remained an elite player for another four years, performing particularly well in 1926, when he batted .324 and scored 91 runs, and 1927, when he earned a 10th-place finish in the league MVP balloting by batting .316, driving in 92 runs, and collecting a career-high 48 doubles. But, after Sewell's offensive production fell off dramatically in 1930 (he batted .289, knocked in just 48 runs, and scored only 44 times in 109 games), the Indians elected to release him at season's end. Sewell left Cleveland with career totals of 30 home runs, 868 RBIs, 857 runs scored, 1,800 hits, 375 doubles, 63 triples, 71 stolen bases, 654 walks and only 99 strikeouts, a batting average of .320, a .398 on-base percentage, and a .425 slugging percentage.

After being released by the Indians, Sewell signed with the Yankees, with whom he spent the final three years of his big-league career manning third base, playing his best ball for them in 1931, when he batted .302 and scored 102 runs. Sewell also batted .272, hit a career-high 11 homers, and scored 95 runs for New York's 1932 World Series championship team. Released by the Yankees following the conclusion of the 1933 campaign, Sewell subsequently announced his retirement, ending his career with 49 home runs, 1,054 RBIs, 1,141 runs scored, 2,226 hits, 436 doubles, 68 triples, 74 stolen bases, a .312 batting average, a .391 on-base percentage, and a .413 slugging percentage.

Following his playing days, Sewell spent two seasons coaching for the Yankees, before returning to Alabama, where he opened a hardware store. He also briefly worked as a spokesman for a local dairy manufacturer. Sewell later returned to Cleveland, where he spent another 10 years with the Indians, first, as a regional scout, and, then, as Southeast scouting supervisor. After leaving the Indians organization in 1962, Sewell spent a year scouting for the New York Mets, before accepting the position of head baseball coach at his alma mater, the University of Alabama. He remained in that post until 1970, when he retired from baseball for good. Sewell spent the remainder of his life in Alabama, passing away at 91 years of age, on March 6, 1990, 13 years after the members of the Veteran's Committee elected him to the Baseball Hall of Fame.

Indians Career Highlights:

Best Season: Sewell performed extremely well for the Indians in both 1924 and 1925, driving in 106 runs, scoring 99 times, batting .316, and leading the league with 45 doubles in the first of those campaigns, before earning a third-place finish in the AL MVP voting the following year by knocking in 98 runs, batting .336, collecting 204 hits, and leading all league shortstops in assists, putouts, and fielding percentage. However, Sewell had his finest all-around season in 1923, when, en route to earning a fourth-place finish in the AL MVP balloting, he ranked among the league leaders in nine different offensive categories, including runs scored (98), hits (195), doubles (41), RBIs (109), batting average (.353), on-base percentage (.456), and slugging percentage (.479), establishing career-high marks in each of the last four categories.

Memorable Moments/Greatest Performances: Sewell helped lead the Indians to a 12-9 win over the St. Louis Browns in the second game of the 1921 regular season by nearly hitting for the cycle, going 3-for-5, with a homer, triple, double, four RBIs, and three runs scored.

Sewell had a big day at the plate against New York on July 21, 1921, collecting three doubles and two singles, driving in a pair of runs, and scoring twice during a lopsided 17-8 victory over the Yankees.

Sewell helped lead the Indians to a 15-1 rout of the Yankees on August 25, 1921, when he scored three times and knocked in four runs with a double and three-run homer off New York starter Bob Shawkey.

Sewell defeated the Boston Red Sox almost single-handedly on June 17, 1922, collecting four hits and driving in four runs during a 5-4 Cleveland win that took 14 innings to complete. After tying the score at 4-4 with a three-run homer in the bottom of the seventh inning, Sewell once again came through in the clutch in the bottom of the 14th, plating the game's winning run with a two-out RBI double.

Sewell had his only 5-for-5 day as a member of the Indians on July 12, 1922, when he hit safely in all five of his trips to the plate and knocked in four runs, in leading the Tribe to an 11-7 win over the Boston Red Sox.

Continuing to feast on Boston pitching, Sewell collected three hits and knocked in five runs during a 12-3 mauling of the Red Sox on August 16, 1923.

Sewell helped lead the Indians to an 8-5 victory over the Philadelphia Athletics on May 11, 1924, by going 4-for-5, with a homer, double, and a career-high six runs batted in.

Sewell equaled his career-high RBI total later in the year, driving in six runs with a single, double, and triple during a 12-1 pasting of the St. Louis Browns on September 27, 1924.

Sewell proved to be the difference in a 7-6, 12-inning win over Washington on August 9, 1925, going 4-for-5, with four RBIs.

Although the Indians lost their June 23, 1928 match-up with the St. Louis Browns by a score of 10-3, Sewell hit two home runs in one game for the only time as a member of the Tribe, driving in all three Cleveland runs with a pair of round-trippers.

Sewell helped lead the Indians to a 12-9 victory over the Detroit Tigers on June 29, 1929, by driving in five runs with a triple and a pair of singles.

Notable Achievements:

- Batted over .300 nine times, topping the .330-mark twice.
- Knocked in more than 100 runs twice.
- Scored more than 100 runs once (101 in 1921).
- Surpassed 200 hits once (204 in 1925).
- Finished in double digits in triples twice.
- Surpassed 30 doubles eight times, topping 40 two-baggers on five occasions.
- Compiled on-base percentage in excess of .400 four times.
- Led AL in: at-bat-to-strikeout ratio six times, doubles once, sacrifice hits once, and games played once.
- Finished second in AL with 98 walks in 1923.

Joe Sewell batted over .300 nine straight times
for the Indians during the 1920s

Courtesy of the Bain News Service Collection at the Library of Congress

- Led AL shortstops in: assists four times, putouts four times, fielding percentage three times, and double plays turned once.
- Led AL third basemen in assists once.
- Holds MLB records for most consecutive games without a strikeout (115) and best career at-bat-to strikeout ratio (62.6).
- Holds Indians single-season record for best at-bat-to-strikeout ratio (152.0 in 1925).
- Holds Indians career record for best at-bat-to-strikeout ratio (56.8).
- Ranks among Indians career leaders in: batting average (9th), RBIs (6th), runs scored (8th), hits (4th), extra-base hits (10th), doubles (4th), total bases (8th), bases on balls (8th), on-base percentage (8th), sacrifice hits (5th), games played (tied-6th), plate appearances (5th), and at-bats (7th).
- Finished in top 10 of AL MVP voting four times, making in into top five twice.
- 1926 Sporting News All-Star selection.
- 1920 AL champion.
- 1920 world champion.
- Elected to Baseball Hall of Fame by members of Veteran's Committee in 1977.

10

OMAR VIZQUEL
1994 - 2004

A superb defensive player who holds MLB records for most double plays turned by a shortstop and fewest errors committed in a season by a shortstop, Omar Vizquel won a total of 11 Gold Gloves over the course of his career, earning eight of those as a member of the Cleveland Indians, with whom he spent 11 of his 24 big-league seasons. Manning arguably the most important position on the diamond for the Tribe from 1994 to 2004, Vizquel won a Gold Glove in each of his first eight seasons in Cleveland, en route to recording the third most assists of any shortstop ever to play the game. A solid offensive performer as well, Vizquel scored more than 100 runs twice, stole more than 30 bases four times, and batted over .280 six times, topping the .300-mark once, with his exceptional all-around play earning him three All-Star selections and helping the Indians capture six division titles and two AL pennants.

Born in Caracas, Venezuela on April 24, 1967, Omar Enrique (Gonzalez) Vizquel spent much of his youth playing soccer, basketball, and volleyball with his friends, developing in the process the athletic skills that later enabled him to pursue a career in baseball. While his participation in basketball and volleyball contributed greatly to the development of his hand-eye coordination, Vizquel explained how competing in soccer, which helped improve his quickness afoot, better prepared him for a career as a middle infielder: "If you're going to play the infield, you need to have good footwork. Your feet and your legs are the start of good defense."

Hoping to follow in the footsteps of fellow Venezuelan shortstops Luis Aparicio and Dave Concepcion, Vizquel began to concentrate primarily on baseball by the time he turned 14. Remaining optimistic even after a coach told him at his first pro tryout, "You should go to the racetrack and be a jockey because you're too small to play baseball," Vizquel, who eventually grew to be 5'9" tall and weigh 170 pounds, began his career with the Leones del Caracas of the Venezuelan Winter League, before signing with the Seattle Mariners as a 16-year-old non-drafted free agent in 1984. He then spent the next five years in the minor leagues, before finally earning a promotion to Seattle in 1989.

Struggling at the plate his first few seasons with the Mariners after laying claim to the starting shortstop job as a rookie, the switch-hitting Vizquel proved to be a liability on offense from 1989 to 1991, failing to bat any higher than .247 or score more than 45 runs in any of those campaigns. However, he began to develop his offensive skills his last two years in Seattle, batting .294 in 1992, before compiling a mark of .255 and scoring 68 runs the following year, while also earning Gold Glove honors for the first of nine straight times. In spite of Vizquel's improvement, though, the Mariners elected to trade him to the Indians for shortstop Felix Fermin and outfielder/first baseman Reggie Jefferson on December 20, 1993.

After being limited by injuries and a player's strike to only 69 games, 33 RBIs, and 39 runs scored in 1994, Vizquel began to emerge as more of a threat on offense the following year, when he batted .266, hit six homers, knocked in 56 runs, scored 87 times, and stole 29 bases for the pennant-winning Indians. Continuing to improve on offense over the course of the next five seasons as he gradually assumed the number two spot in Cleveland's batting order, Vizquel posted batting averages of .297, .280, .288, .333, and .287 from 1996 to 2000, while also averaging 97 runs scored and 36 stolen bases during that time. After beginning that five-year period by hitting nine homers, driving in 64 runs, scoring 98 times, stealing 35 bases, and batting .297 in 1996, Vizquel scored 89 runs and swiped 43 bags the following year. He then earned All-Star honors in each of the next two seasons, performing particularly well in 1999, when, in addition to topping the circuit with 17 sacrifice hits and finishing second in the league with 42 stolen bases, he established career-high marks in runs scored (112), doubles (36), OPS (.833), batting average (.333), and hits (191), ranking among the AL leaders in each of the last two categories. Vizquel again scored more than 100 runs in 2000, crossing the plate 101 times, driving in 66 runs, and batting .287, before experiencing something of an off-year in 2001, when he batted just .255, scored only 84 runs, and stole just 13 bases.

Certainly, the emergence of star shortstops Alex Rodriguez, Derek Jeter, Nomar Garciaparra, and Miguel Tejada during his time in Cleveland prevented Vizquel from receiving the recognition he otherwise would have received. However, while Vizquel lacked the size and power at the plate of the other four men, he proved to be the finest defender in the group, possessing superior quickness and softer hands than any other player at his position. En route to winning nine consecutive Gold Gloves, Vizquel led all AL shortstops in fielding percentage three times, finishing either second or third in the league on four other occasions. Committing fewer than 10 errors in six different seasons, Vizquel made only three defensive miscues in 2000, tying in the process Cal Ripken Jr.'s then American League record for most consecutive games played at shortstop without an error—a streak that lasted a total of 95 games, from September 26, 1999 to July 21, 2000. Often making spectacular plays as well as those of a more routine nature, Vizquel drew praise from sportswriter Bob August, who wrote in the *News-Herald* in 2001, "Vizquel makes a specialty of his magic act. Average players sometimes make great plays, but most of these plays are performed by the artists of their crafts. As a shortstop, Vizquel has provided me with more exciting moments than any other baseball player."

Vizquel spent three more years in Cleveland, earning the last of his three All-Star selections in 2002, when he batted .275, scored 85 runs, and established career-high marks with 14 homers and 72 RBIs. After being limited to only 64 games the following year by off-season knee surgery, Vizquel bounced back in 2004 to bat .291, steal 19 bases, and score 82 runs. A free agent at season's end, the 37-year-old Vizquel signed with the San Francisco Giants, leaving the Indians having hit 60 homers, driven in 584 runs, scored 906 times, amassed 1,616 hits, 288 doubles, 39 triples, and 279 stolen bases, batted .283, compiled a .352 on-base percentage, and posted a .379 slugging percentage as a member of the team.

Vizquel remained in San Francisco for four full seasons, playing his best ball for the Giants in 2006, when he batted .295, scored 88 runs, stole 24 bases, and earned the last of his 11 Gold Gloves. After batting just .222 in a part-time role with the Giants in 2008, Vizquel spent his final four seasons serving in a similar capacity with the Texas Rangers, Chicago White Sox, and Toronto Blue Jays, before announcing his retirement at 45 years of age following the conclusion of the 2012 campaign. Prior to retiring, though, Vizquel expressed the frustration he felt as his range continued to diminish, stating on one occasion, "The ball goes by you, and you start questioning yourself and doubting: 'Wow, I saw the ball there, why couldn't I just get it?' Maybe it was a matter of first-step reaction, or a matter of leaning down to get that ball. Your mind is telling you that you can get to that ball, and your body's not allowing you to get to that ball." Vizquel ended his career with 80 home runs, 951 RBIs, 1,445 runs scored, 2,877 hits, 456 doubles, 77 triples, 404 stolen bases, a .272 batting average, a .336 on-base percentage, and a .352 slugging percentage. Over the course of 24 big-league seasons, he appeared in more games at shortstop (2,709) than any other player in MLB history.

Since retiring as an active player, Vizquel has spent the past few seasons serving as an infield and base-running coach at the major-league level, first for the Los Angeles Angels of Anaheim (2013), and, more recently, for the Detroit Tigers.

Indians Career Highlights:

Best Season: Vizquel had one of his most productive offensive seasons for the Indians in 2002, when he established career-high marks with 14 homers and 72 RBIs, scored 85 runs, and batted .275. He also performed extremely well in 2000, when he hit seven homers, knocked in 66 runs, scored 101 times, batted .287, and committed only three errors in the field, compiling in the process a fielding percentage of .995 that represents the highest single-season mark ever turned in by a shortstop. However, Vizquel had his finest all-around season in 1999, when, en route to earning MVP consideration for the only time in his career (he finished 16th in the voting), he hit five homers, knocked in 66 runs, finished second in the league with 42 stolen bases, and established career-high marks in runs scored (112), hits (191), doubles (36), batting average (.333), on-base percentage (.397), and slugging percentage (.436).

Memorable Moments/Greatest Performances: Vizquel drove in what proved to be the decisive runs of a 15-10 victory over the Boston Red Sox on August 7, 1994, when he cleared the bases with a three-run triple in the top of the 12th inning. He finished the game with three hits, two runs scored, and a career-high six runs batted in.

Vizquel had another huge day against Boston on June 18, 1996, when he led the Indians to a 9-7 win over the Red Sox by driving in six runs with a pair of singles and a grand slam homer.

Vizquel went a perfect 4-for-4 and scored four times during a 6-1 victory over the Chicago White Sox on July 7, 1996.

Omar Vizquel won eight of his 11 Gold Gloves
while playing for the Indians

Courtesy of Jerry Reuss

Vizquel paced the Indians to a 5-1 win over the Cincinnati Reds on June 17, 1997, by driving in all five Tribe runs with a homer and a single.

Vizquel performed brilliantly against the Yankees in the 1997 ALDS, stealing four bases and compiling a batting average of .500 by collecting nine hits in 18 official trips to the plate, with his RBI single in the bottom of the ninth inning of Game Four giving the Indians a 3-2 win that tied the series at two games apiece.

Vizquel used his base-running skills to help the Indians defeat the Chicago White Sox by a score of 13-9 on May 17, 1999, collecting two hits and two walks, scoring three times, and stealing a career-high four bases during the contest.

Vizquel capped off a five-run rally by the Indians in the bottom of the ninth inning with a grand slam home run that gave the Tribe a dramatic 7-4 victory over the Tigers on May 23, 1999.

Vizquel provided further heroics on July 10, 1999, when his two-out, two-run homer in the bottom of the ninth inning gave the Indians an 11-10 win over the Cincinnati Reds.

Vizquel helped the Indians tie the record for the largest comeback win in MLB history on August 5, 2001, when his bases loaded triple in the bottom of the ninth inning tied the score with Seattle at 14-14. The Indians, who once trailed the Mariners by a score of 14-2, ended up winning the game in walk-off fashion in the 11th inning on an RBI single by Jolbert Cabrera. Vizquel finished the contest with four hits and four runs batted in.

Although the Indians lost the 2001 ALDS to Seattle in five games, Vizquel had a tremendous series, batting .409 and collecting six RBIs, all of which came in Game Three, when he led the Tribe to a 17-2 rout of the Mariners by going 4-for-6, with a double and a triple.

Vizquel had his only 5-for-5 day at the plate as a member of the Indians on May 5, 2002, when he collected three doubles and two singles, knocked in a pair of runs, and scored twice during a lopsided 9-2 victory over the Texas Rangers.

Although the Indians ended up losing their June 8, 2002 matchup with the Mets by a score of 8-6, Vizquel starred in defeat, driving in five of the Tribe's six runs with a pair of homers.

Vizquel broke a 2-2 tie with Detroit on May 27, 2003, by recording a straight steal of home in the top of the eighth inning, catching Tigers pitcher Steve Avery by surprise and making it to the plate without a throw. The Indians subsequently scored another two runs in the frame, en route to recording a 5-2 victory over the Tigers.

Vizquel led the Indians to a 22-0 rout of the Yankees on August 31, 2004, by going 6-for-7, with a pair of doubles, four RBIs, and three runs scored.

Notable Achievements:

- Batted over .300 once (.333 in 1999).
- Scored more than 100 runs twice.
- Surpassed 30 doubles four times.
- Stole more than 20 bases six times, topping 30 steals four times and 40 thefts twice.
- Led AL in sacrifice hits three times.
- Finished second in AL with 42 stolen bases in 1999.
- Led AL shortstops in putouts once and fielding percentage three times.
- Ranks among Indians career leaders in: stolen bases (2nd), runs scored (6th), hits (7th), doubles (8th), total bases (10th), games played (10th), plate appearances (6th), and at-bats (5th).
- Holds MLB records for: most double plays turned by a shortstop (1,734), most career games at shortstop (2,709), and fewest errors committed in a season by a shortstop (3 in 2000).
- Recorded second highest fielding percentage of any shortstop in MLB history (.985).
- Recorded third most assists of any shortstop in MLB history (7,676).
- Recorded fifth most assists of any player in MLB history (8,050).
- 1996 Hutch Award winner.
- Eight-time Gold Glove Award winner (1994, 1995, 1996, 1997, 1998, 1999, 2000, and 2001).
- Three-time AL All-Star (1998, 1999, and 2002).
- Two-time AL champion (1995 and 1997).

11

SHOELESS JOE JACKSON
1910 - 1915

His reputation sullied by his alleged involvement in the *Black Sox Scandal* of 1919, Shoeless Joe Jackson spent his remaining days living in infamy, being treated as an outcast by the baseball world and society as a whole. Accused of taking a bribe to throw the 1919 World Series, Jackson subsequently suffered the indignity of being banned from baseball for life by then-commissioner Kenesaw Mountain Landis following the conclusion of the 1920 campaign. More than 65 years after his passing, Jackson's name still evokes feelings of disdain from a large segment of the baseball community, although he has become a far more sympathetic figure to fans of the game over time. Jackson's alleged involvement in the aforementioned fix has also caused baseball fans to associate him most closely with the Chicago White Sox through the years. But, prior to joining the White Sox in 1915, Jackson had some of his greatest seasons for the Cleveland Naps. En route to compiling the highest career batting average in franchise history, Jackson batted over .370 four times, topping the .400-mark once. He also scored more than 100 runs three times, surpassed 200 hits twice, and finished in double digits in triples four times, earning in the process four top-10 finishes in the AL MVP voting. Yet, in spite of his greatness as a player, Jackson remains on the outside looking in when it comes to inclusion in the Baseball Hall of Fame due to Landis's ruling nearly 100 years ago.

Born into abject poverty in Pickens County, South Carolina on July 16, 1888, Joseph Jefferson Wofford Jackson moved with his family to Pelzer, South Carolina while still just a baby. The son of a textile mill worker, Jackson got his first job at the tender age of six, sweeping cotton dust off the wooden floors at nearby Pelzer Mill. In early 1901, the Jackson family relocated once again, this time to the Brandon community of West

Greenville, South Carolina, where young Joseph went to work at Brandon Mill to help support his family. Jackson's early entrance into the work force afforded him little time for a formal education, leaving him almost completely illiterate.

As a youth, Jackson derived what little pleasure he got out of life from baseball. Displaying a natural inclination towards the national pastime at an early age, he began playing on the Brandon Mill men's team at age 13. Despite being the youngest member of the squad, Jackson acquitted himself quite well, often earning tips for his younger brothers, who passed their hats among the crowd every time their older sibling hit a home run. Since the Brandon Mill team played all its games on Saturdays, Jackson's homers became known as "Saturday Specials." Blessed with exceptional all-around skills, Jackson also earned nicknames for his line drives, which became known as "Blue Darters," and his glove, which onlookers referred to as "A place where triples go to die."

Jackson's extraordinary ability eventually earned him a spot on the roster of the semi-pro Greenville Spinners, with whom he acquired his famous nickname in 1908. While breaking in a new pair of cleats, Jackson developed painful blisters on his feet during the first game of a doubleheader. Seeking to ease his discomfort, he removed his spikes before stepping into the batter's box for an at-bat in the nightcap. After he subsequently tripled, a fan of the opposing team shouted, "You shoeless son-of-a-gun," as Jackson pulled into third base. Although he never again appeared "shoeless" in a game, the moniker followed him wherever he went.

Jackson began his professional career shortly thereafter, signing with Connie Mack's Philadelphia Athletics. However, his rise to prominence proved to be a slow and arduous one. Uncomfortable in the big city and ridiculed by his teammates for his inability to read and write, Jackson had a difficult time adjusting to life in Philadelphia. As a result, he struggled terribly at the plate in a pair of brief appearances with the A's in 1908 and 1909, forcing him to spend virtually all of those two seasons in the minor leagues. Finally giving up on Jackson, Mack elected to trade the 22-year-old outfielder to the Cleveland Naps for outfielder Bris Lord and $6,000 on July 30, 1910. After winning the Southern Association batting title, Jackson joined the Naps, for whom he batted .387 in 20 games over the final three weeks of the campaign.

Finding Cleveland far less intimidating than Philadelphia, Jackson also adapted better to his new surroundings because many of his Naps teammates either grew up or played ball in the South. Able to concentrate solely on the game, Jackson earned a starting spot in the Cleveland outfield in 1911, when he put together one of the finest rookie seasons in major league history. In addition to finishing second in the AL with a batting average of .408 that remains the highest mark ever compiled by a first-year player, Jackson topped the circuit with a .468 on-base percentage and ranked among the leaders in RBIs (83), runs scored (126), hits (233), doubles (45), triples (19), total bases (337), stolen bases (41), and slugging percentage (.590). Jackson's extraordinary performance, which earned him a fourth-place finish in the AL MVP voting, prompted Ty Cobb to pay tribute to his newest rival at season's end by proclaiming, "Joe is a grand ball player, and one who will get better and better. There is no denying that he is a better ball player his first year in the big leagues than anyone ever was."

Jackson followed up his superb rookie season with an equally impressive sophomore campaign, earning a ninth-place finish in the MVP balloting by driving in 90 runs, stealing 35 bases, finishing in the league's top three in runs scored (121), doubles (44), batting average (.395), on-base percentage (.458), and slugging percentage (.579), and topping the circuit in hits (226), triples (26), and total bases (331), with his 26 three-baggers establishing a franchise record that still stands. Jackson performed brilliantly again in 1913, finishing runner-up in the MVP voting after placing near the top of the league rankings in home runs (7), RBIs (71), runs scored (109), triples (17), total bases (291), batting average (.373), and on-base percentage (.460), and leading the league in hits (197), doubles (39), slugging percentage (.551), and OPS (1.011).

Blessed with outstanding power at the plate, the 6'1", 200-pound Jackson swung the bat harder than most of his contemporaries, who swore that his line drives sounded different than anyone else's. Ty Cobb recalled years later, "Joe's swing was purely natural—he was the perfect hitter. He batted against spitballs, shine-balls, emery-balls, and all the other trick deliveries. . . . I can still see those line drives whistling to the far precincts. Joe Jackson hit the ball harder than any man ever to play baseball."

Indians pitcher Jim Bagby, who pitched against Jackson after the latter left Cleveland, identified Shoeless Joe as the best hitter he ever faced, stating, "I don't mean, now, that he [Jackson] had the finest average, but he hit the ball better. If Joe was as fast as Cobb, he could have out-hit Ty by forty to seventy points a season. Why, he never beat out more than five infield hits a season. When he hit the ball, it was really hit."

Meanwhile, Tris Speaker suggested, "Jackson was not only a natural hitter, but he had a set style, a grooved swing. I can't ever remember him being in a batting slump. His swing was so perfect that there was little chance of it getting disorganized. He was the greatest natural hitter who ever lived."

While most other players of the period employed a split-grip and punched at the ball, Jackson kept his hands close together near the bottom of the handle and took a full swing. He stood in the batter's box with his feet close together, then strode into the pitcher's offering with a lethal left-handed swing. In discussing his stance years later, Jackson noted, "I used to draw a line three inches from the plate every time I came to bat. I drew a right-angle line at the end of it, right next to the catcher, and put my left foot on it exactly three inches from home plate."

While Jackson built his reputation primarily on his hitting, he also proved to be an exceptional fielder and an outstanding base runner. Playing both left field and right field during his time in Cleveland, Jackson compiled a total of 90 outfield assists over the course of his first three seasons, before opposing players learned not to challenge his powerful throwing arm. Meanwhile, he stole more than 20 bases in each of his first four seasons with the Naps.

Limited by a broken leg to just 122 games in 1914, Jackson experienced a precipitous decline in offensive production, finishing the season with only three home runs, 53 RBIs, 61 runs scored, and 153 hits, although he still managed to amass 13 triples, steal 22 bases, and finish fourth in the league with a .338 batting average. Jackson continued to post rather pedestrian numbers in 1915, batting .327, but knocking in only 45 runs and scoring just 42 times over the first 4½ months of the campaign, before financial difficulties prompted Cleveland owner Charles Somers to part ways with his under-performing star on August 21. After reaching an agreement with the White Sox, Somers signed Jackson to a three-year contract extension at his previous salary, and then sent him to Chicago for $31,500 in cash and three lesser players (pitcher Ed Klepfer and outfielders Braggo Roth and Larry Chappell). Reacting favorably to the trade, Jackson told local sportswriter Henry Edwards, "I think I am in a rut here in Cleveland and would play better somewhere else." In response, Edwards criticized Jackson on his way out of town, writing in the *Cleveland Plain Dealer*, "While he does not admit it, he was becoming a purely individual player who sacrificed team work for Joe Jackson. . . . If he were still the Jackson of 1911, 1912, and 1913, the team would not have let him get away." Jackson left Cleveland having hit 24 homers, driven in 353 runs, scored 474 times, amassed 937 hits, 168 doubles, 89 triples, and 138 stolen bases, batted .375, compiled a .441 on-base percentage, and posted a .542 slugging percentage over parts of six seasons.

After batting just .272 in 45 games with Chicago in 1915, Jackson rebounded the following year, batting .341, knocking in 78 runs, scoring 91 times, finishing second in the league with 202 hits, and topping the circuit with 21 triples and 293 total bases. He then helped lead the White Sox to the pennant in 1917 by batting .301 and ranking among the league leaders with 82 RBIs, 91 runs scored, and 17 triples, before batting .304 during their six-game victory over the New York Giants in the World Series. Jackson subsequently missed most of the 1918 campaign due to the nation's involvement in World War I. However, he returned the following year to lead the White Sox to their second pennant in three seasons by batting .351, knocking in 96 runs, and scoring 79 others. The heavily-favored White Sox then lost the World Series to the Cincinnati Reds, with their uninspired and mistake-prone play raising questions in the minds of many as to the legitimacy of their effort. Chicago failed to make it back to the postseason the following year, even though Jackson had one of his greatest seasons. With the American League using a somewhat livelier ball, Jackson posted career-high marks in home runs (12) and RBIs (121), while also batting .382, scoring 105 runs, amassing 218 hits, and leading the league with 20 triples. Sadly, that 1920 season ended up being Jackson's last in the Major Leagues.

In September of 1920, a Chicago grand jury convened to investigate charges that the White Sox intentionally lost the 1919 World Series to Cincinnati, with Jackson being one of eight Chicago players accused of conspiring with gamblers to "fix" the Series. Court records indicate that, in testimony made before the grand jury on September 28, 1920, Jackson admitted under oath that he agreed to participate in the fix. Contemporary news accounts contend that Jackson told the grand jury:

> *"When a Cincinnati player would bat a ball out in my territory, I'd muff it if I could—that is, fail to catch it. But,*

if it would look too much like crooked work to do that,
I'd be slow and make a throw to the infield that would be
short. My work netted the Cincinnati team several runs
that they never would have had if we had been playing on
the square."

While no such direct quote or testimony to this effect appears in the actual stenographic record of Jackson's grand jury appearance, he did admit to receiving a cash payment of $5,000. He also testified that he had been originally promised a $20,000 bribe. Court records also indicate that several other Chicago players admitted to receiving cash remunerations as well. However, following the mysterious disappearance of their confessions, the eight *Black Sox* won acquittal during their June, 1921 conspiracy trial. Nevertheless, newly appointed baseball commissioner Kenesaw Mountain Landis, in an extraordinarily bold move aimed at restoring public confidence in the game, subsequently suspended all eight players for life.

As a result of Landis's stunning ruling, Shoeless Joe Jackson never played another game of major league baseball. Furthermore, his name remains on the list of those players who are ineligible to be elected to the Hall of Fame. Yet, evidence has continued to surface through the years that puts into question Jackson's true culpability.

Various sources have revealed that Jackson initially refused to take a payment of $5,000, only to have fellow conspirator Lefty Williams toss it on the floor of his hotel room. Jackson then tried to tell White Sox owner Charles Comiskey about the fix, only to have Comiskey refuse to meet with him. In addition, team attorney Alfred Austrian coached Jackson's testimony in an extremely unethical manner before he appeared before the grand jury, reportedly eliciting his admission of guilt by plying him with alcohol, before also getting him to sign a waiver of immunity. Years later, the seven other players implicated in the scandal confirmed that Jackson never attended any of the meetings. In fact, Williams said they only mentioned Jackson's name to give their plot more credibility. Jackson's possible innocence tends to be supported by his performance during the Fall Classic, which included flawless play in the field and a Series-best .375 batting average, 12 hits, six runs batted in, and one home run.

Jackson professed his innocence years later when he told *The Sporting News* in 1942, "Regardless of what anybody says, I was innocent of any wrong-doing. I gave baseball all I had. The Supreme Being is the only one to whom I've got to answer. If I had been out there booting balls and looking foolish at bat against the Reds, there might have been some grounds for suspicion. I think my record in the 1919 World Series will stand up against that of any other man in that Series, or any other World Series in all history."

As for his lifetime banishment, Jackson told *Sport* magazine in October 1949:

> "If I had been the kind of fellow who brooded when things went wrong, I probably would have gone out of my mind when Judge Landis ruled me out of baseball. I would have lived in regret. I would have been bitter and resentful because I felt I had been wronged. But I haven't been resentful at all. I thought when my trial was over that Judge Landis might have restored me to good standing. But he never did. And, until he died, I had never gone before him, sent a representative before him, or placed before him any written matter pleading my case. I gave baseball my best, and, if the game didn't care enough to see me get a square deal, then I wouldn't go out of my way to get back in it. Baseball failed to keep faith with me. When I got notice of my suspension three days before the 1920 season ended— it came on a rained-out day—it read that, if found innocent of any wrongdoing, I would be reinstated. If found guilty, I would be banned for life. I was found innocent, and I was still banned for life."

After being banished from the Major Leagues, Jackson spent another 20 years in baseball, playing and managing with a number of semi-pro teams located mostly in Georgia and South Carolina. After returning to Savannah with his wife in 1922 to open a dry-cleaning business, Jackson eventually moved back to Greenville, South Carolina in 1933, where he owned and operated a barbecue restaurant, before opening "Joe Jackson's Liquor Store," which he and his wife operated until he died of a heart attack in 1951, at the age of 62.

More than 65 years after his passing, it still appears unlikely that Shoeless Joe Jackson's lifetime banishment from baseball will ever be rescinded. As a result, a man with the third-highest batting average in major league history (.356) who is considered by many of his contemporaries to be the greatest natural hitter they ever saw is likely never to gain admittance to Cooperstown. Nevertheless, Jackson's legacy as a truly great player remains undiminished.

Babe Ruth expressed his admiration for Jackson by proclaiming, "I copied Jackson's style because I thought he was the greatest hitter I had ever seen, . . . the greatest natural hitter I ever saw. He's the guy who made me a hitter."

Ty Cobb once told Jackson, "Whenever I got the idea I was a good hitter, I'd stop and take a look at you. Then I knew I could stand some improvement."

Ernie Shore, who faced Jackson as a pitcher with the Red Sox and Yankees, stated, "Everything he [Jackson] hit was really blessed. He could break bones with his shots. Blindfold me and I could still tell you when Joe hit the ball. It had a special crack."

Meanwhile, Connie Mack expressed the sadness he felt over his former player's plight when he noted, "Jackson's fall from grace is one of the real tragedies of baseball. I always thought he was more sinned against than sinning."

Indians (Naps) Career Highlights:

Best Season: Jackson had a tremendous year for the Naps in 1912, finishing in the league's top three in nine different offensive categories, including placing second with a .395 batting average and a 1.036 OPS, and leading the league with 226 hits, 331 total bases, and a franchise-record 26 triples. But he posted slightly better overall numbers as a rookie in 1911, when he earned a fourth-place finish in the AL MVP voting by establishing career-high marks in nine different offensive categories, including batting average (.408), on-base percentage (.468), slugging percentage (.590), runs scored (126), hits (233), and stolen bases (41). In addition to topping the circuit in OBP, Jackson finished second in the league in seven other offensive categories. More than a century later, his .408 batting average and 233 hits both remain single-season franchise records. Excelling in the field as well, Jackson finished second in the league with 32 outfield assists, which established another single-season franchise record that still stands.

Memorable Moments/Greatest Performances: Jackson compiled one of the longest hitting streaks in franchise history in 1911, hitting safely in 28 consecutive games from July 11 to August 12, a period during which

Shoeless Joe Jackson set an MLB record that still stands
by batting .408 as a rookie in 1911

Courtesy of Charles M. Conlon

he went 49-for-109 (.450), with two homers, three triples, 10 doubles, and 37 runs scored.

Jackson helped lead the Naps to a 5-4 victory over the New York Highlanders on August 18, 1911, by going a perfect 4-for-4, with a triple, one RBI, and one run scored.

Jackson led the Naps to a 15-1 pasting of the St. Louis Browns on June 30, 1912, by going 4-for-6, with three triples and four runs scored.

Jackson paced the Naps to a 9-4 victory over the Boston Red Sox on August 21, 1912, by going 4-for-4, with a walk, three RBIs, and four runs scored.

Jackson proved to be the difference in a 7-2 win over the Yankees on May 11, 1913, going 4-for-4 with five runs batted in, with four of those coming on a first-inning grand slam.

Jackson displayed his power during a 9-5 victory over the Yankees on June 4, 1913, driving a Russ Ford fastball off the roof of the right-field grandstand at the Polo Grounds and into the street beyond. Newspapers later claimed that the blast traveled more than 500 feet.

Notable Achievements:

- Batted over .320 six times, surpassing the .370-mark four times and batting .408 in 1911.
- Scored more than 100 runs three times, topping 120 runs scored twice.
- Surpassed 200 hits twice.
- Finished in double digits in triples four times, surpassing 20 three-baggers once (26 in 1912).
- Surpassed 30 doubles three times, topping 40 two-baggers twice.
- Stole more than 20 bases four times, topping 30 steals twice and 40 thefts once (41 in 1911).
- Compiled on-base percentage in excess of .400 four times.
- Posted slugging percentage in excess of .500 four times.
- Posted OPS in excess of 1.000 four times.
- Led AL in: hits twice, triples once, doubles once, on-base percentage once, slugging percentage once, OPS once, and total bases once.
- Finished second in AL in: batting average three times, runs scored once, hits once, doubles twice, total bases twice, on-base percentage twice, slugging percentage twice, and OPS twice.
- Led AL right-fielders with 28 assists in 1913.
- Compiled third-highest career batting average in MLB history (.356).
- Holds Indians single-season records for: highest batting average (.408 in 1911), most hits (233 in 1911), and most triples (26 in 1912).
- Holds Indians career record for highest batting average (.375).
- Ranks among Indians career leaders in: triples (4th), on-base percentage (2nd), slugging percentage (tied-5th), and OPS (2nd).
- Finished in top five of AL MVP voting three times, placing as high as second in 1913.
- Number 35 on *The Sporting News'* 1999 list of Baseball's 100 Greatest Players.

12

HAL TROSKY

1933 – 1941

Once identified by Babe Ruth as the man most likely to mount a serious challenge to his then single-season home run record, Hal Trosky established himself as one of the American League's most potent batsmen during his time in Cleveland. Spending most of his 11-year career with the Indians, Trosky hit more than 30 home runs three times, knocked in well over 100 runs six times, scored more than 100 runs four times, topped 200 hits twice, and batted over .330 on four separate occasions. In addition to setting a single-season franchise record that stood for 63 years by driving in a league-leading 162 runs in 1936, Trosky annually ranked among the AL leaders in homers, doubles, total bases, batting average, slugging percentage, and OPS from 1934 to 1940. Yet, in spite of his prodigious slugging, the powerful first baseman failed to gain the notoriety he deserved due to the fact that he spent most of his peak seasons competing against three of the greatest first sackers in baseball history—Lou Gehrig, Jimmie Foxx, and Hank Greenberg. As a result, Trosky failed to make a single All-Star Game appearance, although he managed to finish in the top 10 of the AL MVP voting twice. Nevertheless, poor health ultimately diminished Trosky's legacy far more than any of those Hall of Fame players.

Born to second-generation German immigrants on November 11, 1912, Harold Arthur Trojovsky grew up on a 420-acre farm just outside his place of birth in Norway, Iowa. After excelling in baseball at local Norway High School, Trojovsky received a contract offer from the St. Louis Cardinals. However, while still considering the Cardinals' bid, he received another proposal from the Cleveland Indians that appealed to him more. Choosing to accept Cleveland's offer, he signed his first contract "Harold Trojovsky," but subsequently elected to use "Trosky" as his last name.

Despite being signed primarily as a pitcher who had the odd habit of hitting cross-handed from the right side of the plate, the righty-throwing Trosky shifted to first base shortly after he joined the Cedar Rapids Bunnies in 1931 at the tender age of 18. After being instructed to retain his grip from a left-handed batting stance, Trosky gradually emerged as a power threat in the minors, batting .331 and hitting 15 home runs in only 68 games with Quincy of the Class B Three-I League in 1932, before being promoted to Cleveland during the latter stages of the ensuing campaign. Appearing in 11 games with the Indians in September 1933, the 20-year-old Trosky batted .295, knocked in eight runs, and hit his first big-league home run.

Supplanting Harley Boss as Cleveland's starting first baseman the following season, Trosky performed brilliantly in his first full year in the majors. Playing every inning of all 154 games, the 6'2", 207-pound Trosky established a new rookie record by hitting 35 home runs, which placed him third in the league rankings, behind only Lou Gehrig and Jimmie Foxx. Trosky also finished among the AL leaders with 142 RBIs, 117 runs scored, 206 hits, 45 doubles, nine triples, 374 total bases, a batting average of .330, a slugging percentage of .598, and an OPS of .987, earning in the process a seventh-place finish in the league MVP voting. Extremely impressed by Trosky's fabulous performance, New York Yankees Business Manager Ed Barrow proclaimed, "Hal Trosky, first baseman of the Indians, has the best chance to succeed Lou Gehrig as the powerhouse of the American League. It is really too bad that our scouts did not like Trosky when he was in the minors. Trosky will go far in his profession, and I have no doubt, in time, he will stand out as the greatest first sacker of the majors."

Although Trosky posted less prolific numbers in 1935, he still managed to hit 26 homers, drive in 113 runs, and bat .271, while once again appearing in every game for the Indians. He followed that up with the most productive offensive season of his career, topping the circuit with 162 RBIs and 405 total bases, finishing second in the league with 42 home runs and a .644 slugging percentage, and also ranking among the leaders with 124 runs scored, 216 hits, 45 doubles, a .343 batting average, and an OPS of 1.026. Yet, with both Lou Gehrig and Jimmie Foxx having outstanding seasons, Trosky failed to land a spot on the AL All-Star Team. He also finished a distant 10th to Gehrig in the league MVP balloting.

Trosky continued his outstanding hitting in 1937, finishing among the AL leaders with 32 home runs and 128 RBIs, while also batting .298 and scoring 104 runs. Although his home-run output fell to 19 the following year, Trosky raised his batting average to .334, knocked in 110 runs, scored 106 others, amassed 40 doubles, and reduced his strikeout total from 60 to 40. He also improved his footwork and overall defense at first base. After leading all AL first sackers with 22 errors in both 1934 and 1936, Trosky never again committed more than 11 defensive miscues in any single season.

Named Indians captain prior to the start of the 1939 campaign, Trosky soon found himself serving as a buffer between his teammates and Cleveland's acerbic manager Oscar Vitt, who tended to alienate himself from his subordinates by constantly berating them. Things eventually became so contentious between the two sides that a group of 11 Cleveland players petitioned team owner Alva Bradley to relieve Vitt of his duties. As one of the dissidents, Trosky received irreparable damage to his reputation when news of the protest leaked out to the press, which subsequently began referring to the episode as the "Crybaby" incident. Still, Trosky and his teammates must have felt somewhat vindicated more than a decade later, in 1951, when the *Cleveland News* published a memo from Bradley concerning the incident that read: "We should have won the pennant [in 1940]. Our real trouble started when a group of eleven players came to my office and made four distinct charges against Vitt and asked for his dismissal. The four charges made against Vitt, on investigations I have made, were one hundred percent correct."

Dealing with an overbearing manager proved to be just one of the problems Trosky encountered after his first few years in Cleveland. Afflicted with severe headaches for the first time in 1939, the slugging first baseman spent much of the season playing in discomfort, making it increasingly difficult for him to bring with him to the park each day the intensity and energy he needed to perform at his usual level. Finally removing himself from the lineup for a period of time midway through the campaign, Trosky ended up appearing in only 122 games. Nevertheless, he finished the year with 25 home runs, 104 RBIs, 89 runs scored, and a .335 batting average.

Although visits to various doctors during the subsequent offseason failed to reveal the source of his discomfort, Trosky's headaches gradually faded over the winter, allowing him to return to the Indians in 1940 eager

Courtesy of the Leslie Jones Collection at the Boston Public Library

Hal Trosky led the American League with 162 RBIs in 1936

to play ball once again. Despite having his season marred by the afore-mentioned "Crybaby" incident, Trosky ended up posting solid numbers, finishing the year with 25 home runs, 93 RBIs, and a .295 batting average. However, his performance fell off considerably during the latter stages of the campaign after he once again began to experience severe headaches that forced him to miss a total of 14 games.

With the frequency and severity of his migraines increasing in 1941, Trosky often felt almost powerless at the plate against a blurry white apparition he said sometimes looked "like a bunch of white feathers." Finally forced to remove himself from the lineup on August 11, Trosky sat out almost two weeks before rejoining the Indians for their last stop in Chicago. His career with the Tribe ended abruptly shortly thereafter, when he fractured his thumb in a collision at first base with White Sox pitcher Ted Lyons. Forced to sit out the final 39 games of the campaign, Trosky finished the year with only 11 homers, 51 RBIs, and a .294 batting average, in just 89 games and 310 official at-bats.

Speaking with Gayle Hayes of the *Des Moines Register* some five months later, Trosky revealed that he did not intend to play baseball in 1942, telling that reporter that it was "for the best interest of the Cleveland club and for myself that I stay out of baseball. . . . I have visited various doctors in the larger cities in the United States and they have not helped me. If, after resting this year, I find that I am better, perhaps I'll try to be reinstated. If I don't get better, then my major league career is over."

Trosky subsequently spent the entire 1942 season on his farm in Iowa devouring news of the war and waiting for a call from the draft board. After the board failed to contact him, Trosky worked out for the Chicago White Sox, who purchased his contract from the Indians in November 1943. Trosky ended his time in Cleveland with 216 home runs, 911 RBIs, 758 runs scored, 1,365 hits, 287 doubles, 53 triples, a .313 batting average, a .379 on-base percentage, and a .551 slugging percentage.

With the army officially declaring Trosky unfit for military service in March 1944 due to his history of headaches, he decided to attempt a comeback with Chicago. However, Trosky found himself unable to regain his earlier form, concluding the 1944 campaign with just 10 home runs, 70 RBIs, and a .241 batting average, in 135 games and 560 total plate appearances. After sitting out the following year, Trosky elected to give baseball one more try in 1946. But he batted just .254 and hit only two home runs in 88 games with the White Sox, prompting him to leave the game for good at season's end. Trosky retired with 228 home runs, 1,012 RBIs, 835 runs scored, 1,561 hits, 331 doubles, 58 triples, a .302 batting average, a .371 on-base percentage, and a .522 slugging percentage.

Following his playing days, Trosky became a scout for the White Sox, traveling the tiny towns of eastern Iowa from 1947 to 1950 hoping to discover untapped talent. After leaving the White Sox in 1950, he spent the next several years working on his farm, before taking up agricultural real estate sales around Cedar Rapids in 1962. Trosky suffered a heart attack in early 1978 that left him dependent on a cane from that point on. He passed away a little over one year later, on June 18, 1979, collapsing from a heart attack so massive that doctors said he died before he even reached the floor. Trosky was 66 years old at the time of his passing.

In discussing his former teammate and good friend years later, Mel Harder said, "I first met Hal in 1933, and he was a truly great player. In my opinion, he was the best first baseman in Cleveland Indians history."

Indians Career Highlights:

Best Season: Trosky had a tremendous rookie year for the Indians in 1934, earning a seventh-place finish in the AL MVP voting by ranking among the league leaders with 35 home runs, 142 RBIs, 117 runs scored, 206 hits, 45 doubles, 374 total bases, a .330 batting average, a .598 slugging percentage, and an OPS of .987. However, he performed even better in 1936, when he established career-high marks in home runs (42), RBIs (162), runs scored (124), hits (216), doubles (45), triples (9), total bases (405), batting average (.343), slugging percentage (.644), and OPS (1.026), leading the league in two of those categories and finishing in the top three in three others.

Memorable Moments/Greatest Performances: Trosky compiled one of the longest hitting streaks in franchise history in 1936, hitting safely in 28 consecutive games from July 5 to August 2, a period during which he went a combined 52-for-126 (.413), with 11 homers, 39 RBIs, and 26 runs scored.

Trosky had his breakout game for the Indians on April 24, 1934, when he went 4-for-5, with a pair of homers, six RBIs, and four runs scored, during a 15-2 pasting of the St. Louis Browns.

Trosky led the Tribe to an 11-7 win over the Philadelphia Athletics on June 14, 1934, by driving in six runs with a pair of homers, including a grand slam in the top of the ninth inning that provided the margin of victory.

Trosky starred in defeat on July 23, 1934, when he went 4-for-5, with a homer, two doubles, five RBIs, and three runs scored, during an 11-9 loss to the Philadelphia Athletics.

Trosky paced the Indians to a 9-2 win over the Detroit Tigers on April 27, 1935, by driving in five runs with a double and a pair of homers.

Although the Indians lost their July 1, 1936 meeting with St. Louis by a score of 16-12, Trosky collected five hits in one game for the only time in his career, going 5-for-6, with three RBIs.

Trosky led the Indians to an 11-4 mauling of the Yankees on July 9, 1936 by collecting two homers and a triple, knocking in three runs, and scoring four times.

Trosky proved to be a one-man wrecking crew against Boston on September 15, 1936, leading the Tribe to a lopsided 13-2 victory over the Red

Sox by going 4-for-4, with a pair of homers, a double, four runs scored, and a career-high seven runs batted in.

Trosky continued to belabor Boston's pitching staff the very next day, going 4-for-4, with a homer, a double, five RBIs, and four runs scored, during a 13-3 pounding of the Red Sox.

Trosky delivered the decisive blow of a 5-3 victory over the Red Sox on August 27, 1939, when his three-run homer in the bottom of the eighth inning made a winner out of Indians starter Willis Hudlin.

Trosky hit three home runs one game twice for the Tribe, doing so for the first time on May 30, 1934, when his three round-trippers and four RBIs led the Indians to a 5-4 win over Chicago. He accomplished the feat again on July 5, 1937, collecting four hits, three homers, and a career-high seven RBIs during a lopsided 14-4 victory over the St. Louis Browns.

Notable Achievements:
- Hit more than 30 home runs three times, topping 40 homers once (42 in 1936).
- Knocked in more than 100 runs six times, surpassing 120 RBIs on three occasions.
- Scored more than 100 runs four times, surpassing 120 runs scored once (124 in 1936).
- Batted over .330 four times.
- Surpassed 200 hits twice.
- Surpassed 30 doubles seven times, topping 40 two-baggers on three occasions.
- Compiled on-base percentage in excess of .400 twice.
- Posted slugging percentage in excess of .500 six times, topping the .600-mark once (.644 in 1936).
- Posted OPS in excess of 1.000 once (1.026 in 1936).
- Led AL in: RBIs once, total bases once, and games played twice.
- Finished second in A.L in: home runs once, RBIs once, total bases once, and slugging percentage once.
- Led AL first basemen in: putouts twice, assists once, and double plays once.
- Holds Indians single-season record for most total bases (405 in 1936).

- Ranks among Indians career leaders in: home runs (5th), RBIs (4th), doubles (9th), extra-base hits (4th), total bases (6th), slugging percentage (4th), and OPS (7th).
- Finished in top 10 of AL MVP voting twice (1934 and 1936).

13

MANNY RAMIREZ
1993 – 2000

Although Manny Ramirez is perhaps more closely associated with the Boston Red Sox, the enigmatic outfielder first gained notoriety as a member of the Cleveland Indians, with whom he began his major-league career in 1993. Starting in right field for the Tribe for the better part of seven seasons, Ramirez gained widespread acclaim during that time as one of the American League's most dangerous and productive hitters, surpassing 30 homers and 100 RBIs five times each, while also batting over .300 on five separate occasions. The Indians' all-time single-season record-holder for most RBIs and highest OPS, Ramirez also holds franchise marks for highest career slugging percentage and OPS, with his prolific hitting earning him three Silver Sluggers, four All-Star selections, two *Sporting News* All-Star nominations, and three top-10 finishes in the AL MVP voting. Meanwhile, Ramirez's potent bat helped lead the Tribe to five division titles and two American League pennants.

Born in Santo Domingo, Dominican Republic on May 30, 1972, Manuel Aristides Ramirez Onelcida moved with his parents to the predominantly Dominican upper Manhattan neighborhood of Washington Heights at the age of 13. Ramirez first gained the attention of major-league scouts while playing third base and center field for George Washington High School's baseball team, which he led to three straight division championships. Performing particularly well as a senior in 1991, Ramirez earned New York City Public School Player of the Year honors by batting .650 and hitting 14 home runs in only 22 games. Proving to be far less successful in the classroom, Ramirez left school without earning a degree after suffering numerous suspensions for truancy and other academic transgressions.

Subsequently selected by the Cleveland Indians with the 13th overall pick of the 1991 MLB Draft, Ramirez advanced rapidly through Cleveland's farm system, making his big-league debut with the parent club in September 1993, after being named *Baseball America's* Minor League Player of the Year for batting .433, hitting 31 homers, and driving in 145 runs, in 129 combined games at the Double-A and Triple-A levels. Labeled a "can't miss" prospect when he arrived in Cleveland, Ramirez struggled at first, batting just .170, hitting two homers, and driving in five runs, in 22 games over the final month of the 1993 campaign. However, he began to live up to the hype that preceded him the following year, when he earned a runner-up finish in the AL Rookie of the Year voting by batting .269, hitting 17 homers, and driving in 60 runs, in only 91 games and 290 official at-bats.

Ramirez emerged as a full-fledged star in his sophomore campaign of 1995, earning the first of his 12 All-Star selections, the first of his nine Silver Sluggers, and a 12th-place finish in the AL MVP balloting by hitting 31 homers, driving in 107 runs, scoring 85 times, and batting .308, before posting extremely similar numbers the following year, when he hit 33 homers, knocked in 112 runs, scored 94 others, batted .309, and amassed a career-high 45 doubles. Meanwhile, even though Ramirez often received criticism for his poor defensive work in the outfield, he managed to finish third among all AL right-fielders in putouts, while leading all players at his position with 19 assists.

Ramirez had another good year for the Indians in 1997, hitting 26 homers, driving in 88 runs, scoring 99 times, and finishing fifth in the league with a .328 batting average, before beginning an exceptional three-year run during which he compiled the following numbers:

> 1998: 45 HR, 145 RBI, 108 Runs Scored, .294 AVG, .377 OBP, .599 SLG, .976 OPS
>
> 1999: 44 HR, **165** RBI, 131 Runs Scored, .333 AVG, .442 OBP, **.663** SLG, **1.105** OPS
>
> 2000: 38 HR, 122 RBI, 92 Runs Scored, .351 AVG, .457 OBP, **.697** SLG, **1.154** OPS

Ramirez ranked among the league leaders in home runs, RBIs, slugging percentage, and OPS all three years, topping the circuit in each of the last two categories twice each. Meanwhile, his league-leading total of 165 RBIs in 1999 established a new franchise record, surpassing the previous mark of 162 set by Hal Trosky in 1936. Ramirez also finished third in the league in batting average in 2000, despite being limited by injuries to only 118 games. Ramirez's superb hitting earning him All-Star honors and a top-10 finish in the AL MVP voting all three years, a Silver Slugger in 1999 and 2000, and the Hank Aaron Award as the American League's best hitter in 1999.

An exceptional fastball hitter, the right-handed swinging Ramirez, who stood six-feet tall and weighed 225 pounds, possessed extraordinarily quick wrists that enabled him to wait longer than most batters before starting his swing, making him an excellent breaking-ball hitter as well. Ramirez also had a keen batting eye, outstanding patience at the plate, and the ability to drive the ball with power to all fields. And, even though he rarely received credit for doing so, Ramirez worked as hard as anyone to perfect his swing, constantly studying video and spending hours in the batting cage every day in an effort to become one of the game's very best hitters. Meanwhile, although Ramirez remained something of a liability on defense, he eventually turned himself into a serviceable outfielder through hard work and dedication.

A free agent following the conclusion of the 2000 campaign, Ramirez elected to sign with the Boston Red Sox for eight years and $160 million, bringing his days in Cleveland to an end. He left the Indians having hit 236 homers, driven in 804 runs, scored 665 others, accumulated 1,086 hits, 237 doubles, and 11 triples, batted .313, compiled an on-base percentage of .407, and posted a slugging percentage of .592 as a member of the team.

Ramirez continued his assault on American League pitching after he arrived in Boston, hitting more than 30 homers and driving in more than 100 runs in each of his first six seasons with the Red Sox, while also batting over .300 five times. After hitting 41 homers, knocking in 125 runs, and batting .306 in 2001, Ramirez reached the seats 33 times, drove home 107 runs, and led the league with a .349 batting average the following year. He also performed magnificently in 2004 and 2005, earning a pair of top-five finishes in the AL MVP balloting by leading the league with 43 homers, knocking in 130 runs, and batting .308 in the first of those campaigns, before batting .292 and ranking among the league leaders with 45 homers and 144 RBIs in 2005.

Although Ramirez's prodigious slugging helped the Red Sox win two World Series, his quirky personality, to which Indians manager Mike Hargrove once referred as "Manny being Manny" in a 1995 *Newsday* article, caused him to be viewed as an eccentric, self-indulgent superstar who put himself before his team, and who marched to the beat of his own drummer. Many of Ramirez's teammates professed great fondness for him, with Nomar Garciaparra once saying, "Manny is really a simple person. He works extremely hard. He just wants to play baseball and go home and be with his family. How can you not respect and love a guy like that?" Derek Lowe added, "He's a kid is really what he is. This is how he's been, and probably how he always will be." Meanwhile, David Ortiz commented, "He's in his own world . . . on his own planet; totally different human being than everyone else."

However, Ramirez's Red Sox teammates became frustrated with him on those occasions when he played lackadaisically and conducted himself in a manner that proved to be detrimental to the rest of the team, with manager Terry Francona stating on one occasion, "There were times when he'd hit a ball and not run. You'd try to stay ahead of him. If you got to a point where he'd beat you to that day off, you might lose him for a week, instead of one day. He was an interesting character, but he could hit, man."

Ramirez's extraordinary offensive production often forced his teammates and Red Sox management to overlook his somewhat bizarre behavior during the team's successful run that lasted from 2004 to 2007. However, he finally wore out his welcome in 2008, when his dissatisfaction over his contract situation prompted him to behave in a manner that made it impossible for him to remain in Boston any longer. Left with no other alternative, the Red Sox completed a three-team trade with the Pirates and Dodgers on July 31, 2008, that sent Ramirez to the Dodgers, who he subsequently helped advance to the playoffs by hitting 17 home runs, driving in 53 runs, and batting .396 over the season's final two months. Although Ramirez continued to perform well for the Dodgers over the course of the next two seasons, Major League Baseball suspended him for 50 games on May 7, 2009, for violating the Joint Drug Prevention and Treatment Program it established with the Players Association in 2004. It also surfaced that Ramirez previously tested positive for performance-enhancing drugs in 2003. However, he received no penalty for his earlier transgression since MLB had yet to institute a formal policy against steroid users at that time.

After being placed on waivers by the Dodgers late in 2010, Ramirez spent the season's final month with the Chicago White Sox. He subsequently signed with Tampa Bay as a free agent prior to the start of the ensuing campaign, but announced his retirement just five games into the season after reportedly testing positive for using a banned performance-enhancing drug in his spring training drug test. Ramirez later attempted to return to the majors, making brief appearances in the farm systems of the Oakland Athletics, Texas Rangers, and Chicago Cubs, before retiring for good after being released by all three teams. He ended his career with 555 home runs, 1,831 runs batted in, 1,544 runs scored, 2,574 hits, 547 doubles, 20 triples, a .312 batting average, a .411 on-base percentage, and a .585 slugging percentage.

After failing in his comeback attempt with Chicago, Ramirez accepted a position in the Cubs organization as a batting consultant in 2015. He remained in that post until January 8, 2017, when the Kōchi Fighting Dogs of the Japanese Shikoku Island League announced that they had reached an agreement with him to play for them in 2017.

Indians Career Highlights:

Best Season: Despite being limited by injuries to only 118 games in 2000, Ramirez performed magnificently for the Indians, hitting 38 homers, driving in 122 runs, scoring 92 times, finishing third in the league with a .351 batting average and a .457 on-base percentage, and topping the circuit with a .697 slugging percentage and an OPS of 1.154, establishing in the process career-high marks in each of the last four categories. Nevertheless, Ramirez compiled his most prolific offensive numbers for the Tribe one year earlier, earning a third-place finish in the 1999 AL MVP voting by ranking among the league leaders with 44 homers, 131 runs scored, 346 total bases, a .333 batting average, and a .442 on-base percentage, while topping the circuit with 165 RBIs, a .663 slugging percentage, and an OPS of 1.105. Ramirez's 165 RBIs, which set a new franchise record, represent the highest total amassed by any player since Jimmie Foxx knocked in 175 runs for the Boston Red Sox in 1938.

Memorable Moments/Greatest Performances: After making his major-league debut just one day earlier, Ramirez starred at the plate for the Indians on September 3, 1993, leading them to a 7-3 win over the Yankees by homering twice, driving in three runs, and scoring three times.

Ramirez paced the Indians to a 9-6 victory over the California Angels on April 11, 1994, by going 3-for-3, with a pair of homers and five RBIs.

Ramirez had another big day at the plate on April 27, 1995, going 4-for-5, with a homer, double, three RBIs, and three runs scored, during an 11-6 win over the Texas Rangers.

Ramirez led the Indians to a 13-4 rout of the Yankees on June 21, 1997, by going 4-for-5 with six RBIs, with his eighth-inning grand slam off Graeme Lloyd breaking the game wide open.

Just five days after homering and knocking in six runs during a 9-1 victory over Kansas City, Ramirez led the Indians to an 11-0 pasting of the Yankees on June 21, 1998, by driving in four runs with a double and a pair of homers.

Ramirez proved to be the Indians' entire offense on July 3, 1998, with his two home runs being the only hits they collected against southpaw Jose Rosado during a 2-1 win over the Royals.

Ramirez homered twice against Bret Saberhagen in Game Three of the 1998 ALDS, in leading the Indians to a 4-3 win over the Boston Red Sox.

Ramirez had an extremely productive day at the plate against Tampa Bay on August 7, 1999, going 3-for-3, with a homer, double, five RBIs, and four runs scored during a 15-10 win over the Devil Rays.

Ramirez led the Indians to a lopsided 18-4 victory over the Toronto Blue Jays on September 24, 1999, by homering twice, scoring three times, and collecting a career-high eight RBIs, with four of those coming on a fifth-inning grand slam.

Ramirez again went deep with the bases loaded during a 14-3 mauling of the Baltimore Orioles on July 29, 2000, finishing the game with two homers, six RBIs, and three runs scored.

Ramirez hit three home runs in one game twice for the Indians, doing so for the first time

during a 7-5 win over the Toronto Blue Jays on September 15, 1998, in which he knocked in five of Cleveland's seven runs.

Ramirez accomplished the feat again on August 25, 1999, when he went 4-for-5, with four RBIs and four runs scored, during a 12-4 victory over the Oakland Athletics.

Courtesy of Jerry Reuss

Manny Ramirez set a new franchise record
when he knocked in 165 runs in 1999

Notable Achievements:

- Hit more than 20 home runs six times, topping 30 homers five times and 40 homers twice.
- Knocked in more than 100 runs five times, surpassing 120 RBIs three times.
- Scored more than 100 runs twice, topping 120 runs scored once.
- Batted over .300 five times, topping the .330-mark twice.
- Surpassed 30 doubles five times, topping 40 two-baggers twice.
- Compiled on-base percentage in excess of .400 four times.
- Posted slugging percentage in excess of .500 seven times, topping the .600-mark twice.
- Posted OPS in excess of 1.000 twice.
- Led AL in: RBIs once, slugging percentage twice, and OPS twice.
- Finished second in AL with .442 on-base percentage in 1999.
- Finished third in AL in: home runs once, batting average once, and on-base percentage once.
- Holds Indians single-season records for most RBIs (165 in 1999) and highest OPS (1.154 in 2000).

- Holds Indians career records for highest slugging percentage (.592) and OPS (.998).
- Ranks among Indians career leaders in: home runs (3rd), RBIs (8th), extra-base hits (8th), on-base percentage (4th), and sacrifice flies (5th).
- Holds MLB records for most post-season home runs (29) and RBIs (78).
- Ranks among MLB all-time leaders with: 21 career grand slams (3rd), .585 career slugging percentage (8th), and .996 career OPS (8th).
- Hit three home runs in one game twice (vs. Toronto Blue Jays on Sept. 15, 1998, and vs. Oakland Athletics on August 25, 1999).
- 1993 *Baseball America* Minor League Player of the Year.
- Finished second in 1994 AL Rookie of the Year voting.
- Two-time AL Player of the Month.
- 1999 AL Hank Aaron Award winner.
- Three-time Silver Slugger winner.
- Finished in top 10 of AL MVP voting three times, making it into top five once (3rd in 1999).
- Two-time *Sporting News* All-Star selection (1995 and 1999).
- Four-time AL All-Star (1995, 1998, 1999, and 2000).
- Two-time AL champion (1995 and 1997).

14

STAN COVELESKI
1916 – 1924

An outstanding right-handed pitcher whose peak years extended from the latter portion of the Dead Ball Era well into the 1920s, Stan Coveleski relied primarily on his exceptional control and sagacious use of the spitball to establish himself as one of the most dominant hurlers of his time. Spending most of his finest seasons in Cleveland, "The Big Pole," as he came to be affectionately known to his teammates, served as the ace of the Indians pitching staff for most of his nine years with the Tribe, winning more than 20 games four times and topping 15 victories on four other occasions. Leading all AL hurlers in numerous statistical categories during his time in Cleveland, Coveleski compiled an ERA under 2.00 twice, posted a WHIP below 1.000 once, threw more than 300 innings three times, and tossed more than 20 complete games on six separate occasions. Meanwhile, his performance in the 1920 Fall Classic, which helped the Indians capture their first world championship, remains one of the most impressive in World Series history.

Born in the coal mining town of Shamokin, Pennsylvania on July 13, 1889, Stanislaus Anthony Kowalewski quit school at the age of 12 to take a job in the local mines, where he spent 12 hours a day, six days a week, hauling timber for the modest sum of $3.75 per week. While the physical nature of his work helped young Stanislaus build up his strength, he spent every free moment working on his pitching skills by throwing rocks at tin cans, eventually developing such superb control that he claimed he had the ability to hit them blindfolded. Returning to school at the behest of a local teacher, who saw him engaging in his favorite hobby one afternoon, Stanislaus began pitching for his school team, performing so well that he began to entertain thoughts of pursuing a career on the diamond.

After relocating with his parents and four older brothers to Lancaster, Pennsylvania in 1909, Coveleski, who anglicized his name as soon as he began his career in organized baseball, signed with Lancaster of the Tri-State League. He spent the next three years pitching for Lancaster, before moving on to Atlantic City, where he won 20 games and compiled an ERA of 2.53 in 1912, making enough of an impression on Connie Mack in the process that the legendary manager of the Philadelphia Athletics signed him to a contract. However, after the 23-year-old Coveleski made a pair of late-season starts for the A's, Mack became convinced that he needed more seasoning and sent him across the country to Spokane in the Northwestern League, believing he had a gentleman's agreement with that organization to retain the young pitcher's rights. Performing exceptionally well on the mound in each of the next two seasons, Coveleski established himself as the circuit's top pitcher, increasing his value to such a degree that Spokane chose to part ways with him only after Portland of the Pacific Coast League offered them five players in exchange for his services following the conclusion of the 1914 campaign. Coveleski then spent one year at Portland, where he developed the spitball for which he later became famous, before being purchased by the Indians at the end of the 1915 season.

Arriving in Cleveland just three months shy of his 27th birthday, Coveleski put together a solid rookie season, going 15-13, with a 3.41 ERA, 11 complete games, and 232 innings pitched for an Indians team that finished sixth in the eight-team American League with a record of 77-77. The 5'11", 170-pound right-hander emerged as one of the junior circuit's top pitchers the following year, helping the Indians improve their record to 88-66 in 1917 by posting a personal mark of 19-14, topping the circuit with nine shutouts, and ranking among the league leaders with a 1.81 ERA, a WHIP of 0.992, 133 strikeouts, 24 complete games, and 298⅓ innings pitched. Even though the nation's involvement in World War I caused the ensuing campaign to end one month early, Coveleski compiled similarly impressive numbers, finishing the year with a record of 22-13, an ERA of 1.82, a WHIP of 1.084, 25 complete games, and 311 innings pitched. He followed that up with another outstanding performance in 1919, helping the Indians finish second in the league for the second straight season by going 24-12, with a 2.61 ERA, 24 complete games, and 286 innings pitched.

Although Coveleski typically threw overhand, he occasionally employed a sidearm delivery when facing right-handed batters. Priding himself on his efficient pitching, Coveleski later recalled, "I was never a strikeout pitcher. Why should I throw eight or nine balls to get a man out when I got away with three or four?" The right-hander also took great pride in his exceptional control, claiming he once pitched seven innings without throwing a ball, with every pitch resulting in either a called strike, a swing-and-a-miss, or contact of some kind. Regarding his use of the spit-ball, which he used to supplement his fastball, curve, and slow ball, Coveleski revealed that he kept alum in his mouth, where it became gummy, before applying the substance to the baseball by wetting his first two fingers. Developing excellent control of his favorite offering, Coveleski had the ability to break his spitter either down, out, or down and out, depending on the action of his wrist. Coveleski also revealed that, even though he went to his mouth before every pitch in an effort to keep opposing hitters off balance, he often used his spitter as a decoy, stating, "I wouldn't throw all spitballs. I'd go maybe two or three innings without throwing a spitter, but I always had them looking for it."

Yet, teammate Joe Sewell suggested that, on at least one occasion, Coveleski used his spitball more often than he might have been willing to admit, claiming:

"He [Coveleski] was one of the best spitball pitchers that I ever saw. Tris Speaker was our manager. We always had a meeting when a club would come into town. But, on this particular day, Covey was going to pitch and Tris Speaker had this roster and says, 'How are you going to pitch to so and so, the leadoff man?' Covey says, 'I'm going to fire that spitter in there.' We discuss it. Speaker says, 'The second man, how are you going to pitch to him?' Covey says, 'I'm going to fire that spitter in there.' We got to about the fourth or fifth hitter and Speaker says, 'Why Covey, you ain't going to throw nothing but a spitball today then?' Covey says, 'That's right.' And he opened up with a spitball and closed up with a spitball."

Sewell then added, "I've seen Coveleski throw that spitball to a right-handed hitter, and he'd fall to the ground, and that ball would break over the plate. It would break from your head down to the ground, like hitting a butterfly."

Although the Major Leagues banned the spitball prior to the start of the 1920 campaign, Coveleski and 16 other pitchers retained the ability to throw it under the grandfather clause. Putting together one of his finest seasons even though his wife of seven years passed away in late May,

Coveleski helped lead the Indians to their first pennant by compiling a record of 24-14 and an ERA of 2.49, throwing 26 complete games and 315 innings, and leading the league with 133 strikeouts and a WHIP of 1.108. He then proved to be the difference in the World Series, earning three complete-game victories over Brooklyn, including a shutout in the series-clincher, to give the Indians their first world championship.

Coveleski surpassed 20 wins for the fourth straight time the following year, going 23-13, with a 3.37 ERA, 28 complete games, and 315 innings pitched for the second-place Indians in 1921, before the team's descent to mediocrity adversely affected his won-lost record in each of the next three seasons. Yet, even though Coveleski compiled an overall mark of just 45-44 from 1922 to 1924, he remained an extremely effective pitcher, performing particularly well in 1923, when he led the league with a 2.76 ERA and five shutouts.

After the Indians finished sixth in the American League in 1924, with Coveleski posting an ERA of 4.04 that represented the highest mark of his career to that point, team management elected to trade him to the defending world champion Washington Senators for a pair of undistinguished players during the subsequent off-season. Revealing his thoughts about leaving Cleveland, Coveleski explained years later, "I never did like Cleveland. Don't know why. Didn't like the town. Now, the people are all right, but I just didn't like the town." Coveleski even admitted that his dissatisfaction with his surroundings eventually began to affect his on-field performance, stating, "You know, I got to a point where I wouldn't hustle any more. See, a player who gets to be with a club too long gets lazy, you know." Coveleski left the Indians having compiled an overall record of 172-123, an ERA of 2.80, and a WHIP of 1.225 as a member of the team. He also recorded 31 shutouts, 193 complete games, 20 saves, and 856 strikeouts in 2,502⅓ innings pitched during his time in Cleveland.

Experiencing something of a rebirth his first year in Washington, Coveleski helped the Senators repeat as AL champions by compiling a record of 20-5 and a league-leading 2.84 ERA, although he failed to earn a victory during Washington's seven-game loss to Pittsburgh in the World Series. After winning another 14 games for the Senators in 1926, Coveleski came down with a sore arm the following year, prompting them to release him midway through the campaign. Signing with the Yankees during the subsequent off-season, Coveleski went 5-1 with a 5.74 ERA for the eventual world champions, before being released in early August. He subsequently announced his retirement, ending his career with a record of 215-142, an ERA of 2.89, a WHIP of 1.251, 38 shutouts, 223 complete games, and 981 strikeouts in 3,082 innings pitched.

Following his playing days, Coveleski moved his family to South Bend, Indiana, where he spent the next few years owning a gas station and coaching a boys' amateur team in his spare time, before retiring to private life. Elected to the Baseball Hall of Fame by the members of the Veteran's Committee in 1969, Coveleski expressed both his appreciation and frustration for having to wait so long when he said, "It makes me feel just swell. I figured I'd make it sooner or later, and I just kept hoping each year would be the one." Coveleski lived another 15 years, passing away at the age of 94, on March 20, 1984, after a lengthy illness. At the time of his death, he was the oldest living Hall of Famer.

Indians Career Highlights:

Best Season: Coveleski pitched his best ball for the Indians from 1917 to 1920, ranking among the league leaders in most statistical categories for pitchers all four years. Although Coveleski failed to top 20 victories for the only time during that period in 1917 (he won 19 games), he performed magnificently, posting career-best marks in ERA (1.81), WHIP (0.992), strikeouts (133), and shutouts (9). Even though Coveleski blanked the opposition just twice the following year, he compiled extremely comparable overall numbers, concluding the campaign with 22 wins, a 1.82 ERA, and a WHIP of 1.084. Nevertheless, Coveleski made his greatest impact in 1920, when he helped lead the Indians to their first pennant by going 24-14, with a 2.49 ERA, 26 complete games, a career-high 315 innings pitched, and a league-leading 133 strikeouts and 1.108 WHIP. He subsequently shone against Brooklyn in the World Series, defeating the Robins three times and allowing just two runs and 15 hits in 27 total innings of work, en route to compiling an ERA of 0.67 and a WHIP of 0.630.

Memorable Moments/Greatest Performances: Coveleski, who hit just one home run in 1,058 career at-bats, reached the seats for the only time in his career on May 30, 1916, when he went deep during a game the Indians eventually lost to the St. Louis Browns by a score of 5-4 in 15 innings.

Coveleski suffered a heartbreaking 1-0 loss to the Chicago White Sox on April 24, 1917, allowing just one hit over eight shutout innings, before yielding a triple to Swede Risberg and a run-scoring sacrifice bunt to Eddie Collins with one man out in the bottom of the ninth.

Some 10 weeks later, on July 7, 1917, Coveleski outpitched Babe Ruth, surrendering just three hits and one run during a 3-1 victory over Ruth and the Red Sox in Cleveland.

Coveleski won a 1-0 pitcher's duel with Detroit's Bernie Boland on September 11, 1917, yielding just three harmless singles to a potent lineup that included Hall of Fame outfielders Ty Cobb and Harry Heilmann.

Coveleski topped that performance eight days later, allowing only two walks and a seventh-inning single by Fritz Maisel, in defeating the Yankees by a score of 2-0 on September 19.

Coveleski hurled another gem in his very next start three days later, surrendering just one run, four hits, and three walks over 11 innings, to earn a 2-1 victory over the Philadelphia Athletics

Coveleski displayed his heart and determination on May 24, 1918, when he worked all 19 innings of a 3-2 marathon win over the Yankees, yielding 12 hits and six walks during the contest.

Coveleski turned in another outstanding effort against New York on July 11, 1918, allowing just three hits and two walks during a complete-game 1-0 victory over the Yankees.

Coveleski turned in a similarly impressive performance against the Red Sox on June 16, 1919, surrendering just three hits and two walks, in winning a 1-0 pitcher's duel with Boston's Carl Mays at Fenway Park.

Coveleski again thwarted Boston's lineup on June 14, 1922, walking only one batter and yielding just three hits during a 3-0 win over the Red Sox.

However, Coveleski's performance in the 1920 World Series would have to be considered the highlight of his career. En route to leading the Indians to a 5-2 series win over Brooklyn in the best-of-nine affair, Coveleski threw three complete-game five-hitters, winning Game One by a score of 3-1 and Game Four by a score of 5-1, before clinching Cleveland's first world championship with a 3-0 win in Game Seven. By allowing just two runs over 27 innings, Coveleski concluded the Fall Classic with a sparkling 0.67 ERA. Reflecting back years later on his complete-game shutout in Game Seven, Coveleski evoked a different era, recalling, "Pitched that game and won it, and walked back alone to the clubhouse.

Stan Coveleski's three victories in the 1920 World Series
gave the Indians their first world championship

And nobody said a word, except maybe 'Nice game, Covey.' Just another
ball game."

Notable Achievements:

- Won more than 20 games four times, surpassing 15 victories on
  four other occasions.
- Posted winning percentage in excess of .600 four times.
- Compiled ERA under 2.00 twice, finishing with mark under 3.00
  three other times.
- Threw more than 300 innings three times, topping 275 innings
  pitched three other times.

- Threw more than 20 complete games six times.
- Tossed nine shutouts in 1917.
- Posted WHIP under 1.000 once (0.992 in 1917).
- Led AL pitchers in: ERA once, shutouts twice, strikeouts once, WHIP once, and starts once.
- Finished second in AL in: wins twice, ERA twice, and starts twice.
- Ranks among Indians career leaders in: wins (4th), innings pitched (5th), complete games (3rd), shutouts (tied-3rd), pitching appearances (10th), and games started (5th).
- 1920 AL champion.
- 1920 world champion.
- Elected to Baseball Hall of Fame by members of Veteran's Committee in 1969.

15

LARRY DOBY
1947 – 1955

With his arrival in Cleveland in July 1947 having been preceded by Jackie Robinson's breaking of baseball's color barrier by some three months, Larry Doby never received the credit he deserved for helping to integrate the American League. Nevertheless, the fact remains that Doby suffered the same indignities that Robinson endured, and without nearly as much media attention and implicit support that the National League's first black player received. As *The New York Times* once wrote, "In glorifying those who are first, the second is often forgotten. . . . Larry Doby integrated all those American League ball parks where Jackie Robinson never appeared. And he did it with class and clout."

Yet, in spite of the tremendous contributions Doby made to baseball, and to society as a whole, by becoming the first black player to perform in the AL, he proved to be more than just a baseball pioneer, establishing himself as one of the junior circuit's most feared sluggers during his time in Cleveland. Annually ranking among the league leaders in home runs, RBIs, and slugging percentage, Doby hit more than 30 homers twice, knocked in more than 100 runs four times, and posted a slugging percentage in excess of .500 on four separate occasions, topping the circuit in each of those categories at least once. Doby also scored more than 100 runs three times, batted over .300 twice, and did a solid job in the outfield, leading all AL center-fielders in fielding percentage twice. In addition to earning seven All-Star selections and a pair of top-10 finishes in the league MVP voting with his outstanding all-around play, Doby helped the Indians win two pennants and one World Series, contributing to his status as one of the most significant figures in franchise history.

Born in Camden, South Carolina on December 13, 1923, Lawrence Eugene Doby moved with his mother and siblings to Paterson, New Jersey as a teenager, several years after his parents divorced. The son of a former semi-pro baseball player, Doby excelled in sports as well, starring in baseball, football, and basketball while attending Paterson's Eastside High School. After accepting an athletic scholarship to play basketball at Long Island University following his graduation from Eastside High, Doby also accepted an offer to play for the Newark Eagles of the Negro National League for the remainder of the 1942 season. Beginning his professional playing career under an assumed name to protect his amateur status, Doby batted .427 while playing second base for the Eagles, prompting him to transfer to Virginia Union University.

Doby put both his college education and playing career on hold after being drafted into the U.S. Navy in 1943. He spent the next two years serving in the South Pacific, before returning to the Eagles following his discharge early in 1946. Picking up right where he left off, Doby batted .341 and finished just one home run behind league leaders Josh Gibson and Johnny Davis in the home-run race, and he was helping Newark win the Negro League World Series. After getting off to a torrid start the following year, Doby elected to alter his plans of pursuing a career as a teacher and coach in New Jersey when Cleveland Indians owner Bill Veeck offered him the opportunity to become the American League's first black player.

Going directly from the Negro Leagues to the majors after signing with Cleveland, Doby never played a single game of minor-league ball, making his debut with the Indians on July 5, 1947. Spending most of the season's final three months coming off the bench as a pinch-hitter, the 23-year-old Doby garnered only 33 plate appearances, batting just .156 and driving in only two runs. However, after being moved from second base to the outfield prior to the start of the ensuing campaign, Doby helped the Indians capture the American League pennant by hitting 14 homers, driving in 66 runs, scoring 83 others, and batting .301, while splitting his time between centerfield and right. He then punctuated his outstanding rookie season by becoming the first African-American player to hit a home run in World Series play, with his game-winning solo shot in Game Four helping the Tribe defeat the Boston Braves in six games.

Joining the Indians less than three months after Jackie Robinson arrived in Brooklyn, Doby received as much verbal abuse and physical threatening as his National League counterpart, although the public never became fully aware of the hardships he had to endure because, as Doby himself put it, "The media didn't want to repeat the same story." Furthermore, unlike the combative Robinson, Doby never displayed the anger he felt inside, stating years later, "My way to react to prejudice was to hit the ball as far as I could."

Remaining calm under the most adverse of conditions, Doby recalled one occasion when, "As I slid into second base, the guy playing shortstop spit on me. But I walked away from it. I knew the racial remarks were from people who were prejudiced, or who wanted to disturb me. I wasn't going to let them upset my play, so I didn't think too much about them."

Even the vast majority of Indians players displayed resentment towards Doby when he first arrived in Cleveland, as he revealed years later when he described his initial meeting with his new teammates: "I walked down that line and stuck out my hand, and very few hands came back in return. Most of the ones that did were cold-fish handshakes, along with a look that said, 'You don't belong here.'"

Doby added, "When I walked into that clubhouse on July 5, 1947, I got a lot of resentment from my teammates, but, after a period of time, they got an opportunity to judge me as to who I was, and not on the color of my skin."

Fortunately, not all of Doby's teammates resented his presence on the ball club, as he later identified Jim Hegan, Joe Gordon, and Bob Lemon as three players who accorded him instant respect, showing little interest in his skin color and treating him like a human being from the outset.

Feeling far more comfortable in his second full season in Cleveland, the left-handed hitting Doby, who stood 6'1" tall and weighed approximately 190 pounds, earned All-Star honors for the first of seven straight times in 1949 by finishing third in the league with 24 homers, driving in 85 runs, scoring 106 others, and batting .280, while continuing to see action at two of the three outfield spots. Inserted in centerfield full-time the following year, Doby emerged as one of the American League's best players, earning an 8th-place finish in the MVP voting by hitting 25 homers, knocking in 102 runs, scoring 110 times, drawing 98 bases on balls, batting .326, and topping the circuit with a .442 on-base percentage and an OPS of .986.

Doby continued his outstanding play in each of the next four seasons, topping 30 homers twice, 100 RBIs three times, and 100 runs scored once, while compiling batting averages of .295, .276, .263, and .272. Performing particularly well in 1952 and 1954, Doby knocked in 104 runs and led the

AL with 32 homers, 104 runs scored, and a .541 slugging percentage in the first of those campaigns, before earning a runner-up finish to Yogi Berra in the 1954 MVP balloting by scoring 94 runs and leading the league with 32 homers and 126 RBIs.

Battling a wrist injury and leg problems that affected his play for the remainder of his career, Doby missed 23 games in 1955, although he still managed to hit 26 homers, drive in 75 runs, score 91 times, and bat .291, earning in the process the last of his seven consecutive All-Star nominations. However, with team management believing that the 32-year-old outfielder had already seen his best days, the Indians elected to trade him to the Chicago White Sox for outfielder Jim Busby and shortstop Chico Carrasquel following the conclusion of the campaign. Doby's impending departure prompted *Cleveland Plain Dealer* columnist Franklin Lewis to write, "He has been a controversial athlete. Highly gifted, he was frequently morose, sullen, and, upon occasion, downright surly to his teammates. . . . He thought of himself, at the beginning, as the symbol of the Negro in his league." In response, Doby stated, "I was looked on as a Black man, not as a human being. I did feel a responsibility to the Black players who came after me, but that was a responsibility, basically, to people, not just to Black people."

Doby ended up spending two years in Chicago, hitting 38 homers and driving in 181 runs for the White Sox during that time, before being reacquired by the Indians prior to the start of the 1958 season. After hitting 13 homers, knocking in 45 runs, and batting .283 in a part-time role with the Tribe that year, Doby found himself on the move once again at season's end when the Indians dealt him to the Detroit Tigers for Tito Francona. He subsequently split the 1959 season between the Tigers and White Sox, batting just .230 in a total of 39 games, before announcing his retirement following the conclusion of the campaign. Doby ended his career with 253 home runs, 970 RBIs, 960 runs scored, 1,515 hits, 243 doubles, 52 triples, 47 stolen bases, a batting average of .283, an on-base percentage of .386, and a slugging percentage of .490. Over parts of 10 seasons with the Indians, he hit 215 homers, knocked in 776 runs, scored 808 times, amassed 1,234 hits, 190 doubles, 45 triples, and 44 stolen bases, batted .286, compiled a .389 on-base percentage, and posted a .500 slugging percentage.

Following his playing days, Doby eventually returned to the game, first as a coach for the Montreal Expos, Cleveland Indians, and Chicago White Sox, before replacing former teammate Bob Lemon as White Sox manager in 1978, thereby becoming just the second African-American skipper in MLB history. After retiring from baseball following the conclusion of the 1979 campaign, Doby spent 10 years serving as the director of communications for the NBA's New Jersey Nets. He also later served as a special assistant to AL President Gene Budig, who, upon his hiring, stated, "Few have done more for baseball than Larry Doby."

Doby lived until June 18, 2003, when he passed away at 79 years of age at his home in Montclair, New Jersey following a lengthy battle with cancer. Following his passing, Bob Feller said of his former teammate, "He was a great American, he served the country in World War II, and he was a great ballplayer. He was kind of like Buzz Aldrin, the second man on the moon, because he was the second African-American player in the majors behind Jackie Robinson. He was just as good of a ballplayer, an exciting player, and a very good teammate."

Choosing to pay tribute to Doby on August 10, 2007, the Indians had every player on their roster wear the former outfielder's retired number 14 when the New York Yankees visited Jacobs Field (now Progressive Field) that day. Commenting on the team's gesture, then Indians pitcher C.C. Sabathia opined, "It's something that definitely needed to be done. I don't think a lot of people know anything about him [Doby], but he was definitely huge. You hear all about Jackie [Robinson] all the time, and people lose sight of the fact that Larry was the first black player in the American League. So he's as much of an icon as Jackie is."

Former Indians teammate Al Rosen agreed, stating:

> *"Jackie [Robinson] was a college educated man who had been an officer in the service and who played at the Triple-A level. Jackie was brought in by Branch Rickey specifically to be the first black player in Major League Baseball. Larry Doby came up as a second baseman who didn't have time to get his full college education, and was forced to play a different position in his first major league season. I think, because of those circumstances, he had a more difficult time than Jackie Robinson. I don't think he has gotten the credit he deserves."*

Indians Career Highlights:

Best Season: Doby proved to be one of the American League's most productive hitters in both 1952 and 1954. After batting .276, finishing second in the league with 104 RBIs, and topping the circuit with 32 homers,

104 RBIs, and a .541 slugging percentage in the first of those campaigns, Doby earned a runner-up finish in the AL MVP voting in 1954 by batting .272, scoring 94 runs, and leading the league with 32 homers and a career-high 126 RBIs. However, Doby posted his best overall numbers in 1950, when he earned his lone *Sporting News* All-Star selection by hitting 25 homers, knocking in 102 runs, scoring 110 times, finishing fourth in the league in batting average (.326) and slugging percentage (.545), and topping the circuit in on-base percentage (.442) and OPS (.986), establishing career-high marks in each of the last five categories.

Memorable Moments/Greatest Performances: Doby made history in Game Four of the 1948 World Series, when he became the first player of African-American descent to hit a home run in the Fall Classic, with his third-inning solo blast off Boston's Johnny Sain proving to be the decisive blow of a 2-1 Cleveland victory. He finished the Series, which the Indians won in six games, with a homer, two RBIs, and a .318 batting average.

Doby hit two home runs in one game for the first time in his career on June 7, 1949, when he reached the seats twice, knocked in four runs, and scored three times during a 13-11 win over the Washington Senators.

Doby led the Indians to a 15-4 pasting of the Philadelphia Athletics on May 16, 1950, by going 3-for-5, with a homer, triple, and career-high six runs batted in.

Doby turned in a memorable performance against Washington on August 2, 1950, when he hit three homers, knocked in five runs, and scored four times during an 11-0 rout of the Senators.

Just three days later, Doby paced the Indians to a 4-2 win over the Yankees by homering twice and driving in three runs.

Doby continued his prolific slugging against St. Louis on August 9, 1950, giving the Tribe a 4-3 victory over the Browns by knocking in all four Cleveland runs with a pair of two-run homers.

Doby again feasted off St. Louis pitching on April 28, 1951, when he homered, singled, knocked in four runs, and scored four times during a lopsided 12-4 victory over the Browns.

Although the Indians suffered a 13-11 defeat at the hands of the Boston Red Sox on June 4, 1952, Doby starred in the loss, hitting for the cycle, scoring three times, and equaling his career-high by driving in six runs.

Larry Doby broke the color barrier in the American League
when he joined the Indians in 1947

Courtesy of Mears Online Auctions

Doby came up big in the clutch for the Indians on August 8, 1952, when his three-run homer in the top of the ninth inning tied the score with St. Louis at 9-9. The Tribe won the contest three innings later, when first baseman Bill Glynn hit a solo blast in the top of the 12th.

Doby had a big day against Boston on June 25, 1953, leading the Indians to a 15-4 win over the Red Sox by going 4-for-5, with two homers, a double, five RBIs, and three runs scored.

Doby capped off a perfect 4-for-4 day at the plate against New York on April 30, 1954, by breaking a 4-4 tie with the Yankees with a bases-loaded single in the top of the 10th inning. The Indians subsequently pushed across three more runs, giving them a 9-4 win over the five-time defending world champions. Doby finished the game with a homer, three singles, four RBIs, and two runs scored.

Doby experienced the finest moment of his second tour of duty with the Indians on August 30, 1958, when his two-run homer in the top of the 14th inning gave the Tribe an 8-6 victory over the Kansas City Athletics. He finished the game with three hits, two homers, three RBIs, and three runs scored.

Notable Achievements:

- Hit more than 20 home runs seven times, topping 30 homers twice.
- Knocked in more than 100 runs four times, topping 120 RBIs once (126 in 1954).
- Scored more than 100 runs three times.
- Batted over .300 twice, topping the .320-mark once (.326 in 1950).
- Topped 100 walks once (101 in 1951).
- Compiled on-base percentage in excess of .400 twice.
- Posted slugging percentage in excess of .500 four times.
- Led AL in: home runs twice, RBIs once, runs scored once, on-base percentage once, slugging percentage once, and OPS once.
- Finished second in AL in: RBIs once, slugging percentage once, and OPS twice.
- Finished third in A.L in: home runs twice, bases on balls once, and on-base percentage once.
- Led AL outfielders in double plays once.
- Led AL center-fielders in double plays once and fielding percentage twice.
- Ranks among Indians career leaders in: home runs (6th), RBIs (9th), runs scored (10th), and bases on balls (6th).
- Hit three home runs in one game vs. Washington Senators on August 2, 1950.
- Hit for cycle vs. Boston Red Sox on June 4, 1952.
- Finished second in 1954 AL MVP voting.

- 1950 *Sporting News* All-Star selection.
- Seven-time AL All-Star (1949, 1950, 1951, 1952, 1953, 1954, and 1955).
- Two-time AL champion (1948 and 1954).
- 1948 world champion.
- Elected to Baseball Hall of Fame by members of Veteran's Committee in 1998.

16

EARLY WYNN
1949 – 1957, 1963

Once called "the toughest pitcher I ever faced" by Ted Williams, Early Wynn proved to be a thorn in the side of opposing hitters throughout his 23-year major-league career, which he split between the Washington Senators, Cleveland Indians, and Chicago White Sox. A notorious head-hunter who routinely threw at the opposition, Wynn struck fear into his opponent with the aggressiveness he displayed on the mound, once responding to the suggestion that he would throw at his own mother by stating, "I would if she were crowding the plate." Extremely talented as well, Wynn surpassed 20 victories five times, doing so on four separate occasions as a member of the Indians, with whom he spent most of his peak seasons. A key member of the Tribe's pitching staff from 1949 to 1957, the burly right-hander compiled an overall record of 164-102 over the course of those nine seasons, posting 23 wins twice and 20 victories two other times. Wynn also compiled an ERA under 3.00 four times, threw more than 250 innings six times, and tossed more than 20 complete games twice during his time in Cleveland, earning in the process three All-Star selections and two top-10 finishes in the AL MVP voting. Meanwhile, Wynn's league-leading 23 victories in 1954 helped the Indians capture just the third pennant in franchise history.

Born in Hartford, Alabama on January 6, 1920, Early Wynn attended Geneva County High School, where he played both football and baseball until a broken leg forced him to concentrate exclusively on the latter sport. With his father having competed in baseball at the semipro level, Wynn once expressed his fondness for the game by proclaiming, "Since the first time I saw my father play semipro ball in Alabama, it has been my greatest ambition and desire to be a big-league ballplayer." Determined to escape a life of picking cotton and peanuts, Wynn showed up at a Washington

Senators tryout camp at the age of 17, making enough of an impression on team scouts to receive a contract offer, after which he decided to quit school. Wynn then spent most of the next five years advancing through Washington's farm system, before finally joining the club during the latter stages of the 1941 campaign. Appearing in a total of five games with the Senators, Wynn compiled a record of 3-1 and an outstanding 1.58 ERA.

Serving as a regular member of Washington's starting rotation from 1942 to 1944, Wynn went a combined 36-45 for the lowly Senators, although he pitched better than his record would seem to indicate, with his finest effort coming in 1943, when he went 18-12 with a 2.91 ERA. After missing all of 1945 while serving in the Army Tank Corp in the Philippines during World War II, Wynn returned to the Senators midway through the 1946 season. Experiencing only a moderate amount of success upon his return, Wynn compiled an overall record of 33-39 from 1946 to 1948, earning the first of his seven All-Star selections in 1947 by winning 17 games for a team that finished next-to-last in the league with a record of just 56-98.

His effectiveness limited somewhat by his over-reliance on his fastball, Wynn nevertheless began to gain a reputation during his time in Washington for his meanness on the mound, which he exhibited with his willingness to pitch inside. Expressing his contempt for opposing hitters on one occasion, Wynn proclaimed, "A pitcher has to look at the hitter as his mortal enemy," quickly adding, "I've got a right to knock down anybody holding a bat."

With Wynn having posted an overall mark of just 72-87 over parts of eight seasons in Washington, the Senators and Indians completed a trade on December 14, 1948, that sent Wynn and first baseman Mickey Vernon to Cleveland, in exchange for first baseman Eddie Robinson and veteran right-handers Joe Haynes and Ed Klieman. While Robinson went on to have some extremely productive years for the Senators and Chicago White Sox, the deal proved to be a steal for the Indians, with Wynn subsequently developing into one of the league's top hurlers under the tutelage of pitching coach Mel Harder, who taught him pitching patterns and how to throw a curveball, slider, and changeup.

After compiling a record of 11-7 and an ERA of 4.15 in his first year with the Tribe, Wynn began an extremely successful seven-year run during which he won at least 17 games each season, topping 20 victories on four separate occasions. He had his first big year for the Indians in 1950, going 18-8, with a league-leading 3.20 ERA and 1.250 WHIP. Wynn followed that up by winning 20 games for the first time in his career in 1951, finishing the season with a record of 20-13, topping the circuit with 274⅓ innings pitched, and ranking among the league leaders with a 3.02 ERA, a WHIP of 1.217, 133 strikeouts, and 21 complete games. He then earned a fifth-place finish in the AL MVP voting in 1952 by going 23-12, with a 2.90 ERA, 153 strikeouts, 19 complete games, and 285 2/3 innings pitched.

Employing a seemingly effortless pitching motion, Wynn gradually gained better command of his pitches under the watchful eye of Harder, enabling him to record more strikeouts during the 1950s (1,544) than any other hurler in the majors, even though he suffered from gout throughout the entire decade He also proved to be quite capable at the bat, compiling a lifetime batting average of .214, while hitting 17 homers and driving in 173 runs over the course of his career, with one of his homers being a pinch-hit grand slam.

Yet, even as Wynn emerged as one of the American League's most accomplished players, he continued to build on his reputation as arguably the circuit's most intimidating pitcher, with his burly, six-foot, 200-pound frame, grizzled appearance, and willingness to knock down opposing hitters adding to his mystique. Although Wynn made a great teammate off the playing field, he assumed a completely different persona once he toed the rubber, once describing the attitude he took with him to the mound by stating, "That space between the white lines—that's my office; that's where I conduct my business. You take a look at the batter's box, and part of it belongs to the hitter. But, when he crowds in just that hair, he's stepping into my office, and nobody comes into my office without an invitation when I'm going to work."

His competitive nature causing him to become incensed when a batter hit a line drive off him early in a game, Wynn typically threw inside to him in subsequent at-bats, and even threw at him as he stood at first base, disguising the beanball as a pick-off throw. Former Senators and Indians teammate Mickey Vernon described one such instance when he recalled, "'We were roommates and good friends. After I was traded back to Washington, I got four hits off of him the first time I faced him, the last one knocking the glove off his hand. When I got to first base, he was steaming. He looked over and said, 'Roommate or not, you've got to go in the dirt

Courtesy of Mears Online Auctions

Early Wynn topped 20 victories in four of his
nine seasons with the Indians

seat next time I see you.' Sure enough, the next time I faced him, the first
pitch was up over my head—to let me know he hadn't forgotten."

After winning 17 games for the Indians in 1953, Wynn helped them
capture the AL pennant the following year by going 23-11, with a 2.73
ERA, 155 strikeouts, 20 complete games, and a league-leading 270 2/3
innings pitched, en route to earning a sixth-place finish in the AL MVP
voting. He remained an effective pitcher for the Tribe for two more years,
compiling a record of 17-11 and an ERA of 2.82 in 1955, before ranking
among the league leaders with a record of 20-9, an ERA of 2.72, a WHIP
of 1.167, four shutouts, 158 strikeouts, 18 complete games, and 277 2/3

innings pitched in 1956. However, after Wynn finished just 14-17 with a 4.31 ERA in 1957, the Indians decided to part ways with the 37-year-old right-hander at season's end, including him in a four-player trade they completed with the White Sox that netted them outfielder Minnie Minoso and third baseman Fred Hatfield.

After struggling his first year in Chicago, Wynn rebounded in 1959 to have one of his finest seasons, helping to lead the White Sox to the pennant by topping the circuit with 22 wins and 255 2/3 innings pitched, with his outstanding performance earning him Cy Young honors and a third-place finish in the AL MVP balloting. Never again a dominant pitcher after that, Wynn compiled an overall record of just 28-29 over the course of the next three seasons, before being released by the White Sox following the conclusion of the 1962 campaign, just one win shy of 300 victories. Signed by the Indians midway through the 1963 season, Wynn attained his 300th victory as a member of the Tribe, going 1-2 the rest of the year, before announcing his retirement. Wynn ended his career with a record of 300-244, an ERA of 3.54, a WHIP of 1.329, 49 shutouts, 289 complete games, and 2,334 strikeouts in 4,564 innings pitched. During his time in Cleveland, he went 164-102, with a 3.24 ERA, a WHIP of 1.274, 24 shutouts, 144 complete games, and 1,277 strikeouts in 2,286 2/3 innings of work.

Following his playing days, Wynn succeeded his mentor, Mel Harder, as Indians pitching coach, spending three years in that role, before assuming the same position with the Minnesota Twins in 1967. After leaving Minnesota, Wynn moved on to Toronto and, later, Chicago, where he spent the better part of a decade broadcasting games for the Blue Jays and White Sox. After retiring from baseball in 1983, Wynn returned to his home in Florida, where he spent the rest of his life, suffering a heart attack and a series of strokes during his final years, before passing away in an assisted-living facility on April 4, 1999, at the age of 79.

Indians Career Highlights:

Best Season: Wynn had an outstanding year for the Indians in 1952, finishing second in the league with 153 strikeouts and a career-high 23 victories, compiling an ERA of 2.90 and a WHIP of 1.299, and ranking among the leaders with four shutouts, 19 complete games, and 285 2/3 innings pitched. He also performed extremely well in 1956, placing in the league's top three in wins (20), winning percentage (.690), ERA (2.72), WHIP (1.167), shutouts (4), and innings pitched (277 2/3), while also tossing 18 complete games. However, Wynn pitched his best ball for the Indians in 1954, when he helped lead them to the pennant by tying teammate Bob Lemon for the league lead with 23 victories, topping the circuit with 270 2/3 innings pitched, and ranking among the leaders in ERA (2.73), WHIP (1.138), strikeouts (155), and complete games (20).

Memorable Moments/Greatest Performances: An excellent hitting pitcher, Wynn often helped his own cause by contributing to his team on offense, doing so on July 17, 1949, when he homered, singled, and scored twice during a 4-2 complete-game win over the Red Sox.

Wynn turned in a tremendous all-around effort against Chicago on August 11, 1951, leading the Indians to a 2-1 win over the White Sox by yielding just four hits and one walk, while also hitting a solo homer in the bottom of the seventh inning that provided the margin of victory.

Wynn did a little bit of everything on September 12, 1952, surrendering just three harmless singles to Boston's lineup and collecting three hits himself during a 5-0 shutout of the Red Sox.

Wynn again excelled both on the mound and at the plate on May 3, 1953, when he homered and allowed just three hits and three walks during a 7-0 shutout of the Washington Senators.

Wynn homered, singled, and yielded just three hits and two walks to New York on June 28, 1953, in defeating the Yankees by a score of 4-1.

Wynn helped his own cause again on September 12, 1956, when his solo homer in the bottom of the sixth inning proved to be the decisive blow of a 2-1 win over the Baltimore Orioles.

Wynn turned in a dominant performance against New York on July 14, 1951, yielding just two hits and two walks during an 8-0 victory over the Yankees.

Wynn again dominated the opposition on May 28, 1954, allowing just two hits and two walks during a 3-0 shutout of the Detroit Tigers.

Wynn tossed a complete-game two-hitter against the Washington Senators on August 26, 1954, defeating his former team by a score of 2-1.

Wynn again yielded just two hits and one run during a 6-1 win over the Yankees on August 31, 1954.

Wynn threw his only one-hitter as a member of the Tribe on May 22, 1955, allowing just four walks and a fourth-inning single to Fred Hatfield during a 4-0 shutout of the Detroit Tigers.

Although Wynn did not pitch well on July 13, 1963, he reached a huge milestone that day, recording the 300th and final victory of his career. Recounting the events surrounding the win, Wynn revealed, "I never slept the night before; the gout was killing me." Expressing his gratitude to Cleveland manager Birdie Tebbetts for lifting him for a pinch-hitter after five innings, Wynn suggested that he otherwise "might have fallen on my face. I was exhausted." Leaving the game with a 5-4 lead after five innings, Wynn recalled, "Jerry Walker relieved me and saved the game for me. He was my roommate and pitched like a man possessed."

Notable Achievements:

- Won at least 20 games four times, surpassing 17 victories on three other occasions.
- Posted winning percentage in excess of .600 seven times.
- Compiled ERA under 3.00 four times.
- Threw more than 250 innings six times.
- Threw more than 20 complete games twice.
- Led AL pitchers in: wins once, ERA once, WHIP once, strikeouts once, innings pitched twice, and starts three times.
- Finished second in AL in: wins twice, winning percentage once, WHIP once, strikeouts three times, shutouts twice, innings pitched twice, and complete games once.
- Ranks among Indians career leaders in: wins (5th), strikeouts (tied-3rd), shutouts (7th), innings pitched (7th), complete games (8th), and games started (7th).
- Finished in top 10 of AL MVP voting twice, making it into top five once (5th in 1952).
- Three-time AL All-Star (1955, 1956, and 1957).
- 1954 AL champion.
- Number 100 on *The Sporting News'* 1999 list of Baseball's 100 Greatest Players.
- Elected to Baseball Hall of Fame by members of BBWAA in 1972.

17

KENNY LOFTON
1992 – 1996, 1998 – 2001, 2007

A winner wherever he went, Kenny Lofton played for teams that advanced to the playoffs in 11 of his 17 big-league seasons. In his three tours of duty with the Indians alone, which covered a total of 9½ seasons, Lofton helped lead the Tribe to six division titles and one American League pennant. Playing the best ball of his career for the Indians during the 1990s, the speedy Lofton succeeded Rickey Henderson as the American League's finest leadoff hitter and foremost base-stealer. In addition to batting over .300 five times for the Tribe, Lofton scored more than 100 runs six times, surpassed 200 hits once, and stole more than 50 bases six times, topping the junior circuit in the last category on five separate occasions. The Indians' all-time leader in stolen bases, Lofton also used his tremendous speed and superior athleticism to his advantage in the outfield, winning four Gold Gloves during his time in Cleveland, with his exceptional all-around play earning him five All-Star selections and one top-five finish in the AL MVP voting.

Born in East Chicago, Indiana on May 31, 1967, Kenneth Lofton grew up in poverty. Raised by his widowed grandmother in the city slums after his unwed teenage mother moved to Alabama, Lofton attended Washington High School, where he starred in baseball and basketball, earning All-State honors in the latter sport. After receiving a basketball scholarship from the University of Arizona, Lofton spent his first two years of college excelling on the hardwood, before finally electing to try out for the school's baseball team as a junior. Although he subsequently appeared in just five games on the diamond for the Wildcats, Lofton made enough of an impression on pro scouts with his speed and athletic ability to be selected by the Houston Astros in the 17th round of the 1988 MLB Draft.

After completing his college education, Lofton began his professional career in earnest in the summer of 1989, spending most of the next three seasons advancing through Houston's farm system, before making a brief appearance with the parent club towards the tail end of the 1991 campaign. However, after batting just .203 in 20 games with the Astros, Lofton found himself headed to Cleveland when Houston traded him to the Indians for pitcher Willie Blair and catcher Eddie Taubensee on December 10, 1991. Upon learning of the trade that sent him to Cleveland, Lofton commented, "I know they [Houston] gave up on me, and now I'm glad they did. One man's trash is another man's treasure."

Inserted into the leadoff spot in the batting order immediately upon his arrival in Cleveland, Lofton ended up performing extremely well for the Tribe in his first full season. After working extensively with Indians first base coach Dave Nelson on refining his base-running technique and bunting skills, the six-foot, 180-pound Lofton went on to bat .285, score 96 runs, and lead the league in stolen bases for the first of five straight times by swiping 66 bags, which established a new single-season franchise record, as well as a new record for American League rookies. Meanwhile, Lofton's 14 assists led all league centerfielders, with his outstanding play earning him a runner-up finish in the 1992 AL Rookie of the Year voting. Improving upon his performance the following year, Lofton began an exceptional four-year run during which he ultimately replaced Rickey Henderson as the junior circuit's top leadoff hitter, compiling the following numbers over the course of those four seasons:

1993: 1 HR, 42 RBI, 116 Runs Scored, 185 Hits, **70** SB, .325 AVG, .408 OBP, .408 SLG

1994: 12 HR, 57 RBI, 105 Runs Scored, **160** Hits, **60** SB, .349 AVG, .412 OBP, .536 SLG

1995: 7 HR, 53 RBI, 93 Runs Scored, 149 Hits, **54** SB, .310 AVG, .362 OBP, .453 SLG

1996: 14 HR, 67 RBI, 132 Runs Scored, 210 Hits, **75** SB, .317 AVG, .372 OBP, .446 SLG

In addition to leading the AL in stolen bases all four years, the lefty-swinging Lofton annually ranked among the league leaders in hits and runs scored, topping the circuit in hits once and placing second in runs scored once. He also finished fourth in the league in batting average in both 1993 and 1994. Meanwhile, Lofton led the AL with 13 triples in 1995, even though he missed nearly a month of the campaign with injuries. Excelling in the outfield as well, Lofton proved to be a spectacular defensive center-fielder who specialized in climbing outfield walls to turn apparent home runs into outs, with his superb glove work earning him Gold Glove honors all four years. Lofton also earned three All-Star selections, one top-five finish in the league MVP voting, and MVP consideration two other times between 1993 and 1996.

Extremely impressed with Lofton's rapid rise to stardom, Milwaukee Brewers manager Phil Garner, who saw him play in the minors, commented, "I remember how raw he was, and I've never seen anybody develop into that type of player that fast. He went from a guy who could hardly get the ball past the infield to a guy who could hit the ball consistently. He always had good speed, but he got lousy jumps and didn't run the bases well. He has turned into a dominant player."

Following Lofton's brilliant 1994 campaign, Indians general manager John Hart gushed, "What a representative for our team and our city. He has the opportunity to be a George Brett-type player here, someone who is synonymous with a franchise."

Expressing his fondness for his adopted city after the Indians won the pennant in 1995, Lofton proclaimed, "I'm glad for the city of Cleveland to be able to experience this, because they haven't experienced this for a long time. The city of Cleveland has grown a lot, and it's improving, and we tried to do this for the city."

Yet, in spite of the mutual love affair that Lofton developed with the city of Cleveland, his impending free agency prompted GM John Hart to trade him to the Atlanta Braves for outfielders Marquis Grissom and David Justice prior to the start of the 1997 campaign. After completing the deal, Hart stated, "We had to make this trade based on the fact that Lofton could be a free agent at the end of this season. We went through it with Albert Belle last year, and Albert left and we had nothing in return. We were not prepared to do that again."

Lofton played well for the Braves in 1997, earning the fourth of his six straight All-Star selections by batting .333, scoring 90 runs, and stealing 27 bases. But, when he became a free agent at season's end, he signed a four-year, $30.6 million deal with the Indians. Upon inking his contract with the Tribe, Lofton said, "It's like I was a ghost for a year. But now I'm back."

Reclaiming his leadoff spot in the batting order after rejoining the Indians, Lofton had an excellent year for the Tribe in 1998, hitting 12 homers, driving in 64 runs, scoring 101 times, batting .282, compiling a .371 on-base percentage, and finishing second in the league with 54 stolen bases. He followed that up by batting .301, scoring 110 runs, and stealing 25 bases in 1999, before batting .278, scoring 107 times, swiping 30 bags, and establishing career-high marks in home runs (15) and RBIs (73) in 2000. But, after Lofton batted just .261, scored only 91 runs, and stole just 16 bases in 2001, the Indians chose not to actively pursue him when he once again became a free agent at season's end.

After signing with the Chicago White Sox, Lofton spent the next six years peddling his services to the highest bidder, splitting his time between the White Sox, Giants, Pirates, Cubs, Yankees, Phillies, Dodgers, and Rangers, before returning to Cleveland for a third tour of duty in July 2007. Playing his best ball during that time for the Pirates and Cubs in 2003, Lofton concluded the campaign with 12 homers, 46 RBIs, 97 runs scored, 30 stolen bases, and a .296 batting average. He also performed well for the Dodgers in 2006, batting .301, scoring 79 runs, and stealing 32 bases in 37 attempts, at 39 years of age. After rejoining the Indians in 2007, Lofton batted .283 and scored 24 runs over the season's final 52 games, before announcing his retirement following the conclusion of the campaign. He ended his career with 130 home runs, 781 RBIs, 1,528 runs scored, 2,428 hits, 383 doubles, 116 triples, 622 stolen bases, a .299 batting average, a .372 on-base percentage, and a .423 slugging percentage. In his 9½ years with the Indians, Lofton hit 87 homers, knocked in 518 runs, scored 975 times, amassed 1,512 hits, 244 doubles, 66 triples, and a franchise-record 452 stolen bases, batted an even .300, compiled an on-base percentage of .375, and posted a slugging percentage of .426.

Since retiring as an active player, Lofton has started his own television production company, which is called FilmPool, Inc. He has also spent time with the Indians during spring training serving as a base-running and outfield coach. In addition, Lofton does color commentary on the Fox Sports West post-game show for the Los Angeles Dodgers.

Indians Career Highlights:

Best Season: Lofton performed brilliantly during the strike-shortened 1994 campaign, earning a fourth-place finish in the AL MVP voting by hitting 12 homers, driving in 57 runs, ranking among the league leaders with 105 runs scored, 32 doubles, nine triples, 246 total bases, a .349 batting average, a .412 on-base percentage, and an OPS of .948, and topping the circuit with 160 hits and 60 stolen bases. However, with a full slate of games, he compiled his best overall numbers in 1996, hitting 14 homers, knocking in 67 runs, batting .317, compiling an on-base percentage of .372, posting a slugging percentage of .446, and establishing career-high marks in hits (210), doubles (35), total bases (295), runs scored (132), and stolen bases (75), with his league-leading total in the last category representing a single-season franchise record.

Memorable Moments/Greatest Performances: Lofton led the Indians to a 13-1 rout of the Toronto Blue Jays on April 16, 1993, by going 4-for-5, with two triples and four runs scored.

Lofton contributed to a 9-8 win over the Chicago White Sox on July 22, 1994, by collecting three hits, homering once, scoring three runs, and stealing four bases.

Lofton ended a 17-inning marathon with the Minnesota Twins in walk-off fashion on May 7, 1995, when he drove home Manny Ramirez with the decisive run of a 10-9 Indians victory with an RBI single to center-field. He finished the game with four hits in 10 trips to the plate.

Lofton collected five hits in one game for the only time as a member of the Indians on July 20, 1996, when he went 5-for-6 and scored twice during a 6-5 win over Minnesota in 11 innings.

Lofton helped lead the Indians to a 10-4 win over the Texas Rangers on May 3, 1999, by going 4-for-5, with a homer and four RBIs.

Lofton, who hit two home runs in one game four times during his career, accomplished the feat on August 20, 2000, when he reached the seats twice and knocked in a career-high six runs, in leading the Indians to a 12-4 victory over the Seattle Mariners.

Lofton turned in a tremendous all-around effort on September 3, 2000, when he went 4-for-7, with a homer, four runs scored, and a career-high five stolen bases, during a 13-inning, 12-11 win over the Baltimore Orioles that he ended with a walk-off solo home run.

Lofton proved to be the difference in a 4-3 victory over the Seattle Mariners on August 26, 2001, going 4-for-5 with a homer, and knocking in all four Cleveland runs.

However, Lofton experienced his finest moment in Game Six of the 1995 ALCS. Lofton, who performed brilliantly throughout the series, leading the Indians to a six-game victory over Seattle by batting .458, with two triples, three RBIs, five stolen bases, and an OPS of 1.142, put on display for all to see his tremendous base-running ability in the eighth inning of that contest. With the Indians already holding a 3-0 lead, Lofton reached base on a bunt single, stole second, and then scored all the way from second on a passed ball by catcher Dan Wilson. Following the game, *The New York Times* described Lofton's effort as "the run that demoralized the Mariners." Some 15 years later, *The Cleveland Plain Dealer* recalled, "Of all the electrifying moments on the Kenny Lofton highlight reel, none captures the essence of the player any better than his one-hundred-eighty-foot dash to glory on October 17, 1995."

Notable Achievements:

- Batted over .300 five times, topping the .320-mark twice.
- Scored more than 100 runs six times, surpassing 130 runs scored once (132 in 1996).
- Topped 200 hits once (210 in 1996).
- Finished in double digits in triples once (13 in 1995).
- Surpassed 30 doubles three times.
- Stole more than 20 bases eight times, topping 50 steals six times and 70 thefts twice.
- Compiled on-base percentage in excess of .400 three times.
- Posted slugging percentage in excess of .500 once (.536 in 1994).
- Led AL in: stolen bases five times, hits once, triples once, and at-bats once.
- Finished second in AL in stolen bases once and runs scored once.
- Finished third in AL in: runs scored twice, hits once, and triples once.
- Led AL outfielders in assists twice.
- Led AL center-fielders in assists four times and double plays twice.
- Holds MLB record for most career postseason stolen bases (34).
- Holds Indians single-season record for most stolen bases (75 in 1996).
- Holds Indians career record for most stolen bases (452).

Courtesy of Jerry Reuss

Kenny Lofton stole more bases than
any other player in franchise history

- Ranks among Indians career leaders in: runs scored (3rd), hits (9th), and at-bats (10th).
- Four-time Gold Glove Award winner (1993, 1994, 1995, and 1996).
- Finished fourth in 1994 AL MVP voting.
- Five-time AL All-Star (1994, 1995, 1996, 1998, and 1999).
- 1995 AL champion.

18

MEL HARDER

1928 - 1947

The longest-tenured player in Indians history, Mel Harder spent his entire 20-year major-league career in Cleveland, appearing in more games during that time than any other pitcher in franchise history. Extremely consistent and durable, Harder won at least 15 games for the Indians eight straight times, surpassing 20 victories on two separate occasions. The right-hander also threw at least 12 complete games and 200 innings in eight consecutive seasons, compiling over the course of his career more wins, innings pitched, and starts than any other hurler to take the mound for the Tribe, with the exception of Bob Feller. Featuring an excellent sinking fastball and one of the best curveballs in the game, Harder did an outstanding job of pitching to contact, performing so well for mostly mediocre Indians teams that he earned four All-Star selections. And, following the conclusion of his playing career, Harder remained in Cleveland for another 16 years, during which time he continued to serve the Indians as one of the sport's most highly regarded pitching coaches.

Born on his family's farm near Beemer, Nebraska on October 15, 1909, Melvin Leroy Harder grew up some 80 miles southeast, in the city of Omaha, where he attended Tech High School. Despite being nearsighted, the bespectacled teen eventually established himself as a top pitching prospect while at Tech High, learning to change speeds and locations on his offerings well enough that he received a contract offer from the minor-league Omaha Buffaloes. Signing with the Buffaloes right out of high school, Harder spent just one season at Omaha, before the St. Louis Cardinals, Chicago White Sox, and Cleveland Indians all came calling. Choosing to sign with the Indians, who received a glowing evaluation of the youngster from scout Cy Slapnicka, Harder began his major-league career at only 18 years of age in 1928, when, working primarily out of the

Cleveland bullpen, he lost his only two decisions and compiled an ERA of 6.61 over 49 innings. Harder subsequently split the ensuing campaign between the Indians and their farm club in New Orleans, continuing to struggle in extremely limited duty at the major-league level.

Harder arrived in the big leagues to stay in 1930, when, functioning as a swingman who made 19 starts and 17 relief appearances, he finished 11-10, with a 4.21 ERA, seven complete games, and 45 strikeouts in 175⅓ innings of work. Assuming a similar role the following year, the 6'1", 195-pound right-hander compiled a record of 13-14 and an ERA of 4.36, completed nine of his 24 starts, and struck out 63 batters in 194 innings of work.

Having improved his ability to locate his pitches over the course of the previous two seasons, Harder earned a regular spot in the Cleveland starting rotation in 1932, which marked the first of eight consecutive seasons in which he surpassed 15 victories, tossed at least 12 complete games, and threw more than 200 innings. In addition to compiling a record of 15-13, Harder completed 17 of his 32 starts and placed in the league's top 10 in ERA (3.75), WHIP (1.355), and innings pitched (254⅔). Although Harder's record slipped to 15-17 in 1933, he actually improved upon his overall performance, leading all AL hurlers with a 2.95 ERA, while also ranking among the league leaders with a WHIP of 1.269 and 253 innings pitched. Harder followed that up with the two finest seasons of his career, earning the first of his four consecutive All-Star selections in 1934 by going 20-12, with a 2.61 ERA, a WHIP of 1.281, 17 complete games, 255⅓ innings pitched, and a league-leading six shutouts, before concluding the ensuing campaign with a mark of 22-11, an ERA of 3.29, a WHIP of 1.274, 17 complete games, four shutouts, and 287⅓ innings pitched.

Although Harder lacked an overpowering fastball, his excellent control, outstanding ball movement, and ability to pitch to spots enabled him to successfully navigate his way through opposing lineups. Employing a smooth overhand delivery that produced a natural sink on his fastball, Harder relied heavily on batters to get themselves out by beating the ball into the ground. He also threw a change-up and a curveball that eventually became his "money pitch," especially to right-handed hitters. When asked who he considered to be the toughest pitcher for him to hit, Joe DiMaggio, who batted just .180 against Harder over the course of his career, responded, "Mel Harder of the Indians because he had a great curve and I had trouble with it."

In discussing his pitching repertoire during a 1998 interview on ESPN, Harder explained, "I didn't have much of a curveball until I got to professional ball. I also had to learn a change-up when I made it to the pros. I got a lot of batters out with that fastball sinker. But, over the years, I had to mix it up more."

Harder became even more dependent on his breaking pitches and exceptional control after he suffered a shoulder injury in July of 1936 that reduced the velocity on his fastball for the remainder of his career. Although he made the All-Star team in both 1936 and 1937, Harder compiled an overall record of just 30-27 over the course of those two seasons, while also posting ERAs of 5.17 and 4.28. However, he rebounded somewhat in 1938, concluding the campaign with a record of 17-10 and an ERA of 3.83 after developing a slider that he added to his repertoire of pitches.

Harder had one more standout season for the Indians, going 15-9 with a 3.50 ERA in 1939, before spending his final eight years in Cleveland toiling in mediocrity. Plagued by occasional arm problems, Harder never again won more than 13 games or threw as many as 200 innings in a season. Nevertheless, he continued to contribute to the Indians, both on and off the field. In addition to posting another 64 victories for the Tribe, Harder became an invaluable source of knowledge to the other members of Cleveland's pitching staff. As one of the team's elder statesmen and most popular players, he also provided guidance to his younger teammates, who often came to him for advice. Perhaps the only blight on Harder's personal record came in 1940, when a group of 11 Indians players went to team owner Alva Bradley to ask for the dismissal of unpopular manager Ossie Vitt. With Harder acting as their spokesman, he received as much criticism as anyone when word of the meeting leaked to the press, causing the unhappy group of players to be nicknamed the "Cleveland Crybabies."

After posting a record of 6-4 and an ERA of 4.50 as a spot-starter in 1947, Harder announced his retirement when the Indians released him at season's end. He finished his career with a record of 223-186, an ERA of 3.80, a WHIP of 1.408, 25 shutouts, 24 saves, 181 complete games, and 1,161 strikeouts in 3,426⅓ innings pitched. Harder subsequently spent the 1948 campaign coaching first base for the Indians, before assuming the role of pitching coach the following year. Remaining in that post for the next 15 seasons, Harder served as mentor to some of the finest pitchers in franchise history, including Bob Lemon, who he helped convert from an infielder into a Hall of Fame hurler; Herb Score, who led the league in

Mel Harder spent more years in Cleveland
than any other player in franchise history

strikeouts in each of his first two seasons after Harder helped him improve
his curveball; and Early Wynn, who later claimed "Mel Harder made me
into a pitcher."

Relieved of his duties following the conclusion of the 1963 campaign
after spending 36 years in the Cleveland organization, Harder continued to
coach at the major-league level for another five seasons, before leaving the
game for good. After having his uniform number 18 retired by the Indians
on July 28, 1990, Harder lived another 12 years, passing away on October
20, 2002, five days after he celebrated his 93rd birthday.

Career Highlights:

Best Season: Even though the Cleveland Chapter of the Baseball Writers Association of America named Harder the Indians Most Valuable Player in 1938 after he helped lead them to a third-place finish by compiling a record of 17-10 and an ERA of 3.83, the right-hander had his two finest seasons in 1934 and 1935. In addition to finishing second in the AL with a career-high 22 victories in the second of those campaigns, Harder ranked among the league leaders with a .667 winning percentage, a 3.29 ERA, a WHIP of 1.274, four shutouts, and a career-high 287⅓ innings pitched. However, he performed even better in 1934, when he went 20-12 with a WHIP of 1.281, threw 255⅓ innings, and established career-best marks in ERA (2.61), complete games (17), and shutouts (6), with the last figure leading all AL hurlers.

Memorable Moments/Greatest Performances: Although Harder struggled on the mound during a 6-4 loss to the Chicago White Sox on July 31, 1935, surrendering 12 hits and six earned runs in seven innings of work, he had an excellent day at the plate, hitting a pair of solo home runs off Chicago starter Ray Phelps.

Even though Harder ended up losing a 1-0 pitcher's duel to Philadelphia's Lefty Grove on July 31, 1932, he performed brilliantly in the first game ever played at Cleveland Municipal Stadium, yielding just one run on five hits, while walking two and recording seven strikeouts. The contest, which drew 80,142 fans to the Indians' new home, set a new record for attendance at a professional baseball game.

Harder out-dueled Washington's Earl Whitehill on July 14, 1934, surrendering just four hits during a 2-0 shutout of the defending American League champions.

Harder turned in another outstanding effort less than two months later, allowing just two hits and three walks during a 1-0 victory over the Detroit Tigers on September 2, 1934.

Harder worked a career-high 14 innings on April 16, 1935, when he yielded eight hits and three walks, en route to earning a complete-game 2-1 victory over the St. Louis Browns.

Harder blanked the New York Yankees on May 9, 1935, surrendering just three harmless singles and one walk during a 5-0 victory in which he also recorded six strikeouts.

Harder hurled another gem some five weeks later, yielding only four walks and a second-inning single by right-fielder Bing Miller during a 4-0 shutout of the Boston Red Sox on June 16, 1935.

Harder helped the Indians complete a sweep of their doubleheader with the Philadelphia Athletics on September 18, 1935, allowing just four hits and striking out six during a lopsided 10-0 victory in Game Two.

Harder turned in his finest effort of the 1938 campaign on September 7, when he surrendered just two hits and three walks during a 1-0 victory over the Detroit Tigers.

Although he issued six bases on balls during the contest, Harder again thwarted Detroit's lineup on September 20, 1942, when he yielded just two hits and recorded eight strikeouts during a 2-0 win over the Tigers.

Harder proved to be one of the finest pitchers in All-Star Game history, throwing a total of 13 scoreless innings in his four appearances in the Mid-summer Classic. Particularly effective in the 1934 contest played at New York's Polo Grounds, Harder earned the victory for the American League by tossing five shutout innings.

Notable Achievements:

- Won at least 20 games twice, surpassing 15 victories on six other occasions.
- Posted winning percentage in excess of .600 five times.
- Compiled ERA under 3.00 twice.
- Threw more than 200 innings eight straight times, topping 250 innings pitched four times.
- Led AL pitchers in: ERA once, shutouts once, assists three times, and putouts four times.
- Finished second in AL in: wins once, ERA once, innings pitched once, shutouts twice, strikeouts-to-walks ratio once, assists once, putouts once, and games started once.
- Holds Indians career record for most pitching appearances (582).
- Ranks among Indians career leaders in: wins (2nd), innings pitched (2nd), complete games (5th), strikeouts (8th), shutouts (6th), and games started (2nd).
- Four-time AL All-Star (1934, 1935, 1936, and 1937).

19

ALBERT BELLE

1989 – 1996

A powerful right-handed hitter who helped restore the Indians to prominence during the 1990s, Albert Belle established himself as one of the most potent batsmen in franchise history during his time in Cleveland. Hitting at least 28 home runs in each of his six full seasons with the Tribe, Belle topped 40 homers twice, establishing a new franchise record in 1995 (since broken), when he led the AL with 50 round-trippers. Belle also batted over .300 three times and knocked in more than 100 runs five times, topping the circuit in RBIs on three separate occasions. Belle's prodigious slugging, which helped the Indians capture two division titles and one American League pennant, earned him four All-Star selections, four *Sporting News* All-Star nominations, four Silver Sluggers, and three top-five finishes in the AL MVP voting. Yet, in spite of his many accomplishments, Belle often found himself being portrayed as a villain in the local media due to his stern countenance, dour disposition, and explosive temper.

Born in Shreveport, Louisiana on August 25, 1966, Albert Jojuan Belle attended Huntington High School, where, in addition to serving as vice president of the local Future Business Leaders of America and a member of the National Honor Society, he excelled in football and baseball, earning All-State honors in the latter sport twice. Offered numerous athletic scholarships as he neared graduation, Belle chose to remain close to home, accepting an offer to attend Louisiana State University on a baseball scholarship.

Starring for the Tigers on the diamond in 1986 and 1987, Belle made First-Team All-SEC both years, before being suspended during the latter stages of his junior year for attacking a heckler at an SEC tournament game. With several organizations subsequently being scared off by Belle's apparent inability to control his temper, the immensely talented outfielder slipped to the second round of the 1987 MLB Draft after he elected to forego his senior year at LSU. Selected by the Cleveland Indians, Belle spent less than two full seasons in the minor leagues, before making his big-league debut with the Tribe on July 15, 1989. Appearing in 62 games over the final 10 weeks of the campaign, Belle hit seven homers, knocked in 37 runs, and batted just .225, earning him a return-trip to the minors at season's end.

After getting off to a slow start in 1990, Belle ended up spending much of the season in alcohol rehab following an infamous locker room tirade in which he destroyed a clubhouse bathroom. Returning to the Indians the following year, Belle performed well in his first full season in the majors after laying claim to the starting left field job, hitting 28 homers and driving in 95 runs, while also batting .282. Yet, he continued to struggle with anger management issues, drawing a six-game suspension at one point during the season for hitting a heckling fan in the chest with a baseball. Although Belle's batting average slipped to .260 in 1992, he once again proved to be the Tribe's most productive hitter, leading the team with 34 homers and 112 RBIs, while also scoring 81 runs. Emerging as a truly dominant hitter the following year, Belle began an exceptional four-year run during which he compiled the following numbers:

1993: 38 HR, **129** *RBI, 93 Runs Scored, 172 Hits, 36 2B, .290 AVG, .370 OBP, .552 SLG*

1994: 36 HR, 101 RBI, 90 Runs Scored, 147 Hits, 35 2B, .357 AVG, .438 OBP, .714 SLG

1995: **50** *HR,* **126** *RBI,* **121** *Runs Scored, 173 Hits,* **52** *2B, .317 AVG, .401 OBP,* **.690** *SLG*

1996: 48 HR, **148** *RBI, 124 Runs Scored, 187 Hits, 38 2B, .311 AVG, .410 OBP, .623 SLG*

In addition to topping the circuit in RBIs in three of the four years, Belle finished third in the league in that category in the strike-shortened campaign of 1994, when he also ranked among the leaders in home runs, hits, doubles, batting average, on-base percentage, slugging percentage, and total bases, leading the league in the last category. Belle also topped the circuit with 377 total bases in 1995, a season in which he became the only player ever to surpass 50 homers and 50 doubles in the same year—a feat made even more impressive by the fact that he accomplished it in a

144-game schedule, since the players' strike delayed the beginning of the campaign. Belle, who struggled somewhat defensively during the early stages of his career, also gradually developed into a competent outfielder, leading all AL left-fielders in assists, putouts, and double plays once each, with his exceptional play earning him four consecutive All-Star selections, four straight Silver Sluggers, three top-three finishes in the league MVP balloting, and *Sporting News* Major League Player of the Year honors in 1995.

Belle, whose cold stare and muscular 6'2", 230-pound frame struck fear into the hearts of opposing pitchers, employed a unique batting stance in which he moved his arms in a circular manner with a slight up and down motion in front of his body before each swing. Approaching each at-bat with a sense of urgency, Belle drew praise from Cleveland manager Mike Hargrove, who told *Sports Illustrated* in May 1996, "When they coined the term tunnel vision, they had Albert Belle in mind." Teammate Sandy Alomar Jr. told that same publication, "There's nobody in here who wants to produce more than he does. Nobody wants to win more. He's just very intense."

In discussing the manner in which Belle approached his craft, former Indians Media Rep Paul DePodesta wrote in the August 4, 1999 edition of the *San Francisco Chronicle*, "Albert has a very intense personality, and that can be a double-edged sword. It contributes to his success, because he's so driven, but it's not something you can just turn on or off. No matter what, he is going to reach his potential as a player, and he is never going to have to wonder if he could have been better, because he's done all he can. It's wound up affecting other parts of his life, but it's made him a Hall of Fame-caliber player."

Belle's intensity, which contributed to his negative portrayal by the media, presented itself in many ways. Meticulous in his preparation, Belle did not allow any pre-game interviews, causing him to be lambasted in the press after he yelled at NBC reporter Hannah Storm in the dugout prior to a game in the 1995 World Series. Belle also liked to keep the clubhouse cool, so much so that he was known to smash the thermostat if someone adjusted its settings. Meanwhile, Belle tried to intimidate the opposition, both verbally and physically, occasionally quarreled with teammates, and did not always hustle, adding to his reputation as a malcontent.

Courtesy of Jerry Reuss

Albert Belle knocked in more than 100 runs
five times for the Indians

Asked to defend his team's enigmatic slugger in an article that appeared in the March 1, 1996 edition of *USA Today*, Cleveland GM John Hart stated, "I've talked about Albert Belle until I'm blue in the face. From the club perspective, we pay him based on productivity and his talent. . . . We've suspended him ourselves, we've sent him to the minor leagues for not running out balls, we've disciplined him, but, at the same time, Albert has grown into a productive player. We don't necessarily pay Albert to have a good image."

Yet, at the same time, those who knew Belle better than most contended that he actually had a much softer side, with Mark Guthrie writing in the *Minneapolis-St. Paul Tribune* on October 13, 1995, "People are shocked when I say Albert is a nice guy, but it's the truth. The only problem Albert has had is he's too competitive. When he gets involved in a game, a competitiveness comes over him that's almost dangerous."

Indians teammate Omar Vizquel echoed those sentiments when he told the *Associated Press* on October 23, 1995, "If you talk to him (Belle) in person, you don't realize how mean he is. He's really a sweet guy. He's like a twelve-year-old. But, when he's on the field and oh-for-three, I don't recommend that you talk to him. Sometimes he throws the cooler around. Sometimes he breaks phones in the clubhouse. There are cookies all over the place. This guy is so unbelievable, he can go three-for-three, go into his last at-bat and pop out, and he's still throwing cookies around."

A free agent following the conclusion of the 1996 campaign, Belle rejected a significant offer from the Indians to sign with the Chicago White Sox, who made him the game's richest player at the time. Belle left Cleveland with career totals of 242 home runs, 751 RBIs, 592 runs scored, 1,014 hits, 223 doubles, and 16 triples, a .295 batting average, a .369 on-base percentage, and a .580 slugging percentage.

Upon inking his deal with the White Sox, Belle told *USA Today*, "Back in 1987, when they drafted me, the Indians were the only team interested in taking a chance on Albert Belle, and I made the most of it. Hopefully they got as much from me as I got from them."

However, Belle proved to be somewhat less diplomatic a few months later, when he told *Sport Magazine*, "The Indians didn't help me in dealing with the media. I think they wanted to keep my market value down. I'm moody. I know that. I've made some mistakes, but, if I was a bad person, would someone want to pay me fifty-five million dollars, and would I have a scholarship fund my mother runs that pays for kids to go to school?"

Belle added, "Leaving wasn't a personal thing where I intentionally wanted to stick it to management or anyone. This is business. I felt I should have been rewarded for helping the Indians turn around a half century of losing. It was a shame they decided to treat me that way, after all I did for them. I helped this team go from a hundred and six losses to basically a hundred and six wins and into the World Series. And what do I get for it? Nothing."

Belle also had a parting shot for the Cleveland media, commenting, "I know the Chicago media will write a lot of bad things, but they'll write a lot of good things too. I can live with that. In Cleveland, all I got was negative press."

Stunned by Belle's departure, the Indians fanbase treated him with disdain the first time he returned to Cleveland as a member of the White Sox, tossing fake dollar bills onto the field, holding up signs, and booing him mercilessly. However, Belle proved to be worth the money the White Sox paid him over the course of the next two seasons, hitting 30 homers, driving in 116 runs, scoring 90 times, and batting .274 in 1997, before earning an eighth-place finish in the AL MVP voting and the last of his five Silver Sluggers in 1998 by hitting 49 homers, knocking in 152 runs, scoring 113 others, amassing 200 hits and 48 doubles, batting .328, and leading the league with 399 total bases, a .655 slugging percentage, and an OPS of 1.055.

Exercising a clause in his contract that allowed him to become a free agent once again, Belle signed another huge deal at the end of 1998, this time with the Baltimore Orioles. Continuing his outstanding production in Baltimore, Belle hit 60 homers and knocked in 220 runs for the Birds the next two years, before a degenerative hip ailment forced him into premature retirement at the age of 34 following the conclusion of the 2000 campaign. He ended his career with 381 home runs, 1,239 RBIs, 974 runs scored, 1,726 hits, 389 doubles, 21 triples, a .295 batting average, a .369 on-base percentage, and a .564 slugging percentage.

Belle, who earned a degree in accounting from LSU following his retirement and currently lives with his family in Arizona, has since made amends with the Indians and their fans, even receiving an invitation to appear at 2012 Spring Training thanks to former teammate Carlos Baerga, before attending a game at Progressive Field later that season. Meanwhile, in assessing Belle as both a player and a person during the latter stages of his career, Ken Griffey Jr. told the *San Francisco Chronicle* in August 1999, "Just look at his numbers; that's all you have to do. He goes out and plays hard. He's really different from how he's portrayed; you guys don't give him a chance. Everything is blown out of proportion."

Indians Career Highlights:

Best Season: Had the 1994 campaign not ended prematurely as the result of a player's strike, Belle likely would have compiled the best numbers of his career. As it is, he posted career-high marks in batting average (.357), on-base percentage (.438), and slugging percentage (.714), finishing either second or third in the AL in all three categories, while topping the circuit with 294 total bases and also placing in the league's top three in home runs (36), RBIs (101), hits (147), and doubles (35). Belle had another huge year in 1996, batting .311, posting an OPS of 1.033, leading the league with 148 RBIs, and also ranking among the leaders with 48 homers, 124 runs scored, and 375 total bases. Nevertheless, Belle compiled the most prolific offensive numbers of his career in 1995, when, in addition to batting .317 and posting an OPS of 1.091, he led the league with 50 homers, 126 RBIs, 121 runs scored, 52 doubles, 377 total bases, and a .690 slugging percentage, becoming in the process the only player in MLB history to surpass 50 home runs and 50 doubles in the same season.

Memorable Moments/Greatest Performances: Belle gave an early indication of what lay ahead for AL pitchers less than two weeks into his big-league career, when he delivered the decisive blow of a 7-3 victory over the Yankees on July 24, 1989, by homering with the bases loaded in the bottom of the seventh inning.

Belle proved to be the difference in a 10-6 win over Oakland on May 25, 1992, hitting a pair of homers, knocking in four runs, and scoring four times.

Belle defeated California almost single-handedly on May 3, 1993, leading the Indians to a 5-4 win over the Angels by driving in four runs with a pair of homers, with his two-out, three-run blast in the bottom of the eighth inning providing the margin of victory.

Belle actually made a habit out of hitting game-winning home runs, delivering one such blow on May 19, 1994, when his two-run shot in the bottom of the 13th inning gave the Indians a 4-2 victory over the Milwaukee Brewers.

Belle again came through in the clutch on June 28, 1994, when his solo homer in the bottom of the ninth inning gave the Indians a 9-8 win over the Baltimore Orioles.

Belle provided further heroics on July 18, 1995, when his grand slam homer in the bottom of the ninth inning gave the Indians a 7-5 walk-off win over the California Angels.

Belle hit another dramatic ninth-inning homer on July 31, 1996, when his two-out, bases loaded blast off Toronto reliever Bill Risley gave the Tribe a 4-2 walk-off win over the Blue Jays.

Belle also delivered what proved to be the decisive blow of a 9-4 victory over the Baltimore Orioles in Game Three of the 1996 ALDS, when his seventh-inning grand slam off reliever Armando Benitez gave the Indians an 8-4 lead that they protected the rest of the way.

In addition to his late-game heroics, Belle hit three home runs in one game twice as a member of the Indians, doing so for the first time during a 12-inning, 12-9 win over the Seattle Mariners on September 6, 1992, in which he knocked in a total of five runs.

Belle accomplished the feat again on September 19, 1995, when he hit three solo homers during an 8-2 win over the Chicago White Sox.

Notable Achievements:

- Hit more than 30 home runs five times, topping 40 homers twice and 50 homers once.
- Knocked in more than 100 runs five times, surpassing 120 RBIs on three occasions.
- Scored more than 120 runs twice.
- Batted over .300 three times, topping the .350-mark once (.357 in 1994).
- Topped 30 doubles five times, surpassing 50 two-baggers once (52 in 1995).
- Stole more than 20 bases once (23 in 1993).
- Compiled on-base percentage in excess of .400 three times.
- Posted slugging percentage in excess of .500 five times, topping .600-mark three times and .700-mark once (.714 in 1994).
- Posted OPS in excess of 1.000 three times.
- Led AL in: home runs once, RBIs three times, runs scored once, doubles once, extra-base hits twice, total bases twice, slugging percentage once, and sacrifice flies once.

- Finished second in AL in: doubles once, total bases once, batting average once, slugging percentage once, and OPS twice.
- Finished third in AL in: home runs once, RBIs once, hits once, and on-base percentage once.
- Led AL outfielders in double plays once.
- Led AL left-fielders in: putouts once, assists once, and double plays once.
- Holds Indians single-season records for highest slugging percentage (.714 in 1994) and most extra-base hits (103 in 1995).
- Ranks among Indians career leaders in: home runs (2nd), RBIs (10th), extra-base hits (9th), slugging percentage (2nd), OPS (5th), and sacrifice flies (6th).
- Hit three home runs in one game twice (vs. Seattle Mariners on Sept. 6, 1992, and vs. Chicago White Sox on Sept. 19, 1995).
- Three-time AL Player of the Month.
- Four-time Silver Slugger winner (1993, 1994, 1995, and 1996).
- Finished in top 10 of AL MVP voting four times, finishing in top five three times, and placing as high as second once (1995).
- 1995 *Sporting News* Major League Player of the Year.
- Four-time *Sporting News* All-Star selection (1993, 1994, 1995, and 1996).
- Four-time AL All-Star (1993, 1994, 1995, and 1996).
- 1995 AL champion.

20

AL ROSEN
1947 - 1956

His period of dominance limited to a few short seasons by an injured back and a badly-mangled finger that forced him into premature retirement at only 32 years of age, Al Rosen failed to compile the Hall-of-Fame type numbers for which he appeared headed after his first few years in Cleveland. Nevertheless, the slugging third baseman wielded one of the most potent bats in all of baseball from 1950 to 1954, topping 30 homers twice, batting over .300 three times, and knocking in more than 100 runs five straight times, in helping the Indians capture one pennant and post three second-place finishes. Annually ranking among the AL leaders in both home runs and RBIs throughout the period, Rosen topped the junior circuit in each category twice, capturing league MVP honors in 1953, when he came within a percentage point of winning the American League Triple Crown. In all, Rosen earned two top-10 finishes in the MVP voting, two *Sporting News* All-Star nominations, and four consecutive trips to the All-Star Game before he decided to call it quits following the conclusion of the 1956 campaign.

Born in Spartanburg, South Carolina on February 29, 1924, Albert Leonard Rosen moved with his mother and brother to Miami, Florida at only 18 months of age after being abandoned by his father. Raised by his grandmother, mother, and aunt, Rosen attended Riverside Elementary School, Ada Merritt Junior High School, and Miami Senior High School for a year, before enrolling at Florida Military Academy in St. Petersburgh, Florida, where he distinguished himself in baseball, football, basketball, and boxing. After suffering from asthma as a child, Rosen spent much of his youth trying to dispel the stereotype that Jews didn't make good athletes, recalling years later, "Sports were always my addiction."

Although Rosen eventually gained fame for his skills on the baseball diamond, he earlier developed a reputation as a tough guy by entering the ring as an amateur boxer, where he had his nose broken 11 times before finally deciding to concentrate on the less violent sport of baseball. Hoping to follow in the footsteps of his childhood idols Hank Greenberg and Lou Gehrig after enrolling at the University of Florida in Gainesville following his graduation from Florida Military Academy, Rosen played baseball for the Gators as a freshman. However, he left college prior to the start of his sophomore year once he signed with the Cleveland Indians as a 17-year-old amateur free agent early in 1942. Rosen then spent one year playing in the minor leagues, before enlisting in the United States Navy, for whom he spent the next three years fighting in the Pacific.

Returning to the world of professional baseball following his discharge from the military, Rosen spent 1946 with the Pittsfield Electrics, earning the nickname the "Hebrew Hammer" by leading the Canadian-American League with 15 homers, 86 RBIs, and 19 triples, while also batting .323. He followed that up by capturing Texas League MVP honors as a member of the Oklahoma City Indians in 1947, topping the circuit in eight different offensive categories, including RBIs (141) and batting average (.349). Yet, in spite of his prolific slugging, Rosen spent virtually all of the next two seasons toiling in the minor leagues since the Indians considered him no immediate threat to incumbent third baseman Ken Keltner, whose defensive skills far surpassed those possessed by the talented but extremely raw youngster.

However, after appearing in a total of only 35 games at the major-league level over the course of the three previous seasons, the 26-year-old Rosen received his big break when the Indians parted ways with Keltner prior to the start of the 1950 campaign. Making the most of his opportunity, Rosen established a new American League record for rookies by topping the circuit with 37 homers, while also batting .287, compiling an on-base percentage of .405, and ranking among the league leaders with 116 RBIs, 100 runs scored, 100 bases on balls, 301 total bases, a .543 slugging percentage, and an OPS of .948. He also sufficiently improved his work at the hot corner to lead all AL third basemen with 322 assists.

Rosen continued to establish himself as one of the American League's top sluggers over the course of the next two seasons, teaming up with Larry Doby to give the Indians arguably the junior circuit's most formidable one-two punch. Although Rosen batted just .265 in 1951, he hit 24 homers, knocked in 102 runs, scored 82 others, walked 85 times, and hit four grand slams, setting in the process a single-season Indians record that remained a franchise mark until Travis Hafner homered with the bases loaded five times in 2006. Rosen then earned a 10th-place finish in the AL MVP balloting and All-Star honors for the first of four straight times in 1952 by placing near the top of the league rankings with 28 homers, 101 runs scored, 171 hits, 32 doubles, a .302 batting average, a .524 slugging percentage, and a .911 OPS, while also topping the circuit with 105 RBIs and 297 total bases. He also struck out only 54 times in 649 total plate appearances, which represented an unusually low total for a slugger such as him. In fact, displaying a keen batting eye and a tremendous amount of patience at the plate, Rosen struck out fewer than 50 times in four of his seven full seasons, never fanning more than 72 times in any single campaign.

As Rosen made a name for himself as one of the league's most feared batsmen, he also became known as a fierce competitor who had the courage to stand up to the torrent of abuse he received for being the game's most notable player of Jewish descent. Discussing years later the obstacles he faced, particularly during the early stages of his career, Rosen revealed:

> *"I can only tell you this: there was anti-Semitism throughout my playing days, and it came from the stands, it came from the managers, the coaches, and players. But as time went on, and particularly after the birth of Israel as a nation, I think that a new aura took over and people had more respect for Jewish athletes, or Jews generally, because it showed once again that Jews were not to be taken lightly and that they could fight as well as be bookkeepers and accountants and that sort of thing. The kind of taunting and things like that that I heard personally from the benches softened a great deal after 1946."*

Still, there were times after he reached the Major Leagues that the muscular 5'10", 180-pound Rosen experienced the kind of verbal abuse that made it necessary for him to stand up to those who insulted his ancestry. On one particular occasion, a member of the Chicago White Sox called the former amateur boxer a "Jew bastard." White Sox pitcher Saul Rogovin, also of Jewish descent, recalled that an angry Rosen responded by striding belligerently towards the Chicago dugout and challenging the "son of a bitch" to a fight. The Chicago player backed down.

Another time, Rosen challenged an opposing player who had "slurred his religion" to fight him under the stands. When a Red Sox catcher called him anti-Semitic names, Rosen called time and "started towards him, to take him on." Hank Greenberg, who served as general manager in Cleveland throughout most of Rosen's tenure with the team, recalled that the third baseman "wanted to go into the stands and murder" fans who hurled anti-Semitic insults at him. Rosen himself was later quoted as saying, "There's a time that you let it be known that enough is enough. . . . You flatten them."

While Rosen stood up for himself verbally whenever he found it necessary to do so, he made an even bigger statement with his bat in 1953. Experiencing the greatest season of his career, the right-handed hitting slugger finished among the American League leaders with 201 hits and a .422 on-base percentage, while topping the circuit with 43 homers, 145 runs batted in, 115 runs scored, 367 total bases, a .613 slugging percentage, and an OPS of 1.034. He also finished an extremely close second to Washington's Mickey Vernon in the AL batting race, compiling a mark of .336 that left him just one percentage point behind Vernon's league-leading figure of .337. Having barely missed out on capturing the Triple Crown, Rosen had to settle for being named the unanimous winner of the league MVP Award.

Rosen's extraordinary performance earned him praise from Yankee manager Casey Stengel, who said of the Cleveland third baseman, "That young feller, that feller's a ball player. He'll give you the works every time. Gets all the hits, gives you the hard tag in the field. That feller's a real competitor, you bet your sweet curse life."

Indians pitcher Early Wynn also paid tribute to his teammate, telling writer Roger Kahn, "People think Mickey Mantle is the toughest hitter in the league, but I can usually get him out if I don't make a mistake. The real toughest clutch hitter is Berra. As you change speeds and move around, Berra moves right with you. Rosen does the same thing, but fortunately he's playing third behind me, so I don't have to pitch to him. Believe me, the two best clutch hitters in the game are Berra and Rosen. Most of us pitchers wish to hell they'd switch to golf."

Rosen picked up right where he left off early the following year, batting .372 and leading the league with 11 homers and 44 RBIs after the first 35 games of the 1954 campaign. However, his career took a sudden turn for the worse when he suffered an injury while putting his own interests aside for the betterment of his team.

Seeking to get spring sensation Rudy Regalado into the lineup, Cleveland manager Al Lopez asked Rosen to play first base for a few weeks in order to allow the youngster to get some playing time at third. The shift in positions proved disastrous for Rosen, who broke his right index finger on a line drive hit by Chicago's Jungle Jim Rivera after having his vision obscured by the runner at first base. Although Rosen sat out a few days, he returned to the lineup well before the swollen finger healed. Looking back on the incident, Rosen said, "Today, they would have sent me to the hospital, X-rayed me, and put me on the disabled list. . . . I was equally at fault. I wanted to play." Rosen's premature return caused the condition of his finger to worsen, with the slugger later stating, "It was mangled. All of a sudden, I was just another out."

Al Rosen captured AL MVP honors in 1953 when he came within percentage points of winning the Triple Crown

Rosen batted with his broken finger sticking in the air, unable to wrap it around the bat. Yet, even though he spent the remainder of the year playing in pain, he managed to hit 24 homers, drive in 102 runs, and bat an even .300, helping the Indians capture the American League pennant in the process. Despite his heroic efforts, though, Rosen had his salary cut from $42,500 to $37,500 by general manager Hank Greenberg at season's end. With his finger still bothering him, Rosen found himself unable to regain his earlier form when he returned to his more familiar position of third base full time in 1955. With Rosen finishing the year with just 21 homers, 81 RBIs, and a .244 batting average, the Indians cut his salary by another $5,000 following the conclusion of the campaign.

Feeling somewhat angry and resentful, and hampered by numerous physical ailments that included back problems and whiplash that resulted from an automobile accident that occurred just prior to the start of 1955 spring training, Rosen found himself growing increasingly disenchanted with his profession. No longer deriving a great deal of pleasure from playing the game, Rosen played just one more year, hitting 15 homers, driving in 61 runs, and batting .267 in 1956, before announcing his retirement at only 32 years of age at season's end. He finished his career with 192 home runs, 717 RBIs, 603 runs scored, 1,063 hits, 165 doubles, 20 triples, a .285 batting average, a .384 on-base percentage, and a .495 slugging percentage.

Following his playing days, Rosen became a stockbroker, continuing in that field until he chose to re-enter baseball 20 years later as President of the New York Yankees. He remained in that post for two years, before assuming the position of General Manager of the Houston Astros from 1980 to 1985. From Houston, he moved on to San Francisco, where his clever maneuvering as Giants GM enabled the team to capture the NL West title in 1987 and the NL pennant in 1989. Rosen held his GM position with the Giants from 1985 to 1992, after which he retired to his home in Rancho Mirage, California. Rosen spent the remainder of his life there, passing away from natural causes on March 13, 2015, two weeks after he turned 91 years of age.

Career Highlights:

Best Season: Rosen performed exceptionally well for the Indians as a rookie in 1950, batting .287, driving in 116 runs, scoring 100 times, and leading the American League with 37 homers. However, he unquestionably had his finest season in 1953, when, en route to earning league MVP and *Sporting News* Major League Player of the Year honors, he established career-high marks in 10 different offensive categories, including home runs (43), RBIs (145), batting average (.336), runs scored (115), hits (201), on-base percentage (.422), slugging percentage (.613), and total bases (367), topping the circuit in six of those.

Memorable Moments/Greatest Performances: Rosen provided the game-winning blow in a 7-6 victory over the Washington Senators on June 25, 1950, when his grand slam homer in the bottom of the eighth inning turned a 4-3 deficit into a 7-4 lead.

Rosen led the Indians to a 7-4 win over Detroit on July 1, 1950, by driving in five runs with a pair of homers.

Rosen proved to be the difference in a 7-3 victory over the St. Louis Browns on August 21, 1953, going 3-for-4, with two homers, five RBIs, and three runs scored.

Batting in the unfamiliar position of leadoff on September 25, 1953, Rosen led the Indians to a 12-3 mauling of the Tigers by going 4-for-6, with two homers, four RBIs, and three runs scored.

Despite playing with a badly-injured finger, Rosen led the American League to an 11-9 victory over the NL in the 1954 All-Star Game by driving in five runs with a pair of homers. Recalling his performance years later, Rosen stated, "I had one of those days you dream about."

Rosen turned in an outstanding all-around effort against Baltimore on June 27, 1956, going 4-for-6, with a homer, double, stolen base, two RBIs, and three runs scored, during an 11-inning, 12-11 win over the Orioles.

Rosen, though, had the greatest day of his career on April 29, 1952, when he led the Indians to a 21-9 rout of the Philadelphia Athletics by going 4-for-6, with three homers, seven RBIs, and four runs scored.

Notable Achievements:

- Hit more than 20 home runs six times, topping 30 homers twice and 40 homers once (43 in 1953).
- Knocked in more than 100 runs five times, topping 140 RBIs once (145 in 1953).
- Scored more than 100 runs three times.
- Batted over .300 three times, topping the .330-mark once (.336 in 1953).
- Surpassed 200 hits once (201 in 1953).

- Surpassed 30 doubles twice.
- Topped 100 walks once (100 in 1950).
- Compiled on-base percentage in excess of .400 three times.
- Posted slugging percentage in excess of .500 four times, topping the .600-mark once (.613 in 1953).
- Posted OPS in excess of 1.000 once (1.034 in 1953).
- Led AL in: home runs twice, RBIs twice, runs scored once, total bases twice, slugging percentage once, and OPS once.
- Finished second in AL in batting average once and on-base percentage once.
- Finished third in AL in: runs scored once, hits once, slugging percentage once, and OPS once.
- Led AL third basemen in assists twice and double plays once.
- Ranks ninth in Indians history with 192 career home runs.
- Hit three home runs in one game vs. Philadelphia Athletics on April 29, 1952.
- 1953 AL MVP.
- 1953 *Sporting News* Major League Player of the Year.
- Two-time *Sporting News* All-Star selection (1953 and 1954).
- Four-time AL All-Star (1952, 1953, 1954, and 1955).
- Two-time AL champion (1948 and 1954).
- 1948 world champion.

21

MIKE GARCIA
1948 – 1959

Easily the most overlooked and underappreciated member of the Indians' magnificent group of starters that became known as the "Big Four," Mike Garcia spent most of his time in Cleveland pitching in the shadow of Hall of Fame hurlers Bob Feller, Bob Lemon, and Early Wynn. Yet, even though the relative brevity of Garcia's career prevented him from receiving the widespread acclaim bestowed upon his more famous teammates, he proved to be every bit as effective in his prime. En route to compiling an overall record of 104-57 for the Tribe between 1949 and 1954, the hard-throwing right-hander won at least 18 games four straight times, topping 20 victories on two separate occasions. Garcia also posted an ERA under 3.00 three times, leading the league in that category twice, while topping the circuit in shutouts twice as well, with his outstanding mound work earning him three All-Star selections and one top-10 finish in the league MVP voting. Meanwhile, Garcia's strong pitching helped the Indians win one pennant and finish second to the Yankees five other times.

Born to Mexican immigrant parents in San Gabriel, California on November 17, 1923, Edward Miguel Garcia grew up some 200 miles north, in Orosi, California, a small farming community located just outside Fresno. After starring on the mound for three years at Orosi High School, Garcia transferred to nearby Visalia, where he spent his senior year pitching for his new school, while also performing for a local semi-pro team. Discovered by Cleveland scout Willis Butler while playing semi-pro ball, Garcia signed with the Indians following his graduation in 1942, after which he spent one season pitching for the Appleton Papermakers, Cleveland's Class-D affiliate in the Wisconsin State League, before being drafted into the United States Army. He subsequently spent the next three years stringing up telephone wire for the Army, before being discharged early in 1946.

Resuming his baseball career following his discharge, Garcia spent the next three years advancing through Cleveland's farm system, performing well at all levels, before finally being summoned to the big leagues late in 1948. Appearing in just one game for the eventual world champions, Garcia allowed three hits and recorded one strikeout in two scoreless innings of work. He then began the ensuing campaign in the bullpen, before being inserted into the starting rotation in late July. Putting together an outstanding rookie season, the 25-year-old Garcia compiled a record of 14-5 and a league-leading 2.36 ERA, tossed five shutouts and eight complete games, and threw 175⅔ innings.

Garcia's strong performance prompted Indians General Manager Hank Greenberg and pitching coach Mel Harder to express a considerable amount of optimism heading into the 1950 season, with Greenberg proclaiming, "Garcia has all the potentialities of a really great pitcher. I see no reason he should not reach greatness this season." However, Garcia ended up being something of a disappointment, finishing the year just 11-11, with a 3.86 ERA.

After working hard during the subsequent off-season to gain better control of the curveball Harder taught him two years earlier, Garcia developed into an elite pitcher in 1951, joining Feller, Lemon, and Wynn in giving the Indians arguably the strongest starting rotation in all of baseball. In addition to compiling a record of 20-13 that gave him the fourth-most wins in the AL, Garcia threw 15 complete games and ranked among the league leaders with a 3.15 ERA, 254 innings pitched, and a WHIP of 1.264. He followed that up with an even stronger performance in 1952, earning a ninth-place finish in the AL MVP voting and the first of his three consecutive All-Star nominations by going 22-11, with a 2.37 ERA, 143 strikeouts, 19 complete games, 292⅓ innings pitched, and a league-leading six shutouts.

Assigned the moniker "Big Bear" by teammate Joe Gordon because of his large frame, the 6'1", 220-pound Garcia threw extremely hard when he first entered the league, with his first manager, Lou Boudreau, once stating, "I didn't see Bob Feller at his fastest, but there can't be many of them as fast as Mike right now." Meanwhile, infielder George Strickland described his longtime roommate as "a big, strong, powerful pitcher who threw a very heavy ball."

George Brace Courtesy of Mears Online Auctions

Mike Garcia served as one of the key members of
the Indians' "Big Four" during his time in Cleveland

Former Indians manager Al Lopez agreed with Strickland's assessment, recalling, "He [Garcia] threw such a 'heavy' ball, when you hit it, it felt like you were hitting a rock."

Fellow Indians pitcher Bob Lemon added, "Hitting a Garcia pitch was like hitting a shotput," also suggesting, "Mike was a sneak. His physical size belied really fine control."

Garcia, who liked to work to the corners of the plate rather than up and down in the strike zone, also used a slider to complement his fastball, which bore down and in on right-handed hitters. But he didn't become a complete pitcher until he gained better command of the curveball he learned from pitching coach Mel Harder, with Cleveland sportswriter Hal Lebovitz writing years later, "Garcia, until the day he died, would tell me how much of his success he owed to Harder." Garcia also once admitted to throwing an occasional spitball, claiming, "Maybe a dozen in my life. I'm sure plenty of the great pitchers did."

Garcia continued his strong pitching in 1953, compiling a record of 18-9 and an ERA of 3.25, while also placing near the top of the league rankings in complete games (21) and innings pitched (271⅔). He then helped lead the Indians to the AL pennant in 1954 by going 19-8, with a league-leading 2.64 ERA, 1.125 WHIP, and five shutouts, earning in the process his final All-Star selection and a 19th-place finish in the league MVP balloting.

However, the 1954 campaign proved to be Garcia's last as a dominant pitcher. After posting an overall record of just 34-33 over the course of the next three seasons, Garcia slipped on a wet mound at 1958 spring training, causing him to wrench his back, and forcing him to undergo season-ending surgery a few weeks later to repair a slipped disc. Hardly the same pitcher when he returned to the Tribe the following year, Garcia finished just 3-6 with a 4.00 ERA, before being released by the Indians at season's end. He subsequently signed with the Chicago White Sox, for whom he appeared in only 15 games in 1960, before making 16 relief appearances with the Washington Senators the following year. Released by Washington in early September 1961, Garcia announced his retirement shortly thereafter, ending his career with a record of 142-97, an ERA of 3.27, a WHIP of 1.318, 27 shutouts, 24 saves, 111 complete games, and 1,117 strikeouts in 2,174⅔ innings pitched, compiling virtually all those numbers as a member of the Indians.

Unfortunately, Garcia's post-playing days did not prove to be particularly happy ones. After returning to Cleveland, where he spent many years operating a dry-cleaning store in the suburb of Parma, Garcia developed diabetes, which resulted in kidney disease and heart damage by the time he reached his fifties. Forced to undergo dialysis several times weekly, Garcia eventually had to sell his business to help pay his medical bills. Fighting a losing battle, Garcia finally succumbed to his illness at 62 years of age, on January 13, 1986, on his 35th wedding anniversary.

Following the passing of his longtime teammate, Bob Lemon said, "Mike was so darn consistent. He did more than his share, and I hope the Cleveland fans remember that."

Indians Career Highlights:

Best Season: A strong argument could certainly be made that Garcia pitched his best ball for the Indians in 1954, when, in addition to compiling a record of 19-8, throwing 258⅔ innings, and tossing 13 complete games, he led all AL hurlers with a 2.64 ERA, five shutouts, and a career-best WHIP of 1.125. However, he made his greatest overall impact in 1952, earning a ninth-place finish in the MVP voting by finishing third in the league in wins (22), placing second in ERA (2.37) and innings pitched (292⅓), topping the circuit in shutouts (6), and also ranking among the leaders in winning percentage (.667), strikeouts (143), complete games (19), and WHIP (1.269), establishing in the process career-best marks in wins, shutouts, and innings pitched.

Memorable Moments/Greatest Performances: Garcia turned in his first dominant pitching performance for the Indians on September 4, 1949, when he recorded nine strikeouts and yielded just four hits and one walk during a 5-0 complete-game shutout of the St. Louis Browns.

Garcia won a 1-0 pitcher's duel with Philadelphia's Sam Zoldak on July 20, 1951, surrendering just four hits and one walk over 10 innings, while also recording seven strikeouts and getting three hits himself. The Indians won the contest in the bottom of the 10th when Bobby Avila doubled home Dale Mitchell from first base with the game's only run.

Garcia helped his own cause on August 7, 1951, when he hit one of his two career home runs during a 5-1 complete-game victory over the St. Louis Browns in which he allowed just four hits and struck out six batters. Garcia delivered his homer with two men on base in the bottom of the sixth inning.

Garcia dominated the New York Yankee lineup on June 13, 1952, recording 10 strikeouts and yielding just four hits and two walks during a complete-game 7-1 win.

Garcia turned in another superb effort exactly one month later, surrendering just two hits and two walks during a 1-0 shutout of the Washington Senators at Griffith Stadium on July 13.

Garcia proved to be equally dominant against Philadelphia on September 11, 1952, once again allowing just two hits and two walks, in defeating the Athletics by a score of 1-0.

Garcia hurled another gem against Philadelphia on May 16, 1954, yielding just two walks and a fourth-inning single to shortstop Joe DeMaestri during a 6-0, one-hit shutout of the Athletics.

Continuing to dominate Philadelphia's lineup on June 5, 1954, Garcia allowed just two hits and walked six batters in 11 innings of work, in earning a 4-1 victory over the Athletics.

Although he yielded seven hits and four walks during the contest, Garcia recorded a career-high 12 strikeouts during a 7-0 win over the Washington Senators on June 4, 1956.

Garcia again baffled Washington's lineup on September 18, 1956, when he recorded eight strikeouts and surrendered only three hits and one walk during a 6-0 victory over the Senators.

Notable Achievements:

- Won more than 20 games twice, topping 18 victories two other times.
- Posted winning percentage in excess of .600 six times, topping the .700-mark twice.
- Compiled ERA below 3.00 three times.
- Threw more than 250 innings four times.
- Threw more than 20 complete games once (21 in 1953).
- Led AL pitchers in: ERA twice, WHIP once, shutouts twice, and starts once.
- Finished second in AL in: ERA once, shutouts once, and innings pitched twice.
- Ranks among Indians career leaders in: wins (9th), strikeouts (10th), shutouts (5th), innings pitched (9th), pitching appearances (6th), and games started (9th).
- Finished ninth in 1952 AL MVP voting.
- Three-time AL All-Star (1952, 1953, and 1954).
- Two-time A.L champion (1948 and 1954).
- 1948 world champion.

22

WES FERRELL

1927 - 1933

A durable right-handed pitcher who split his peak years between the Cleveland Indians and Boston Red Sox, Wes Ferrell won at least 20 games six times over the course of 15 big-league seasons, doing so four straight times as a member of the Indians. Spending the first half of his career in Cleveland, Ferrell won a total of 102 games for the Tribe, en route to earning one *Sporting News* All-Star selection and a spot on the American League's inaugural All-Star team. In addition to surpassing 20 victories four times for the Indians, Ferrell tossed at least 25 complete games on three separate occasions and threw more than 200 innings five straight times, establishing himself in the process as one of the junior circuit's hardest working pitchers. Excelling at the bat as well, Ferrell became equally well known for his hitting ability, compiling a lifetime batting average of .280, while setting major league records for most home runs in a career (38) and in a season (9) by a pitcher.

Born in Greensboro, North Carolina on February 2, 1908, Wesley Cheek Ferrell grew up on his family's farm in nearby Guilford, where he spent most of his free time playing baseball with his six brothers. Recalling his favorite form of childhood recreation, Ferrell explained in an interview with author Donald Honig years later, "We'd go out into the fields after harvest time and hit for hours. Just hit an old beat-up nickel ball as far at it'd go and chase it down and throw it around. Saturday and Sunday were our big days, of course. That's when we played team ball, around the countryside here."

Starring in both baseball and basketball at Guilford High School, Ferrell also spent his high school years playing baseball for several amateur teams in the Guilford County League. After enrolling at the Oak Ridge Institute following his graduation in 1926, Ferrell continued to star in multiple sports until he began playing semi-pro ball in East Douglas, Massachusetts one year later. Offered contracts by the Cleveland Indians and Detroit Tigers shortly thereafter, Ferrell ultimately elected to sign with the Indians, who he joined during the latter stages of the 1927 campaign, allowing three runs and three hits in just one inning of work. Ferrell subsequently spent virtually all of 1928 in the minor leagues, compiling a record of 20-8 and an ERA of 2.74 for Terre Haute in the Three-I League, before making two starts for the Indians in late September.

After earning a spot in Cleveland's starting rotation the following spring, the 21-year-old Ferrell went on to have an outstanding rookie season, concluding the 1929 campaign with a record of 21-10 that placed him second in the league in wins and third in winning percentage (.677). He also threw 242⅔ innings and finished in the league's top 10 in ERA (3.60) and complete games (18). The early success experienced by the 6'2", 195-pound Ferrell, whose size, control, and seemingly effortless pitching motion led a number of contemporary witnesses to compare him with Christy Mathewson, prompted noted columnist F.C. Lane to write in the March 1930 edition of *Baseball Magazine*, "His [Ferrell's] best ball, of course, is his fast ball. But he also has a most serviceable curve, such a curve as many pitchers fail to acquire in years of patient practice. And, as young and inexperienced as he is, he has developed a baffling change of pace."

Ferrell performed even better in 1930, earning his lone *Sporting News* All-Star nomination by finishing second in the league with 25 wins (he went 25-13), a 3.31 ERA, 25 complete games, and 296⅔ innings pitched, while also ranking among the leaders with a career-high 143 strikeouts. He followed that up with another outstanding year in 1931, earning an 11th-place finish in the AL MVP voting by going 22-12, with a 3.75 ERA, 276⅓ innings pitched, and a league-leading 27 complete games.

In addition to excelling on the mound, Ferrell gradually began to make a name for himself as a dangerous hitter his first few seasons in Cleveland. After batting .297, driving in 14 runs, and scoring 19 times, in only 118 official plate appearances in 1930, Ferrell emerged as a true threat on offense the following year, when he batted .319, hit nine homers, knocked in 30 runs, and scored 24 times, in just 116 official at-bats. In fact, Ferrell became so well known for his offensive prowess that the teams for which he played often used him as a pinch-hitter.

Equally famous for his bad temper and fierce competitive spirit, Ferrell displayed little tolerance when the players behind him committed defensive miscues or an umpire made what he considered to be a bad call. Growing increasingly impatient with the mistakes of others as he evolved into one of the league's top pitchers, Ferrell did not hesitate to speak his mind when he became angry, with his complaints eventually leading to friction between himself and his teammates and manager, Roger Peckinpaugh. As one observer noted, "Ferrell is too easily provoked. He has the experience, the ability, and all the necessary requisites to be of greater value to his club and himself if he would remain undisturbed when the breaks of the game turn against him." Ferrell's temperamental nature became apparent for all to see during a game against the Boston Red Sox on August 30, 1932, when Peckinpaugh came out to the mound to remove him from the contest. Refusing to hand over the ball to his manager, Ferrell subsequently found himself being suspended for 10 days without pay for insubordination.

Although Ferrell continued to perform well for the Indians in 1932, ranking among the league leaders with a record of 23-13, an ERA of 3.66, 26 complete games, and 287⅔ innings pitched, he experienced a growing level of anxiety due to the intermittent soreness he felt in his pitching arm. With one reporter noting that Ferrell became increasingly dependent on his breaking pitches as the season progressed, he asked the pitcher if he considered himself to be just as effective as he had been two seasons earlier. In response, Ferrell stated, "No. I have had bad trouble with my pitching shoulder for two seasons. There is some sort of infection there, or nerve restriction. Some days my shoulder tightens up and I can't throw the ball as fast as when the shoulder is free."

With Ferrell once again experiencing discomfort in his pitching shoulder in 1933, he started only 26 games, compiling a record of just 11-12 and an ERA of 4.21, although his reputation as one of the American League's premier pitchers earned him a spot on the junior circuit's first All-Star team. Remaining extremely concerned over his physical condition, Ferrell told F.C. Lane during an interview that appeared in the June 1933 issue of *Baseball Magazine*, "It isn't only the pain, however, it's the mental unrest. It's the worry, the fear that perhaps the arm will not come around, and it weighs on a pitcher. Plenty of times it has kept me awake nights."

With Ferrell struggling on the mound and growing increasingly contentious towards his teammates and manager, the Indians decided to part ways with the enigmatic right-hander on May 25, 1934, trading him to the Boston Red Sox, along with outfielder Dick Porter, for pitcher Bob Weiland, outfielder Bob Seeds, and $25,000 in cash. Ferrell left Cleveland with an overall record of 102-62, an ERA of 3.67, a WHIP of 1.437, 8 shutouts, 113 complete games, and 516 strikeouts in 1,321⅓ innings pitched. He also batted .274, hit 19 homers, and knocked in 100 runs in only 599 official at-bats as a member of the Indians.

Ferrell ended up experiencing something of a rebirth in Boston, giving the Red Sox three excellent years. No longer a power pitcher, Ferrell relied heavily on his breaking ball, knowledge of opposing hitters, and older brother and new battery mate, Rick, to compile an overall record of 59-34 from 1934 to 1936, surpassing 20 victories in two of those seasons. Particularly effective in 1935, Ferrell led all AL hurlers with 25 wins, 31 complete games, and 322⅓ innings pitched, earning in the process a runner-up finish to Detroit's Hank Greenberg in the league MVP voting. However, after getting off to a slow start in 1937, Ferrell found himself headed to Washington, where he spent most of the next two seasons pitching for the Senators. Released by Washington during the latter stages of the 1938 campaign, Ferrell subsequently split the next three seasons between the New York Yankees, Brooklyn Dodgers, and Boston Braves, before announcing his retirement after being released by the Braves on May 8, 1941. Ferrell ended his career with a record of 193-128, a 4.04 ERA, a WHIP of 1.481, 17 shutouts, 227 complete games, and 985 strikeouts in 2,623 innings of work. He earned two All-Star selections and a pair of top-10 finishes in the AL MVP voting.

Following his playing days, Ferrell entered into a career in managing, spending the next several years piloting a number of minor-league teams based in the southeast. He also made several sound real estate investments, enabling him to live comfortably until he passed away at 68 years of age, on December 9, 1976.

Indians Career Highlights:

Best Season: Ferrell pitched his best ball for the Indians in 1930, when he finished second in the AL in wins (25), ERA (3.31), complete games (25), and innings pitched (296⅔), while also ranking among the league leaders in winning percentage (.658) and strikeouts (143). However, he had his finest all-around season the following year, when, in addition to topping the circuit with 27 complete games and finishing among the

Courtesy of MEARS Online Auctions

Wes Ferrel won more than 20 games
four straight times for the Indians

leaders with 22 victories, a .647 winning percentage, 123 strikeouts, and
276⅓ innings pitched, he batted .319, hit nine homers, knocked in 30 runs,
and scored 24 others, establishing in the process the all-time single-season
record for most home runs by a pitcher.

Memorable Moments/Greatest Performances: Ferrell had a big day
at the plate against Chicago on August 31, 1931, leading the Indians to a
lopsided 15-5 victory over the White Sox by going 3-for-4, with a pair of
homers, five RBIs, and four runs scored, while also going the distance on
the mound.

Ferrell again helped his own cause on June 30, 1932, going 3-for-4, with a double, three RBIs, and one run scored, during a complete-game 7-4 victory over the Detroit Tigers.

Ferrell turned in his first dominant pitching performance for the Indians on August 17, 1929, when he out-dueled Philadelphia's Rube Walberg, allowing just four hits and one unearned run during a 2-1 complete-game win over the Athletics.

Ferrell hurled another gem a little over one month later, yielding just a pair of singles and a walk during a 4-0 shutout of the St. Louis Browns on September 29, 1929.

Ferrell got the best of New York right-hander Red Ruffing on June 8, 1931, surrendering just three hits and two walks during a 4-1 win over the Yankees, with former Indians teammate Joe Sewell reaching him for two of New York's three safeties.

Ferrell dominated Boston's lineup on August 6, 1932, yielding just two walks and a fourth-inning infield single to first baseman Dale Alexander during a 3-0 shutout of the Red Sox.

Ferrell topped that performance, though, on April 29, 1931, when he no-hit St. Louis, defeating the Browns by a score of 9-0. Ferrell, who recorded eight strikeouts on the day, issued three walks during the contest, with two other Browns reaching base on errors by Cleveland shortstop Bill Hunnefield. Making the victory even sweeter, Ferrell contributed to his own cause by going 2-for-4 at the plate, with a homer, double, four RBIs, and two runs scored.

Notable Achievements:

- Won more than 20 games four straight times, surpassing 25 victories once (25 in 1930).
- Posted winning percentage in excess of .600 four times.
- Threw more than 275 innings three times.
- Threw more than 25 complete games three times.
- Led AL pitchers in: complete games once, assists once, and putouts once.
- Finished second in AL in: wins three times, ERA once, innings pitched once, and complete games twice.
- Ranks ninth in Indians history with .622 winning percentage.

- Holds Major League records for most home runs hit by a pitcher in a career (38) and in a season (9 in 1931).
- Threw no-hitter vs. St. Louis Browns on April 29, 1931.
- 1930 *Sporting News* All-Star selection.
- 1933 AL All-Star selection.

23

KEN KELTNER
1937 – 1944, 1946 – 1949

Although he is remembered primarily for the role he played in ending Joe DiMaggio's record-setting 56-game hitting streak, Ken Keltner accomplished a great deal more during his time in Cleveland. Combining solid hitting with superb defense, Keltner proved to be the American League's top third baseman for much of the 1940s. In addition to surpassing 20 home runs three times, Keltner knocked in more than 100 runs twice, topping 90 RBIs two other times. He also batted over .300 once and led all AL third sackers in putouts once, assists four times, double plays five times, and fielding percentage on three separate occasions, with his .965 career fielding percentage representing the third highest mark ever posted by a major league third baseman at the time of his retirement in 1950. Keltner's stellar all-around play, which helped lead the Indians to their second world championship in 1948, earned him seven All-Star selections and MVP consideration in four of his 11 full seasons in Cleveland.

Born in Milwaukee, Wisconsin on October 31, 1916, Kenneth Frederick Keltner attended Boy's Technical High School, after which he took a job working as a truck driver. Discovered while playing fast-pitch softball in his spare time by the minor league Milwaukee Brewers in 1936, Keltner began his professional playing career with his hometown team later that year. Ascending rapidly through the minors, Keltner received an invitation from the Cleveland Indians to attend their spring training camp in 1938. After winning the team's starting third base job, the 21-year-old Keltner went on to have an outstanding rookie season, earning a 14th-place finish in the AL MVP voting by hitting 26 homers, driving in 113 runs, scoring 86 times, collecting 31 doubles and nine triples, and compiling a batting average of .276.

Although the six-foot, 190-pound Keltner subsequently hit only 13 home runs in his sophomore campaign of 1939, he posted excellent overall numbers, finishing the year with 97 RBIs, 84 runs scored, 191 hits, 35 doubles, 11 triples, and a .325 batting average, while also leading all players at his position in putouts, double plays, and fielding percentage. Starting all 154 games for the Indians at third base, Keltner earned a 12th-place finish in the league MVP balloting with his solid all-around play. He followed that up with a subpar performance in 1940, hitting 15 homers, driving in 77 runs, and batting just .254. Nevertheless, Keltner's outstanding glove work at third helped him earn a spot on the AL All-Star team for the first of five straight times. Increasing his offensive output in 1941, Keltner hit 23 homers, knocked in 84 runs, scored 83 others, and batted .269. But, it was with his glove that Keltner truly excelled, leading all AL third basemen in assists, double plays, and fielding percentage, while etching his name into baseball lore on July 17 of that year, when his two outstanding defensive plays at third thwarted Joe DiMaggio's attempt to extend his record hitting streak to 57 games.

Generally considered to be the finest defensive third baseman of his time, Keltner often toyed with opposing batters, holding the ball until the last possible moment, before gunning them out at first base with his powerful and extremely accurate throwing arm. In discussing the man who spent most of his career playing behind him at third, Bob Feller said, "Keltner was simply the best in the American League. He could go to his right better than anyone and had a great, great arm."

Ossie Bluege, a Washington Senators coach and former third baseman, praised Keltner during a 1942 spring training interview with Shirley Povich of the *Washington Post*, stating:

> *"Ken Keltner's skill may not be generally appreciated, but every man who ever played third knows that Keltner is a swell performer. The test is in the plays he makes, and nobody else in the league is close to him. Keltner makes whatever kind of a throw is needed to get his man. When it's an easy play, he takes his time. If he has to hurry the throw, it doesn't bother him because he has a strong, true arm. He throws from on balance, off balance, underhand, or with a wrist flip on bunts. The man who can't do all of these things can't be called a good third baseman. Keltner probably plays a closer third base than any other*

man in the league. Only a really good third baseman can play close."

Povich agreed with Bluege's assessment, offering, "My man on the Cleveland club is Ken Keltner, who so far outstrips every other third baseman in the league that it is no contest. Keltner not only is the best fielding third baseman, but he is the biggest batting threat among 'em. We'd say he's the best ballplayer on the club."

The right-handed hitting Keltner possessed good power to all fields, often taking advantage of the dimensions at League Park, noting on one occasion, "I did learn to hit to right field a lot to take advantage of that short right field wall in Cleveland." He also proved to be a solid contact hitter, striking out more than 50 times in a season just four times his entire career.

Although Keltner totaled only 23 home runs from 1942 to 1944, he continued his string of five straight All-Star Game appearances, performing particularly well in the last of those campaigns, when he hit 13 homers, knocked in 91 runs, scored 74 times, batted .295, and finished second in the league with a career-high 41 doubles, while also leading all players at his position in assists and double plays.

After missing the entire 1945 campaign while serving in the United States Navy during World War II, Keltner returned to the Indians the following year, posting subpar numbers in both 1946 and 1947. However, he rebounded in 1948 to have arguably the finest season of his career. Starting 153 out of a possible 156 games at third for the Tribe, Keltner finished third in the league with 31 homers, knocked in 119 runs, scored 91 others, and batted .297, earning in the process his final All-Star nomination and a 14th-place finish in the AL MVP balloting. He then helped the Indians defeat Boston in a one-game playoff to determine the league champion by collecting three hits during the Tribe's 8-3 victory, including a game-changing three-run homer over Fenway Park's "Green Monster."

Limited by injuries to 80 games in 1949, Keltner concluded the campaign with just eight homers, 30 RBIs, 35 runs scored, and a .232 batting average, prompting the Indians to release him at season's end. Replaced by Al Rosen in Cleveland, Keltner signed with the Red Sox, for whom he appeared in only 13 games in 1950, before being released in early June. Although Keltner spent the following year playing for the Sacramento Solons in the Pacific Coast League, he never again donned a major league uniform, ending his big-league career at only 33 years of age, with 163 home runs, 852 RBIs, 737 runs scored, 1,570 hits, 308 doubles, 69 triples, a .276 batting average, a .338 on-base percentage, and a .441 slugging percentage.

Ken Keltner helped bring an end to Joe Di Maggio's 56-game hitting streak in 1941 with his stellar defensive play at third base

After retiring as an active player, Keltner spent the next several years scouting for the Indians and Red Sox, before leaving the game for good. He spent his remaining years living in his home state of Wisconsin, eventually moving into an assisted living facility when he became too ill to care for himself. Keltner passed away on December 12, 1991, less than two months after he celebrated his 75th birthday, after suffering a fatal heart attack. Two years later, former teammate Lou Boudreau said of Keltner in his 1993 autobiography, "He was a real professional, one of the best third basemen I've ever seen and, in my opinion, one who also belongs in the Hall of Fame."

Indians Career Highlights:

Best Season: It could certainly be argued that Keltner had his finest all-around season for the Indians in 1939, when, en route to earning a 12th-place finish in the league MVP voting, he hit 13 homers, knocked in 97 runs, scored 84 times, collected 35 doubles and 11 triples, compiled an OPS of .868, posted career-high marks in hits (191) and batting average (.325), and led all AL third basemen in putouts, double plays, and fielding percentage. Nevertheless, Keltner compiled slightly better overall numbers in 1948, when he helped lead the Tribe to the pennant by batting .297 and establishing career-best marks in homers (31), RBIs (119), runs scored (91), walks (89), total bases (291), on-base percentage (.395), slugging percentage (.522), and OPS (.917), earning in the process a 14th-place finish in the MVP balloting.

Memorable Moments/Greatest Performances: Keltner had his breakout game for the Indians on May 3, 1938, when he led them to a 10-9 win over the Washington Senators by homering twice and driving in a career-high six runs.

Although the Indians suffered an 8-5 defeat at the hands of the Senators on June 22, 1939, Keltner starred in the loss, going 5-for-5, with a homer and two RBIs.

Keltner had one of the most productive days of his career on July 31, 1940, when he helped lead the Indians to a 12-11 victory over the Red Sox by going 4-for-5, with a grand slam homer, five RBIs, and three runs scored.

Keltner matched his career-high RBI total on August 20, 1940, when he knocked in six runs during a come-from-behind 11-6 win over the Red Sox at Fenway Park, keying the Tribe's comeback with an eighth-inning grand slam.

Keltner delivered another big hit for the Indians on May 30, 1942, concluding a 4-for-5 afternoon with a two-out RBI double in the bottom of the ninth inning that gave the Tribe a 5-4 victory over the St. Louis Browns.

Keltner celebrated Independence Day in 1942 by going 5-for-5, with two RBIs and three runs scored, in leading the Indians to a 10-3 win over the Detroit Tigers.

Keltner paced the Indians to a 7-1 victory over the White Sox on April 17, 1946, by driving in four runs with a double and a pair of homers.

Keltner gave the Indians a 4-3 victory over the Yankees on May 20, 1946, when he put the finishing touches on a 4-for-5 day at the plate by hitting a game-winning solo home run in the bottom of the ninth inning.

Just two days after homering twice during an 8-2 win over Detroit, Keltner accomplished the feat again on April 25, 1948, leading the Indians to a 7-4 victory over the Tigers by going 3-for-4, with a pair of homers, four RBIs, and three runs scored.

Keltner continued his slugging in the month of May, reaching the seats twice during a 10-inning, 4-1 win over the Red Sox at Fenway Park on May 9, 1948, with his second solo homer of the contest producing what proved to be the game-winning run.

Keltner again victimized Boston pitchers on May 25, 1939, when he led the Indians to an 11-0 rout of the Red Sox by hitting three home runs, all of which came with the bases empty.

Although teammate Lou Boudreau appropriately received much of the credit for the Indians' 8-3 victory over Boston in 1948's one-game playoff, Keltner contributed significantly to the win as well, collecting three hits and giving the Tribe a 4-1 lead in the top of the fourth inning by hitting a towering three-run homer into the netting atop Fenway Park's "Green Monster" in left field.

Still, Keltner is remembered more than anything for the two outstanding defensive plays he made at third base on July 17, 1941, that helped end Joe DiMaggio's record 56-game hitting streak. Fully aware that DiMaggio had no intention of bunting, and also knowing that the previous evening's rainfall in Cleveland made it difficult for batters to get out of the box quickly, Keltner wisely chose to play the Yankee Clipper extremely deep and close to the third-base line every time he stepped up to the plate. Keltner's strategy paid off since DiMaggio hit two hard smashes down the third-base line that he backhanded behind the bag, before throwing to first base just in time to nip Joltin' Joe by a half step. DiMaggio ended up grounding into a double play in his final at-bat, thereby bringing to a close his record-setting streak.

Notable Achievements:

- Hit more than 20 home runs three times, topping 30 homers once (31 in 1948).
- Knocked in more than 100 runs twice.
- Batted over .300 once (.325 in 1939).
- Finished in double digits in triples three times.
- Surpassed 30 doubles six times, topping 40 two-baggers once (41 in 1944).
- Posted slugging percentage in excess of .500 once (.522 in 1948).
- Finished second in AL with 41 doubles in 1944.
- Finished third in AL in: home runs once, hits once, and triples once.
- Led AL third basemen in: assists four times, putouts once, fielding percentage three times, and double plays five times.
- Ranks among Indians career leaders in: RBIs (7th), hits (8th), doubles (6th), total bases (5th), games played (tied-6th), plate appearances (9th), and at-bats (6th).
- Hit three home runs in one game vs. Boston Red Sox on May 25, 1939.
- Seven-time AL All-Star (1940, 1941, 1942, 1943, 1944, 1946, and 1948).
- 1948 AL champion.
- 1948 world champion.

24

SAM MCDOWELL
1961 – 1971

Perhaps the most naturally gifted pitcher ever to don an Indians uniform, Sam McDowell proved to be the closest thing the American League had to Sandy Koufax for much of the 1960s. Featuring an overpowering fastball, an exceptional curve, and an outstanding slider, McDowell dominated AL hitters from 1964 to 1970, fanning more than 300 batters in two of those seven seasons, en route to topping the junior circuit in strikeouts five times. An imposing figure on the mound, the 6'5", 215-pound left-hander also compiled an ERA under 3.00 six times, leading the league in that category once. Meanwhile, despite pitching for mostly mediocre Indians teams, McDowell won at least 17 games three times, posting 20 victories in 1970, when he earned a third-place finish in the AL Cy Young voting and recognition as *The Sporting News* American League Pitcher of the Year. Still, McDowell's career has to be considered something of a disappointment since he likely would have accomplished so much more had injuries and an addiction to alcohol not brought his period of dominance to a premature end.

Born in Pittsburgh, Pennsylvania on September 21, 1942, Samuel Edward McDowell attended Central Catholic High School, where he starred in baseball, basketball, football, and track. Particularly proficient on the diamond, McDowell garnered a significant amount of attention from major-league scouts with his superb pitching, which included tossing a pair of no-hitters and a one-hitter at the Colt World Series as a junior. Continuing to dominate the opposition in his senior year of 1960, McDowell struck out 152 batters in 63 innings of work and did not surrender a single earned run, en route to compiling a perfect 8-0 record.

Signed to a $75,000 bonus by the Cleveland Indians, who outbid 12 other teams for his services following his graduation, McDowell reported to his first spring training in Tucson, Arizona, where Bob Dolgan, Indians beat writer for the *Cleveland Plain Dealer*, assigned him the moniker "Sudden Sam" due to the manner in which he delivered his overpowering fastball from an unusually calm pitching motion. Yet, in spite of the tremendous "stuff" he possessed at such a young age, it took McDowell several years to learn how to locate his pitches, forcing him to spend most of the next three seasons in the minor leagues. Although McDowell spent parts of the 1962 and 1963 campaigns in Cleveland, compiling an overall record of 6-12 during that time, he didn't join the Indians for good until 1964, when he finally gained better command of his fastball. Asked to explain the abrupt turnaround years later, McDowell commented, "During those first four years, I listened to everybody and anybody who had a theory on pitching, and I tried to do everything they told me. I made up my mind to stop listening to everybody and figure out a few things on my own. I made up my mind I wasn't going to worry about my wildness; that I would throw where I wanted. By the middle of the season, I could do it most of the time, at least with my fastball."

Gradually working his way into the Indians starting rotation over the course of the 1964 season, McDowell ended up compiling a record of 11-6 and an ERA of 2.70, while also striking out 177 batters in only 173⅓ innings of work. Emerging as one of the American League's best pitchers the following year, McDowell earned the first of his six All-Star selections by going 17-11 with a WHIP of 1.136, and leading the league with a 2.18 ERA and 325 strikeouts. However, he continued to struggle with his control at times, topping the circuit in bases on balls allowed for the first of five times by issuing 132 walks in 273 innings pitched.

With Cleveland pitching coach Early Wynn preaching the effectiveness of the high fastball, McDowell relied heavily on his upper-90s heater to put away opposing batters. However, he also possessed an excellent 12-to-6 curveball and a good slider that he often used instead, stating on one occasion, "It's no fun throwing fastballs to guys who can't hit them. The real challenge is getting them out on the stuff they can hit." Although McDowell often did opposing hitters a favor by throwing them off-speed pitches, the combination of his size, blazing fastball, and effective wildness made him easily the American League's most intimidating pitcher.

Still, Oakland slugger Reggie Jackson expressed his fondness for McDowell when he said, "I like Sudden and I think he's got the greatest fastball, curveball, slider, and changeup I ever saw. I call him 'Instant Heat.'

Courtesy of Cleveland Indians

Sam McDowell led the American League
in strikeouts five times while pitching for the Indians

Sudden simplifies things out there. You know he's gonna challenge you, his strength against yours, and either you beat him or he beats you. And he won't throw at you, either, because he's too nice a guy. He knows that, with his fastball, he could kill you if he ever hit you."

Plagued by arm problems for much of 1966, McDowell missed more than a month of the season, limiting him to only 28 starts and a record of 9-8, although he still managed to lead the league with 225 strikeouts and five shutouts. Fully healthy by the start of the 1967 campaign, McDowell nevertheless suffered through a disappointing season in which he finished just 13-15, with a 3.85 ERA. However, he returned to top form the following year, ranking among the league leaders with 269 innings pitched and a 1.81 ERA, posting a career-best WHIP of 1.082, and topping the circuit with 283 strikeouts, although Cleveland's feeble offense relegated him to a record of just 15-14. With the Indians scoring one run or less in 12 of his losses, McDowell chose not to throw his teammates under the bus, instead showing his support for them by stating, "What can I do? I know the guys are trying hard—I feel sorry for them. It's just one of those unexplainable things. Next year the situation might just be the opposite."

McDowell performed extremely well again in 1969, compiling a record of 18-14 and an ERA of 2.94, while leading the league with 279 strikeouts and ranking among the leaders with a WHIP of 1.137, four shutouts, 18 complete games, and 285 innings pitched. However, he pitched even better the following year, earning a third-place finish in the AL Cy Young balloting and his lone *Sporting News* All-Star selection by going 20-12, with a 2.92 ERA, 19 complete games, and a league-leading 305 innings pitched and 304 strikeouts.

Unfortunately, the 1970 campaign proved to be McDowell's last as an elite pitcher. After holding out for more money during the subsequent off-season, McDowell ended up compiling a record of just 13-17 and an ERA of 3.40, throwing only eight complete games and 214⅔ innings, and recording just 192 strikeouts in 1971, although his reputation enabled him to make the All-Star team for the sixth and final time in his career. Furthermore, McDowell's behavior became increasingly erratic as the season progressed, causing him to eventually wear out his welcome in Cleveland. After demanding a trade at season's end, McDowell found himself headed to the West Coast when Indians general manager Gabe Paul dealt him to the San Francisco Giants for star pitcher Gaylord Perry and infielder Frank Duffy on November 29, 1971. McDowell left Cleveland with a career record of 122-109, an ERA of 2.99, a WHIP of 1.268, 22 shutouts, 97 complete games, and 2,159 strikeouts in 2,109⅔ innings pitched, placing him second only to Bob Feller in strikeouts in franchise history.

Due to soreness in his pitching shoulder and persistent back and neck pains, McDowell accomplished very little the rest of his career, compiling an overall mark of just 19-25 over the course of his final four seasons, which he split between the Giants, Yankees, and Pittsburgh Pirates. Even more than his physical woes, though, McDowell suffered from a growing dependence on alcohol, which he later admitted when he disclosed, "The last four years of my career, I was a full-blown, third-stage alcoholic." McDowell went on to say, "I was the biggest, most hopeless, and most violent drunk in baseball during my fifteen years in the majors. That is a fair statement, I think, until some other lush comes out of the closet with his own story to tell."

McDowell, who has been sober since 1979, now openly discusses his earlier demons, revealing, "I knew I had this habit, but I didn't know it was an illness. I didn't know I had been lying to myself all those years, and that I had one of the worst diseases known to mankind. All I knew was that I was sick and tired of being tired and sick."

Recalling the level of subterfuge to which he stooped in order to deceive his managers, McDowell claims:

> "Everywhere I pitched, it was a con game I was playing—my drinking against their innocence of how really big a boozer I was. I was in a continual alcoholic state, semicontrolled by a little ritual I had. . . . Two days before I was to pitch, I stopped drinking. I could control it for that long. I ran the outfield and sweated out, and only my close buddies were the wiser. After taking my pitching turn, I was into the booze day and night for the next two, three days."

Admitting that "I didn't leave the game. I was kicked out finally, after bouncing around from the Cleveland Indians, to the San Francisco Giants, to the Yankees, and, finally, to the Pirates," McDowell lost his wife and two children because of his illness, prompting him to seek the help of his parents, who took him into their home after a failed business venture left him desolate and broke. Looking back at his feelings at the time, McDowell recalls:

> "There was a horrendous inner pain, far more devastating than any physical pain. There was the feeling of always being alone, of always being on the outside, of something being wrong and you can never find out what. I can't say I chose to sober up, or chose to get help. I quite frankly didn't think there was any hope. I didn't feel there was any way of helping me. I honestly thought I was going insane. . . . My parents and brothers pulled me through. They refused to let me lie to myself."

McDowell eventually checked himself into Gateway Rehab, a rehabilitation facility located outside of Pittsburgh, where he conquered his inner demons. After repaying his debts, he enrolled at the University of Pittsburgh, where he earned associate degrees in sports psychology and addiction. McDowell later returned to the Major Leagues as a sports addiction counselor with the Toronto Blue Jays and Texas Rangers, earning a World Series ring while working with the Blue Jays in 1993. He has since remarried and started a retirement community for former players in Clermont, Florida, for which he serves as chairman and CEO.

In discussing his current state of mind, McDowell says, "I don't think about the past very much. Today is all I care about. I've been very lucky because I believe seriously in my heart that this had to be, that my calling in life is what I am right now."

Indians Career Highlights:

Best Season: McDowell earned *Sporting News* AL Pitcher of the Year honors in 1970 by going 20-12, with a 2.92 ERA, a WHIP of 1.203, a career-high 19 complete games, and a league-leading 304 strikeouts and 305 innings pitched. Particularly effective from May 10 to July 23, McDowell posted a record of 12-1 in his 17 starts over that 10-week period. He also performed magnificently in 1968, when, despite being limited by poor run support to a record of 15-14, he recorded a league-leading 283 strikeouts and established career-best marks in ERA (1.81) and WHIP (1.082). Nevertheless, McDowell pitched his best ball for the Indians in 1965, when he compiled a record of 17-11, posted a WHIP of 1.136, finished second in the league with 14 complete games and 273 innings pitched, and topped the circuit with 325 strikeouts and an ERA of 2.18.

Memorable Moments/Greatest Performances: McDowell turned in the first dominant pitching performance of his career on April 16, 1963, when he allowed just two hits and recorded 13 strikeouts during a 3-0 shutout of the Washington Senators.

McDowell recorded a 2-1, 10-inning victory over the Detroit Tigers on June 5, 1965, surrendering five walks, just four hits and one unearned run, and striking out 15 batters.

McDowell yielded just two hits and four walks during a 5-0 shutout of the California Angels on June 20, 1965.

McDowell tossed the first of his four career one-hitters on August 31, 1965, recording 11 strikeouts and allowing just four walks, one unearned run, and a fourth-inning single by Kansas City second baseman Dick Green during an 8-1 victory over the Athletics.

Although the Indians ended up losing to the Baltimore Orioles by a score of 1-0 in 11 innings four days later, McDowell turned in another brilliant effort, recording a career-high 16 strikeouts and yielding just two hits and four walks over the first 10 innings. After the game, Baltimore shortstop Luis Aparicio said of McDowell, "He just overpowered us. I'm glad I'm a right-handed batter. I never saw anybody so fast."

McDowell threw consecutive one-hit shutouts in 1966, allowing just a sixth-inning single to Kansas City center-fielder Jose Tartabull during a 2-0 win over the Athletics on April 25, before fanning 10 batters and surrendering only a third-inning double to Chicago second baseman Don Buford during a 1-0 victory over the White Sox on May 1.

McDowell continued his brilliant pitching in his next start, striking out 10 batters and yielding just seven hits, three walks, and one run over the first 12 innings of a May 6, 1966 contest the Indians eventually lost to the Orioles by a score of 3-2 in 15 innings.

McDowell recorded 13 strikeouts and surrendered just two hits and two walks during a 5-0 shutout of the California Angels on July 1, 1966.

McDowell established a new American League record in May 1968, when he struck out a total of 30 batters in successive games. After recording 16 strikeouts and allowing just three hits and one unearned run during a 3-1 win over the Athletics on May 1, McDowell fanned 14 batters, en route to defeating the Yankees by a score of 3-2 five days later.

McDowell recorded seven strikeouts and yielded just two hits, in defeating the Kansas City Royals by a score of 4-1 on May 20, 1969.

McDowell again allowed just two hits during a 3-0 shutout of the Angels on June 8, 1969.

McDowell threw his last one-hitter on August 19, 1969, when he recorded 10 strikeouts and surrendered just two walks and a fourth-inning infield single to Bert Campaneris during a 3-0 shutout of the Oakland Athletics.

McDowell again dominated Oakland's lineup on May 29, 1970, when he struck out 13 batters and yielded just two hits and three bases on balls during a 2-1 victory over the Athletics.

McDowell followed that up with another superb outing, recording eight strikeouts and allowing just two hits and one walk during a 4-1 win over the Milwaukee Brewers on June 2.

McDowell turned in another dominant performance on July 19, 1970, when he recorded 14 strikeouts and yielded just three hits during a 3-1 win over the Minnesota Twins.

McDowell tossed his final two-hitter as a member of the Indians on June 13, 1971, when he struck out nine batters, issued four bases on balls, and surrendered only a sixth-inning double by shortstop Rick Auerbach and a seventh-inning single by center-fielder Dave May during an 11-0 rout of the Milwaukee Brewers.

Notable Achievements:

- Won 20 games once, surpassing 17 victories two other times.
- Posted winning percentage in excess of .600 three times.
- Compiled ERA under 3.00 six times, posting mark under 2.00 once (1.81 in 1968).
- Struck out more than 300 batters twice, topping 200 strikeouts four other times.
- Threw more than 300 innings once, surpassing 250 innings pitched three other times.
- Led AL pitchers in: ERA once, strikeouts five times, shutouts once, and innings pitched once.
- Finished second in AL in: ERA once, strikeouts once, innings pitched once, and complete games twice.
- Ranks among Indians career leaders in: strikeouts (2nd), shutouts (8th), innings pitched (10th), fewest hits allowed per nine innings pitched (2nd), most strikeouts per nine innings pitched (4th), and games started (8th).
- Finished third in 1970 AL Cy Young voting.
- 1970 *Sporting News* AL Pitcher of the Year.
- 1970 *Sporting News* All-Star selection.
- Six-time AL All-Star (1965, 1966, 1968, 1969, 1970, and 1971).

25

ROCKY COLAVITO
1955 – 1959, 1965 – 1967

Handsome, charismatic, and extremely talented, Rocky Colavito established himself as one of the most popular players in Indians history during his time in Cleveland, which included two tours of duty with the club. After ingratiating himself to Indians fans with his colorful persona and prolific slugging during the early stages of his career, Colavito returned to Cleveland in 1965, at which time he renewed his love affair with the hometown fans. Hitting a total of 190 home runs over parts of eight seasons with the Tribe, Colavito surpassed 20 homers six times, slugging more than 40 round-trippers twice. Colavito also knocked in more than 100 runs three times and batted over .300 once, earning in the process three All-Star selections and three top-five finishes in the AL MVP voting. Nearly 60 years after the Indians foolishly traded the popular outfielder to the Detroit Tigers for Harvey Kuenn, the lack of overall success they have experienced since making that infamous deal continues to be referred to by some as "The Curse of Rocky Colavito."

Born in the Bronx, New York on August 10, 1933, Rocco Domenico Colavito, like most young Italian boys of the day, grew up idolizing Joe DiMaggio. Hoping to follow in his hero's footsteps, young Rocco dropped out of Theodore Roosevelt High School after his sophomore year to pursue his dream of playing in the Major Leagues. Looking back at his decision years later, Colavito admitted, "It was a big mistake. I didn't want kids to say, 'He dropped out of school and he made the big leagues.'"

A gifted athlete with outstanding power at the plate and an exceptional throwing arm, Colavito began playing semipro baseball immediately after leaving school. Eventually given a tryout at Yankee Stadium by the Indians, Colavito signed with Cleveland at the tender age of 17 in 1951, after appealing a ruling in place at the time that prohibited a player from signing a professional contract until his class graduated. Cleveland scout Mike McNally later recalled, "We had a tryout in the Bronx for about eight or ten kids. I saw Rocky make a throw from the outfield. That was enough for me. I don't think I have ever seen a stronger arm."

After initially being assigned to Daytona Beach of the Class D Florida State League, Colavito gradually worked his way up to Reading in the Eastern League, where a lengthy slump forced him to adopt a new batting style. Having watched Colavito struggle at the plate for weeks as he attempted to mimic his hero, Joe DiMaggio, by copying his open batting stance, Reading manager Kerby Farrell told the young outfielder, "Rocky, we've gone far enough with you on this DiMaggio stuff. Let's try to be Colavito." Farrell subsequently had Colavito move his feet closer together and employ a slight crouch while awaiting the pitcher's offering, resulting in an offensive resurgence by the right-handed hitting slugger, who went on to top the circuit with 28 home runs and 121 RBIs.

With Larry Doby, Dale Mitchell, and Al Smith holding down the starting outfield jobs in Cleveland, the 20-year-old Colavito returned to the minors for another year of seasoning in 1954, performing extremely well at the Triple-A level, where he slugged another 38 homers. After spending most of the ensuing campaign in the minors as well, Colavito finally joined the Indians in September 1955, making a favorable impression on team management by hitting safely in four of his nine trips to the plate, compiling in the process a batting average of .444.

Colavito began the following year in the Pacific Coast League, where he once exhibited his powerful throwing arm by hurling a ball over the center-field wall from home plate, a distance that measured a total of 436 feet. Rejoining the Indians in early June, Colavito laid claim to the starting right-field job, after which he went on to bat .276, hit 21 homers, and knock in 65 runs, in only 101 games and 322 official at-bats, beginning in the process a string of 11 consecutive seasons in which he hit more than 20 home runs. He followed that up with another solid performance in 1957, finishing his first full season with 25 homers, 84 RBIs, and a .252 batting average, while also placing fourth in the league with 12 outfield assists and leading all players at his position in putouts for the first of five times.

After being convinced by Cleveland manager Joe Gordon to cut down on his swing the following year, Colavito emerged as one of baseball's top sluggers, finishing second in the AL with 41 homers and 113 RBIs, placing

Courtesy of Mears Online Auctions

Rocky Colavito established himself as one of the most popular players in franchise history during his time in Cleveland

third in the league with 303 total bases and an OPS of 1.024, topping the circuit with a slugging percentage of .620, and batting .303. Colavito also ranked third in the league with 14 outfield assists and led all AL outfielders with six double plays, his outstanding all-around play earning him a third-place finish in the league MVP balloting. Although Colavito's batting average dropped nearly 50 points, to .257 in 1959, he earned a fourth-place finish in the MVP voting and the first of his six All-Star selections by scoring 90 runs, finishing second in the league with 111 RBIs, topping the circuit with 42 homers and 301 total bases, and leading all AL right-fielders with 311 putouts.

Colavito's ability to hit home runs in huge bunches made him one of the American League's most feared sluggers. Despite being predominantly a pull hitter, the right-handed swinging Colavito possessed power to all fields, as New York Yankees right-hander Bob Turley suggested when he said, "There isn't a park he can't drive 'em out of with his power. . . . Even if you fool him on a pitch, he can still hit the ball out of the park."

Although Colavito suffered from flat feet, limiting his speed on the base paths and range in the outfield, he caught nearly everything he reached, leading all players at his position in fielding percentage on three separate occasions. Meanwhile, base runners rarely challenged his powerful right arm, which opposing players compared favorably to that of Roberto Clemente.

Colavito's playing ability, muscular 6′3″, 200-pound frame, matinee idol looks, and charisma turned him into an icon in the city of Cleveland before long. Boys emulated him on the sandlots, copying his batting stance and the manner in which he flexed his bat behind his back before stepping into the batter's box. Girls doted on him. And fans of all ages appreciated his work ethic and accommodating nature, which made him accessible to the many people who sought his autograph after each game.

The level of popularity Colavito reached during his time in Cleveland made it difficult for Indians fans to accept the announcement made on April 17, 1960—just two days before the opening of the regular season—that their favorite player had been dealt to the Detroit Tigers for defending AL batting champion Harvey Kuenn. While Cleveland GM Frank "Trader" Lane attempted to quell the anger subsequently expressed by Indians fans by proclaiming to the press, "What's all the fuss about? All I did was trade hamburger for steak," Tigers GM Bill DeWitt jokingly responded that he liked hamburger. The Detroit fans and media similarly rejoiced, with Edgar Hayes, sports editor of the *Detroit Times*, writing, "The Tigers lost thirty games by one run last season due to the lack of a long-ball hitter. This deal strengthens the Tigers and weakens the Indians. Colavito hit eight home runs in spring training this year, while the entire Detroit club has hit only fourteen."

The trade turned out to be a steal for the Tigers, who benefited greatly from Colavito's ability to hit the long ball. After experiencing something of an off-year in 1960, hitting 35 homers, but driving in only 87 runs and batting just .249, Colavito rebounded in 1961 to bat .290 and rank among the league leaders with 45 home runs, 140 RBIs, 129 runs scored, 113 walks, and an OPS of .982. He followed that up with two more excellent years for the Tigers, hitting 37 homers, driving in 112 runs, scoring 90 times, and batting .273 in 1962, before reaching the seats 22 times, knocking in 91 runs, scoring 91 others, and batting .271 in 1963. Meanwhile, Kuenn ended up spending just one year in Cleveland, batting .308, but hitting just nine homers, driving in only 54 runs, and scoring just 65 times for the Tribe in 1960, before being dealt to the San Francisco Giants for veteran pitcher Johnny Antonelli and promising young outfielder Willie Kirkland following the conclusion of the campaign.

With Colavito failing to develop the same rapport with the fans of Detroit that he shared with Indians fans, the Tigers elected to part ways with him on November 18, 1963, trading him to Kansas City for three players. Colavito ended up spending one productive season in Kansas City, hitting 34 homers and driving in 102 runs for the Athletics in 1964, before being reacquired by the Indians prior to the start of the 1965 campaign, as part of a three-team trade that also included the Chicago White Sox. From the Indians' perspective, the deal essentially sent Colavito back to Cleveland, in exchange for catcher John Romano and talented youngsters Tommie Agee and Tommy John. Upon making the trade, Kansas City general manager Pat Friday praised Colavito, stating, "He is a great player, and he was a favorite with the fans here. I never have known a player who hustled as consistently and as much as Colavito."

Meanwhile, Indians GM Gabe Paul claimed that he finally succeeded in reacquiring Colavito after spending the previous few years trying to right the earlier wrong made by former GM Frank Lane, revealing, "I made more than a hundred offers to Detroit when Colavito was there."

Cleveland fans subsequently expressed their glee over Colavito's impending return by flooding the team's switchboards, as well as those of the local newspapers. Colavito also looked forward to returning to Cleveland, saying, "I'm glad to be going home—and I do mean home. Every year, when I went into Cleveland with the Tigers or Athletics, I would say to myself, 'Wouldn't it be nice to be playing here again?'"

Colavito performed well in his first year back, when, appearing in all 162 games for the Indians, he earned his fifth All-Star selection and a fifth-place finish in the AL MVP voting by hitting 26 homers, scoring 92 runs, batting .287, and leading the league with 108 RBIs and 93 bases on balls, while also going the entire season without committing a single error in the outfield. Hampered by a sore shoulder in 1966, Colavito still managed to earn All-Star honors for the final time by hitting 30 homers, although he knocked in only 72 runs and batted just .238. After getting off to a slow start the following year, Colavito found himself headed to Chicago when the White Sox acquired him for a pair of nondescript players on July 29, 1967. He left Cleveland having hit 190 homers, driven in 574 runs, scored 464 times, amassed 851 hits, 136 doubles, and nine triples, batted .267, compiled a .361 on-base percentage, and posted a .495 slugging percentage as a member of the Indians.

Colavito spent the remainder of the year in Chicago, before splitting the 1968 campaign between the Dodgers and Yankees. Choosing to announce his retirement after being released by the Yankees on September 30, 1968, Colavito ended his career with 374 home runs, 1,159 RBIs, 971 runs scored, 1,730 hits, 283 doubles, 21 triples, a .266 batting average, a .359 on-base percentage, and a .489 slugging percentage. He retired as the AL's third-leading right-handed home run hitter, trailing only Jimmie Foxx and Harmon Killebrew at the time.

Following his playing career, Colavito returned to Cleveland, where he spent three years working as a TV analyst for station WJW. He also served as a member of the Indians' coaching staff for three seasons, before later assuming a similar role with the Kansas City Royals during the early 1980s. Unfortunately, Colavito, who currently resides in Berks County, Pennsylvania, has experienced serious health problems in recent years, having his right leg amputated just below the knee on August 11, 2015, after spending the previous several years suffering from Type-2 Diabetes. Never one to feel sorry for himself, Colavito says, "They had to take the leg off, but I still have the knee. I'm so grateful for that. There have been no infections. The surgery went great. I don't want anyone's pity." He then added, "What can you do? No one wants to hear anyone cry about it. It's just life, I guess."

Voted the most memorable personality in Indians history in 1976, Colavito received the additional distinction of being immortalized by Cleveland sportswriter Terry Pluto in the latter's 1994 best-selling book entitled,

The Curse of Rocky Colavito, which details the difficulties the Indians encountered after they traded away the popular outfielder to the Tigers in 1960. In describing the qualities that endeared Colavito to the fans of Cleveland, Pluto wrote, "He was everything a ballplayer should be: dark, handsome eyes, and raw-boned build; and he hit home runs at a remarkable rate."

Indians Career Highlights:

Best Season: Although Colavito led the American League with 42 home runs and 301 total bases in 1959, he played his best ball for the Indians one year earlier, earning a third-place finish in the 1958 AL MVP voting by posting career-high marks in batting average (.303), on-base percentage (.405), slugging percentage (.620), and OPS (1.024), while also placing near the top of the league rankings with 41 home runs, 113 RBIs, and 303 total bases.

Memorable Moments/Greatest Performances: Colavito made his first start in the big leagues a memorable one, going 4-for-4, with a pair of doubles and two runs scored, during a 7-0 win over the Detroit Tigers on September 24, 1955.

Colavito again went 4-for-4 on August 10, 1956, when he homered, doubled, singled twice, and scored four times during an 11-0 rout of the Kansas City Athletics.

Colavito powered the Indians to a 4-1 victory over Washington on August 26, 1956, driving in all four Tribe runs with a homer and a double.

Colavito again feasted off Washington pitching on July 17, 1958, hitting a pair of homers and knocking in four runs, in leading the Indians to an 8-3 win over the Senators.

Colavito hit a pair of late-inning solo home runs that brought the Indians back from a 2-0 deficit to Kansas City on August 31, 1958, with his second round-tripper coming with two men out in the top of the ninth inning. Minnie Minoso gave the Tribe a 3-2 victory with a solo blast of his own in the top of the 11th.

Colavito gave the Indians a 5-4 win over the Boston Red Sox on September 12, 1958, when he knocked in the game's decisive runs with a seventh-inning grand slam.

Just four days after leading the Indians to a 7-6 victory over the Yankees by going 4-for-5, with a homer, two RBIs, and two runs scored, Colavito homered twice, drove in four runs, and scored three times during a 12-6 win over the Red Sox on May 16, 1959.

Colavito led the Indians to back-to-back wins over Detroit later in the year, homering twice and knocking in three runs during an 8-7 victory over the Tigers on July 11, 1959, before driving in four runs with a pair of homers, in pacing them to an 8-4 win over the Tigers the following day.

Colavito reached the seats twice and knocked in four runs during a 6-3 victory over the Yankees and Hall of Fame left-hander Whitey Ford on August 25, 1959.

Colavito also had several big days at the plate during his second tour of duty with the Indians, with the first of those coming on May 30, 1965, when he went 4-for-5, with a homer and five RBIs, during a lopsided 10-2 victory over the Detroit Tigers.

Colavito led the Indians to a convincing 8-0 win over the Baltimore Orioles on July 2, 1965, by driving in five runs with a homer, double, and single.

However, Colavito unquestionably had the greatest day of his career on June 10, 1959, when he powered the Indians to an 11-8 victory over the Orioles by becoming just the eighth player in MLB history to hit four home runs in one game. Colavito, who also knocked in six runs and scored five times during the contest, later said, "Honest, I was just trying to meet the ball. . . . No, I wasn't going for a fourth. I thought I had a pretty good night already, hitting three."

Notable Achievements:

- Hit more than 20 home runs six times, topping 30 homers three times and 40 homers twice.
- Knocked in more than 100 runs three times.
- Batted over .300 once (.303 in 1958).
- Compiled on-base percentage in excess of .400 once (.405 in 1958).
- Posted slugging percentage in excess of .500 three times, topping the .600-mark once (.620 in 1958).
- Posted OPS in excess of 1.000 once (1.024 in 1958).

- Led AL in: home runs once, RBIs once, extra-base hits twice, total bases once, bases on balls once, and slugging percentage once.
- Finished second in AL in: home runs once, RBIs twice, and on-base percentage once.
- Finished third in A.L in: hits once, total bases once, and OPS once.
- Led AL outfielders in double plays once and fielding percentage once.
- Led AL right-fielders in: putouts twice, double plays once, and fielding percentage once.
- Ranks 10th in Indians history with 190 career home runs.
- Hit four home runs in one game vs. Baltimore Orioles on June 10, 1959.
- Finished in top five of AL MVP voting three times.
- Three-time AL All-Star (1959, 1965, and 1966).

26

ANDRE THORNTON
1977 – 1987

An imposing right-handed hitter who served as the main source of power on mostly bad Indians teams during the 1970s and 1980s, Andre Thornton spent 10 of his 14 big-league seasons in Cleveland, establishing himself during that time as one of the top sluggers in franchise history. Overcoming personal tragedy and a rash of serious injuries, Thorton hit more than 20 home runs in six of his eight full seasons with the Tribe, surpassing 30 homers on three separate occasions. Thornton also knocked in more than 100 runs twice, en route to earning two All-Star selections, one Silver Slugger Award, and AL Comeback Player of the Year honors in 1982, when he finished third in the junior circuit with a career-high 116 RBIs. A solid defender as well before injuries forced him to spend the second half of his career manning the designated hitter (DH) position, Thornton proved to be one of the few bright spots on Indians teams that posted a winning record just twice in his 10 years with the club.

Born in Tuskegee, Alabama on August 13, 1949, Andre Thornton grew up in Phoenixville, Pennsylvania after moving there with his family in 1955. Although Thornton established himself as a three-sport star while attending Phoenixville Area High School, excelling in baseball, basketball, and football, he proved to be even more proficient in the game of pool, spending much of his free time in the local pool halls. After signing with the Philadelphia Phillies as an amateur free agent in 1967, Thornton spent six long years in the minor leagues, beginning his ascent to the majors as an outfielder/first baseman with the Class-A Huron (South Dakota) Phillies in the Northern League. Looking back at his earliest days as a pro, Thornton recalls, "Going from Philadelphia to South Dakota was a culture shock. There weren't any blacks in Huron, except on the baseball team. I lived in a house with five players. We rented it and slept in the basement. One of my roommates was [future Indians teammate] Toby Harrah."

Enlisting in the National Guard while rising through Philadelphia's farm system, Thornton established a strong connection to religion that helped him persevere through the difficult times that lay ahead, revealing, "The Army is where I found Christ. I had seen baseball. I had seen the streets. I was watching the result of the senseless killing going on in Vietnam. They tell you to work hard and you'll get a piece of the American Pie. They tell you things are equal. Well, I grew up knowing none of that was true. Reality was a cold place. Several times I had been in the depths of despair. None of it made any sense."

Traded from the Phillies to the Braves, who eventually dealt him to the Chicago Cubs for Joe Pepitone, Thornton finally made it to the big leagues in late July 1973, compiling a batting average of .200 in extremely limited duty over the final two months of the campaign. Gradually working his way into the starting lineup the following year, Thornton posted decent offensive numbers for the Cubs, hitting 10 homers and driving in 46 runs, in just over 300 official at-bats, while playing first base and also serving as an occasional pinch-hitter. Making an extremely favorable impression on Chicago manager Jim Marshall during that time, Thornton drew praise from his skipper, who commented, "He's come a long way in just this one season and has yet to reach his potential. He's going to be an even better hitter. But I don't know how much better he can be in the field. He's an outstanding fielder right now."

Although Thornton subsequently performed well for the Cubs in 1975, hitting 18 homers, driving in 60 runs, and batting .293, Chicago elected to trade him to the Montreal Expos early the following year. Relegated to a part-time role in Montreal, Thornton suffered through a dismal 1976 campaign in which he hit just 11 homers, knocked in only 38 runs, and batted just .194, prompting the Expos to trade him to the Indians for pitcher Jackie Brown. Upon acquiring Thornton, Cleveland General Manager Phil Seghi stated, "I consider him a real big addition to our team. He's a good player, and potentially a twenty-five-homer man. He's still a young man, a right-handed hitter, which we need, and a very good glove man."

Inserted at first base full-time upon his arrival in Cleveland, Thornton posted solid numbers for the Tribe in 1977, leading the team with 28 homers and 77 runs scored, finishing second on the club with 70 RBIs, and batting .263. However, just as Thornton appeared to be hitting his stride, he experienced personal tragedy on October 17, 1977, when he lost his wife and young daughter in an automobile accident. With Thornton driving his wife, three-year-old daughter, and four-year-old son to a wedding in West Chester, Pennsylvania, a sudden snowstorm and high winds pushed the family van across the icy road and flipped it over into a ditch on the Pennsylvania turnpike. After being taken to the hospital, Thornton learned that his son had survived the accident, but that his wife and daughter had perished. Looking back years later at his devastating loss, Thornton revealed, "It was then that I truly felt the power of God. I sensed Him telling me 'I will never leave you or forsake you.' I told my son it was just him and me now, but I don't know if he understood because he was so young."

Thornton's faith and inner strength helped him return to the Indians more focused than ever in 1978, enabling him to finish fourth in the league with 33 homers, 105 RBIs, 97 runs scored, and an OPS of .893, while also batting .262 and ranking among the top players at his position in putouts, assists, and fielding percentage. Thornton's strong performance prompted Boston's Carl Yastrzemski to comment, "He's always had great power. Now he's hitting the ball hard all the time, even on outs." Baltimore's Jim Palmer added, "When I face Cleveland, I just want to be able to pitch around Thornton. He'll turn my one-oh win into a two-one loss." Meanwhile, in addressing the 6'3", 215-pound Thornton's surprising quickness, agility, and soft hands in the field, Indians manager Jeff Torborg said, "Andy really is impressive. The more you watch him, he's an excellent first baseman."

Although Thornton subsequently batted just .233 in 1979, he hit 26 homers, drove in 93 runs, and scored 89 times, earning in the process Major League Baseball's prestigious Roberto Clemente Award, presented annually to the player who "best exemplifies the game of baseball, sportsmanship, community involvement, and the individual's contribution to his team." Thornton then missed the entire 1980 campaign while undergoing two surgeries to repair a knee that he injured during spring training. His injury woes continued the following year, when he appeared in only 69 games after breaking his hand during the preseason.

With the Indians having acquired Mike Hargrove during his absence, Thornton became the Tribe's full-time DH in 1982. In discussing his new role, Thornton suggested, "Certainly, if you're a full-time DH, your focus is going to be centralized on hitting and focusing on what you need to do from that position. You have to look at it just like any other position on the field. Everybody has a responsibility. Your responsibility as a DH is to try to drive in runs."

Adapting extremely well to his new role, Thornton scored 90 runs, batted .273, and ranked among the league leaders with 32 homers, 116 RBIs, and 109 bases on balls, en route to earning his first All-Star selection and AL Comeback Player of the Year honors. In assessing his performance, Thornton stated, "All I needed was my health. If I could stay sound, I knew I could produce. Just check my record. If I don't get hurt, I can put up some good numbers. To me, this season was gratifying, but it certainly didn't shock me."

Cleveland GM Phil Seghi agreed, commenting, "I know that Thornton has been hurt quite a bit. But every injury has been a serious one—broken bones, knee troubles. The man wants to play. When he can, he is one of the best power hitters in the game."

The one true power threat in the Indians lineup for much of his time in Cleveland, Thornton presented a menacing figure to opposing pitchers as he stood in the batter's box, crowding the plate, with his hulking arms dangling over the strike zone. But he also proved to be an extremely selective hitter who rarely swung at bad pitches, drawing more than 90 bases on balls in four different seasons, en route to compiling a lifetime on-base percentage of .360. Meanwhile, Thornton's humility and dedication to his profession helped make him one of the most respected players in the game.

Thornton remained the Indians' full-time designated hitter for another four years, averaging 22 home runs and 83 RBIs during that time. Performing particularly well in 1984, Thornton earned his second All-Star nomination and lone Silver Slugger by hitting 33 homers, driving in 99 runs, scoring 91 times, and batting .271. Released by the Indians following the conclusion of the 1987 campaign after losing his starting DH job to Pat Tabler, Thornton announced his retirement, ending his career with 253 home runs, 895 RBIs, 792 runs scored, 1,342 hits, 244 doubles, 22 triples, a .254 batting average, a .360 on-base percentage, and a .452 slugging percentage. During his time in Cleveland, he hit 214 homers, knocked in 749 runs, scored 650 others, amassed 1,095 hits, 193 doubles, and 12 triples, batted .254, compiled a .355 on-base percentage, and posted a .453 slugging percentage.

Following his retirement, Thornton, who lived in Cleveland year-round during his playing days, chose to remain in the area, beginning a new career as a successful businessman and motivational speaker, often sharing his Christian faith with others. Inducted into the Indians Hall of Fame in 2007, Thornton accepted the honor with grace and dignity, stating, "To spend eleven years with the Indians and compile a record that people think is worthy of their Hall of Fame. . . . I'm just humbled by it."

Indians Career Highlights:

Best Season: Thornton posted excellent power numbers for the Indians in both 1978 and 1984, concluding the first of those campaigns with 33 home runs, 105 RBIs, 97 runs scored, and a .516 slugging percentage, before earning his lone Silver Slugger in the second by hitting 33 homers, driving in 99 runs, scoring 91 times, and compiling a slugging percentage of .484. However, he had his finest all-around season in 1982, when he hit 32 homers, scored 90 runs, batted .273, and established career-high marks in hits (161), RBIs (116), and bases on balls (109), finishing third in the league in each of the last two categories.

Memorable Moments/Greatest Performances: Thornton had his first big day at the plate for the Indians on June 17, 1977, when he homered twice and knocked in six runs during a 12-inning, 8-5 win over the Detroit Tigers, with his two-out, three-run blast in the bottom of the 12th giving the Tribe the victory.

Thornton again hit two homers during a 4-2 win over the Tigers on June 24, 1977, driving in all four Cleveland runs with a pair of round-trippers and a sacrifice fly.

After Toby Harrah tied the score earlier in the frame with a two-out, two-run homer, Thornton gave the Indians an 11-10 victory over the California Angels on June 12, 1979, by driving home Bobby Bonds from second base with an RBI single in the bottom of the ninth inning. Thornton finished the game with three hits and four runs batted in.

Thornton helped lead the Indians to a lopsided 14-2 victory over the Oakland Athletics on May 9, 1982, by hitting a pair of two-run homers and scoring three times.

Thornton proved to be the difference in a 12-inning, 5-1 win over the Milwaukee Brewers on July 29, 1982, driving in all five Cleveland runs with an RBI single in the top of the fourth inning and a grand slam homer in the final frame.

Although the Indians lost their September 8, 1984 meeting with Oakland by a score of 9-5, Thornton starred in defeat, having the only 5-for-5 day of his career at the plate.

Courtesy of Cleveland Indians

Playing for mostly losing teams, Andre Thornton hit more than 30 home runs for the Indians on three separate occasions

Thornton capped off a three-hit, five-RBI game against Detroit on August 15, 1985, by hitting a three-run homer in the top of the ninth inning that gave the Indians a 7-6 win over the Tigers.

After leading the Indians to a 9-5 victory over the Yankees one day earlier by hitting a pair of two-run homers, Thornton collected three hits and five RBIs during a 15-8 win over the Oakland Athletics on September 17, 1985.

Thornton turned in one of his most memorable performances on April 22, 1978, when, during a 13-4 victory over the Boston Red Sox, he became just the sixth player in Indians history to hit for the cycle. Looking back on his atypical day, Thornton said the game stood out to him for a couple of reasons. "One, it [hitting for the cycle] was something unusual for a player—any player—but especially for me because I wasn't the fastest guy in the world. And second, each hit came off a different Boston pitcher [Allen Ripley, Bob Stanley, Jim Wright, and Tom Burgmeier]."

Notable Achievements:

- Hit more than 20 home runs six times, topping 30 homers on three occasions.
- Knocked in more than 100 runs twice.
- Surpassed 30 doubles once (31 in 1979).
- Topped 100 walks once (109 in 1982).
- Posted slugging percentage in excess of .500 twice.
- Finished third in AL in: home runs once, RBIs once, and bases on balls once.
- Ranks among Indians career leaders in home runs (7th) and bases on balls (7th).
- Hit for cycle vs. Boston Red Sox on April 22, 1978.
- 1979 Roberto Clemente Award winner.
- 1982 *Sporting News* AL Comeback Player of the Year.
- 1982 Hutch Award winner.
- 1984 Silver Slugger winner.
- Two-time AL All-Star (1982 and 1984).

27

CHARLIE JAMIESON
1919 – 1932

A solid line drive hitter with good speed and an excellent throwing arm in the outfield, Charlie Jamieson spent most of his 18-year major-league career in Cleveland, serving as the Indians starting left-fielder throughout the entire decade of the 1920s. En route to earning a place among the franchise's career leaders in numerous statistical categories, Jamieson batted over .300 nine times, topped 200 hits twice, amassed more than 30 doubles four times and 10 triples three times, and scored more than 100 runs on two separate occasions. Along the way, the diminutive outfielder earned two top-10 finishes in the A.L MVP voting, placing as high as third in 1924, when he finished second in the American League with a career-high batting average of .359. An outstanding defender as well, Jamieson accumulated a total of 153 assists in left field over the course of his career—a figure that places him seventh all-time among players at that position. Jamieson accomplished all he did during his time in Cleveland even though he did not become a member of the Indians starting outfield until after he celebrated his 27th birthday.

Born in Paterson, New Jersey on February 7, 1893, Charles Devine Jamieson attended Paterson High School, while at the same time playing semi-pro ball with a local team called the Lafayettes. After being offered $250 a month to join the International League's Buffalo Bisons prior to the start of the 1912 season, Jamieson began his pro career, oddly enough, as a starting pitcher. Performing well in that role, Jamieson compiled an overall record of 27-17 over the course of the next two seasons, before moving to the outfield in 1914. After batting .307 for Buffalo in 1915, Jamieson made his major league debut with the Washington Senators, who purchased him during the latter stages of the campaign.

Having compiled a batting average of .279 in 17 games with Washington in 1915, Jamieson made enough of an impression to earn a roster spot the following season, after which he spent the next year-and-a-half serving the Senators as a backup outfielder, before being placed on waivers midway through the 1917 season. Subsequently claimed by the Philadelphia Athletics, Jamieson spent the rest of the year starting in right field for the A's, compiling a batting average of .267, driving in 27 runs, and scoring 41 others in 85 games and 345 official at-bats. Jamieson remained in Philadelphia one more year, batting just .202 for the Athletics in 1918, before being traded to the Indians, along with third baseman Larry Gardner and pitcher Elmer Myers, for outfielder Braggo Roth and cash prior to the start of the ensuing campaign.

Seeing very little action his first year in Cleveland, Jamieson garnered only 17 at-bats in 1919, although he performed extremely well in his primary role as a pinch-hitter, posting a batting average of .353. Inserted into the starting lineup midway through the 1920 season after earlier splitting time in left field with Jack Graney and Joe Evans, Jamieson went on to claim the job for his own by batting .319, driving in 40 runs, and scoring 69 others, in 108 games and 370 official plate appearances. He then helped lead the Indians to their first world championship by batting .333 against the Brooklyn Robins in the World Series.

Despite having already celebrated his 28th birthday by the start of the 1921 campaign, Jamieson played the best ball of his career for the Indians over the course of the next few seasons. After batting .310 and scoring 94 runs in his first year as a full-time starter, Jamieson hit .323, scored 87 runs, and collected 183 hits from his leadoff spot in the batting order in 1922. He then earned a sixth-place finish in the AL MVP voting in 1923 by ranking among the league leaders with 130 runs scored, a .345 batting average, 12 triples, 36 doubles, 80 walks, and 18 stolen bases, while topping the circuit with 222 hits. Jamieson followed that up with an equally impressive performance in 1924, earning a third-place finish in the MVP balloting by finishing second in the league with 213 hits and a batting average of .359, scoring 98 runs, and stealing a career-high 21 bases.

Standing only 5′8″ tall and weighing just 165 pounds, the left-handed hitting Jamieson possessed very little power at the plate, accumulating only 18 home runs over the course of his career. But he proved to be an excellent line drive hitter and a solid run-producer at the top of the Indians lineup, batting well over .300 five straight times at one point, never hitting

Courtesy of the Bain News Service Collection at the Library of Congress

Charlie Jamieson batted over .300 for the Indians nine times

any lower than .291 from 1920 to 1931, and scoring more than 90 runs on four separate occasions. A strong defender as well, the speedy Jamieson did an outstanding job of covering the expansive left field at League Park, annually ranking among the top players at his position in putouts, assists, double plays, and fielding percentage. In fact, he led the league in each of those categories at least once during his time in Cleveland.

Jamieson remained the Indians starting left-fielder for another six years, during which time he batted over .300 three more times. Performing particularly well in 1925, Jamieson batted .296 and placed near the top of the league rankings with 109 runs scored. He followed that up by batting .299 and scoring 89 runs in 1926, before his playing time gradually began to diminish over the course of the next four seasons. Relegated to pinch-hitting duties by 1931 after losing his starting job to Joe Vosmik, Jamieson spent his final two seasons in Cleveland fulfilling that role, before being released by the Indians following the conclusion of the 1932 campaign. Upon his release, *The Plain Dealer's* Gordon Cobbledick wrote, "They come and they go in baseball, a racket wherein there's no place for either the aged or the incompetent, and you can't be mourning long for any of them. But, still, without allowing yourself to grow too sentimental about it, you find yourself wishing old Jamie could have stuck around for another fourteen years. He's that kind of a guy and that kind of a ballplayer."

The extremely popular Jamieson ended his time in Cleveland with 18 home runs, 490 RBIs, 942 runs scored, 1,753 hits, 296 doubles, 74 triples, 107 stolen bases, a .316 batting average, a .388 on-base percentage, and a .406 slugging percentage. Including his years in Washington and Philadelphia, he knocked in 550 runs, scored 1,062 times, amassed 1,990 hits, 322 doubles, 80 triples, and 131 stolen bases, batted .303, compiled a .378 on-base percentage, and posted a .385 slugging percentage.

Following his release by the Indians, Jamieson, who once said, "I'm going to play ball as long as they'll let me—major, minor, semi-pro, and sandlot," spent one season playing for the Jersey City Skeeters in the International League, before managing the Paterson Smart Set of the Paterson East Side Park Club for much of the 1930s. After finally leaving the game, Jamieson retired to his hometown of Paterson, New Jersey, where he lived until October 27, 1969, when he passed away at the age of 76.

Indians Career Highlights:

Best Season: Although Jamieson earned a third-place finish in the 1924 AL MVP voting by scoring 98 runs, stealing 21 bases, and finishing second in the league with 213 hits and a career-high .359 batting average, he actually posted better overall numbers the previous season. In addition to topping the circuit with 222 hits in 1923, Jamieson ranked among the league leaders in batting average (.345), stolen bases (18), doubles (36), triples (12), total bases (288), walks (80), runs scored (130), and on-base percentage (.422), establishing career-high marks in each of the last six categories. He also led all AL left-fielders with a .974 fielding percentage and a career-best 360 putouts, earning in the process a sixth-place finish in the league MVP voting.

Memorable Moments/Greatest Performances: The only outfielder in MLB history to initiate two triple plays in one season, Jamieson accomplished the feat within a span of roughly two weeks in 1928. After starting a triple play in the ninth inning of a 4-3 loss to the Chicago White Sox on May 23, Jamieson duplicated his earlier effort during a 7-3 loss to the Yankees on June 9.

Jamieson led the Indians to an 8-4 victory over the St. Louis Browns on September 27, 1920, by going 4-for-5, with a double, triple, three RBIs, and three runs scored.

Jamieson hit one of his 18 career home runs during a lopsided 17-3 victory over the Philadelphia Athletics on September 15, 1921, going 4-for-5, with a homer, triple, three RBIs, and a career-high five runs scored.

Jamieson helped lead the Indians to a 17-4 pounding of the Boston Red Sox on June 6, 1923, by going 4-for-5, with a double, triple, and four runs scored.

Jamieson again tormented Boston pitchers one month later, collecting three hits, including a triple, driving in three runs, and scoring four times during a 27-3 massacre of the Red Sox on July 7, 1923.

Jamieson had a big day at the plate against the Yankees on July 17, 1923, going 5-for-5, with two RBIs and two runs scored, during a lopsided 13-0 victory over the eventual World Series champions.

Jamieson exacted a measure of revenge against his former team on August 7, 1923, when he helped lead the Indians to a 22-2 dismantling of the Washington Senators by going 4-for-5, with a triple, two RBIs, and three runs scored.

Jamieson hit safely in five of his six trips to the plate and scored three runs during a lopsided 12-4 victory over the St. Louis Browns on September 2, 1924.

Jamieson had another big game against St. Louis on April 14, 1925, when he homered, collected three singles, knocked in a pair of runs, and scored four times during a 21-14 win over the Browns that featured a 12-run uprising by the Indians in the eighth inning.

Jamieson helped pace the Indians to an 11-5 win over the Washington Senators on June 9, 1926, by going 4-for-4, with a triple, a pair of doubles, three RBIs, and three runs scored.

Jamieson continued his assault on Washington pitching later in the year, going 5-for-5 and scoring three runs, in leading the Indians to an 8-5 victory over the Senators on August 7, 1926.

Jamieson had his last big day at the plate for the Indians on September 17, 1930, when he went 4-for-5, knocked in three runs, and scored three others during a 13-7 win over Washington.

Notable Achievements:

- Batted over .300 nine times, topping the .320-mark three times and surpassing .340 twice.
- Scored more than 100 runs twice, scoring 130 times in 1923.
- Surpassed 200 hits twice.
- Finished in double digits in triples three times.
- Surpassed 30 doubles four times.
- Stole more than 20 bases once (21 in 1924).
- Compiled on-base percentage in excess of .400 twice.
- Led AL in: hits once, plate appearances once, and at-bats once.
- Finished second in AL with .359 batting average and 213 hits in 1924.
- Led AL outfielders with 22 assists in 1928.
- Led AL left-fielders in: putouts once, assists once, fielding percent twice, and double plays three times.
- Ranks seventh all-time among MLB left-fielders with 153 assists.
- Ranks among Indians career leaders in: runs scored (4th), hits (5th), doubles (7th), triples (tied-10th), total bases (9th), bases on balls (10th), sacrifice hits (tied-9th), games played (9th), plate appearances (8th), and at-bats (8th).1920 world champion.
- Finished in top 10 of AL MVP voting twice, making it into top five once (third in 1924).
- 1920 AL champion.
- 1920 world champion.

28

ELMER FLICK
1902 - 1910

Although he is remembered most as the player that Cleveland re-fused to trade for a young Ty Cobb and as the man who won the American League batting title with the lowest average prior to 1968, Elmer Flick carved out an extremely successful career for himself during the Dead Ball Era that eventually landed him in Cooperstown. Building his reputation on his hard-hitting and fleetness afoot, Flick spent his first four big-league seasons starring for the Philadelphia Phillies in the NL, before jumping to the rival American League, where he spent the remainder of his career excelling in right field for the Cleveland Naps. Batting over .300 in four of his six full seasons with the Naps, Flick compiled a batting average of .299 during his time in Cleveland, leading the league with a mark of .308 in 1905. He also finished in double digits in triples and stole more than 20 bases six times each, topping the junior circuit in three-baggers three times and thefts twice. Yet, Flick likely would have accomplished considerably more over the course of his career had a mysterious gastrointestinal ail-ment not brought his playing days to a premature end.

Born in Bedford, Ohio on January 11, 1876, Elmer Harrison Flick starred in multiple sports while attending Bedford High School, excelling in baseball, football, boxing, and wrestling. Particularly proficient on the diamond, Flick made a name for himself as a slugging catcher for his high school team, while also spending most of his teenage years playing for the local semi-pro team.

Choosing to pursue a career in organized ball, Flick made his profes-sional debut as an outfielder with Youngstown (Ohio) in 1896, recalling years later, "In my first game for Youngstown, I hit a ninth-inning homer with one on, to win, two to one. That's when they first started to call me 'Elmer Flick, the demon of the stick.'"

After one more year in the minors, Flick joined the Philadelphia Phillies, who initially expected him to serve them primarily as a backup. But the 22-year-old outfielder made an extremely favorable impression during spring training, with local writer Francis Richter suggesting, "Flick is going to make the outfielders hustle to hold their positions. He is the fastest and most promising youngster the Phillies have ever had."

Before long, Flick worked his way into the starting lineup, concluding his rookie campaign of 1898 with eight home runs, 81 RBIs, 84 runs scored, and a .302 batting average. He improved upon those numbers the following year, driving in 98 runs, scoring 98 times, and batting .342, before having the finest season of his career in 1900, when he ranked among the NL leaders in every major offensive category, topping the circuit with 110 RBIs, and finishing a close second in the batting race to Honus Wagner with a mark of .367. Interestingly enough, Flick engaged in a fistfight with teammate Napoleon Lajoie earlier in the year that resulted in the latter missing five weeks with a broken jaw.

After performing well for the Phillies again in 1901, Flick accepted a lucrative offer to jump to the infant American League, where he joined former teammate Lajoie on the Philadelphia Athletics. However, after Flick appeared in 11 games with the Athletics that spring, a court order prohibited him and Lajoie from playing for any team other than the Phillies in the city of Philadelphia, making them ineligible to appear in any of their new team's home games. The two men circumvented that ruling, though, by signing with Cleveland—an action that kept them off the field only when the Naps traveled to the City of Brotherly Love.

Despite being limited to only 110 games in 1902 by the legal machinations that took place during the early stages of the campaign, the left-handed hitting Flick, who usually batted either first or third in the Cleveland lineup, had a solid year for the Naps, hitting .297, with two home runs, 61 RBIs, 70 runs scored, 11 triples, and 20 stolen bases. He followed that up by hitting two homers, driving in 51 runs, scoring 81 times, batting .296, amassing 16 triples, and stealing 24 bases in 1903. Flick then began a string of four straight seasons in which he accumulated at least 17 triples, stole more than 35 bases, and batted over .300, compiling marks of .306, .308, .311, and .302 from 1904 to 1907. Performing particularly well in 1905 and 1906, Flick led the league with 18 triples, a .308 batting average, a .462 slugging percentage, and an OPS of .845 in the first of those campaigns, before batting .311 and topping the circuit with 98 runs

Courtesy of the Bain News Service Collection at the Library of Congress

Elmer Flick led the AL in triples three times
and stolen bases twice while playing for the Indians

scored, 22 triples, and 39 steals the following year. Flick's league-leading mark of .308 in 1905 remained the lowest average compiled by a batting champion until 1968, when Carl Yastrzemski won the AL batting title with an average of .301.

Although Flick stood approximately 5′8″ tall and weighed only 165 pounds, he had good extra-base power, which, combined with his outstanding speed, enabled him to annually rank among the league leaders in triples. He also possessed a strong throwing arm, compiling more than 20 outfield assists on five separate occasions over the course of his career. In discussing Flick in the *St. Petersburg Times* years later, Branch Rickey recalled, "I remember him well from my early years as an American League catcher with St. Louis and New York. Flick, then playing for Cleveland, was an outstanding hitter. We couldn't get him out. He was a flash on the bases, an adroit right fielder and one of the finest gentlemen then in the game."

Yet, in spite of his outstanding play, Flick remained dissatisfied with his situation in Cleveland, developing a distaste for the southern cooking he found himself being exposed to during spring training, and developing even more of an aversion for the hot eastern road trips the Naps made during the regular season. Flick's unhappiness prompted team management to consider trading him to the Detroit Tigers on two separate occasions, once for abrasive 21-year-old outfielder Ty Cobb. But, both times, the Naps decided not to part with Flick.

While southern cuisine and eastern travel both contributed to Flick's growing discontentment, the outfielder eventually found himself being troubled much more by his failing health. In a revealing article published in the July 22, 1907, issue of the *Cleveland Press*, Flick disclosed that "playing the game day in and day out was ruining his health," that he was "on the verge of physical collapse," and that "the time of his retirement was not far distant." Less than eight months later, Flick came down with a gastrointestinal illness that caused him to miss almost the entire 1908 season, and most of the next two seasons as well. He lost weight, his power and speed diminished, and the pain became so severe that, at times, he thought he didn't have very much longer to live. Flick later admitted, "My last three years with the Naps were awful. I shouldn't have played at all." Although Flick's doctors initially found it difficult to identify the source of his discomfort, he later revealed that they claimed he suffered from acute gastritis, which forced him to take pills for the rest of his life.

After Flick appeared in just 99 games, accumulated only 338 official at-bats, and posted a composite batting average of just .254 from 1908 to 1910, the Naps released him, bringing his major-league career to an end. During his time in Cleveland, Flick amassed 19 home runs, 376 RBIs, 535 runs scored, 1,058 hits, 164 doubles, 106 triples, and 207 stolen bases, batted .299, compiled an on-base percentage of .371, and posted a slugging percentage of .422. Over the course of his career, he hit 48 homers, drove in 756 runs, scored 950 others, collected 1,752 hits, 268 doubles, 164 triples, and 330 stolen bases, batted .313, compiled a .389 on-base percentage, and posted a .445 slugging percentage.

After refusing to report to Kansas City of the American Association following his release by the Naps, Flick spent parts of the next two seasons playing for that league's Toledo Mud Hens, before retiring from baseball and returning to Bedford in 1912. In retirement, Flick farmed, hunted, and raised trotting horses. He also later scouted for the Indians and became involved in selling real estate.

Although the memory of Flick's accomplishments grew increasingly dim in the years that followed, Ty Cobb's passing in 1961 revived interest in the man who the Naps once refused to trade for the Georgia Peach. The renewed attention, in turn, led to Flick being voted into the Hall of Fame by the members of the Veteran's Committee in 1963. During his induction speech, the 87-year-old Flick told the crowd in attendance, "This is a bigger day than I've ever had before. I'm not going to find the words to explain how I feel." Flick lived another eight years, dying from congestive heart failure on January 9, 1971, just two days shy of his 95th birthday. He also suffered from mycosis fungoides, a malignant lymphoma, which contributed to his death.

Indians (Naps) Career Highlights:

Best Season: Flick won his only batting title in 1905, when he led the AL with a mark of .308. He also knocked in 64 runs, scored 72 times, amassed 29 doubles, stole 35 bases, and finished first in the league with 18 triples, a .462 slugging percentage, and an OPS of .845. Nevertheless, Flick compiled slightly better overall numbers the following year, when, appearing in all of his team's games for the only time in his career, he drove in 62 runs, ranked among the league leaders with 194 hits, 34 doubles, 275 total bases, a .311 batting average, a .372 on-base percentage, and a .441 slugging percentage, and topped the circuit with 98 runs scored, 22 triples, and 39 stolen bases.

Memorable Moments/Greatest Performances: During a 6-2 victory over the Chicago White Sox on July 6, 1902, Flick accomplished the rare feat of collecting three triples in one game.

Flick was involved in another rarity less than two weeks later, when he walked five times during a 14-4 win over the Boston Red Sox on July 18.

Notable Achievements:

- Batted over .300 four times.
- Finished in double digits in triples six times, topping 20 three-baggers once (22 in 1906).
- Surpassed 30 doubles twice.

- Stole more than 20 bases six times, topping 30 steals four times and 40 thefts once (41 in 1907).
- Led AL in: batting average once, runs scored once, triples three times, stolen bases twice, slugging percentage once, and OPS once.
- Finished second in AL in: runs scored once, total bases once, stolen bases once, and on-base percentage once.
- Ranks among Indians career leaders in triples (3rd) and stolen bases (6th).
- Elected to Baseball Hall of Fame by members of Veteran's Committee in 1963.

29

ROBERTO ALOMAR
1999 – 2001

One of the finest all-around players of his generation, Roberto Alomar spent most of his peak seasons starring at second base for the Toronto Blue Jays and Baltimore Orioles. Combining outstanding hitting with superb defense and exceptional base-running, Alomar earned eight consecutive All-Star selections, seven Gold Gloves, two Silver Sluggers, and three top-10 finishes in the AL MVP voting while playing for the Blue Jays and Orioles. Continuing to excel in all facets of the game after he arrived in Cleveland in 1999, Alomar earned All-Star and Gold Glove honors in each of his three seasons with the Indians, while also claiming two more Silver Sluggers, two *Sporting News* All-Star nominations, and a pair of top-five finishes in the league MVP balloting. In addition to hitting more than 20 homers and driving in more than 100 runs twice each for the Tribe, Alomar batted over .300, scored more than 100 runs, and stole more than 30 bases in each of his three seasons with the Indians, leading them to two AL Central titles in the process.

Born in Ponce, Puerto Rico on February 5, 1968, Roberto Velazquez Alomar had baseball in his blood. As the son of former major league infielder Sandy Alomar and the younger brother of big league receiver Sandy Jr., Roberto received exposure to the game at an early age. After growing up in Salinas, Puerto Rico, where he attended Luis Munoz Rivera High School, Alomar signed with the San Diego Padres as a 17-year-old amateur free agent in 1985. He then spent the next three years advancing through San Diego's farm system, winning the California League batting championship in 1986 with a mark of .346, before joining the Padres in 1988. Laying claim to the starting second base job upon his arrival in San Diego, Alomar spent his earliest days in the big leagues playing alongside his older brother and performing under the watchful eye of his father, who served the team as a coach. Having a solid rookie year for the Padres, Alomar hit nine homers, knocked in 41 runs, scored 84 times, batted .266, and stole 24 bases, although, in spite of the excellent range he displayed at second base, he also committed 16 defensive miscues, which represented the second highest total of any NL second sacker.

Continuing to perform somewhat erratically in the field during his sophomore campaign of 1989, Alomar led all players at his position with 28 errors. However, the 21-year-old switch-hitter also developed into an excellent offensive player, batting .295, driving in 56 runs, scoring 82 others, and ranking among the league leaders with 184 hits and 42 stolen bases. In addition to putting up solid numbers again in 1990 (.287, 80 runs scored, and 24 steals), Alomar displayed greater consistency in the field, enabling him to earn the first of his 12 consecutive All-Star nominations.

Included in a four-player trade the Padres completed with the Blue Jays following the conclusion of the 1990 campaign that also sent Joe Carter to Toronto, in exchange for shortstop Tony Fernandez and slugging first baseman Fred McGriff, Alomar subsequently developed into an elite player during his time in Toronto, earning All-Star and Gold Glove honors five straight times, while also finishing in the top 10 of the AL MVP voting on three occasions. Performing particularly well for Toronto in 1993, Alomar led the Blue Jays to their second straight world championship by hitting 17 homers, driving in 93 runs, and ranking among the league leaders with 109 runs scored, 192 hits, 55 stolen bases, and a batting average of .326 during the regular season, before batting .480 and knocking in six runs against Philadelphia in the World Series. Making an extremely favorable impression on new teammate Dave Winfield his first year with the Blue Jays, Alomar drew praise from the future Hall of Famer, who commented, "Everybody can see the skills on the field. He's acrobatic, flamboyant, he's got his style."

After earning his fifth straight Gold Glove with the Blue Jays in 1995 by committing just four errors in 643 total chances, en route to compiling a career-best .994 fielding average and establishing new records for AL second basemen for consecutive errorless games (104) and errorless chances (482), Alomar signed a lucrative free-agent deal with the Baltimore Orioles prior to the start of the 1996 season. Continuing his exceptional all-around play his first year in Baltimore, Alomar established new career highs with 22 homers, 94 RBIs, 132 runs scored, 43 doubles, a .328 batting average, and an OPS of .938, while also teaming up with Cal

Ripken Jr. to give the Orioles the league's best double-play combination. Expressing his admiration for Alomar years later, Ripken Jr. stated, "He is one of the most talented guys I ever played with and against. He was great at the plate and in the field and made plays at second base that I never saw anyone else make."

Yet, in spite of his brilliant play on the field, Alomar found himself being villified by the media and fans everywhere for his actions during an ugly late-season incident that permanently damaged his previously spotless reputation. During a September 27th game against the Blue Jays, Alomar got into a heated exchange with home plate umpire John Hirschbeck over a called third strike. Towards the end of the argument, Alomar showed his disdain for Hirschbeck by spitting in his face. The Baltimore second baseman later attempted to defend his actions by saying that Hirschbeck had uttered a racial slur during the altercation, and that the umpire had become "real bitter" since his son died in 1993 of Adrenoleukodystrophy (ALD), a rare brain disease. Upon hearing this public disclosure of his personal life, Hirschbeck had to be physically restrained from confronting Alomar in the players' locker room.

Alomar's unsavory actions resulted in a five-game suspension at the start of the 1997 season. He attempted to restore his tarnished image by donating $50,000 to ALD research, while also burying the hatchet with Hirschbeck prior to the start of an April 22, 1997 contest by standing at home plate and shaking hands with the umpire in front of the crowd. But, in spite of his efforts, Alomar's popularity throughout the league waned, and he never again felt comfortable in the city of Baltimore. Although Alomar played well for the Orioles over the course of the next two seasons, earning two more All-Star selections and another Gold Glove, he appeared to be badly in need of a change in scenery after batting just .282 and driving in only 56 runs in 1998.

With Alomar becoming a free agent again following the conclusion of the 1998 campaign, he decided to join his older brother, Sandy Jr., in Cleveland. Inspired by his new surroundings, Alomar put together arguably the finest all-around season of his career. In addition to winning his third Silver Slugger by hitting 24 homers, driving in 120 runs, leading the league with 138 runs scored, batting .323, collecting 182 hits and 40 doubles, stealing 37 bases, and walking 99 times, Alomar earned his eighth Gold Glove by committing only six errors in the field all year, with his superb play also earning him a third-place finish in the AL MVP voting. He followed that up with another outstanding performance in 2000, hitting 19 homers. knocking in 89 runs, scoring 111 times, batting .310, amassing 189 hits and 40 doubles, and finishing second in the league with 39 stolen bases, en route to earning the last of his four Silver Sluggers. Meanwhile, Alomar again earned Gold Glove honors by teaming up with Omar Vizquel to form arguably the greatest double-play combination in the history of the game.

As exceptional an offensive player as the six-foot, 185-pound Alomar proved to be over the course of his career, perhaps his greatest strength lay in his defense. Blessed with superb range, sure hands, a powerful throwing arm, and the quickness of a gazelle, Alomar had the ability to turn apparent base hits into outs in any number of ways. His quickness enabled him to go deep into the hole, dive for the ball, rise to his feet in the blink of an eye, whirl, and toss out the incredulous batter at first base. Meanwhile, his tremendous athleticism and strong throwing arm allowed him to field balls behind second base and fire laser beams to first, depriving many an opposing batter of an apparent hit.

Alomar had another sensational year for the Indians in 2001, earning a fourth-place finish in the AL MVP balloting and the last of his 10 Gold Gloves by hitting 20 homers, driving in 100 runs, stealing 30 bases, and ranking among the league leaders with 113 runs scored, 193 hits, 12 triples, a .336 batting average, a .415 on-base percentage, and an OPS of .956, while also committing only five errors in the field, en route to leading all players at his position with a .993 fielding percentage. However, the 2001 campaign ended up being Alomar's last in Cleveland. With the Indians in a rebuilding mode, they elected to trade the 34-year-old second baseman to the New York Mets for outfielders Matt Lawton and Alex Escobar, pitcher Jerrod Riggan, and two players to be named later on December 11, 2001. Alomar left Cleveland having hit 63 homers, driven in 309 runs, scored 362 others, accumulated 564 hits, 114 doubles, 17 triples, and 106 stolen bases, batted .323, compiled a .405 on-base percentage, and posted a .515 slugging percentage as a member of the Tribe.

Displaying little passion for the game after he arrived in New York, Alomar failed to perform at the same lofty level for the Mets, prompting them to trade him to the Chicago White Sox midway through the 2003 campaign. Continuing his uninspired play in Chicago, Alomar split the 2004 season between the White Sox and Arizona Diamondbacks, before announcing his retirement early in 2005 after being plagued by back and vision troubles. He ended his career with 210 home runs, 1,134 RBIs, 1,508 runs scored, 2,724 hits, 504 doubles, 80 triples, 474 stolen bases, a .300 batting average, a .371 on-base percentage, and a .443 slugging percentage. Among MLB second basemen, Alomar ranks seventh all-time in assists, eighth in double plays, 15th in putouts, and third in games played.

Although Alomar's unfortunate altercation with John Hirschbeck in 1996 prevented him from gaining admittance to the Baseball Hall of Fame the first time his name appeared on the ballot in 2010, he took his rightful place among the game's immortals the following year, when the members of the BBWAA entered his name on 90 percent of the ballots they cast. Expressing his agreement with that decision, fellow Hall of Famer Orlando Cepeda proclaimed, "I've seen a lot of second basemen in my time. My father played in the Negro Leagues and the Caribbean Winter League, where I saw Cool Papa Bell play. I played with Julian Javier, Felix Millan, and Cookie Rojas. I played against Bill Mazeroski and Joe Morgan. In All-Star games, I saw Rod Carew. As good as they were, none of them were as good as Roberto Alomar. I've been watching baseball for sixty years, and he's the best I've ever seen."

Indians Career Highlights:

Best Season: Although Alomar performed brilliantly his entire time in Cleveland, he played especially well in 1999 and 2001, earning a third-place finish in the AL MVP voting and a Silver Slugger in the first of those campaigns by batting .323, posting an OPS of .955, collecting 182 hits, 40 doubles, 300 total bases, and 37 steals, and establishing career-high marks in home runs (24), RBIs (120), and runs scored (138), with the last figure leading the American League. Equally outstanding in 2001, Alomar earned a fourth-place finish in the MVP balloting by hitting 20 homers, driving in 100 runs, stealing 30 bases, amassing 311 total bases, and ranking among the league leaders with 113 runs scored, 193 hits, 12 triples, a .336 batting average, a .415 on-base percentage, and a career-high OPS of .956. Alomar also won a Gold Glove each season, leading all AL second basemen in fielding percentage both years, with marks of .992 and .993, respectively. While either campaign would have made a good choice, I ultimately settled on 1999 for one reason. Even though the Indians exited the postseason tournament quickly both years, losing to Boston in the ALDS in 1999, before being eliminated by Seattle in the opening round two years later, Alomar performed much better against the Red Sox, batting .368, with three RBIs, four runs scored, four doubles, and two steals, while batting just .190 against the Mariners.

Memorable Moments/Greatest Performances: Alomar came up a double shy of hitting for the cycle on May 7, 1999, homering, tripling, singling, driving in five runs, and scoring twice during a 20-11 come-from-behind victory over the Tampa Bay Devil Rays. The Indians, who trailed by scores of 9-2 and 11-6 earlier in the contest, scored the game's final 14 runs, with Alomar's two-out grand slam in the bottom of the eighth inning putting the finishing touches on their memorable comeback.

Exactly one week later, on May 14, 1999, Alomar led the Indians to a 4-2 win over the Detroit Tigers by going 4-for-5, with a homer, three RBIs, and a stolen base.

Alomar paced the Tribe to a 13-10 victory over the Chicago White Sox on July 31, 1999, by driving in five runs with a pair of homers.

Alomar provided the margin of victory in a 7-6 win over the Baltimore Orioles on September 3, 1999, concluding a two-hit, five-RBI day at the plate with a three-run homer in the top of the seventh inning that drove in the final three runs of the contest.

Alomar proved to be the difference in a 6-2 victory over the Tampa Bay Devil Rays on September 6, 2000, hitting a pair of homers, driving in three runs, and scoring three times.

Alomar starred again just three days later, leading the Indians to a 9-3 rout of the White Sox on September 9, 2000, by going 4-for-5, with three doubles, three RBIs, and two runs scored.

Alomar had the only 5-for-5 day of his career on July 3, 2001, when he led the Indians to a convincing 9-1 win over the Boston Red Sox by hitting safely in all five of his trips to the plate.

Alomar had an extremely productive day at the plate against Texas on August 12, 2001, leading the Indians to a 13-2 pasting of the Rangers by going 3-for-5, with a double, triple, four RBIs, and three runs scored.

Notable Achievements:

- Hit more than 20 home runs twice.
- Knocked in more than 100 runs twice, topping 120 RBIs once (120 in 1999).

Courtesy of Sportsmemorabilia.com

Roberto Alomar earned All-Star and Gold Glove honors
in each of his three seasons with the Indians

- Scored more than 100 runs three times, topping 130 runs scored once (138 in 1999).
- Batted over .300 three times, topping the .320-mark twice.
- Finished in double digits in triples once (12 in 2001).
- Surpassed 30 doubles three times, topping 40 two-baggers twice.
- Stole more than 30 bases three times.
- Compiled on-base percentage in excess of .400 twice.
- Posted slugging percentage in excess of .500 twice.
- Led AL in runs scored once and sacrifice flies once.
- Finished second in AL in triples once and stolen bases once.
- Finished third in AL with batting average of .336 in 2001.

- Led AL second basemen in assists once and fielding percentage twice.
- Holds Indians career record for highest successful stolen base percentage (86.89%).
- Ranks among Indians career leaders in: batting average (tied-6th), on-base percentage (tied-5th), slugging percentage (9th), and OPS (8th).
- Two-time Silver Slugger winner (1999 and 2000).
- Three-time Gold Glove winner (1999, 2000, and 2001).
- Finished in top five of AL MVP voting twice (1999 and 2001).
- Two-time *Sporting News* All-Star selection (1999 and 2000).
- Three-time AL All-Star (1999, 2000, and 2001).
- Elected to Baseball Hall of Fame by members of BBWAA in 2011.

30

JEFF HEATH

1936 – 1945

Hindered by his own immaturity, a poor attitude, and a terrible temper, Jeff Heath never quite reached the level of excellence for which he appeared headed when he first arrived in Cleveland in 1936. His own worst enemy, Heath dwelled on the negative and fought with fans, reporters, and teammates alike, preventing him from focusing on the game the way he needed to in order to fulfill his enormous potential. Nevertheless, the talented outfielder still managed to compile a batting average in excess of .300 four times, surpass 20 home runs and 100 RBIs twice each, amass more than 30 doubles four times, and accumulate more than 10 triples three times as a member of the Indians, becoming in 1941 the first American League player to top 20 homers, 20 triples, and 20 doubles in the same season. Once described by Indians manager Oscar Vitt as "the best natural hitter I've seen since Joe Jackson," Heath ended up earning one top-10 finish in the AL MVP voting and two All-Star selections during his time in Cleveland. Yet, had Heath not been plagued by personal demons throughout his career, he likely would have accomplished so much more.

Born in Fort William, Ontario, Canada on April 1, 1915, John Geoffrey Heath moved with his parents to Victoria, British Columbia at the age of one, before the family finally settled in Seattle, Washington seven months later. Establishing himself as an outstanding all-around athlete while attending local Garfield High School, Heath excelled on the baseball diamond as an outfielder and also earned All-City honors in football as a fullback. But, after sustaining numerous injuries to his ankles and knees while competing on the gridiron, Heath ultimately chose to pursue a career in baseball, turning down scholarship offers from several major universities, including Oregon, California, and Alabama.

After graduating from Garfield High in 1934, Heath spent two semesters studying business administration at the University of Washington, before signing with the Yakima Indians of the semi-pro Northwest League. Having compiled a batting average of .390 in 75 games with Yakima, the left-handed hitting Heath subsequently signed with the Cleveland Indians, in whose farm system he spent most of the next two seasons, although he also appeared in a total of 32 games at the major-league level over the course of the 1936 and 1937 campaigns.

Arriving in Cleveland to stay in 1938, Heath laid claim to the Indians starting left field job during spring training, with one columnist writing: "Vitt finally decided to use Jeff Heath, the chap with the bulging muscles, in his left pasture. There are few better hitters in the American League than the husky from Washington. Jeff is not the most graceful ball-hawk in captivity, and he may toss to the wrong base, but, put a bat in his hands, and the opposition's pitcher will tremble."

Living up to his advanced billing, Heath performed exceptionally well for the Indians as a rookie, hitting 21 homers, driving in 112 runs, scoring 104 times, finishing second in the league with a batting average of .343, and topping the circuit with 18 triples. Already being referred to as "The Natural" and "a future Hall of Famer" by several Cleveland sportswriters by season's end, Heath had all the physical tools to fulfill that prophecy. A muscular 5'11", 200-pounder with broad shoulders and a thick neck, Heath drove the ball well to all parts of the ball park with his powerful left-handed swing. He also possessed good speed on the base paths, a strong throwing arm, and did a solid job in the outfield.

Yet, in spite of his immense physical talent, Heath failed to maintain the same level of offensive production in either of the next two seasons. After missing the first few weeks of the 1939 campaign due to a lengthy hold-out, he finished the year with a .292 batting average and just 14 home runs, 69 RBIs, and 64 runs scored. Believing that those numbers represented a departure from the norm, Heath proclaimed prior to the start of the 1940 season, "I'm going to show 'em I'm no flash in the pan. Last year, I was over-swinging and taking my eye off the ball. I'm not going to do that this season." However, Heath ended up suffering through a horrendous 1940 campaign in which he batted just .219, with only 14 homers, 50 RBIs, and 55 runs scored.

Heath's poor performance, coupled with his questionable behavior off the playing field, prompted the local scribes to label him a troublemaker. In addition to annoying several of his teammates with his constant demands for more money, Heath developed an increasingly contentious relationship with the fans and sportswriters, with his legendary temper often getting the best of him.

The first such instance took place on August 27, 1939, when, after striking out against Boston's Denny Galenhouse, Heath threw his bat in frustration. With his lumber subsequently landing in one of the nearby box seats and glancing off *Cleveland Press* editor Lou Seltzer, home plate umpire Bill McGowan ejected Heath from the contest. Returning to the Cleveland dugout, an irate Heath got into a fist-fight with teammate Johnny Broacca. The very next day, after Heath fouled out on a 3-0 pitch he should have taken, a fan yelled, "Why don't you throw your bat in the stands again?" In response, the temperamental outfielder charged the man and punched him in the chest.

Heath also feuded with Cleveland sportswriter Ed McAuley, who he threatened with physical violence after the latter wrote that he lacked team spirit and did not always hustle. Meanwhile, roommate Bob Feller revealed that Heath once knocked out with one punch a cameraman who offended him.

Putting aside those many distractions, Heath returned to top form in 1941, earning an eighth-place finish in the AL MVP voting and the first of his two All-Star selections by ranking among the league leaders in nine different offensive categories, including home runs (24), RBIs (123), batting average (.340), hits (199), total bases (343), and triples (20), topping the circuit in the last category. Extremely impressed with Heath's spirited play, new Indians manager Roger Peckinpaugh went against common opinion when he suggested, "If every man on this ball club showed the determination and hustle that Jeff Heath has shown me, we'd be so far ahead you'd think we were in another league."

Heath's dark side surfaced once again, though, after he hit just 10 homers, knocked in only 76 runs, and batted just .278 in 1942, with the enigmatic outfielder subsequently blaming his decline in offensive production on the vast dimensions of Cleveland Municipal Stadium. However, Indians player-manager Lou Boudreau, who replaced Peckinpaugh at the helm prior to the start of the campaign, laid the blame squarely on

Heath's shoulders, telling *Baseball Digest* in 1943 that his left-fielder did not always deliver maximum effort, or work hard enough, and that he tended to give up once he became frustrated, claiming that, on one occasion, he let a ball drop in front of him without making any effort to catch it.

Excused from military duty due to problems with his knees, Heath remained in Cleveland during the nation's involvement in World War II, earning his second All-Star selection in 1943, when he batted .274, hit 18 homers, and knocked in 79 runs, in only 118 games. Limited by injuries to just 60 games in 1944, Heath hit only five homers and drove in just 33 runs, although he compiled an impressive batting average of .331. After missing the first 40 games of the ensuing campaign while holding out for more money, Heath went on to post solid numbers for the Tribe, finishing the year with 15 home runs, 61 RBIs, and a .305 batting average. But, with team management having grown weary of Heath's contentious personality, the Indians elected to trade the 30-year-old outfielder to the Washington Senators for fellow outfielder George Case on December 14, 1945. Heath left Cleveland with career totals of 122 home runs, 619 RBIs, 546 runs scored, 1,040 hits, 194 doubles, 83 triples, and 52 stolen bases, a lifetime batting average of .298, an on-base percentage of .366, and a slugging percentage of .506.

Reporting on Heath's acquisition by the Senators, the Associated Press wrote:

> "Heath's performance may be the key to the Senators' fate. The husky Canadian is the kind of slugger Washington was crying for last fall. He can break up a ball game with one mighty swish of his bat but, to put it mildly, there always has been an uncertain quality about him. Big Jeff was dissatisfied in Cleveland, didn't like the ballpark, didn't like the management, didn't like anything. Still, he has been a most valuable hitter, perhaps one of the best in the game when he is settled down to business."

Heath ended up remaining in Washington for less than three months before he wore out his welcome there as well. Dealt to the St. Louis Browns midway through the 1946 campaign, Heath spent the next year-and-a-half in St. Louis, posting solid numbers for the Browns in 1947, when he hit 27 homers, knocked in 85 runs, and batted .251. Sold to the Boston Braves during the subsequent offseason, Heath helped the Braves capture the National League pennant in 1948 by hitting 20 homers, driving in 76 runs, and batting .319. However, he broke his leg during the latter stages of the campaign, relegating him to the role of a backup the following year. After being released by the Braves on October 13, 1949, Heath never again appeared in a major league game, ending his career with 194 home runs, 887 RBIs, 777 runs scored, 1,447 hits, 279 doubles, 102 triples, 56 stolen bases, a batting average of .293, a .370 on-base percentage, and a .509 slugging percentage.

Shortly after Heath left Boston, Cleveland sportswriter Franklin Lewis wrote, "There was the inimitable Heath who . . . should have been one of the greatest players in history. But there were no valves on his temper. He grinned in the manner of a schoolboy or he snarled with the viciousness of a tiger."

Two years later, Lewis asked Heath what he would do differently if he had his career to do over again. In response, Heath stated, "I wouldn't gag around as much. I shouldn't have popped off. It's all right for little guys to talk loud, but not a big ox like me."

Reflecting back on Heath's failure to live up to his enormous potential, Bob Feller expressed the belief that his onetime roommate did not take baseball—or life—seriously enough. Meanwhile, Indians pitcher Harry Eisenstat told *The Cleveland Plain Dealer*, "If he'd go oh-for-four, he'd complain that the pitcher wasn't very good. He'd keep talking about it. He dwelled on the negative."

Following his release by Boston, Heath appeared in 57 games for the Pacific Coast League's Seattle Rainiers in 1950, before retiring from professional baseball. He subsequently tried his hand at dairy farming and selling real estate, before returning to the game, first as a scout for the Indians, and, later, as a color commentator for the Rainiers. After suffering a heart attack at only 42 years of age in 1957, Heath lived another 18 years, passing away at the age of 60 on December 9, 1975, following another heart attack. In an obituary that subsequently appeared in the *Cleveland News*, Howard Preston said of Heath, "He was a mixture of gentleness and brute strength, angel and devil, but withal an exciting fellow for what he might have been, as well as for what he was."

Indians Career Highlights:

Best Season: Heath performed exceptionally well as a rookie in 1938, hitting 21 homers, driving in 112 runs, scoring 104 times, finishing second in the AL with a .343 batting average, topping the circuit with 18 triples, and also ranking among the league leaders with a .602 slugging percentage and an OPS of .985. However, he had his finest all-around season in 1941, when he hit 24 homers, amassed 32 doubles, stole a career-high 18 bases, batted .340, compiled a slugging percentage of .586, topped the circuit with 20 triples, and finished second in the league with 123 RBIs, 199 hits, and 343 total bases, with his 24 homers, 20 triples, and 32 doubles making him the first player in American League history to top the 20-mark in all three categories in the same season.

Memorable Moments/Greatest Performances: Heath had his break-out game for the Indians on September 23, 1936, when he went 3-for-5, with a triple, four RBIs, and three runs scored, during a lopsided 17-2 victory over the Chicago White Sox.

Heath had another big day at the plate against Chicago on August 12, 1938, helping to lead the Indians to a 12-9 win over the White Sox by going 4-for-6, with a homer, three RBIs, and three runs scored.

Continuing to feast off Chicago pitching, Heath led the Tribe to an 8-2 win over the White Sox on August 20, 1938, by going 3-for-4, with a homer and a career-high five runs scored.

Heath hit two home runs in one game for the first time in his career 10 days later, reaching the seats twice and driving in four runs during a 10-8 victory over Philadelphia on August 30, 1938.

Heath provided much of the offensive firepower for the Indians during a 5-4 win over the Boston Red Sox on September 17, 1938, going 4-for-4, with a homer and four runs scored.

Heath tied a major-league record on July 25, 1939, when he delivered two pinch hits in one inning during a 12-8 win over the Philadelphia Athletics, contributing to a nine-run rally in the top of the ninth by driving in three runs with a double and a triple.

Heath flexed his muscles on May 25, 1941, when, during a 6-0 win over the St. Louis Browns, he became the first player to homer into the upper deck at Cleveland Municipal Stadium, driving a Johnny Allen offering deep into the right field stands. He finished the game 3-for-4, with a homer, triple, two RBIs, and two runs scored.

Heath led the Indians to an 11-4 victory over the Philadelphia Athletics on August 27, 1941, by driving in a career-high seven runs with a triple and a pair of three-run homers.

Courtesy of Lelands Auctions

In 1941, Jeff Heath became the first AL player to top 20 homers, 20 triples, and 20 doubles in the same season

Heath had a big game against St. Louis on September 21, 1941, going 4-for-5, with a pair of doubles and five RBIs, during a 14-0 pasting of the Browns.

Heath nearly hit for the cycle on May 2, 1942, going 3-for-4, with a double, triple, homer, and five RBIs, during a lopsided 12-3 victory over the Washington Senators.

Heath delivered the decisive blow of a 14-inning, 7-5 win over the Yankees on August 18, 1943, sending the fans at League Park home happy by hitting a game-winning two-run homer off New York reliever Marius Russo in the bottom of the 14th. He finished the game with three hits and five runs batted in.

Notable Achievements:

- Hit more than 20 home runs twice.
- Knocked in more than 100 runs twice.
- Scored more than 100 runs once (104 in 1938).
- Batted over .300 four times, topping the .330-mark on three occasions.
- Finished in double digits in triples three times, accumulating 20 three-baggers in 1941.
- Surpassed 30 doubles four times.
- Topped 20 home runs, 20 triples, and 20 doubles in 1941.
- Compiled on-base percentage in excess of .400 once (.402 in 1944).
- Posted slugging percentage in excess of .500 three times, compiling mark in excess of .600 once (.602 in 1938).
- Led AL in triples twice.
- Finished second in AL in: batting average once, RBIs once, hits once, triples once, and total bases once.
- Ranks fifth in Indians history with 83 career triples.
- Finished in top 10 of AL MVP voting once (8th in 1941).
- Two-time AL All-Star (1941 and 1943).

31

CARLOS BAERGA
1990 – 1996, 1999

A key contributor to the resurgence the Indians experienced during the 1990s, Carlos Baerga proved to be an extremely influential figure during his time in Cleveland. An outstanding team leader, Baerga used his charismatic personality and positive outlook to help alter the mindset of a ball club that had grown accustomed to losing. An excellent player as well, Baerga batted over .300 four times and surpassed 20 home runs and 100 RBIs twice each, en route to earning two Silver Sluggers, three AL All-Star nominations, and a pair of *Sporting News* All-Star selections. And, even though Baerga played for only one pennant-winning Indians team before departing for New York during the latter stages of the 1996 campaign, he left his imprint on a Tribe squad that went on to win five consecutive AL Central titles.

Born in Santurce, Puerto Rico on November 4, 1968, Carlos Obed (Ortiz) Baerga attended Barbara Ann Rooshart High School in Rio Piedras, Puerto Rico, where he starred on the diamond while also competing in the local amateur leagues. After signing with the San Diego Padres on his 17th birthday, Baerga spent the next four years advancing through San Diego's farm system, performing well at each level with the bat, but struggling in the field while splitting his time between second base, shortstop, and third.

Traded to the Indians, along with catcher Sandy Alomar Jr. and outfielder Chris James, in exchange for power-hitting outfielder Joe Carter on December 6, 1989, Baerga arrived in Cleveland having never appeared in a single major-league game. Recalling his thoughts upon learning of the deal that sent him to the Indians, Baerga stated, "When they told me that I got traded with Sandy Alomar and Chris James for Joe Carter, it was something special. A lot went through my mind. I went to spring training, but I never thought that I was going to make the team because Jerry Browne was coming off of a good year. We also had Brooke Jacoby and Felix Fermin, so I thought that I was going back to Triple-A, but they gave me the opportunity."

Baerga spent most of his first season with the Indians filling in at second base and shortstop, hitting seven homers, driving in 47 runs, scoring 46 times, and batting .260, in 108 games and 312 official at-bats. Improving his play dramatically after returning to the team following a brief stint in the minors in early August, Baerga batted .319 in the season's final 41 games, although he performed erratically in the field, committing a total of 17 errors on the year.

After spending the first few months of the 1991 campaign manning third base for the Tribe, Baerga moved to second base during the season's second half, finishing the year with 11 homers, 69 RBIs, a batting average of .288, and a team-leading 80 runs scored. Emerging as a full-fledged star the following year, Baerga earned his first All-Star selection by hitting 20 homers, knocking in 105 runs, scoring 92 times, finishing second in the AL with 205 hits, and also ranking among the leaders with a .312 batting average. Baerga continued his rise to elite status in 1993, earning a 10th-place finish in the AL MVP voting, his second straight trip to the All-Star Game, his first Silver Slugger, and the first of his two *Sporting News* All-Star selections by hitting 21 homers, scoring 105 runs, and ranking among the league leaders with 114 RBIs, 200 hits, and a .321 batting average. By batting over .300 and surpassing 20 home runs, 100 RBIs, and 200 hits for the second consecutive season, the switch-hitting Baerga joined the legendary Rogers Hornsby as the only second basemen in MLB history to reach each of those marks in successive seasons. Looking back at his accomplishment, Baerga said, "Getting two hundred hits with 100 RBIs and a .300 batting average is hard to do. Nobody in the American League had ever done it before, just Rogers Hornsby. For me to be able to do that was something very special."

Although Baerga stood 5'11" tall and weighed only 170 pounds, he possessed good power, driving the ball well to the outfield gaps from both sides of the plate. One of the junior circuit's more difficult men to strike out, Baerga fanned more than 50 times in just six of his 14 big-league seasons. A notorious bad-ball hitter, Baerga also rarely walked, never drawing more than 48 bases on balls in any single campaign. In discussing Baerga's batting skills, former Montreal Expos manager Felipe Alou suggested, "He can get a hit anytime he wants. He has a base-hit swing. He has a bat that knows how to get a hit."

Baerga also proved to be a somewhat underrated defender. Although he never developed into one of the league's top glove men at his position, typically committing somewhere between 15 and 20 errors a season, he had good range and quickness, leading all AL second sackers in assists three times, putouts twice, and double plays turned once.

Meanwhile, Baerga developed a reputation before long for his dedication to his profession and willingness to play hurt, with Texas Rangers catcher Ivan Rodriguez saying of his fellow countryman, "He likes to play baseball hard. He plays every day. He can play sore; he can play hurt. And he's a man who hits three hundred every year."

Baerga, who his teammates called "Papi" because of his paternal instincts, also became known for his exceptional leadership ability, particularly among the Latin ball players. In showing his support for his teammate, Candy Maldonado noted, "Besides being the star player he has become, he is a superstar away from the field. . . . He has been blessed with the ability not only to play, but also to communicate and have the charisma to attract people who are going to contribute to his plans and to things he wants to do."

A leader of Latin players on other teams as well, Baerga drew praise from Orlando Merced of the Pittsburgh Pirates, who claimed that he played in the Puerto Rican winter league in 1995-96 solely because of Baerga, stating, "I didn't play in Puerto Rico for five years. He got the message across to me that 'people in Puerto Rico really want to see you play.' He talked to me, and I realized the people there need to see my playing."

Indians manager Mike Hargrove also held Baerga in high esteem, suggesting, "He's more than just a leader of the Latin players. All of the players look up to Carlos."

Baerga continued to perform extremely well for the Indians in 1994, concluding the strike-shortened campaign with 19 home runs, 80 RBIs, 81 runs scored, a .314 batting average, and a career-high 32 doubles, earning in the process his second straight Silver Slugger. He followed that up with another big year in 1995, helping the Indians capture their first pennant since 1954 by hitting 15 homers, driving in 90 runs, scoring 87 others, and batting .314, with his outstanding play earning him *Sporting News* All-Star honors for the second time and his third and final All-Star selection.

Baerga then helped the Indians advance to the World Series, which they lost to the Atlanta Braves in six games, by homering once, knocking in four runs, and batting .400 against Seattle in the ALCS.

The 1995 campaign ended up being Baerga's last full season in Cleveland. Displaying a somewhat lackadaisical attitude following the Tribe's loss to Atlanta in the Fall Classic, Baerga subsequently spent many of his evenings drinking and partying until all hours of the night in the local discos, causing him to report to 1996 spring training out of shape. Often seen speaking on his cell phone during batting practice, Baerga further angered team management by getting off to an extremely slow start. After hitting just 10 homers, driving in only 55 runs, and batting just .267 through the season's first 100 games, Baerga found himself headed to New York when the Indians traded him and infielder Alvaro Espinosa to the Mets for infielders Jeff Kent and Jose Vizcaino on July 29, 1996.

Shocked and disappointed to be leaving Cleveland, Baerga had a difficult time resigning himself to playing for a poor Mets team. Further hampered by knee problems that plagued him throughout the remainder of his career, Baerga never regained his power stroke. Although he improved his performance somewhat his last two years in New York after batting just .193 for the Mets during the final two months of the 1996 campaign, Baerga failed to recapture his earlier glory, prompting New York to allow him to file for free agency at the end of 1998. After signing with the San Diego Padres, Baerga spent the rest of his playing career serving as a back-up for five different major-league teams, one independent league ball club, and one team in the Korean League, returning to Cleveland briefly for a second tour of duty in 1999. Experiencing his greatest amount of success during that time with Arizona in 2003, Baerga batted .343 and knocked in 39 runs, in just 207 official at-bats with the Diamondbacks, before announcing his retirement two years later after spending 2005 with the Washington Nationals. Baerga ended his career with 134 home runs, 774 RBIs, 731 runs scored, 1,583 hits, 279 doubles, 17 triples, 59 stolen bases, a .291 batting average, a .332 on-base percentage, and a .423 slugging percentage. During his time in Cleveland, he hit 104 homers, knocked in 565 runs, scored 549 times, accumulated 1,097 hits, 190 doubles, 15 triples, and 49 stolen bases, batted .299, compiled a .339 on-base percentage, and posted a .444 slugging percentage.

Since retiring as an active player, Baerga has assumed the position of color commentator for Monday Night Baseball's ESPN Dos telecasts. He

Courtesy of George Kitrinos

Carlos Baerga is one of only two second basemen
in MLB history to bat over .300 and surpass 20 homers,
100 RBIs, and 200 hits in consecutive seasons

also appears as an analyst on Beisbol Esta Noche on ESPN Deportes and
on ESPN Latin America.

Indians Career Highlights:

Best Season: Although Baerga appeared to be on the verge of establishing career-high marks in several offensive categories before a player's strike brought the 1994 season to a premature end, he compiled the best overall numbers of his career in 1993, concluding the campaign with 21 homers, 105 runs scored, 303 total bases, and an OPS of .840, finishing second in the league with 200 hits, and ranking among the leaders with 114 RBIs and a .321 batting average.

Memorable Moments/Greatest Performances: Baerga helped lead the Indians to a 12-7 victory over the Yankees on September 20, 1990, by going 4-for-5, with a triple, three doubles, three RBIs, and three runs scored.

Although the Indians suffered a 10-7 defeat at the hands of the Oakland Athletics on July 23, 1991, Baerga had the only 5-for-5 day of his career, collecting a double and four singles, driving in one run, and scoring three times during the loss.

Baerga once again starred in defeat on April 11, 1992, collecting six hits during a 7-5, 19-inning loss to the Boston Red Sox.

Baerga defeated Kansas City almost single-handedly on July 19, 1992, going 4-for-5, with a homer, double, and three RBIs, during a 4-3 win over the Royals, with his RBI single in the top of the ninth inning driving in the game's winning run.

Baerga again came up big in the clutch for the Indians on August 26, 1992, when his two-run double in the top of the 10th inning drove in the decisive runs of a 6-3 win over Seattle.

Baerga made history on April 8, 1993, when, during a 15-5 trouncing of the Yankees, he became the first player in major-league history to homer from both sides of the plate in the same inning. Accomplishing the feat in the seventh inning of the contest, Baerga first reached the seats against left-hander Steve Howe, before driving an offering from right-hander Steve Farr out of the ball park later in the frame. Baerga, who finished the game 4-for-5, with three RBIs and four runs scored, later said, "The two home runs in the same inning was special because it was against the Yankees, which was a team I wanted to beat all the time. When I hit the second one, I never knew it was a record. There were so many great switch hitters before me, like Eddie Murray and Mickey Mantle, I figured one of them had done it. It was special. I got the two balls after the ball game, and they put it on the scoreboard and I thought, 'Wow, I just did something no one has ever done before.'"

Baerga had perhaps his greatest day at the plate during a 9-5 loss to the Detroit Tigers on June 17, 1993, hitting three homers and driving in five runs.

Baerga led the Indians to a 9-5 victory over the Oakland Athletics on July 20, 1993, by going 3-for-5, with a homer, five RBIs, and three runs scored.

Baerga gave the Indians an 8-6 win over the Milwaukee Brewers on August 12, 1993, by hitting a three-run homer in the top of the 11th inning.

Notable Achievements:

- Hit more than 20 home runs twice.
- Knocked in more than 100 runs twice.
- Scored more than 100 runs once (105 in 1993).
- Batted over .300 four times, topping the .320-mark once (.321 in 1993).
- Surpassed 200 hits twice.
- Topped 30 doubles twice.
- Posted slugging percentage in excess of .500 once (.525 in 1994).
- Finished second in AL in hits twice and sacrifice flies once.
- Led AL second basemen in: assists three times, putouts twice, and double plays once.
- Ranks third in Indians history with 48 career sacrifice flies.
- Hit three home runs in one game vs. Detroit Tigers on June 17, 1993.
- First player in MLB history to switch-hit home runs in same inning (vs. Yankees on 4/8/93).
- Finished 10th in 1993 AL MVP voting.
- Two-time Silver Slugger winner (1993 and 1994).
- Two-time *Sporting News* All-Star selection (1993 and 1995).
- Three-time AL All-Star (1992, 1993, and 1995).
- 1995 AL champion.

32

TRAVIS HAFNER
2003 – 2012

One of the American League's most feared hitters before injuries brought his days as a premier slugger to an end, Travis Hafner spent his first four full seasons in Cleveland serving as the Indians' primary power threat. Averaging 32 home runs and 109 RBIs for the Tribe from 2004 to 2007, the massive designated hitter topped 40 homers once and 100 RBIs four straight times, en route to earning two top-10 finishes in the AL MVP voting. Hafner also batted over .300 three times and led the league in slugging percentage and OPS once each, establishing himself in the process as one of the junior circuit's most potent batsmen. An outstanding run-producer, Hafner performed especially well with men on base, exhibiting his ability to excel in such situations in 2006, when he tied a major-league record by hitting six grand slam home runs.

Born in Jamestown, North Dakota on June 3, 1977, Travis Lee Hafner grew up on a farm in Wells County, where he attended tiny Sykeston High School, which didn't have a baseball team. Unable to participate in his favorite sport, Hafner instead concentrated on developing his basketball skills, earning All-Region honors on the hardwood, while also excelling in the discus and triple jump in track and field. After enrolling at Cowley County Community College in Arkansas City, Kansas following his graduation, Hafner spent the next two years starring at first base for the school's baseball team, prompting the Texas Rangers to select him in the 31st round of the 1996 MLB Draft. Hafner, though, elected to return to college for one more year, before beginning his pro career in the Texas organization after leading Cowley County to the JUCO World Series championship in 1997.

His path to the majors blocked by fellow first baseman Rafael Palmeiro, Hafner ended up spending the better part of the next six seasons in the minor leagues, before finally arriving in Texas in August 2002. Garnering 62 official at-bats over the final two months of the campaign, Hafner batted .242, knocked in six runs, and hit his first big-league homer, while serving the Rangers primarily as a DH and pinch-hitter.

Included in a four-player trade the Rangers completed with the Indians during the subsequent off-season that also sent Aaron Myette to Cleveland, in exchange for Einar Diaz and Ryan Drese, Hafner soon acquired the nickname "Pronk," which represented a combination of the monikers "Project" (which the coaching staff considered him to be), and "Donkey" (which referred to the manner in which he rumbled around the bases like a donkey). Taking everything in stride, the 6'3", 240-pound Hafner enjoyed the camaraderie of the Cleveland clubhouse and voiced no objections to the derisive remarks directed towards him that made him out to be a dumb jock, even sporting a t-shirt at times that said, "I'm not very smart, but I can lift heavy things."

Taking over at first base for the departed Jim Thome upon his arrival in Cleveland, Hafner posted decent numbers as a rookie, concluding the 2003 campaign with a .254 batting average, 14 homers, and 40 RBIs, although an injured foot limited him to only 91 games, half of which he spent at the DH position. Looking back at his first year with the Indians, Hafner recalled, "Everyone made a big deal of me replacing him [Thome]. I know that you can't replace a guy like that. I was just focused on establishing myself as a major leaguer."

Serving the Indians almost exclusively as a designated hitter the following year, Hafner had a breakout season, hitting 28 homers, driving in 109 runs, scoring 96 times, batting .311, and compiling an OPS of .993, despite playing the second half with bone spurs in his right elbow that needed to be surgically removed at season's end. He followed that up with a similarly productive 2005 campaign in which he hit 33 homers, knocked in 108 runs, scored 94 others, batted .305, and finished third in the league with a .408 on-base percentage and a .595 slugging percentage, earning in the process a fifth-place finish in the AL MVP voting.

Even though Hafner's slowness afoot and lack of agility in the field forced the Indians to employ him primarily as a DH, his patience at the plate and prodigious power made him a tremendous asset to them on offense. Possessing a keen batting eye, Hafner rarely offered at bad pitches, enabling him to draw more than 100 bases on balls two different times.

Meanwhile, his incredibly strong forearms, wrists, and hands allowed him to wait longer than most batters before starting his swing, giving him the ability to drive the ball out of any part of the park.

Hafner continued his assault on AL pitching in 2006, finishing third in the league with 42 homers, driving in 117 runs, scoring 100 times, batting .308, topping the circuit with a .659 slugging percentage and an OPS of 1.097, and becoming just the second player in MLB history to hit as many as six grand slams in a season, with his outstanding performance earning him an eighth-place finish in the MVP balloting. Although his batting average slipped to .266 the following year, Hafner had another extremely productive season, hitting 24 homers, knocking in 100 runs, scoring 80 others, and posting an OPS of .837.

Unfortunately, the 2007 campaign ended up being Hafner's last as a true offensive force. Plagued by a sore right shoulder in subsequent seasons that forced him to miss a significant amount of playing time, Hafner never regained his power stroke. Further hampered by back, knee, foot, ankle, and hand injuries, the one-time slugger appeared in more than 100 games for the Tribe just once between 2008 and 2012, totaling just 59 home runs and 214 RBIs over the course of those five seasons, before signing with the Yankees as a free agent following the conclusion of the 2012 campaign when the Indians declined to pick up the option on his contract. Hafner left Cleveland having hit 200 homers, driven in 688 runs, scored 582 times, amassed 1,039 hits, 238 doubles, and 11 triples, batted .278, compiled a .382 on-base percentage, and posted a .509 slugging percentage as a member of the team.

Hafner spent just one year in New York, hitting 12 homers, driving in 37 runs, and batting .202 for the Yankees in a part-time role in 2013, before announcing his retirement after becoming a free agent again at season's end. Over parts of 12 big-league seasons, he hit 213 homers, knocked in 731 runs, scored 619 times, accumulated 1,107 hits, 250 doubles, and 13 triples, batted .273, compiled a .382 on-base percentage, and posted a .509 slugging percentage.

After retiring as an active player, Hafner became a volunteer assistant coach at the University of Notre Dame. More recently, he accepted a position with the Indians as a special assistant in both player development and scouting. In addition to evaluating players for the draft, free agency, and trades, Hafner works with Cleveland minor league hitters, primarily during spring training.

Indians Career Highlights:

Best Season: Hafner posted big numbers for the Indians in both 2004 and 2005, finishing the first of those seasons with 28 homers, 109 RBIs, 96 runs scored, a batting average of .311, and an OPS of .993, before hitting 33 homers, driving in 108 runs, scoring 94 times, compiling a batting average of .305, and posting an OPS of 1.003 the following year. Nevertheless, the 2006 campaign would have to be considered the finest of his career. In addition to batting .308, scoring 100 runs, and ranking among the league leaders with 42 homers, 117 RBIs, 100 walks, and a .439 on-base percentage, Hafner topped the circuit with a slugging percentage of .659 and an OPS of 1.097, earning in the process one of his two top-10 finishes in the AL MVP voting. Furthermore, Hafner became the first player in MLB history to hit five grand slam home runs before the All-Star break, en route to tying the all-time single-season mark of six previously set by Don Mattingly in 1987.

Memorable Moments/Greatest Performances: Hafner had one of his greatest days at the plate on August 14, 2003, when he hit for the cycle, knocked in two runs, and scored three times during an 8-3 victory over the Twins in Minnesota.

Hafner had another huge game on July 20, 2004, when he homered three times, singled, and knocked in six runs during a 14-5 win over the Angels in Anaheim.

Some two weeks later, on August 4, 2004, Hafner led the Indians to a 14-5 rout of the Toronto Blue Jays by going 4-for-5, with a pair of homers, a double, six RBIs, and three runs scored.

Hafner celebrated Independence Day in 2005 by going 4-for-5, with two homers, five RBIs, and three runs scored, during a 9-3 pasting of the Detroit Tigers.

Exactly one year later, on July 4, 2006, Hafner led a 19-1 massacre of the Yankees by homering twice, driving in four runs, and scoring four times.

Hafner hit a number of memorable home runs during his time in Cleveland, with the first of those coming on July 19, 2004, when his three-run homer off Troy Percival in the top of the 10th inning gave the Indians an 8-5 win over the Anaheim Angels.

Hafner delivered another game-winning blast on June 28, 2005, when his grand slam homer in the top of the ninth inning off Boston closer Keith Foulke gave the Tribe a 12-8 win over the Red Sox.

Hafner again came up big in the clutch on August 30, 2006, bringing the Indians even with Toronto at 2-2 in the bottom of the eighth inning with his second solo homer of the contest. The Tribe won the game by a score of 3-2 two frames later on a walk-off homer by Jhonny Peralta.

Hafner provided further heroics on September 4, 2007, when his two-run homer off Minnesota closer Joe Nathan in the top of the 11th inning gave the Indians a 7-5 win over the Twins.

Hafner continued to come through in pressure situations in that year's postseason, driving in the winning run of a 2-1 victory over the Yankees in Game Two of the 2007 ALDS (also known as the "bug game") with a bases loaded single off Luiz Vizcaino in the bottom of the 11th inning.

Hafner delivered perhaps his most memorable hit, though, on July 7, 2011, when his grand slam homer off Luis Perez in the bottom of the ninth inning gave the Indians a 5-4, walk-off win over the Toronto Blue Jays.

Notable Achievements:

- Hit more than 20 home runs four times, topping 30 homers twice and 40 homers once.
- Knocked in more than 100 runs four times.
- Scored more than 100 runs once.
- Batted over .300 three times.
- Topped 30 doubles three times, surpassing 40 two-baggers twice.
- Drew more than 100 bases on balls twice.
- Compiled on-base percentage in excess of .400 three times.
- Posted slugging percentage in excess of .500 three times, topping the .600-mark once (.659 in 2006).
- Posted OPS in excess of 1.000 twice.
- Led AL in slugging percentage once and OPS once.
- Finished second in AL in on-base percentage once and OPS twice.

Courtesy of Keith Allison

Travis Hafner knocked in more than 100 runs
four straight times for the Indians

- Finished third in AL in: home runs once, on-base percentage twice, and slugging percentage once.
- Holds share of MLB record for most grand slams in a season (six in 2006).
- Ranks among Indians career leaders in home runs (8th) and slugging percentage (10th).
- Hit for cycle vs. Minnesota Twins on August 14, 2003.
- Hit three home runs in one game vs. Anaheim Angels on July 20, 2004.
- Two-time AL Player of the Month.
- Finished in top 10 of AL MVP voting twice, making it into top five once (5th in 2005).

33

SANDY ALOMAR JR.

1990 – 2000

A key member of Indians teams that captured five division titles and two American League pennants, Sandy Alomar Jr. spent 11 seasons in Cleveland, establishing himself during that time as arguably the best catcher in franchise history. Despite being plagued by injuries throughout most of his career, Alomar served as the glue that helped hold together Tribe squads that finished first in the AL Central five straight times from 1995 to 1999, earning in the process six All-Star selections and one Gold Glove. And, in spite of his injuries, Alomar managed to hit more than 20 home runs once, bat over .300 three times, and post a slugging percentage in excess of .500 twice, leaving us to wonder what he might have accomplished had he remained healthy.

Born in Salinas, Puerto Rico on June 18, 1966, Santos (Velazquez) Alomar attended Luis Munoz Rivera High School, before signing with the San Diego Padres as an undrafted free agent. Establishing himself as a top prospect while advancing through San Diego's farm system, Alomar earned *Baseball America* Minor League Player of the Year honors in both 1988 and 1989, although he found his path to the big leagues blocked by Padres catcher Benito Santiago. After appearing in a total of only eight games with the Padres during the latter stages of the previous two campaigns, Alomar finally received his reprieve on December 6, 1989, when the Indians sent power-hitting outfielder Joe Carter to San Diego, in exchange for Alomar, infielder Carlos Baerga, and outfielder Chris James.

Laying claim to the starting job behind home plate as soon as he arrived in Cleveland, the 23-year-old Alomar became the first rookie receiver to start an All-Star game, win a Gold Glove, and be named AL Rookie of the Year. In addition to hitting nine homers, driving in 66 runs, scoring 60 times, collecting 26 doubles, batting .290, and compiling an

OPS of .744, Alomar did an expert job of handling Cleveland's pitching staff. Meanwhile, he often displayed his powerful throwing arm by tossing out attempted base stealers from his knees.

Even though Alomar made the AL All-Star team in 1991 and 1992 as well, he found his playing time and offensive production reduced significantly by a series of injuries that made him the only player in the majors to spend time on the disabled list in each of the next five seasons. After missing much of the 1991 campaign with a rotator cuff injury, Alomar seriously injured his left knee in 1992, limiting him to only 89 games. An injured back then sidelined Alomar for most of the 1993 season, before an assortment of ailments kept him off the field for significant portions of both 1994 and 1995. Still, Alomar performed well for the Indians whenever he took the field in each of the last two seasons, batting .288, hitting 14 homers, and driving in 43 runs, in only 80 games and 292 official at-bats in 1994, before batting an even .300, hitting 10 homers, and knocking in 35 runs, in just 66 games and 203 at-bats the following year.

Choosing to make light of his misfortune, Alomar quipped, "When I won the Rookie of the Year award, everybody referred to [younger brother] Roberto as Sandy's brother. But, since then, I've become known as Roberto's brother."

Acknowledging his older sibling's bad luck, Roberto commented, "It's been real frustrating for Sandy. I know he can do much better than he's done. But he has played through the pain."

Able to remain relatively healthy in 1996, Alomar earned his fourth All-Star selection by hitting 11 homers, knocking in 50 runs, and batting .263. He followed that up with the finest season of his career, helping the Indians capture their second pennant in three years by hitting 21 homers, driving in 83 runs, amassing 37 doubles, batting .324, and posting an OPS of .900, en route to earning his fifth All-Star nomination and a 14th-place finish in the AL MVP voting. Alomar continued his exceptional play in the postseason, delivering one of the most dramatic home runs in franchise history in Game Four of the ALDS, when his game-tying, eighth-inning blast off Yankee closer Mariano Rivera breathed new life into the Indians, who subsequently went on to defeat New York in five games.

Crediting Alomar's greater patience at the plate for his outstanding season, Indians hitting coach Charlie Manuel noted, "He's always been a contact hitter who would chase bad pitches and get himself out. This season, he's working the count more and hitting better pitches harder. Sandy's learning that he's a much better hitter than he thought he was."

The right-handed hitting Alomar, who stood 6'5" tall and weighed 210 pounds, possessed decent power at the plate, although he proved to be more of a gap-to-gap hitter than a true home-run threat over the course of his career. Displaying very little patience as a hitter, Alomar never walked more than 25 times in any single season. However, he also did not strike out very much, never fanning more than 48 times in a season.

Alomar remained the Indians' full-time starting catcher for one more year, batting just .235, hitting only six homers, and driving in just 44 runs in 1998, before missing significant portions of each of the next two seasons with injuries. After concluding the 2000 campaign with seven home runs, 42 RBIs, and a batting average of .289, Alomar signed with the Chicago White Sox as a free agent. He left Cleveland with career totals of 92 home runs, 453 RBIs, 416 runs scored, 944 hits, 194 doubles, and 8 triples, a .277 batting average, a .315 on-base percentage, and a .419 slugging percentage.

Alomar spent parts of the next four seasons with the White Sox, although he also played briefly for the Colorado Rockies in 2002. After becoming a free agent again at the end of 2004, Alomar signed with the Texas Rangers, with whom he spent one season serving as a part-time player, before splitting the next two seasons between the Dodgers, White Sox, and Mets. After appearing in only eight games with the Mets in 2007, Alomar announced his retirement, ending his career with 112 home runs, 588 RBIs, 520 runs scored, 1,236 hits, 249 doubles, 10 triples, a .273 batting average, a .309 on-base percentage, and a .406 slugging percentage.

Named catching instructor for the Mets upon his retirement, Alomar continued to function in that role for two years, before returning to Cleveland as first base coach in 2009. Alomar remained in that position for the next three years, until the Indians promoted him to bench coach prior to the start of the 2012 campaign. He has since returned to the first base coach's box, where he remains a valuable member of manager Terry Francona's coaching staff.

Indians Career Highlights:

Best Season: Alomar had easily his best season for the Indians in 1997, when he established career-high marks in virtually every offensive

Courtesy of George Kitrinos

Sandy Alomar Jr. helped lead the Indians
to five division titles and two AL pennants

category, including home runs (21), RBIs (83), runs scored (63), doubles (37), batting average (.324), on-base percentage (.354), and slugging percentage (.545), putting together at one point during the campaign a 30-game hitting streak that ranks as the second-longest in franchise history. Continuing his success in the postseason, Alomar hit two homers, knocked in five runs, and batted .316 against the Yankees in the ALDS, before hitting another pair of homers, driving in 10 runs, and batting .367 against the Florida Marlins in the World Series. Alomar also earned All-Star Game MVP honors by hitting a two-run homer into the left field bleachers at his home ballpark in the bottom of the seventh inning that gave the American League a 3-1 victory over the NL

Memorable Moments/Greatest Performances: As previously mentioned, Alomar recorded a 30-game hitting streak in 1997—one that lasted from May 25 to July 6, a period during which he went 49-116 (.422), with two homers, 14 doubles, 16 RBIs, and 19 runs scored.

Alomar had his breakout game for the Indians on April 21, 1990, when he homered, doubled, and knocked in five runs during an 8-4 win over the Chicago White Sox.

Alomar helped lead the Indians to a 10-5 victory over the Yankees on May 3, 1990, by going 3-for-4, with five RBIs.

Alomar had another big day at the plate against the Yankees on April 17, 1992, when he went 4-for-5, with a homer, double, three RBIs, and three runs scored, during an 11-1 Indians win.

Alomar hit two home runs in one game for the first of three times as a member of the Indians on July 20, 1995, when he collected three hits, three RBIs, and three runs scored during a 6-3 win over the Texas Rangers.

Alomar delivered many game-winning hits for the Indians through the years, with one of those coming on August 25, 1995, when his solo homer in the bottom of the 11th inning gave the Tribe a 6-5 victory over the Detroit Tigers.

Alomar went on a brief power surge in April 1997, tying a franchise record by homering in five straight games.

Alomar helped lead the Indians to a 15-3 pasting of the Anaheim Angels on April 11, 1997, by going 4-for-5 and scoring a career-high four times.

Alomar feasted off Boston pitching on June 6, 1997, collecting four doubles and scoring twice during a 7-3 victory over the Red Sox.

Alomar helped the Indians overcome an early 9-2 deficit to the Yankees on September 23, 1997, by driving in four runs with a homer and two singles, with his two-out RBI single to center-field in the bottom of the ninth inning giving the Tribe a memorable 10-9 comeback win.

Alomar led the Indians to a 7-2 victory over Minnesota just three days later by driving in four runs with a pair of homers.

Although Alomar struggled at the plate against Baltimore in the 1997 ALCS, he had a huge Game Four, leading the Indians to an 8-7 win by collecting three hits, homering, and driving in four runs, including the game-winner in the bottom of the ninth inning.

Alomar provided further heroics on May 3, 1998, when he gave the Indians a 10-8 win over the Tampa Bay Devil Rays by hitting a grand slam home run off reliever Roberto Hernandez with two men out in the bottom of the ninth inning.

Still, there is little doubt that Alomar experienced the most memorable moment of his career in Game Four of the 1997 ALDS against the Yankees, when his two-out, opposite field solo home run off Mariano Rivera in the bottom of the eighth inning tied the score at 2-2. The Indians, who appeared to be on the verge of elimination, subsequently won the contest in the ensuing frame on an RBI single by Omar Vizquel.

Notable Achievements:

- Hit more than 20 home runs once (21 in 1997).
- Batted over .300 three times, topping the .320-mark once (.324 in 1997).
- Surpassed 30 doubles once (37 in 1997).
- Posted slugging percentage in excess of .500 twice.
- Hit safely in 30 consecutive games from May 25 to July 6, 1997.
- 1990 AL Rookie of the Year.
- 1990 Gold Glove Award winner.
- 1997 All-Star Game MVP.
- Six-time AL All-Star (1990, 1991, 1992, 1996, 1997, and 1998).
- Two-time AL champion (1995 and 1997).

34

GEORGE UHLE
1919 – 1928, 1936

The anchor of Cleveland's starting rotation for nearly a decade, George Uhle proved himself to be a true workhorse from 1921 to 1928, leading all AL hurlers in games started three times and complete games and innings pitched twice each over the course of those eight seasons. Meanwhile, even though Uhle, who Babe Ruth identified as the toughest pitcher he ever faced, spent most of his time in Cleveland pitching for mediocre Indians teams, he won more than 20 games three times, surpassing 25 victories twice, en route to leading the league in that category on two separate occasions. In addition to ranking among the franchise's all-time leaders in wins, innings pitched, complete games, and starts, Uhle excelled as a hitter, compiling a lifetime batting average of .289 that represents the highest mark ever posted by a pitcher who never played another position.

Born in Cleveland, Ohio on September 18, 1898, George Ernest Uhle attended Cleveland West High School, before beginning his career in baseball at the semi-pro level following his graduation. After playing for several teams in the Cleveland area, Uhle took a job at Standard Parts, working for the company during the week and pitching for its ball club on weekends. Looking back at the time he spent with Standard Parts, Uhle recalled, "We were as good as any Double-A or Triple-A club in the minors. We had five former major leaguers, all Clevelanders, playing for us: Jim and Frank Delehanty, Del Young, Glenn Liebhardt, and Heinie Berger."

Granted a tryout with the hometown Indians at 1919 spring training due to Liebhardt's relationship with Cleveland President Ernest Barnard, Uhle made enough of an impression on manager Lee Fohl that he earned a spot on the team's major-league roster, stating years later, "I made them put in the contract that they couldn't send me to the minors. If I wasn't good enough for the majors, I wanted my release. I figured I could do better working at Standard Parts."

The right-handed throwing Uhle, who relied primarily on a fastball and side-arm curve, also made an extremely favorable impression on staff ace Jim Bagby, who told his teammates, "Boys, I want to tell you that we are going to have a mean pitcher in that boy Uhle. I have seen some real stuff in my day, but if that side-arm ball of his does not get him by, I'm going to be a greatly surprised man."

Uhle ended up having a solid rookie year for the Indians, concluding the 1919 campaign with a record of 10-5 and an ERA of 2.91, while working as both a starter and a reliever. However, he struggled terribly the following season, later recalling, "I went ten-to-five that first year, but they began to pound me, and I couldn't get anybody out during the first part of 1920." Informed by Browns' pitcher Urban Shocker that his lack of success stemmed from the fact that he tipped off his pitches to opposing batters with his delivery, Uhle eventually changed his motion to home plate, enabling him to right himself during the season's second half. Nevertheless, he finished the year with a disappointing 4-5 record and an inordinately high 5.21 ERA.

After assuming a regular spot in the starting rotation in 1921, Uhle emerged as one of the team's most reliable pitchers, finishing the season with a record of 16-13, an ERA of 4.01, 13 complete games, and 238 innings pitched. Assuming an even more prominent role the following year, Uhle compiled a record of 22-16 and an ERA of 4.07, led all AL hurlers with 40 starts and five shutouts, and also ranked among the league leaders with 23 complete games and 287⅓ innings pitched. Uhle then established himself as the ace of Cleveland's pitching staff in 1923, when he earned an eighth-place finish in the AL MVP voting by posting a record of 26-16 that gave him the most wins of any pitcher in the league. He also compiled an ERA of 3.77 and topped the circuit in starts (44), complete games (30), and innings pitched (357⅔). Meanwhile, as Uhle rose to prominence among AL hurlers, he also became known as one of the league's best-hitting pitchers, establishing career-high marks in both batting average (.361) and RBIs (22).

Unfortunately, Uhle's heavy workload in 1922 and 1923 adversely affected his performance in each of the next two seasons. Plagued by arm problems in 1924, Uhle missed a significant amount of time, starting only

25 games, and finishing the year just 9-15 with an ERA of 4.77. Although somewhat healthier the following year, Uhle made only 26 starts, compiling a record of 13-11 and an ERA of 4.10.

Fully recovered by the start of the 1926 campaign, Uhle went on to have the finest season of his career. In addition to leading all AL pitchers with 27 victories (he finished 27-11), Uhle placed second in ERA (2.83), strikeouts (159), and shutouts (3), and topped the circuit in winning percentage (.711), complete games (32), innings pitched (318⅓), and starts (36), earning in the process a spot on *The Sporting News* Major League All-Star team. Once again, though, the heavy workload caused Uhle to develop arm problems, limiting him to only 22 starts, 153⅓ innings, and a record of 8-9 in 1927.

Uhle encountered further problems in 1928, when he incurred the wrath of new Indians manager Roger Peckinpaugh by failing to keep himself in top condition. Complaining of discomfort in his right arm due to the pressure being placed on a nerve by a misplaced ligament, Uhle received little sympathy from team management, which countered that his failure to observe training rules caused his arm to lose much of its strength. Suspended for the rest of the season by Peckinpaugh on September 9, Uhle finished the year with a record of 12-17 and an ERA of 4.07. With ill feelings continuing to exist on both sides, the Indians elected to trade Uhle to Detroit for shortstop Jackie Tavener and pitcher Ken Holloway during the subsequent off-season. After making the deal, Cleveland General Manager Billy Evans said, "George wasn't a particularly good influence on one or two other players. If his removal will help them to play better ball, it will add just that much to the advantage we gain by trading him. We had high hopes for Uhle last spring. We gave him an increase of $5,000 over what he made in 1927, thinking that would give him an incentive to go in and pitch. When it didn't, we simply had to quit on him."

Upon learning of the trade, Uhle chose to take the high road, stating, "I've always been an admirer of [Tigers manager] Stanley Harris. A change often does one good, and I'll give my best to the Tigers."

Uhle ended up spending four full seasons in Detroit, before being dealt to the New York Giants during the early stages of the 1933 campaign. During that time, the veteran right-hander compiled an overall record of 44-41 and an ERA of 3.91 for the Tigers, posting double-digit wins for them in each of his first three seasons. While in Detroit, Uhle also discovered

Courtesy of the Bain News Service Collection at the Library of Congress

George Uhle led all AL hurlers in wins twice
during his time in Cleveland

a new pitch, which eventually became known as the slider. After spending most of 1932 working out of the Detroit bullpen, Uhle split the next two seasons between the Giants and Yankees, before spending all of 1935 pitching and coaching for the Toledo Mud Hens of the American Association. He then returned to Cleveland in 1936, appearing in seven games with the Indians, before announcing his retirement at season's end. Uhle finished his career with a record of 200-166, an ERA of 3.99, a WHIP of 1.405, 21 shutouts, 27 saves, 232 complete games, and 1,135 strikeouts in 3,119⅔ innings pitched. As a member of the Indians, he compiled a record of 147-119, an ERA of 3.92, and a WHIP of 1.432, saved 16 games, tossed 16 shutouts and 167 complete games, and recorded 763 strikeouts in 2,200⅓ innings of work.

After retiring as an active player, Uhle spent the next several years serving as a pitching coach, first for the Indians, and later for Buffalo in the International League, the Cubs in the National League, and the Senators back in the AL Following his career in baseball, Uhle remained active, working as a manufacturer's representative for Arrow Aluminum Company until shortly before he lost his 20-year battle with emphysema on February 26, 1985. Uhle was 86 years old at the time of his passing.

Indians Career Highlights:

Best Season: Uhle had a tremendous all-around year for the Indians in 1923, earning an eighth-place finish in the AL MVP voting by leading the league with 26 wins, 30 complete games, 357⅔ innings pitched, and a franchise-record 44 starts, while also establishing career-high marks in batting average (.361), RBIs (22), runs scored (23), hits (52), doubles (10), triples (3), on-base percentage (.391), and slugging percentage (.472) on offense, with his 52 hits representing a single-season record for pitchers. Nevertheless, Uhle experienced his greatest success on the mound in 1926. In addition to leading all AL hurlers in wins (27), winning percentage (.711), complete games (32), innings pitched (318⅓), and starts (36), Uhle finished second in ERA (2.83), strikeouts (159), and shutouts (3), and posted a WHIP of 1.313 that also placed him among the league leaders.

Memorable Moments/Greatest Performances: One of the best hitting pitchers in baseball history, Uhle turned in a number of memorable performances at the plate, with the first of those coming on April 28, 1921, when he collected three hits and a career-high six RBIs during an 18-5 victory over Detroit, driving in four of those runs with a fourth-inning grand slam.

Uhle had another big day on offense against Detroit on June 1, 1923, when he helped pace the Indians to a 17-4 win over the Tigers by going 4-for-4, with three doubles, three RBIs, and four runs scored.

Uhle again helped his own cause on August 19, 1923, when he went 4-for-5, with a pair of doubles and five RBIs, during a 16-3 drubbing of the Philadelphia Athletics.

Although Uhle issued six walks during the contest, he dominated New York's lineup on September 24, 1921, allowing just four harmless singles during a lopsided 9-0 victory over the eventual American League champion Yankees.

Uhle turned in another strong outing against New York on August 22, 1922, yielding just two hits, two walks, and a pair of runs during a 6-2 win over the Yankees.

Uhle had an exceptional all-around game against St. Louis on May 27, 1925, going 2-for-4 at the plate and surrendering only three hits and two unearned runs during a complete-game, 4-2, 10-inning win over the Browns.

Uhle threw a gem against Philadelphia on July 28, 1926, when he allowed just four hits and struck out seven during a 2-0 victory over the Athletics.

Uhle turned in an equally impressive performance against St. Louis on June 26, 1927, yielding just four hits and recording seven strikeouts during a 2-0 win over the Browns.

However, Uhle pitched the greatest game of his career on May 13, 1928, when he surrendered just one walk and a second-inning double to right field by Mickey Cochrane, in defeating the Philadelphia Athletics by a score of 2-0. Uhle also recorded six strikeouts during the contest.

Notable Achievements:

- Won more than 20 games three times, topping 25 victories twice.
- Posted winning percentage in excess of .600 three times, topping .700-mark once (.711 in 1926).
- Compiled ERA under 3.00 twice.
- Threw more than 300 innings twice, topping 275 innings pitched one other time.
- Threw more than 20 complete games three times, completing at least 30 of his starts twice.
- Led AL pitchers in: wins twice, winning percentage once, innings pitched twice, complete games twice, and starts three times.

- Finished second in AL in: ERA once, strikeouts once, and shutouts once.
- Holds Indians single-season record for most starts (44 in 1923).
- Ranks among Indians career leaders in: wins (8th); innings pitched (8th); complete games (6th); and games started (10th).
- Batted over .300 five times.
- Holds highest lifetime batting average (.289) of any pitcher who never played another position.
- Finished eighth in 1923 AL MVP voting.
- 1926 *Sporting News* All-Star selection.
- 1920 AL champion.
- 1920 world champion.

35

JOE VOSMIK
1930 – 1936

An outstanding line drive hitter who spent his first six seasons in the big leagues manning left field for his hometown Cleveland Indians, Joe Vosmik joined Earl Averill during the 1930s in giving the Tribe one of the most formidable outfield tandems in all of baseball. En route to compiling a lifetime batting average of .313 as a member of the Indians, Vosmik batted well over .300 four times, compiling a mark of .348 in 1935 that nearly won him the American League batting title. The hard-hitting outfielder also knocked in more than 100 runs twice, amassed more than 200 hits once, topped 30 doubles four times, and accumulated 20 triples once during his time in Cleveland, leading the AL in each of the last three categories in his banner year of 1935, when he finished third in the league MVP voting. Yet, Vosmik would have accomplished considerably more for the Indians had they not foolishly decided to part ways with him following the conclusion of the 1936 campaign.

Born to Bohemian immigrant parents in Cleveland, Ohio on April 4, 1910, Joseph Franklin Vosmik developed a love of baseball at a very young age. After displaying an interest in the national pastime as an infant, Vosmik spent much of his youth trying to sneak into Dunn Field (later called League Park) to watch the Indians play, recalling years later, "When I was in the fourth grade, I began playing truant to go to the Indians' ball park and watch the big-league players. Soon after, I began finding ways and means of sneaking into the stadium, but, most of the time, I was kicked out as soon as I got in. But I had made up my mind to be a professional ballplayer and nothing discouraged me."

Vosmik began playing semi-pro ball while attending East Tech High School, pitching and manning first base for Ruggles Jewelry at the tender age of 15. Following his graduation from East Tech in 1926, Vosmik moved onto a higher level of competition, joining Rotbart Jewelers in the Cleveland Municipal League, where he gradually transitioned to the outfield. Vosmik received his big break in 1928, when Indians manager Roger Peckinpaugh advised Cleveland GM Billy Evans to sign him after watching him compete in a city league game.

Beginning his professional career one year later with the Class D Frederick (MD) Warriors in the Blue Ridge League, the 19-year-old Vosmik acquitted himself extremely well at the plate, batting .381 and accumulating 39 doubles and 24 triples, in only 408 official at-bats. Yet, even though he possessed good running speed, Vosmik still had a lot to learn about playing the outfield. In an effort to improve his defense, Vosmik spent the subsequent offseason working with legendary center fielder Tris Speaker, who helped turn him into a far more competent outfielder. Meanwhile, Vosmik continued to impress everyone with his outstanding hitting, compiling a batting average of .397 and driving in 116 runs for the Terre Haute Tots of the Class B League in 1930, before being summoned to Cleveland in mid-September. Appearing in nine games with the Indians over the final two weeks of the campaign, Vosmik collected six hits in 26 official trips to the plate, giving him a batting average of .231 in his first taste of big-league play.

Making a favorable impression on team management the following spring, Vosmik laid claim to the starting left field job, with *The Hartford Courant* predicting that the "big, blonde youngster" (Vosmik stood six feet tall and weighed 185 pounds) "may be the find of 1931." Proving that newspaper to be prophetic, Vosmik went on to have an exceptional rookie season, hitting seven homers, driving in 117 runs, scoring 80 times, batting .320, collecting 36 doubles, and ranking among the league leaders with 189 hits and 14 triples. The right-handed hitting outfielder posted excellent numbers again in 1932, concluding the campaign with 10 homers, 97 RBIs, 106 runs scored, 194 hits, and a batting average of .312, while also leading all players at his position with a career-high 425 putouts and .989 fielding percentage. However, a bout with the flu that affected his vision and a broken hand he suffered on Labor Day hampered Vosmik's performance in 1933, limiting him to only 119 games and just four homers, 56 RBIs, 53 runs scored, and a batting average of .263.

Although injuries once again plagued Vosmik in 1934, the 24-year-old outfielder rebounded in a big way, batting .341, driving in 78 runs, and scoring 71 times, in only 104 games and 405 official at-bats. Fully healthy

Courtesy of the Leslie Jones Collection at the Boston Public Library

Joe Vosmik nearly won the AL batting title
with a mark of .348 in 1935

by the start of the 1935 season, Vosmik posted the best offensive numbers of his career, scoring 93 runs, leading the league with 216 hits, 47 doubles, and 20 triples, and ranking among the leaders with 110 RBIs, 333 total bases, a .408 on-base percentage, a .537 slugging percentage, and a .348 batting average, which placed him a close second in the AL batting race to Washington's Buddy Myer, who topped the circuit with a mark of .349.

Vosmik's superb hitting, which earned him All-Star honors for the only time in his career and a third-place finish in the AL MVP voting, behind only Hank Greenberg and Wes Ferrell, prompted new Indians manager Steve O'Neill to proclaim, "Joe Vosmik can hit any pitcher in any league. He has quick wrists and rips the ball to all fields. He has that sixth sense and was made to hit a baseball."

Despite missing two weeks of the ensuing campaign due to injury, Vosmik turned in another strong performance, finishing the year with seven homers, 94 RBIs, 76 runs scored, and a .287 batting average. But, with the Indians finishing fifth in the league, 22½ games behind the pennant-winning Yankees, they decided to make a number of changes during the subsequent offseason, with Vosmik figuring prominently in one of those moves. Choosing to part ways with one of their best players, the Indians completed a trade with the Browns on January 17, 1937, that sent Vosmik, pitcher Oral Hildebrand, and infielder Bill Knickerbocker to St. Louis, in exchange for slugging outfielder Moose Solters, veteran shortstop Lyn Lary, and journeyman pitcher Ivy Andrews. Vosmik left Cleveland having compiled 44 homers, 556 RBIs, 480 runs scored, 1,003 hits, 206 doubles, 65 triples, a .313 batting average, a .376 on-base percentage, and a .459 slugging percentage as a member of the Indians.

Vosmik ended up spending just one season in St. Louis, amassing 193 hits and 47 doubles, batting .325, and driving in 93 runs for the Browns in 1937, before being dealt to the Boston Red Sox prior to the start of the ensuing campaign. He then spent two years in Boston, having his best year for the Red Sox in 1938, when he batted .324, scored 121 runs, and led the league with 201 hits. Sold to the Dodgers at the end of 1939, Vosmik appeared in only 116 games his first year in Brooklyn, before being temporarily blinded during the subsequent offseason when a bottle of medicine exploded in his face. Although Vosmik eventually recovered, he never regained his batting eye, prompting the Dodgers to release him midway through the 1941 campaign.

Still believing that he had a lot of baseball left in him, the 31-year-old Vosmik spent parts of the next four seasons playing in the American Association, before briefly returning to the majors as a member of the Washington Senators in 1944. But, after batting just .194 in 14 games with the Senators, Vosmik announced his retirement, ending his career with 65 home runs, 874 RBIs, 818 runs scored, 1,682 hits, 335 doubles,

92 triples, a .307 batting average, a .369 on-base percentage, and a .438 slugging percentage.

Following his playing days, Vosmik managed in the minor leagues for four years, before resigning his post in 1950 after being hospitalized with ulcers and pneumonia. He then scouted for the Indians and, later, sold automobiles until he passed away at the age of 51, on January 27, 1962, after contracting pneumonia following the removal of a cancerous lung tumor.

Indians Career Highlights:

Best Season: Vosmik performed extremely well for the Indians in each of his first two seasons, batting .320, driving in 117 runs, scoring 80 times, and colleting 189 hits and 14 triples as a rookie in 1931, before hitting .312, knocking in 97 runs, scoring 106 others, and ranking among the league leaders with 194 hits and 39 doubles the following year. However, he had his finest all-around season in 1935, when he knocked in 110 runs, scored 93 times, topped the circuit with 216 hits, 47 doubles, and 20 triples, finished second in the league with a .348 batting average, and also ranked among the leaders with 333 total bases, a .408 on-base percentage, a .537 slugging percentage, and an OPS of .946.

Memorable Moments/Greatest Performances: Vosmik had the only 5-for-5 day of his career on April 18, 1931, when he collected a triple, three doubles, and a single during a lopsided 11-2 victory over the Chicago White Sox.

Vosmik helped lead the Indians to a 12-0 rout of the St. Louis Browns on May 26, 1931, by going 4-for-5, with four RBIs and one run scored.

Vosmik came up big in the clutch for the Indians on April 23, 1932, when his two-run homer in the bottom of the eighth inning tied the score with Detroit at 7-7. The Indians won the game in the ensuing frame on an RBI single by Earl Averill. Vosmik finished the contest with three hits, four RBIs, and two runs scored.

Vosmik had a huge day at the plate against Boston on June 15, 1932, leading the Indians to a 9-3 win over the Red Sox by going 4-for-5, with a double, triple, and career-high six RBIs.

Vosmik helped pace the Indians to a 12-1 win over the Chicago White Sox on May 1, 1934, by going 4-for-5, with a homer, double, two RBIs, and career-best four runs scored.

Vosmik starred during a 12-2 rout of the Philadelphia Athletics on May 24, 1935, going 5-for-6, with two RBIs and one run scored.

Vosmik hit two home runs in one game for the only time in his career on May 2, 1936, when he reached the seats twice, singled twice, and knocked in four runs during a 7-3 win over Boston.

Vosmik gave the Indians an 8-7 victory over the Red Sox on June 26, 1936, when he hit a solo homer with one man out in the bottom of the 10th inning. He finished the game 3-for-5, with three RBIs and two runs scored.

Notable Achievements:

- Batted over .300 four times, topping the .320-mark three times and surpassing .340 twice.
- Knocked in more than 100 runs twice.
- Scored more than 100 runs once (106 in 1932).
- Surpassed 200 hits once (216 in 1935).
- Finished in double digits in triples four times, reaching the 20-mark once (20 in 1935).
- Surpassed 30 doubles four times, topping 40 two-baggers once (47 in 1935).
- Compiled on-base percentage in excess of .400 once (.408 in 1935).
- Posted slugging percentage in excess of .500 once (.537 in 1935).
- Led AL in: hits once, doubles once, and triples once.
- Finished second in AL with .348 batting average in 1935.
- Led AL outfielders in fielding percentage once.
- Led AL left-fielders in putouts once and fielding percentage twice.
- Finished third in 1935 AL MVP voting.
- 1935 AL All-Star.

36

VICTOR MARTINEZ
2002 - 2009

An outstanding hitter who proved to be the most productive offensive receiver in franchise history during his time in Cleveland, Victor Martinez spent parts of eight seasons with the Indians, serving as the team's primary catcher in five of those. Playing his best ball for the Tribe from 2004 to 2007, the switch-hitting Martinez surpassed 20 homers in three of those four seasons, knocked in more than 100 runs twice, and batted over .300 three times, earning in the process one Silver Slugger, one top-10 finish in the AL MVP voting, and three All-Star selections. Gradually establishing himself as the Indians' emotional leader as well, Martinez helped lead the club to one division title and more than 90 victories on two separate occasions, before being dealt to Boston just prior to the July 2009 trade deadline.

Born in Ciudad Bolivar, Venezuela on December 23, 1978, Victor Jesus Martinez grew up in a one-parent home after his father died suddenly of a massive heart attack while he was still just a young boy. Receiving his earliest lessons on the diamond in softball games played on the field across the street from his house, Martinez manned the shortstop position whenever possible, hoping to follow in the footsteps of his childhood idol, fellow Venezuelan Ozzie Guillen. After learning how to switch-hit at an early age, Martinez soon found himself competing against adults as a teenager, with his beefy, six-foot frame and powerful throwing arm enabling him to hold his own against men much older than himself.

Discovered by Cleveland scout Luis Aponte while competing in his homeland, Martinez signed with the Indians as a 17-year-old amateur free agent in 1996. Assigned to the Indians' club in the newly formed Venezuelan Summer League (VSL) the following year, Martinez moved from shortstop to catcher after being told by coach Minnie Mendoza that the

Cleveland farm system lacked depth behind home plate. Adapting well to his new position, Martinez made great strides in his first year as a receiver, while also compiling a league-leading batting average of .344. After spending one more year in the VSL, Martinez traveled to the United States, where he spent the next two seasons further developing his catching skills, before winning a pair of batting titles and minor-league MVP awards in 2001 and 2002. Particularly impressive in the last of those campaigns, Martinez earned Eastern League MVP and Indians Minor League Player of the Year honors by hitting 22 homers and topping the circuit with 84 runs scored and a .336 batting average while playing for Class-AA Akron.

After appearing in 12 games with the Indians during the latter stages of the 2002 campaign, Martinez spent the first half of the 2003 season back in the minors, before being recalled by the Tribe towards the end of June. Splitting time behind home plate with Josh Bard the rest of the year, Martinez batted .289, homered once, and knocked in 16 runs, in 49 games and 159 official at-bats.

Anointed the Indians' starting catcher after spending a considerable amount of time in the weight room during the subsequent off-season, Martinez posted outstanding numbers for the Tribe in his first full season, earning All-Star and Silver Slugger honors in 2004 by hitting 23 homers, driving in 108 runs, amassing 38 doubles, and batting .283 as the club's cleanup hitter. He followed that up with another excellent year in 2005, hitting 20 homers, knocking in 80 runs, and leading the team with a batting average of .305, prompting Indians manager Eric Wedge to state, "We knew he was a good hitter, but we didn't expect him to come this fast."

On the other hand, Martinez displayed only average defensive skills behind home plate, throwing out just under 25 percent of attempted base-stealers his first two seasons as a full-time starter, en route to allowing more stolen bases than any other AL receiver during that time. However, he also ranked among the league leaders in putouts and assists by a catcher both years and did a solid job of handling the Indians' young pitching staff. Commenting on Martinez's overall performance, Cleveland GM Mark Shapiro said, "There's a premium for the position he plays, and the teammate he is, and I think the leader he is going to be."

Proving Shapiro to be prophetic, Martinez emerged as the Indians' emotional leader before long, with his pre-game practice of looking every starting player in the eyes before taking the field and giving them each an elaborate, customized handshake soon becoming a team ritual. A leader behind the plate as well, Martinez took wins and losses personally, with his attitude and interpersonal skills making him the heart and soul of the team in many ways.

Although Martinez remained the Indians' primary receiver in 2006 and 2007, he also spent some time at first base both seasons, concluding the first of those campaigns with 16 homers, 93 RBIs, 82 runs scored, 181 hits, 37 doubles, a .316 batting average, a .391 on-base percentage, and a .465 slugging percentage. Posting similarly impressive numbers in 2007, Martinez led the Tribe to the AL Central title by hitting 25 homers, ranking among the league leaders with 114 RBIs, scoring 78 times, amassing 40 doubles, batting .301, compiling a .374 on-base percentage, and posting a .505 slugging percentage, with his strong performance earning him All-Star honors for the second time and a seventh-place finish in the AL MVP voting.

Yet, in spite of the outstanding offensive numbers the 6'2", 210-pound Martinez compiled each season, he did not consider himself to be a slugger in the truest sense of the word, stating on one occasion, "In my mind, I don't see myself as a power hitter. But, once in a while, you put the ball in the air and it keeps going."

In describing his approach once he stepped into the batter's box, Martinez said, "Every time I go to the plate, I'm just trying to put a good swing on the ball. Anytime you can do that, good things will happen."

A determined run-producer from both sides of the plate, Martinez proved to be something of a free-swinger with the bases empty. However, he altered his approach with men on base, shortening his swing and becoming far more disciplined as a hitter. Commenting on Martinez's ability to hit with men in scoring position, Mark Shapiro noted, "Victor reminds me of Manny Ramirez in that he just drives in runs."

After serving as one of the Indians' top offensive threats in each of the previous four seasons, Martinez missed more than half of the 2008 campaign due to injury, finishing the year with just two home runs, 35 RBIs, and a .278 batting average. Healthy again in 2009, Martinez posted solid numbers through the end of July, hitting 15 homers, driving in 67 runs, and batting .284. But, with the Indians struggling and Martinez set to become a free agent at the end of the 2010 season, the Tribe completed a trade with the Red Sox on July 31 that sent arguably their best hitter to Boston, in exchange for pitchers Justin Masterson, Nick Hagadone, and Bryan Price.

Upon learning of the deal, Martinez expressed his sadness to be leaving Cleveland to the local press corps. Wearing sunglasses to hide his tears and a black cap and T-shirt to capture his mood, Martinez told the assembled media, "This is the toughest day of my career. This is my house, and I feel like I'm leaving my house. . . . This organization brought me to the big leagues. It made me a better person and player. I always wanted to wear one uniform in my career . . . but tomorrow is another day, and we've got to move on."

Cleveland GM Mark Shapiro revealed that he, too, found the parting of ways to be quite an emotional experience, stating, "It's a challenging personal moment for me, [assistant GM] Chris Antonetti, and our organization. I was there the first week we signed Victor in Venezuela. I know he will be a friend well beyond his playing days and my GM days."

Martinez left the Indians having hit 103 homers, driven in 518 runs, scored 413 times, amassed 900 hits, 191 doubles and two triples, batted .297, compiled a .369 on-base percentage, and posted a .463 slugging percentage as a member of the team.

Martinez ended up performing well for the Red Sox during his relatively brief stay in Beantown, hitting eight homers, driving in 41 runs, and batting .336 over the final two months of the 2009 campaign, before earning All-Star honors the following year by hitting 20 homers, knocking in 79 runs, and batting .302. However, after becoming a free agent at the end of 2010, he signed with the Detroit Tigers, with whom he has spent the past seven seasons serving primarily as a DH. Playing his best ball during that time in 2011 and 2014, Martinez batted .330 and knocked in 103 runs in the first of those campaigns, before earning All-Star honors and a runner-up finish in the AL MVP balloting three years later by hitting 32 homers, driving in 103 runs, finishing second in the league with a .335 batting average and a .565 slugging percentage, and topping the circuit with a .409 on-base percentage and an OPS of .974.

Since Martinez will enter the 2018 season at 39 years of age, it remains to be seen how much longer he intends to play. Adding to the uncertainty of his situation is the fact that he spent some time on the disabled list this past season after being hospitalized with an irregular heartbeat. Nevertheless, as of this writing, Martinez boasts career totals of 237 home runs;

Courtesy of Pristine Auctions

Victor Martinez earned three All-Star selections
as a member of the Indians

1,124 RBIs; 882 runs scored; 2,036 hits; 402 doubles; and three triples; a batting average of .298; an on-base percentage of .364; and a slugging percentage of .462.Indians

Career Highlights:

Best Season: Martinez performed extremely well for the Indians in both 2004 and 2006, concluding the first of those campaigns with 23 homers, 108 RBIs, a .283 batting average, and an OPS of .851, before hitting 16 homers, driving in 93 runs, batting .316, and posting an OPS of .856 two years later. However, Martinez compiled his best overall numbers as a member of the team in 2007, when he earned a seventh-place finish in the league MVP voting by hitting 25 homers, driving in a career-high 114 runs, amassing 40 doubles, batting .301, and compiling an OPS of .879.

Memorable Moments/Greatest Performances: Martinez homered, doubled, singled twice, and scored a career-high four runs during a lopsided 9-3 victory over the Toronto Blue Jays on August 26, 2005.

Although the Indians lost their June 10, 2006 meeting with the Chicago White Sox by a score of 4-3 in 11 innings, Martinez starred in defeat, hitting a pair of homers and knocking in all three Cleveland runs, with his solo shot in the top of the 11th temporarily giving the Tribe a 3-2 lead.

Martinez helped lead the Indians to a 19-1 rout of the Yankees on July 4, 2006, by going 5-for-6, with a homer, double, three RBIs, and two runs scored.

Martinez had a big offensive day against Boston on May 6, 2009, going 3-for-5, with a homer, double, four RBIs, and three runs scored, during a 9-2 win over the Red Sox.

Martinez again starred at the plate a little over one week later, leading the Indians to an 11-7 victory over the Tampa Bay Rays on May 14, 2009, by going 4-for-5, with a pair of doubles, four RBIs, and two runs scored.

Martinez hit a number of big home runs for the Indians, with one of those coming on June 1, 2007, when he brought them to within one run of Detroit with a three-run shot in the bottom of the ninth inning. The Tribe subsequently scored another two times, to come away with a thrilling, 12-11 come-from-behind victory over the Tigers.

Martinez delivered another big three-run homer on September 16, 2008, when his three-run blast in the bottom of the 11th inning gave the Indians a 12-9 walk-off win over the Minnesota Twins. Martinez finished the game with three hits, three RBIs, and three runs scored.

Martinez again provided the margin of victory during an 8-7 win over the Kansas City Royals on April 21, 2009, concluding a 4-for-5 evening with a two-run homer in the bottom of the eighth inning that drove home the game's winning runs.

However, Martinez had his most memorable game as a member of the Indians on July 16, 2004, when he led the Tribe to an 18-6 rout of the Seattle Mariners by going 5-for-5, with three homers and a career-high seven runs batted in.

Notable Achievements:

- Hit more than 20 home runs three times.
- Knocked in more than 100 runs twice.
- Batted over .300 three times.
- Surpassed 30 doubles four times, topping 40 two-baggers once (40 in 2007).
- Posted slugging percentage in excess of .500 once (.505 in 2007).

- Led AL with 11 sacrifice flies in 2007.
- Led AL catchers with 61 assists in 2004.
- Hit three home runs in one game vs. Seattle Mariners on July 16, 2004.
- 2004 Silver Slugger winner.
- Finished seventh in 2007 AL MVP voting.
- Three-time AL All-Star (2004, 2007, and 2009).

37

BOBBY AVILA

1949 – 1958

An outstanding contact hitter who rarely struck out and occasionally hit for power, Bobby Avila established himself as one of the American League's top second basemen during his time in Cleveland, earning three All-Star selections and two top-10 finishes in the league MVP voting in his first five seasons as a full-time starter. One of the first Mexican players to arrive in the United States, Avila eventually became the first Latin player to win a batting title when he topped the junior circuit with a mark of .341 in 1954, helping the Indians capture the American League pennant in the process. An extremely consistent performer until injuries began to take their toll on him later in his career, Avila batted over .300 two other times as well, while also scoring more than 100 runs twice. Meanwhile, Avila's excellent glove work at second enabled him to lead all AL second sackers in assists twice and fielding percentage once, gaining him general recognition as one of the league's most complete players at his position.

Born in Veracruz, Mexico on April 2, 1924, Roberto Francisco Avila spent much of his youth playing soccer, competing professionally at the age of 16, although he retained inside of him a strong desire to eventually become a bullfighter. After finding a book written by former major league pitcher Jack Coombs, Avila taught himself to play baseball, which soon became his first love. Beginning his career on the diamond as a third baseman with Cordoba in the Veracruz State League in 1942, Avila moved on to the Mexican League before long, where he spent the next five seasons manning shortstop and second base for the Pueblo Pericos. After gradually improving his batting average from .250 to .347 during that time, Avila decided to make baseball his livelihood, even though he previously spent three years studying engineering at the University of Mexico.

Arriving in the United States in 1948, Avila initially turned down offers from the Brooklyn Dodgers and Washington Senators, before finally accepting $17,500 to sign with the Indians. Subsequently assigned to Cleveland's Triple-A affiliate in the International League, Avila batted just .220 in 56 games with the Baltimore Orioles, before a hernia brought his season to a premature end. In addition to his health problems and struggles at the plate, Avila found his transition to American baseball further hampered by his unfamiliarity with the English language, which prompted his first minor-league manager, Tommy Thomas, to describe him as "a stranger in a strange land." Looking back years later at that particular period in his life, Avila recalled, "It was very hard for me at first. Any Latin ballplayer who comes here must fight the language."

After undergoing surgery to repair his hernia during the subsequent off-season, Avila joined the Indians, who found themselves forced to add him to their roster due to the bonus rules of the day. Seeing very little action over the course of the 1949 campaign, Avila appeared in only 31 games, mostly as a late-inning replacement, compiling a batting average of .214 in just 14 official plate appearances. However, he used his time on the bench to learn the English language and familiarize himself with American customs. Pitcher Mike Garcia, US-born but also of Mexican heritage, roomed with Avila on the road. In discussing the progress his roommate made during his early days with the Indians, Garcia remembered, "At first, Bobby didn't speak a lick of English. All he would do was point and say, 'Como se llama eso?' meaning 'What's that?'"

As Avila grew increasingly comfortable in his new surroundings, he began to display his worth on the playing field, garnering significantly more playing time during the latter stages of the 1950 campaign as injuries and advancing age began to slow 35-year-old starting second baseman Joe Gordon. Performing well over the season's final two months, Avila finished the year with a .299 batting average, 21 RBIs, and 39 runs scored, in 80 games and 201 official at-bats.

Following the release of Gordon at season's end, Avila became the Indians' full-time starter at second—a role he maintained for the next eight seasons. Having an excellent year for the Tribe in 1951, the right-handed hitting Avila earned a 10th-place finish in the AL MVP voting by batting .304, hitting 10 homers, driving in 58 runs, scoring 76 times, and finishing fourth in the league with 14 stolen bases. He earned his first All-Star selection the following year by batting an even .300, topping the circuit with 11 triples, and finishing second in the league with 102 runs scored and 179 hits. Avila had another solid season in 1953, batting .286, scoring 85 runs, and striking out only 27 times in 634 total plate appearances, which gave him an at-bat-to-strikeout ratio of 20.7 that represented the sixth-best mark in the league.

The success Avila experienced after being inserted into the starting lineup prompted Cleveland GM Hank Greenberg to say of his second baseman, "He has that something extra that makes a great hitter. Call it competitive instinct. . . . He's always fighting the pitcher, never choking up and never giving an inch. . . . In a tough spot, I'm always glad to see Bobby coming to the plate."

Indians manager Al Lopez also praised Avila, stating that he had "a fine swing, a sharp eye, a good spirit of competition . . . and a world of confidence in himself."

In addition to establishing himself as one of the American League's better offensive players his first few years in Cleveland, the 5'10", 175-pound Avila developed a reputation as a daring base-runner and an excellent defender, annually ranking among the top players at his position in putouts, assists, double plays, and fielding percentage. Particularly adept at turning the double play, Avila employed the same agility he used in soccer to improve his footwork around the bag. He also used his soccer training to perfect the art of sliding into a base while simultaneously attempting to kick the baseball out of the fielder's glove—a practice that angered many opposing players.

After performing well for the Indians in each of the three previous seasons, Avila had a career-year in 1954, helping the Tribe post a franchise-best 111 victories during the regular season by hitting 15 homers, driving in 67 runs, topping the circuit with a .341 batting average, and also ranking among the league leaders with 112 runs scored, 189 hits, and an OPS of .880. With the Indians finishing eight games ahead of the second-place Yankees in the AL pennant race, Avila earned a third-place finish in the league MVP balloting, his lone *Sporting News* All-Star selection, and recognition as *The Sporting News* AL Player of the Year. Avila, who spent most of the year batting second in the Cleveland lineup, accomplished all he did despite breaking his thumb in early June when New York's Hank Bauer slid into him at second base. Recounting his banner year during an interview for "Splendor on the Diamond," Avila, whose batting average

Courtesy of MEARS Online Auctions

Bobby Avila won the AL batting title in 1954 with a mark of .341

stood at .396 prior to the injury, recalled, "I started to hit well early, and, once you're hitting well, you build confidence. I felt like I could hit anybody."

Negatively impacted by a lengthy pre-season holdout, the departure of his roommate, mentor, and close friend Hank Majeski, who the Indians traded to Baltimore in early July, and a rash of health problems that included a sprained right toe and a corneal cyst in his right eye, Avila failed to perform at the same lofty level in 1955. Nevertheless, he earned the last of his three All-Star nominations by hitting 13 homers, driving in 61 runs, scoring 83 others, and batting .272.

Plagued by injuries in each of the next three seasons as well, an aging Avila never regained his earlier form, compiling batting averages of .224, .268, and .253 for the Indians from 1956 to 1958, before being dealt to the Baltimore Orioles for career minor leaguer Russ Heman and $30,000 following the conclusion of the 1958 campaign. After splitting the 1959 season between the Orioles, Red Sox, and Milwaukee Braves, Avila returned to his homeland when the Braves optioned him to the Mexico City Tigers of the Mexican League. Avila ended his big-league career with 80 home runs, 467 RBIs, 725 runs scored, 1,296 hits, 185 doubles, 35 triples, 78 stolen bases, a .281 batting average, a .359 on-base percentage, and a .388 slugging percentage, compiling virtually all those numbers while playing for the Indians.

Avila played one more season in Mexico, batting .333 and scoring a record 125 runs in 1960, before announcing his retirement. He later summed up his baseball career by stating, "I loved the game. And I was real honest about my job. Nobody could ever say they saw Bobby Avila drunk or playing around. I was honest about my career, and I gave it everything I had."

Following his playing days, Avila became involved in politics, serving in Mexico's congress during the 1960s and 1970s, and as mayor of Veracruz from 1976 to 1979. Avila also purchased the Veracruz Eagles and served as president of the Mexican League for a period of time during the early 1980s. He died in Veracruz of complications from diabetes and a lung ailment at the age of 80, on October 26, 2004.

Speaking of his fellow countryman, Los Angeles Dodgers great Fernando Valenzuela claimed, "Everybody knows who Avila was in Mexico. He was an inspiration, of course, for Mexican ballplayers to follow to the States and play in the Major Leagues. He did a good job. Everybody knows and recognizes what he did."

Indians Career Highlights:

Best Season: There is little doubt that Avila had his finest season in 1954, when he established career-high marks in home runs (15), RBIs (67), runs scored (112), hits (189), doubles (27), batting average (.341), on-base percentage (.402), slugging percentage (.477), and OPS (.880), earning in the process a third-place finish in the AL MVP balloting, with only Yogi Berra and teammate Larry Doby receiving more votes.

Memorable Moments/Greatest Performances: Avila helped lead the Indians to a convincing 16-0 win over the Washington Senators on May 24, 1951, by going 4-for-5, with three RBIs and three runs scored from his leadoff spot in the batting order.

Avila came up big in the clutch for the Indians on July 31, 1951, when he broke a 3-3 tie with Washington in the top of the ninth inning by driving in a pair of runs with an opposite field single. With the Senators failing to score in the bottom of the frame, Avila's hit proved to be the game-winner. He finished the contest with three hits and four RBIs.

Avila provided further heroics some three weeks later, when he gave the Indians a 6-5 win over the Washington Senators on August 22, 1951, by hitting a walk-off homer in the bottom of the 14th inning with two men out and no one on base.

Avila had one of the most productive days of his career on June 6, 1952, when he went 4-for-5, with a homer, double, and five RBIs, during a lopsided 11-4 victory over Philadelphia.

Avila gave the Indians a 6-3 win over the Detroit Tigers on September 17, 1954, when he hit a two-out bases loaded homer off right-hander Ned Garver in the top of the seventh inning.

Avila had a huge game against Kansas City on August 12, 1955, driving in a career-high six runs with a pair of homers and a single during a 17-1 mauling of the Athletics.

However, Avila turned in his most memorable performance on June 20, 1951, when he went 5-for-6, with three homers, four RBIs, and four runs scored, during a 14-8 win over the Red Sox.

Notable Achievements:

- Batted over .300 three times, topping the .340-mark once (.341 in 1954).
- Scored more than 100 runs twice.
- Finished in double digits in triples once (11 in 1952).
- Compiled on-base percentage in excess of .400 once (.402 in 1954).

- Led AL in: batting average once, triples once, and sacrifice hits twice.
- Finished second in AL in hits once and runs scored once.
- Led AL second basemen in assists twice and fielding percentage once.
- Finished third in 1954 AL MVP voting.
- 1954 *Sporting News* AL Player of the Year.
- 1954 *Sporting News* All-Star selection.
- Three-time AL All-Star (1952, 1954, and 1955).
- 1954 AL champion.

38

DALE MITCHELL
1946 - 1956

An outstanding line-drive hitter with superb bat control, Dale Mitchell compiled the third-highest batting average in all of Major League Baseball during the period that extended from 1943 to 1960, posting a mark of .312 that placed him behind only legendary sluggers Ted Williams and Stan Musial. Spending most of his time with the Indians hitting out of the leadoff spot in the batting order, Mitchell topped the .300-mark six times between 1947 and 1953, while also amassing more than 200 hits twice and surpassing 20 triples once. One of the finest contact hitters of his time, the left-handed swinging Mitchell also struck out only 119 times in more than 4,300 total plate appearances, enabling him to compile a 2.91 walk-to-strikeout ratio over the course of his career that ranks as the eighth best in MLB history. A solid outfielder as well, Mitchell earned two All-Star selections with his strong all-around play, helping the Indians win two pennants and one world championship in the process. Yet, in spite of the many contributions he made to the team during his time in Cleveland, Mitchell is remembered most for making the final out in Don Larsen's perfect game in the 1956 World Series as a member of the Brooklyn Dodgers.

Born in the small rural town of Colony, Oklahoma on August 23, 1921, Loren Dale Mitchell attended Cloud Chief High School, some 20 miles from his home, where he excelled in baseball, basketball, and track, earning All-State honors in the first two sports, while setting a state record by recording a time of 9.8 seconds in the 100-yard dash. Continuing to star in multiple sports after enrolling at the University of Oklahoma, Mitchell played outfield for the school's baseball team and also ran track. Meanwhile, he spent one summer fine-tuning his hitting skills by playing semi-pro ball with the Oklahoma Natural Gas club, recalling years later, "I had a habit of stepping away at the plate and pulling the bat with my body. . . . [Coach] Roy Deal taught me how to spread my stance and hit with my wrists. This enabled me to hit outside balls and, thus, bat better against southpaw pitching." With an improved approach at the plate, Mitchell went on to set Sooner records by batting .507 as a senior, while also posting a mark of .467 over the course of his college career.

Temporarily abandoning his dream of pursuing a career in pro ball after being drafted into the United States Army Air Force late in 1942, Mitchell spent most of the next three years serving in Europe during World War II, before being discharged from the military following Germany's surrender in 1945. Subsequently signed by the Indians as an amateur free agent early in 1946, Mitchell made his minor-league debut with Cleveland's Double-A affiliate in Oklahoma City on June 3, 1946, compiling a league-leading .337 batting average over the course of the next 3½ months, before being summoned to the big leagues in mid-September. Appearing in 11 games with the Indians during the season's final two weeks, Mitchell made an extremely favorable impression on team management by posting a batting average of .432 in 44 official plate appearances.

Making the Cleveland roster the following year, Mitchell began the season as the team's starting center-fielder after working extensively during spring training with coach Tris Speaker, who taught the speedy but inexperienced youngster the correct way to break for line drives and fly balls, the proper way to field base hits, and how to get more leverage on his throws to home plate and the infield. However, after Mitchell got off to a slow start, the Indians demoted him to Oklahoma City. Refusing to report to the minor-league club, Mitchell sat at home until the Tribe called him back on June 2. Excelling upon his return to Cleveland, Mitchell subsequently ran off a 22-game hitting streak, allowing him to conclude the campaign with a .316 batting average that placed him sixth in the league rankings. He also scored 69 runs in 123 games and struck out only 14 times in 518 total plate appearances, prompting Speaker to say of his pupil, "The man has one of the best batting eyes in baseball."

Establishing himself as the Indians' leadoff hitter and full-time starter in left field in 1948, Mitchell helped the Tribe capture the AL pennant by driving in 56 runs, scoring 82 times, finishing second in the league with 204 hits, placing third in the batting race to Ted Williams and teammate Lou Boudreau with a mark of .336, posting a career-high OPS of .814, and leading all players at his position with 10 assists and a .991 fielding percentage. He followed that up with another outstanding performance in

1949, earning his first All-Star selection by knocking in 56 runs, scoring 81 others, batting .317, and topping the circuit with 203 hits and 23 triples, which represented the highest total compiled by an American League player since Earle Combs banged out 23 three-baggers for the Yankees in 1927. Mitchell also led all AL outfielders with a .994 fielding percentage

Courtesy of the Cleveland Memory Project

Dale Mitchell served as the leadoff hitter
for Cleveland's 1948 world championship team

and struck out only 11 times in 685 total plate appearances, giving him easily the league's best at-bat-to-strikeout ratio (58.2).

Although the 6'1", 195-pound Mitchell had decent power, he preferred to focus on meeting the ball, rather than driving it great distances. Primarily a line-drive hitter who hit the ball to all parts of the ballpark, Mitchell concentrated on driving the ball to left-center or straightaway center, prompting most teams to defend against him as if he were a right-handed pull-hitter. He also used his outstanding speed to his advantage, often collecting infield hits by bouncing the ball into the shortstop hole or over the pitcher's mound. Yet, even though Mitchell never hit more than 13 home runs in any single season, he had good extra-base power, telling reporters in 1949, "I have learned to relax at the plate. When I feel I am getting tight, I step out of the box and drop my bat. This has helped me to get more power. I fool 'em now and get more punch in my swing." Commenting on Mitchell's all-around hitting ability following the conclusion of the 1949 campaign, Indians player-manager Lou Boudreau said, "If anyone ever hits four hundred, Dale Mitchell will be the man."

Mitchell continued to perform well for the Tribe in each of the next four seasons, posting batting averages of .308, .290, .323, and .300 from 1950 to 1953, while twice scoring more than 80 runs, and earning his second and final All-Star selection in 1952, when his .323 average left him just four points behind league-leader Ferris Fain. Reduced to the role of a backup after Al Smith claimed the starting left-field job in 1954, Mitchell spent his final 2½ years in Cleveland serving the Indians as a pinch-hitter deluxe, before being sold to the Brooklyn Dodgers on July 29, 1956. He remained in Brooklyn until season's end, announcing his retirement after the Dodgers lost the World Series to the Yankees in seven games. Prior to that, though, Mitchell became a part of baseball history in Game Five of that year's Fall Classic, when, pinch-hitting for Brooklyn pitcher Sal Maglie with two men out in the top of the ninth inning, he took a called third strike on a Don Larsen pitch he always maintained was really a ball, thereby ending the only perfect game in Series history. Announcing his retirement shortly thereafter, Mitchell ended his career with 41 homers, 403 RBIs, 555 runs scored, 1,244 hits, 169 doubles, 61 triples, 45 stolen bases, a .312 batting average, a .368 on-base percentage, a .416 slugging percentage, 346 bases on balls and only 119 strikeouts, compiling virtually all those numbers while playing for the Indians.

Following his playing days, Mitchell worked in the oil and cement industries, before retiring in the early 1980s. He suffered a fatal heart attack not long after, passing away on January 5, 1987, a little over four months after he celebrated his 65th birthday.

Indians Career Highlights:

Best Season: Mitchell had a big year for the Indians in 1948, helping them capture the AL pennant by driving in 56 runs, scoring 82 times, and establishing career-high marks in doubles (30), hits (204), batting average (.336), and OPS (.814). Nevertheless, the 1949 campaign would have to be considered his finest all-around season. In addition to knocking in 56 runs, scoring 81 others, and finishing fourth in the league with a .317 batting average, Mitchell topped the circuit with 203 hits and 23 triples, with his 23 three-baggers representing the sixth-highest total in American League history. He also struck out only 11 times in 685 total plate appearances, giving him a career-best and league-leading at-bat-to-strikeout ratio of 58.2.

Memorable Moments/Greatest Performances: Mitchell put together four hitting streaks of more than 20 games during his time in Cleveland, with the longest of those lasting from July 20 to August 15, 1951, a 23-game stretch during which he went 41-for-94 (.436), with a homer, three triples, five doubles, 15 RBIs, and 19 runs scored.

Mitchell made perhaps his most memorable defensive play on June 30, 1948, when he helped preserve Bob Lemon's no-hitter with a spectacular catch in left field. With Detroit third baseman George Kell leading off the bottom of the seventh inning with a drive to deep left, Mitchell used his sprinter's speed to race back to the fence, before spearing the ball and crashing into the wall, holding onto the sphere despite hitting the ground hard. Lemon subsequently recorded the final eight outs, giving him the only no-hitter of his career.

Mitchell helped lead the Indians to a convincing 11-1 victory over the Philadelphia Athletics on June 6, 1948, by going 4-for-6, with a double and a career-high five runs batted in.

Mitchell had another big day at the plate on September 18, 1948, going 4-for-5, with a triple, double, and two runs scored, during a 10-1 win over the Washington Senators.

Mitchell delivered the decisive blow of a 7-3 victory over the Philadelphia Athletics on June 22, 1949, when he drove in three runs with a bases-loaded triple in the top of the 14th inning. He finished the game with four hits, three RBIs, and one run scored.

Mitchell collected five hits in one game for the first time in his career on August 4, 1949, when he went 5-for-6, with a triple, one RBI, and one run scored, during a 14-1 rout of the Senators.

Mitchell paced the Indians to an 8-1 win over the St. Louis Browns on September 3, 1950, by going 3-for-5, with a homer, double, four RBIs, and two runs scored.

Mitchell recorded the only grand slam of his career during a 12-4 victory over the Browns on April 28, 1951.

Mitchell homered twice in one game for the only time on August 18, 1951, when he led the Indians to a 7-0 win over the White Sox by going 4-for-4, with a pair of homers and four RBIs.

Mitchell went a perfect 5-for-5 at the plate during a 6-4 win over the Yankees on August 22, 1952.

Mitchell made his last big-league home run a memorable one, with his two-run, pinch-hit homer in the top of the seventh inning against Detroit on September 18, 1954, giving the Indians a 3-2 win over the Tigers that clinched the pennant for the Tribe.

Notable Achievements:

- Batted over .300 six times, topping the .320-mark twice.
- Surpassed 200 hits twice.
- Finished in double digits in triples twice, topping 20 three-baggers once (23 in 1949).
- Surpassed 30 doubles once (30 in 1948).
- Led AL in: hits once, triples once, and at-bats once.
- Finished second in AL in batting average once and hits once.
- Led AL outfielders in fielding percentage twice.
- Led AL left-fielders in assists once and fielding percentage three times.
- Two-time AL All-Star (1949 and 1952).
- Two-time AL champion (1948 and 1954).
- 1948 world champion.

39

JIM BAGBY
1916 - 1922

A key member of Cleveland's first world championship team of 1920, Jim Bagby established a single-season franchise record that year by posting 31 victories, while also leading all AL pitchers in winning percentage, complete games, and innings pitched. Although the right-handed hurler failed to ascend to such heights at any other point during his career, he proved to be much more than just a one-year wonder, winning at least 17 games three other times and compiling an overall record of 88-52 for the Indians from 1917 to 1920. Noted for his "fade-away" pitch and outstanding control, Bagby also compiled an ERA under 3.00 five straight times, threw more than 300 innings twice, and tossed more than 20 complete games on four separate occasions. And, even though Bagby made a name for himself as a starting pitcher, he also did a creditable job for the Indians coming out of the bullpen, finishing among the AL leaders in saves five times.

Born in Barnett, Georgia on October 5, 1889, James Charles Jacob Bagby broke into professional baseball with the Augusta Tourists of the Class C Sally League in 1910, before being transferred shortly thereafter to the Hattiesburg Timberjacks of the Class D Cotton States League, with whom he spent the remainder of the season compiling a record of 5-11. Rejoining Hattiesburg the following year, the 21-year-old Bagby won 22 games for the Timberjacks, prompting the Cincinnati Reds to purchase his contract prior to the start of the 1912 season. Failing to make much of an impression in his five appearances with the Reds during the early stages of the campaign, Bagby returned to the minor leagues, where he spent the next three seasons.

Having won a total of 39 games in his final two years at New Orleans (a minor-league affiliate of the Indians), Bagby found himself back in the majors at the start of the 1916 season. Serving the Indians as both a starter and a reliever over the course of his first full season, Bagby posted respectable numbers as a rookie, finishing the year with a record of 16-17, an ERA of 2.61, three shutouts, 14 complete games, and 272⅔ innings pitched. Although Bagby continued to come out of the bullpen occasionally in 1917, finishing second in the league with seven saves, he joined Stan Coveleski at the top of Cleveland's starting rotation, establishing himself as one of the junior circuit's best pitchers by going 23-13, with a 1.99 ERA, 8 shutouts, 26 complete games, and 320⅔ innings pitched.

Continuing to perform well in each of the next two seasons, Bagby went 17-16, with a 2.69 ERA, 23 complete games, and 271⅓ innings pitched in 1918, before compiling a record of 17-11 and an ERA of 2.80, tossing 21 complete games, and throwing 241⅓ innings the following year. Bagby subsequently exceeded all expectations in 1920, when he put together the finest season of his career, enabling the Indians to edge out the White Sox and Yankees in a tight, three-team pennant race by compiling a league-leading record of 31-12, while also ranking among the leaders in ERA (2.89) and WHIP (1.228), and topping the circuit with 30 complete games and 339⅔ innings pitched. He then helped the Indians claim their first world championship by winning one of his two starts and compiling an ERA of 1.80 against Brooklyn in the World Series.

Nicknamed "Sarge" by his teammates, who assigned that moniker to him after watching a Broadway play that featured a character named "Sergeant Jimmy Bagby," the six-foot, 175-pound Bagby did not throw particularly hard, never fanning more than 88 batters in any single season. However, he had excellent control and one of the best breaking balls in the game, which made him extremely effective against left-handed hitters. Identified by Ty Cobb as "the smartest pitcher I ever faced," Bagby delighted in facing the top hitters, telling the *Richmond Times-Dispatch* years later, "It's a funny thing, but my record shows the really great hitters never damaged me nearly as much as some of the ordinary batters." Perhaps much of the success Bagby experienced against the game's finest batsmen can be attributed to the fact that he approached them cautiously, making a study of hitters and remembering their strengths and weaknesses.

Unfortunately, the massive workload he assumed in 1920 took its toll on Bagby, who never again pitched to an elite level. After going 14-12, with a 4.70 ERA and only 13 complete games the following year, Bagby suffered through a dismal 1922 campaign made even more unpleasant by

Courtesy of the Bain News Service Collection at the Library of Congress

Jim Bagby posted a franchise-record 31 wins
for Cleveland's 1920 world championship ball club

an emergency appendectomy he underwent in August. With Bagby winning just four of his nine decisions and compiling an inordinately high 6.32 ERA, the Indians sold him to Pittsburgh at season's end. He left Cleveland having compiled an overall record of 122-86 as a member of the team, along with an ERA of 3.03, a WHIP of 1.265, 16 shutouts, 131 complete games, 424 strikeouts in 1,735⅔ innings pitched, and 26 saves.

Bagby subsequently spent just one season in Pittsburgh, compiling a record of 3-2 and an ERA of 5.24 for the Pirates in 1923, before being released at the end of the year. He finished his big-league career with a record of 127-89, an ERA of 3.11, and a WHIP of 1.286. After leaving Pittsburgh, Bagby spent seven seasons pitching in the minor leagues, before finally announcing his retirement following the conclusion of the 1930 campaign. In retirement, he ran a dry- cleaning establishment in Atlanta for 14 years, then a gas station for another year. However, the lure of baseball proved to be quite strong, prompting Bagby to return to the game as an umpire in the Coastal Plain League in 1941. Promoted to the Piedmont League the following year, Bagby continued to serve in that capacity until he suffered a debilitating stroke that forced him to relinquish his duties. After making a partial recovery, he took a job working for the Atlanta department stores J. M. High Co. and Davidson's. Bagby passed away at 64 years of age, on July 28, 1954, after suffering another stroke at his home in Marietta Georgia. Eight years earlier, his son, Jim Bagby Jr., appeared in the 1946 World Series as a member of the Boston Red Sox, making them the first father/son tandem ever to play in the Fall Classic.

Indians Career Highlights:

Best Season: It could be argued that Bagby pitched his best ball for the Indians in 1917, when, in addition to finishing third among AL pitchers with 23 victories, he ranked fourth in innings pitched (320⅔), fifth in complete games (26), sixth in ERA (1.99), seventh in WHIP (1.091), second in shutouts (8), and second in saves (7), establishing career-best marks in each of the last four categories. Nevertheless, the 1920 campaign is generally considered to be Bagby's signature season—and with good reason. Although the American League's use of a livelier ball in 1920 caused Bagby's ERA and WHIP to be significantly higher than the marks he posted in each category three years earlier, he compiled the best overall numbers of his career en route to leading the Indians to their first pennant, topping the junior circuit with 31 wins, a .721 winning percentage, 30 complete games, and 339⅔ innings pitched, while also finishing fifth in ERA (2.89) and fourth in WHIP (1.228). Bagby also had an excellent year at the plate, batting .252, homering once, and establishing career-high marks in RBIs (14), runs scored (17), hits (33), doubles (7), and triples (3).

Memorable Moments/Greatest Performances: An excellent hitting pitcher who batted .218 over the course of his career, Bagby twice collected four hits in one game, doing so for the first time on August 21, 1917, when he doubled once, singled three times, knocked in two runs, and scored three others during a 16-3 rout of the Philadelphia Athletics. Bagby accomplished the feat a second time almost exactly three years later, going 4-for-5 during a lopsided 15-3 victory over the Athletics on August 27, 1920.

Bagby performed heroically on June 8, 1916, when he came out of the bullpen to pitch 10 scoreless innings against Washington in a game that ended in a 14-inning, 5-5 tie. Entering the fray in the top of the fifth inning with the Indians trailing by a score of 5-2, Bagby surrendered no runs and just four hits the rest of the way, allowing his teammates to tie the contest with three runs in the bottom of the ninth inning.

Bagby turned in one of his most dominant performances on June 2, 1917, surrendering just three hits during a 5-0 shutout of the defending world champion Boston Red Sox.

Bagby hurled another gem nearly three weeks later, winning a 1-0 pitcher's duel with Chicago's Ed Cicotte on June 21 during which he allowed just three hits and a pair of walks.

Three starts later, on June 30, 1917, Bagby began a string of 38 consecutive scoreless innings that lasted more than two weeks. The streak included three straight shutouts, with Bagby's finest effort coming on July 8, when he won a 1-0 pitcher's duel with Boston's Dutch Leonard, surrendering just four hits during the contest.

Although a matchup of staff aces resulted in a 1-0 loss to Walter Johnson and the Washington Senators on May 11, 1918, Bagby pitched brilliantly, going the distance and surrendering just four hits and three walks to the Nats, who scored the game's only run in the bottom of the sixth inning when Johnson tripled and came home on an RBI single by Washington left-fielder Howie Shanks. Bagby also collected two of Cleveland's five hits off Johnson, getting a single and double in his three trips to the plate.

Bagby turned in perhaps his finest performance of the 1920 campaign on September 15, when he allowed just three hits and one base on balls during a 14-0 mauling of the Athletics.

Although Bagby did not pitch particularly well on September 28, 1920, yielding 10 hits and five runs during a 9-5 victory over the St. Louis Browns, he made history by becoming the only pitcher ever to win 30 games in a season for the Indians.

Bagby further endeared himself to the fans of Cleveland in his very next start, clinching the pennant for the Indians with a complete-game 10-1 victory over the Detroit Tigers on the next-to-last day of the regular season.

However, Bagby experienced the most memorable moment of his career in Game Five of the 1920 World Series, when, after dropping a 3-0 decision to Hall of Fame pitcher Burleigh Grimes in Game Two, he contributed to an 8-1 victory over Grimes and the Brooklyn Robins four days later by going 2-for-4, with a homer and three RBIs, with his three-run blast in the bottom of the fourth inning making him the first pitcher in the history of the Fall Classic to go deep.

Notable Achievements:

- Won 31 games in 1920, posting more than 20 victories one other time (23 in 1917).
- Posted winning percentage in excess of .600 three times, topping the .700-mark once (.721 in 1920).
- Compiled ERA under 2.00 once, finishing with mark under 3.00 four other times.
- Threw more than 300 innings twice, topping 270 innings pitched two other times.
- Threw more than 20 complete games four times, completing 30 of his starts once.
- Tossed eight shutouts in 1917.
- Led AL pitchers in: wins once, winning percentage once, innings pitched once, complete games once, appearances twice, and putouts twice.
- Finished second in AL in: shutouts once, saves twice, pitching appearances once, and games started once.
- Holds Indians single-season record for most wins (31 in 1920).
- Ranks 10th in Indians history with 131 complete games.
- 1920 AL champion.
- 1920 world champion.

40

JOE CARTER
1984 – 1989

Although he is remembered most for his game-winning, walk-off home run in Game Six of the 1993 World Series that gave the Toronto Blue Jays their second straight world championship, Joe Carter first rose to prominence as a member of the Cleveland Indians. Easily the best player on some of the worst Indians teams in recent memory, Carter spent six seasons in Cleveland, hitting more than 25 homers four straight times, driving in more than 100 runs three times, stealing more than 20 bases four times, and batting over .300 once, en route to earning one top-10 finish in the AL MVP voting and MVP consideration on two other occasions.

Possessing a rare combination of power and speed, Carter became the first player in franchise history to hit more than 30 home runs and steal more than 30 bases in the same season in 1987, when he reached the seats 32 times and swiped 31 bags. An outstanding clutch hitter as well, Carter annually ranked among the AL leaders in RBIs, topping the circuit in that category once, and placing in the league's top 10 on three other occasions during his time in Cleveland. Yet, Carter perhaps made his greatest contribution to the Indians by serving as the centerpiece of a trade that helped make them the dominant team in the AL Central for much of the 1990s.

Born in Oklahoma City, Oklahoma on March 7, 1960, Joseph Chris Carter attended Millwood High School, where he starred in baseball, basketball, football, and track, with head football coach Leodies Robinson recalling years later, "He was probably the best all-around athlete to ever come out of this neighborhood." Continuing to praise Carter, who played quarterback for the Knights during his time at Millwood, Robinson claimed, "He had a rifle for an arm. His teammates would run forty yards down the field before looking back to catch one of his passes." Carter also played shortstop on the school's baseball team, with his home runs often landing in the trailer park adjacent to Millwood, some 375 feet from home plate.

After high school, Carter enrolled at Wichita State University, where he initially planned to compete in both football and baseball, before eventually deciding to focus exclusively on further developing his diamond skills. Proving that he made the right choice, Carter went on to earn First-Team All-American honors twice and gain recognition as the *Sporting News* College Player of the Year as a junior in 1981, when he hit 24 homers, batted .411, and set a then single-season collegiate record by driving in 120 runs. Coach Gene Stephenson, who helped mold Carter into a solid outfielder, later said of his protégé, "I knew he was a player the first time I saw him. When you see a guy of his speed, with that size, it's only a matter of time. He was very raw in high school, but anyone who saw him play could tell he had the tools. The physical talent was there. It just needed direction."

Electing to leave Wichita State after his junior year, Carter entered the 1981 MLB Draft, where the Chicago Cubs selected him with the second overall pick. He subsequently spent most of the next three years advancing through Chicago's farm system, receiving a brief trial with the Cubs in 1983, before being sent back down to the minors at the start of the ensuing campaign. The 24-year-old Carter finally received his big break on June 13, 1984, when the Cubs included him in a seven-player trade they completed with the Indians that sent Carter, fellow outfielder Mel Hall, pitcher Don Schulze, and minor-league pitcher Darryl Banks to Cleveland, in exchange for catcher Ron Hassey and pitchers Rick Sutcliffe and George Frazier. While some speculated that the Indians made the deal in order to decrease their payroll, GM Phil Seghi disagreed, stating, "Money had nothing to do with this. The trade follows the pattern we began in the winter. We want to get the best young players we can and see what they can do. Hall and Carter are outfielders with some pop. Carter is a good prospect and Hall hit seventeen homers for the Cubs. Carter hits for power and average. Carter and Hall can also run."

Summoned to Cleveland shortly after being acquired by the Indians, Carter spent the rest of the year playing all over the outfield, although left-field remained his primary position. Acquitting himself extremely well in his first lengthy exposure to big-league pitching, the right-handed hitting Carter batted .275, hit 13 homers, and knocked in 41 runs, in only 66 games and 244 official at-bats. Impressed with his new teammate, Pat

in 1987, Joe Carter became the first player in franchise history to surpass 30 homers and 30 steals in the same season

Tabler noted, "He has a lot of talent. I'll tell you, he has a heckuva lot of talent—and he is still learning."

Although Carter also saw some action in right field and at first base in 1985, he again spent most of his time in left field, finishing his first full season with 15 homers, 59 RBIs, 64 runs scored, 24 stolen bases, and a .262 batting average. He followed that up with the finest all-around season of his career, earning a ninth-place finish in the 1986 AL MVP voting by hitting 29 homers, stealing 29 bases, batting .302, topping the circuit with

121 RBIs, and placing in the league's top five with 108 runs scored, 200 hits, nine triples, and 341 total bases. Even though Carter subsequently posted somewhat less impressive overall numbers in 1987, he had another very good year, batting .264, driving in 106 runs, hitting 32 homers, and stealing 31 bases, becoming in the process the first Indians player to top 30 homers and 30 steals in the same season. Commenting on his teammate's ability to drive in runs, Cleveland center-fielder Brett Butler stated, "The man's an RBI machine. He's unbelievable. Every time you looked up, it seemed he was knocking someone in. He cranks out RBIs like no one I've ever seen, game after game. Like a machine."

Yet, in spite of the excellent power and outstanding run-production the 6'3", 215-pound Carter gave the Indians, he had his weaknesses. A notorious free-swinger who displayed very little patience at the plate, Carter often expanded the strike zone, never walking more than 49 times in any single season over the course of his career, while striking out more than 100 times on seven separate occasions. Furthermore, even though Carter possessed good speed and a very strong throwing arm, he never developed into anything more than a marginal defensive outfielder, with his inability to properly judge fly balls eventually forcing him to spend a significant amount of time playing first base or serving as his team's designated hitter.

Carter remained Cleveland's primary offensive threat for two more years, batting .271, stealing 27 bases, and leading the team with 27 home runs and 98 RBIs in 1988, before placing near the top of the league rankings with 35 homers, 105 RBIs, and 303 total bases in 1989, despite batting just .243. However, with Carter approaching free agency and the Indians desperately seeking to improve their fortunes in order to convince city officials to provide additional funding for a new stadium, Cleveland GM Hank Peters completed a trade with the San Diego Padres on December 6, 1989 that sent his team's best player to San Diego, in exchange for outfielder Chris James and a pair of top prospects—catcher Sandy Alomar Jr. and infielder Carlos Baerga. While James never amounted to much, Alomar and Baerga ended up serving as cornerstones of Indians teams that spent most of the 1990s contending for the American League pennant. Carter, who hit 151 homers, knocked in 530 runs, scored 456 times, accumulated 876 hits, 164 doubles, 22 triples, and 126 stolen bases, batted .269, compiled a .309 on-base percentage, and posted a .472 slugging percentage during his time in Cleveland, averaged 28 home runs, 98 RBIs, 85 runs scored, and 25 stolen bases in his five full seasons with the Indians.

Looking back years later on the Indians' situation when he departed for San Diego, Carter recalls, "When I left, I said nothing was going to change in Cleveland until they got a new stadium and started signing their young players to long-term deals. That eventually happened, and, when I came back here, it was great. Cleveland was hopping."

Carter ended up spending just one year with the Padres, hitting 24 homers, driving in 115 runs, and batting .232 for them in 1990, before being traded to the Toronto Blue Jays at season's end. He subsequently spent seven productive seasons playing north of the border, topping 30 homers four times and 100 RBIs six times, en route to earning five All-Star selections, two Silver Sluggers, and three top-10 finishes in the league MVP voting. After signing with the Baltimore Orioles as a free agent following the conclusion of the 1997 campaign, Carter spent one more year in the big leagues, splitting the 1998 season between the Orioles and San Francisco Giants, before announcing his retirement at season's end. Over the course of his career, he hit 396 homers, knocked in 1,445 runs, scored 1,170 times, amassed 2,184 hits, 432 doubles, 53 triples, and 231 stolen bases, batted .259, compiled a .306 on-base percentage, and posted a .464 slugging percentage.

Following his playing days, Carter embarked on a brief career in broadcasting, serving as a color commentator for the Toronto Blue Jays on CTV Sportsnet from 1999 to 2000, before spending the next two years working alongside play-by-play man Chip Caray on Chicago Cubs telecasts for WGN-TV. He currently devotes much of his time to doing charitable works for the Children's Aid Foundation.

Indians Career Highlights:

Best Season: Although Carter became the first Indians player to surpass 30 home runs and 30 stolen bases in the same season the following year, he played his best ball for the Tribe in 1986, when, in addition to hitting 29 homers, stealing 29 bases, batting .302, and compiling an OPS of .849, he led the American League with 121 RBIs and ranked among the leaders with 108 runs scored, 200 hits, nine triples, and 341 total bases, posting career-high marks in each of the last seven categories. Carter, whose outstanding performance earned him recognition as the Indians Man of the Year, later said, "As far as doing everything, that [1986] was my best year."

Memorable Moments/Greatest Performances: Carter proved to be a one-man wrecking crew on August 12, 1984, when he led the Indians to a 6-0 win over the Yankees by driving in all six Tribe runs with a pair of homers off left-hander Ron Guidry, with the second of those coming with the bases loaded.

Carter had the first 5-for-5 day of his career on June 10, 1986, when he hit safely in all five of his trips to the plate and knocked in four runs during an 8-7 win over the Oakland Athletics.

Carter helped lead the Indians to a 15-4 rout of Milwaukee on September 4, 1986, by collecting four hits, driving in four runs with a fourth-inning grand slam, and scoring three times.

Just two days later, Carter went 5-for-6, with a pair of homers, four RBIs, and a career-high five runs scored, during a 17-9 win over the Brewers.

Carter gave the Indians a 6-4 victory over Kansas City on July 7, 1987, when he capped off a three-hit, four-RBI day at the plate by hitting a two-run, walk-off homer off Royals closer Dan Quisenberry in the bottom of the ninth inning.

Carter led the Indians to a 15-2 pasting of the Boston Red Sox on September 5, 1987, by going 4-for-6, with a pair of homers, five RBIs, and four runs scored.

Carter paced the Indians to a lopsided 10-2 victory over the Minnesota Twins on April 23, 1988, by driving in six runs with a pair of homers and a double.

Carter continued his power surge three days later, homering twice and knocking in five runs during a 12-6 win over the Seattle Mariners on April 26.

Carter, who established an American League record by hitting three home runs in one game five times over the course of his career, did so four times while playing for the Indians, accomplishing the feat for the first time during a 7-3 victory over the Red Sox on August 29, 1986, during which he went a perfect 5-for-5 at the plate, with four runs batted in.

Although the Indians suffered a 12-8 defeat at the hands of the Red Sox on May 28, 1987, Carter again reached the seats three times, finishing the game with four hits and five RBIs.

Carter helped lead the Indians to a 7-3 win over the Texas Rangers on June 24, 1989, by hitting three solo homers.

Carter homered three times in one game for the final time as a member of the Indians on July 19, 1989, when reached the seats three times and knocked in six runs during a 10-1 mauling of the Minnesota Twins.

Notable Achievements:

- Hit more than 20 home runs four times, topping 30 homers twice.
- Knocked in more than 100 runs three times, topping 120 RBIs once (121 in 1986).
- Scored more than 100 runs once (108 in 1986).
- Batted over .300 once (.302 in 1986).
- Surpassed 200 hits once (200 in 1986).
- Surpassed 30 doubles three times.
- Stole more than 20 bases four times, topping 30 steals once (31 in 1987).
- Posted slugging percentage in excess of .500 once (.514 in 1986).
- Hit more than 30 home runs and stole more than 30 bases in same season once (1987).
- Led AL with 121 RBIs in 1986.
- Finished second in AL with 35 home runs in 1989.
- Finished third in A.L in triples once and total bases twice.
- Hit three home runs in one game four times (vs. Boston on August 29, 1986; vs. Boston on May 28, 1987; vs. Texas on June 24, 1989; vs. Minnesota on July 19, 1989).

41

C.C. SABATHIA
2001 – 2008

An outstanding left-handed pitcher who continued to perform at an elite level after he left the Indians, C.C. Sabathia established himself as one of the American League's top hurlers during his time in Cleveland, posting double-digit wins in each of his seven full seasons with the Tribe. Extremely durable, Sabathia not only surpassed 15 victories on three separate occasions for the Indians, but he also made at least 30 starts six times and threw more than 200 innings twice, leading all AL hurlers in innings pitched in 2007, when he earned Cy Young honors by finishing second in the circuit with 19 wins. Although Sabathia's impending free agency prompted the Indians to part ways with him at the height of his career, he nevertheless helped lead them to a pair of division titles before departing for Milwaukee and, later, New York.

Born in Vallejo, California on July 21, 1980, Carsten Charles Sabathia Jr. grew up rooting for the San Francisco Giants and Oakland A's, with some of his favorite players being Will Clark, Matt Williams, Jose Canseco, Mark McGwire, and Dave Stewart. An outstanding all-around athlete, Sabathia starred in baseball, basketball, and football at Vallejo High School, excelling on the diamond as a pitcher and first baseman, the hardwood as a power forward, and the gridiron as a tight end. Heavily recruited by UCLA and the University of Hawaii, Sabathia eventually signed a letter of intent to attend the latter institution on a football scholarship. However, after being listed as the top high school prospect in Northern California by *Baseball America*, Sabathia changed his plans when the Indians selected him in the first round of the 1998 MLB Draft, with the 20th overall pick.

Advancing rapidly through Cleveland's farm system, Sabathia spent less than three full seasons in the minors, before joining the Indians at the start of the 2001 campaign after being named the franchise's Minor

Courtesy of Keith Allison

C.C. Sabathia earned AL Cy Young honors in 2007 when he won
19 games and led the league in starts and innings pitched

League Player of the Year in 2000. Despite being the youngest player in the majors, the 20-year-old Sabathia performed extremely well in his first big-league season, earning a runner-up finish in the AL Rookie of the Year voting by compiling a record of 17-5, 171 strikeouts, and a 4.39 ERA for an Indians team that captured the AL Central title. Sabathia followed that up with a solid sophomore campaign in which he went 13-11 with a 4.37 ERA, before earning the first of his three All-Star selections as a member of the Tribe in 2003 by going 13-9 with a 3.60 ERA. Extremely impressed with the young southpaw's performance, Indians manager Eric Wedge commented, "For as young as he is, he has a great deal of experience. He's been through a great deal, and he's done nothing but continue to mature and be the pitcher that you see him right now."

Meanwhile, Cleveland GM Mark Shapiro suggested, "C.C. is one of our better ball players and one of our better people."

Yet, in spite of his early success, Sabathia proved to be a source of concern to team management due to the lack of poise he displayed on the mound at times. Prone to mental melt downs if things did not go his way, Sabathia often allowed bad situations to grow worse if one of his team-mates committed an error behind him, an umpire made what he perceived to be a bad call, or an opposing batter hit a home run off a good pitch. Continuing to display an inability to overcome adversity in 2004, the 24-year-old left-hander finished just 11-10 with a 4.12 ERA. However, Sabathia finally began to exhibit a new level of maturity the following year, when he finished 15-10, with a 4.03 ERA and a total of 161 strikeouts that placed him seventh in the league rankings. Sabathia made further advancements in 2006, when, despite going just 12-11 due to poor run support, he finished third in the AL with a 3.22 ERA, topped the circuit with six complete games and two shutouts, and ranked among the league leaders with a WHIP of 1.173 and 172 strikeouts. Sabathia pitched as well as he did even though he spent the entire year pitching in discomfort, straining an oblique on Opening Day and later developing pain in his right knee that forced him to undergo arthroscopic surgery at season's end.

Fully healthy by the start of 2007 campaign, Sabathia took his game to a whole new level. More mature and focused than ever before, the 6'6", 290-pound southpaw found a way to emerge victorious even on those days when he lacked his best stuff, finishing the season with a record of 19-7 that gave him the second most wins of any AL hurler. He also topped the circuit with 241 innings pitched and 34 starts, led the league with a strikeouts-to-walks ratio of 5.649, and ranked among the leaders in winning percentage (.731), ERA (3.21), WHIP (1.141), strikeouts (209), and complete games (4), with his excellent pitching earning him AL Cy Young and *Sporting News* AL Pitcher of the Year honors, a 14th-place finish in the league MVP voting, and recognition as the winner of the Warren Spahn Award, presented annually to the best left-handed pitcher in the Major Leagues.

Sabathia predicated much of his success in 2007 on his impeccable control and outstanding repertoire of pitches. Issuing only 37 bases on balls in 241 total innings of work, Sabathia allowed just 1.382 walks per nine innings pitched, placing him second only to teammate Paul Byrd in the AL rankings in that category. Meanwhile, in addition to his mid-90s mph cut-fastball, Sabathia threw a low-to-mid 90s mph two-seam/sinker fastball, a 74-76 mph curve ball, a 78-82 mph slider that he used to strike out left-handers, and an 82-84 mph change-up that he used to fan right-handed batters. Surprisingly quick on the mound as well for a man his size, Sabathia did an excellent job of fielding his position, often converting hard-hit balls through the middle and slow rollers into outs.

Although Sabathia subsequently posted a mark of just 6-8 through the first three months of the 2008 campaign, he pitched much better than his record would seem to indicate, compiling an ERA of 3.83 and striking out 123 batters in 122⅓ innings of work. But, with the 27-year-old left-hander scheduled to become a free agent at season's end, the Indians completed a trade with the Brewers on July 7, 2008, that sent Sabathia to Milwaukee, in exchange for Matt LaPorta, Zach Jackson, Rob Bryson, and a player to be named later, who ended up being Michael Brantley. Sabathia left Cleveland with a career record of 106-71, an ERA of 3.83, a WHIP of 1.265, 19 complete games, seven shutouts, and 1,265 strikeouts in 1,528⅔ innings pitched.

Even though Sabathia turned his season around after he arrived in Milwaukee, leading the Brewers into the playoffs and earning a sixth-place finish in the NL MVP balloting by compiling a record of 11-2 and an ERA of 1.65 over the final three months of the campaign, he remained loyal to the fans of Cleveland, taking out a large $12,870 ad in the sports section of the July 30, 2008 edition of *The Cleveland Plain Dealer* that expressed his gratitude for the way Indians fans treated him and the members of his family. The ad, which everyone in the Sabathia family signed, read: "Thank you for ten great years. . . . You've touched our lives with your kindness, love and generosity. We are forever grateful! It's been a privilege and an honor!"

Sabathia's superb pitching during the second half of the 2008 campaign earned him a seven-year, $161 million free agent contract with the New York Yankees at season's end that made him the game's highest-paid pitcher at the time. Giving the eventual World Series champion Yankees a solid return on their investment his first year in pinstripes, Sabathia earned a fourth-place finish in the AL Cy Young voting by posting a league-leading 19 victories, before being named ALCS MVP after defeating the Angels twice. He followed that up by winning 21, 19, and 15 games the next three years, en route to earning two more top-five finishes in the Cy Young balloting and his final three All-Star selections. Hampered by an injured knee, a decrease in velocity on his fastball, and a growing addiction to alcohol that eventually forced him to check himself into an alcohol treatment center, Sabathia failed to perform at the same lofty level the next few seasons, compiling an overall record of just 32-39 for New York from 2013 to 2016. However, he turned things around this past season, concluding the 2017 campaign with a mark of 14-5 and an ERA of 3.69 that would seem to make him an extremely attractive free agent option for any team looking for left-handed starting pitching. Sabathia will enter the 2018 season with a career record of 237-146, an ERA of 3.70, a WHIP of 1.251, 38 complete games, 12 shutouts, and 2,846 strikeouts in 3,317 total innings pitched, with his 2,846 strikeouts placing him third all-time among left-handed pitchers, behind only Randy Johnson and Steve Carlton.

Indians Career Highlights:

Best Season: Sabathia unquestionably pitched his best ball for the Indians during his Cy Young campaign of 2007, when, in addition to compiling a record of 19-7 that gave him the second most wins of any AL hurler, he led the league with 34 starts, 241 innings pitched, and a strikeouts-to-walks-ratio of 5.65, and also ranked among the leaders with a 3.21 ERA, a WHIP of 1.141, 209 strikeouts, and four complete games.

Memorable Moments/Greatest Performances: An excellent hitting pitcher, particularly during the early stages of his career, Sabathia compiled a batting average of .300 and homered twice in 40 official trips to the plate as a member of the Indians, reaching the seats for the first time on May 21, 2005, when his two-run homer in the top of the fourth inning proved to be the decisive blow of a 5-3 victory over the Cincinnati Reds.

Sabathia got the win, allowing two earned runs and seven hits over six strong innings.

Sabathia hit his only other home run for the Indians during a June 21, 2008 contest against the Dodgers that the Tribe ended up winning by a score of 7-2 in 11 innings. Sabathia, who delivered his blow off Chan Ho Park in the third inning, also performed brilliantly on the mound, recording 10 strikeouts and yielding just five hits and one run in seven innings of work.

Although the Indians eventually lost their September 28, 2001 match-up with the Minnesota Twins by a score of 1-0, Sabathia turned in an excellent effort, striking out 11 batters and surrendering just four hits and four walks over seven shutout innings.

Sabathia went the distance against Minnesota on July 3, 2003, yielding just four hits, one walk, and one run during a 4-1 win over the Twins.

Sabathia tossed his first complete-game shutout against Tampa Bay on August 15, 2003, recording nine strikeouts and surrendering just four hits and three walks during a 1-0 victory over the Devil Rays.

Sabathia earned a 4-1 complete-game victory over the Detroit Tigers on September 7, 2005, by striking out 10 batters and allowing just four hits.

Sabathia dominated Pittsburgh's lineup on May 19, 2006, recording nine strikeouts and yielding just three hits and one walk during a 4-1 complete-game win over the Pirates.

Sabathia struck out seven batters and surrendered just three harmless singles during a complete-game 9-0 shutout of the Orioles on July 7, 2006.

Sabathia turned in a similarly dominant performance against the Chicago White Sox on September 26, 2006, recording 11 strikeouts and allowing just four hits over the first eight innings of a 6-0 Indians victory.

Sabathia threw a five-hit shutout against Oakland on May 14, 2008, allowing just two walks and striking out 11 batters during a 2-0 Cleveland win.

Notable Achievements:

- Won at least 15 games three times, posting 19 victories in 2007.
- Posted winning percentage in excess of .700 twice.
- Struck out more than 200 batters once (209 in 2007).

- Threw more than 200 innings twice.
- Led AL pitchers in: shutouts once, complete games once, innings pitched once, and starts once.
- Finished second in AL in wins once and complete games once.
- Finished third in AL in winning percentage twice and ERA once.
- Ranks among Indians career leaders in strikeouts (5th) and strikeouts-to-walks ratio (9th).
- Finished second in 2001 AL Rookie of the Year voting.
- July 2001 AL Rookie of the Month.
- May 2006 AL Pitcher of the Month.
- 2001 *Sporting News* AL Rookie Pitcher of the Year.
- 2007 Warren Spahn Award winner.
- 2007 AL Cy Young Award winner.
- 2007 *Sporting News* AL Pitcher of the Year.
- Three-time AL All-Star (2003, 2004, and 2007).

42

JULIO FRANCO
1983 - 1988, 1996 - 1997

Best known for being the oldest regular position player in MLB history, Julio Franco spent 23 long years in the majors, appearing in his final game at the ripe old age of 49. Although Franco played for seven different teams over the course of his career, he first made a name for himself as a member of the Cleveland Indians, whose uniform he wore from 1983 to 1988, before returning to the club for a second tour of duty in 1996. Spending nearly eight full seasons in Cleveland, Franco batted over .300 four times for the Tribe, earning in the process one of his five Silver Sluggers. An outstanding base runner as well during the early stages of his career, Franco also stole more than 30 bases twice and scored more than 80 runs five times for the Indians. And, even though he initially struggled somewhat with his fielding, Franco eventually turned himself into a solid defender, particularly after he moved from shortstop to second base prior to the start of the 1988 campaign.

Born in Hato Mayor del Rey in the Dominican Republic on August 23, 1958, Julio Cesar Franco grew up in Consuelo, San Pedro de Macoris, where he attended Divine Providence School. After signing with the Phillies in 1978, Franco spent most of the next five years advancing through Philadelphia's farm system, before finally being summoned to the big leagues after hitting 21 homers and batting .300 for Triple-A Oklahoma City in 1982. Appearing in a total of 16 games with the Phillies, eight of which he started at shortstop, Franco compiled a batting average of .276, hitting safely in eight of his 29 official trips to the plate.

Acquired by the Indians during the subsequent off-season in a trade that sent him and four other players to Cleveland in exchange for promising young outfielder Von Hayes, Franco laid claim to the Indians' starting shortstop job shortly after he joined the team. Performing well for the

Tribe in his first full big-league season, Franco earned a runner-up finish in the AL Rookie of the Year balloting by hitting eight homers, driving in 80 runs, scoring 68 times, stealing 32 bases, and batting .273. He followed that up with another solid year in 1984, knocking in 79 runs, scoring 82 others, swiping 19 bases, batting .286, and ranking among the league leaders with 188 hits. Yet, while Franco provided a spark on offense, he proved to be something of a liability with the glove, committing a total of 64 defensive miscues over the course of his first two seasons, while displaying only average range at shortstop.

Franco continued to struggle in the field in 1985, leading all players at his position with 36 errors for the second straight time. However, he also emerged as one of the league's better hitters, concluding the campaign with 90 RBIs, 97 runs scored, 183 hits, and a .288 batting average.

Franco, who stood six-feet tall and weighed only 165 pounds during his initial tour of duty with the Indians, employed a long, whip-like swing and used an extremely heavy bat, in spite of his relatively lean frame. He also employed a rather unique batting stance in which he kept his knees close together and held his bat over his head, with the barrel end pointing towards the pitcher. An extremely aggressive hitter, Franco typically struck out far more often than he walked, although he gradually developed more patience at the plate as his career progressed. Quite popular with the hometown fans, Franco nevertheless rubbed some of his teammates the wrong way, with Indians manager Pat Corrales stating in the May 6, 1985 edition of *The Sporting News*, "Julio Franco is the kind of guy you want to kiss one time and kick the next."

Franco continued to produce on offense in each of the next three seasons, compiling batting averages of .306, .319, and .303, scoring more than 80 runs each year, stealing more than 25 bases twice, and winning his first Silver Slugger in 1988. He also improved his fielding dramatically, cutting his error total in half in 1986 and 1987, before committing only 14 defensive miscues after being shifted to second base prior to the start of the 1988 campaign. However, with Franco developing a somewhat contentious relationship with new Indians manager Doc Edwards, the team elected to trade him to the Texas Rangers for infielder Jerry Browne, first baseman Pete O'Brien, and outfielder Oddibe McDowell on December 6, 1988, prompting Franco to later tell *The Sporting News*, "They just wanted to see the bad things. They always said I was a troublemaker. I'm not that way."

Courtesy of Jerry Reuss

Julio Franco batter over .300 four times and stole more than
30 bases twice during his time in Cleveland

Franco ended up playing the best ball of his career for the Rangers over the course of the next five seasons, earning three All-Star selections and three Silver Sluggers. Performing particularly well in 1991, Franco won the AL batting title with a mark of .341, while also establishing career-high marks in runs scored (108), hits (201), and stolen bases (36). Franco also developed into more of a power threat at the plate after adding some 15 or 20 pounds of muscle onto his frame, hitting as many as 15 home runs for the Rangers in 1991.

After five years in Texas, the 35-year-old Franco spent the remainder of his career serving as a hired gun, offering his services to the highest bidder through free agency. Signing a one-year deal with the Chicago White Sox prior to the start of the strike-shortened 1994 campaign, Franco had a huge year while playing first base for the Sox, batting .319, hitting 20 homers, and driving in 98 runs, in only 112 games. He then spent one year in Japan, before rejoining the Indians in 1996. Serving the Tribe primarily as a first baseman and designated hitter for most of the next two seasons, Franco performed well for the Indians in 1996, when, once again appearing in only 112 games, he hit 14 homers, knocked in 76 runs, scored 72 times, and batted .322. Released by the Indians after assuming a part-time role for much of the ensuing campaign, Franco signed with the Milwaukee Brewers, with whom he spent the remainder of the year. He then split the next 10 seasons between the Chiba Lotte team in Japan, the Samsung Lions in South Korea, the Angelopolis Tigers and the Quintana Roo Tigers of the Mexican League, the Atlanta Braves, and the New York Mets, before finally announcing his retirement in May 2008. Franco ended his major-league career with 173 home runs, 1,194 RBIs, 1,285 runs scored, 2,586 hits, 407 doubles, 54 triples, 281 stolen bases, a batting average of .298, an on-base percentage of .365, and a slugging percentage of .417. During his time with the Indians, he hit 62 homers, knocked in 530 runs, scored 619 others, amassed 1,272 hits, 189 doubles, 33 triples, and 147 stolen bases, batted .297, compiled a .352 on-base percentage, and posted a .400 slugging percentage.

Since retiring as an active player, Franco has entered into a career in managing, spending one year piloting the rookie-level Gulf Coast League Mets, four years managing in the Mexican League, and the last few seasons managing in Japan.

Indians Career Highlights:

Best Season: Franco posted excellent offensive numbers for the Indians in 1985, concluding the campaign with 90 RBIs, 97 runs scored, 183 hits, 33 doubles, and a .288 batting average. However, he also committed a league-leading 36 errors at shortstop. Meanwhile, although a hyperextended right elbow limited Franco to only 128 games in 1987, he still managed to score 86 runs, steal 32 bases, and compile a batting average of

.319 and an OPS of .818, posting in the process the best overall numbers of his career, to that point. At the same time, Franco improved his fielding significantly, committing just 18 defensive miscues. All things considered, Franco had his finest all-around season as a member of the Indians in 1987.

Memorable Moments/Greatest Performances: Franco helped lead the Indians to a 12-8 victory over the Detroit Tigers on June 18, 1983, by going 3-for-4, with a pair of doubles and a career-high five RBIs.

Franco collected three hits and again knocked in five runs during a convincing 10-4 win over the Baltimore Orioles on August 3, 1985.

Franco delivered the decisive blow of a 7-4 victory over Boston on August 28, 1985, putting the Tribe ahead to stay with a seventh-inning grand slam off Red Sox reliever Mark Clear.

Franco had the first 5-for-5 day of his career on July 9, 1986, hitting safely in all five of his trips to the plate during a 6-3 win over the Chicago White Sox.

Franco capped off a 4-for-4 day at the plate against Boston on June 22, 1988, by hitting a solo homer in the bottom of the eighth inning that proved to be the game-winning blow of a 3-1 Cleveland victory.

Franco knocked in five runs for the final time as a member of the Indians during a 12-2 rout of Baltimore on July 27, 1988, also scoring twice and collecting three doubles during the contest.

Franco collected five hits and scored the game-winning run in the bottom of the 13th inning, in leading the Indians to a 4-3 victory over the Chicago White Sox on September 2, 1988.

Franco delivered one of his most memorable hits as a member of the Indians during his second tour of duty with the club, giving them a 6-5 win over the Milwaukee Brewers on May 21, 1996, by hitting a two-out, walk-off homer in the bottom of the ninth inning.

Franco hit two home runs in one game for the only time as a member of the Indians later in the year, doing so during an 11-2 blowout of the Angels on September 12, 1996.

Notable Achievements:

- Batted over .300 four times, topping the .320-mark once (.322 in 1996).

- Compiled on-base percentage in excess of .400 once (.407 in 1996).
- Surpassed 30 doubles twice.
- Stole more than 30 bases twice.
- Led AL with 658 at-bats in 1984.
- Finished second in 1983 AL Rookie of the Year voting.
- 1988 Silver Slugger winner.

43

COREY KLUBER
2011 – Present

One of the American League's most dominant hurlers the past few seasons, Corey Kluber has served as the ace of the Indians' pitching staff since 2014, when he captured A.L. Cy Young honors for the first of two times by topping the junior circuit with 18 victories. In addition to winning 18 games two other times over the course of the last four years, Kluber has compiled an ERA under 3.00 twice, thrown more than 200 innings four times, and struck out more than 200 batters each season, earning in the process two All-Star selections and three top-three finishes in the Cy Young voting. Meanwhile, Kluber's brilliant pitching nearly led the Indians to their first world championship in 68 years in 2016.

Born in Birmingham, Alabama on April 10, 1986, Corey Scott Kluber attended Coppell High School in Coppell, Texas, where he starred on the mound for his school's baseball team. Overused by his high school coach, Don English, Kluber developed a stress fracture in his elbow, forcing him to undergo surgery during which he had two screws inserted in his injured arm. After subsequently going undrafted in the 2004 MLB Draft, Kluber enrolled at Stetson University in DeLand, Florida, where he spent the next three years establishing himself as one of the top pitchers in the Atlantic Sun Conference. Performing particularly well as a junior in 2007, the talented young right-hander earned Conference Pitcher of the Year and American Baseball Coaches Association All-Atlantic Region Second-Team honors by compiling a record of 12-2, an ERA of 2.05, and 117 strikeouts.

Kluber's outstanding mound work prompted the San Diego Padres to select him in the fourth round of the 2007 MLB Draft, after which he spent most of the next four seasons advancing through San Diego's farm system, before being included in a three-team trade the Padres completed with the Indians and Cardinals on July 31, 2010, that sent Ryan Ludwick from St. Louis to San Diego, Jake Westbrook from Cleveland to St. Louis, and Kluber from San Diego to Cleveland. After spending the remainder of the 2010 campaign with the Tribe's Double-A affiliate in Akron, Kluber advanced to Triple-A Columbus the following year, where he struggled somewhat, posting a record of 7-11 and an ERA of 5.56. Nevertheless, the Indians summoned him to Cleveland in September, after which Kluber pitched ineffectively in his three appearances with the big club, compiling an ERA of 8.31 and allowing six hits and three walks in just over four innings of work.

Returned to the minors in 2012, Kluber spent most of the year at Columbus, before being recalled by the Indians in August. Making 12 starts for the Tribe over the final two months of the campaign, Kluber won just two of his seven decisions and compiled an unimpressive ERA of 5.14, although he also struck out 54 batters over 63 innings. After beginning the following season back in the minors, Kluber joined the Indians for good when Brett Myers suffered an elbow injury. Making the most of his opportunity, Kluber posted a record of 11-5 and an ERA of 3.85, while also recording 136 strikeouts in 147⅓ innings of work.

A regular member of the Indians' starting rotation by the start of the 2014 season, Kluber soon emerged as the ace of the Tribe's pitching staff, leading all AL hurlers with 34 starts, while also compiling a record of 18-9 that tied him with Max Scherzer and Jered Weaver for the most wins in the league. Kluber also finished second in the circuit with 269 strikeouts and three complete games, placed third in ERA (2.44) and innings pitched (235⅔), and ranked sixth in WHIP (1.095), with his exceptional pitching earning him an 11th-place finish in the AL MVP voting and a close decision over Seattle's Felix Hernandez in the Cy Young balloting.

Although poor run support caused Kluber to finish just 9-16 in 2015, he pitched much better than his record would seem to indicate, compiling an ERA of 3.49, leading the league with four complete games, and also ranking among the leaders with 245 strikeouts, a WHIP of 1.054, and 222 innings pitched. Pitching for a stronger Indians team the following year, Kluber concluded the campaign with a mark of 18-9 that gave him the third most wins of any AL hurler. He also topped the circuit with two shutouts and ranked among the league leaders with an ERA of 3.14, a WHIP of 1.056, 227 strikeouts, three complete games, and 215 innings pitched, earning in the process his first All-Star selection and a third-place finish in the Cy Young voting. Kluber then performed brilliantly in the postseason, working seven scoreless innings against Boston in Game Two of the ALDS, before going 1-1 with a 1.59 ERA against Toronto in the ALCS and defeating Chicago twice in the World Series, although the Indians ultimately lost to the Cubs in seven games.

During his time in Cleveland, Kluber has become known for his stoic demeanor on the mound, his fierce competitive spirit, and his varied arsenal of pitches that prompted fellow hurler Chris Sale to say, "He has the nastiest stuff I've ever seen—really." Included in Kluber's repertoire are a mid-90s sinker he often uses as a set-up pitch and a low-to-mid-80s slider he uses as a strikeout pitch to both right-handed and left-handed hitters. He also throws a mid-90s four-seam fastball, a mid-80s change-up with a huge vertical drop, and a 90-mph cut fastball that acts very much like a sinker, breaking down-and-in on lefties, and down-and-away from righties.

After getting off to a poor start in 2017, Kluber spent nearly a month on the disabled list with a lower back strain. Unable to ply his craft, Kluber suffered mentally, as well as physically, later revealing, "I hated it. I also knew it was something I had to do. I couldn't pitch with the injury. I was only going to hurt the team by going in there."

However, after returning to the Indians on June 1, Kluber performed magnificently the rest of the year, concluding the campaign with a record of 18-4, striking out 265 batters in 203⅔ innings of work, and leading all AL pitchers with an .818 winning percentage, an ERA of 2.25, a WHIP of 0.869, five complete games, and three shutouts, earning in the process Cy Young honors for the second time. Commenting on his teammate's sensational pitching, Michael Brantley suggested, "He's been as good as I've ever seen him, and he's been good for a long time."

Heading into the 2018 season, Kluber has compiled a career record of 76-48, an ERA of 3.13, a WHIP of 1.086, 15 complete games, six shutouts, and 1,201 strikeouts in 1,091 total innings of work. Since he is still only 31 years old as of this writing, Kluber should be able to improve upon those figures considerably before his time in Cleveland comes to an end, thereby giving him an excellent chance of also advancing several places in these rankings.

Career Highlights:

Best Season: Although Kluber had a big year for the Indians in 2016, earning his first All-Star selection and a third-place finish in the A.L. Cy Young voting by tossing a league-leading two shutouts and ranking among the leaders with 18 wins, a 3.14 ERA, a WHIP of 1.056, 227 strikeouts, 215 innings pitched, and three complete games, he performed even better in each of his two Cy Young campaigns. En route to winning the award for the first time in 2014, Kluber led all AL pitchers with 18 wins and also ranked among the leaders with an ERA of 2.44, a WHIP of 1.095, 269 strikeouts, and 235⅔ innings pitched, establishing career-high marks in each of the last two categories. Nevertheless, Kluber managed to top that performance this past season, earning Cy Young honors again by placing second in the league with 265 strikeouts, while also finishing first among AL hurlers with career-best marks in wins (18), winning percentage (.818), ERA (2.25), WHIP (0.869), complete games (5), and shutouts (3), with his ratio of 12.070 strikeouts per nine innings pitched setting a new single-season franchise record. Named AL Pitcher of the Month three times over the course of the campaign, Kluber proved to be particularly effective in June and September, going 4-0, with a 1.26 ERA, a WHIP of 0.67, and an average of 13.4 strikeouts per nine innings pitched in the first of those months, before compiling a perfect 5-0 record, a miniscule 0.84 ERA, and 50 strikeouts in 43 innings of work during the final month of the regular season.

Memorable Moments/Greatest Performances: Kluber earned the first complete-game victory of his career on April 24, 2014, when he surrendered just four hits and recorded 11 strikeouts during a 5-1 win over the Kansas City Royals.

Although the Indians eventually suffered a 4-3 defeat at the hands of the Chicago White Sox on May 4, 2014, Kluber pitched brilliantly over the first eight innings of the contest, striking out 13 batters and yielding just three hits and one run.

Kluber again failed to earn a decision in spite of his exceptional mound work on July 24, 2014, when he recorded 10 strikeouts and allowed just two hits and one unearned run over the first nine innings of a game the Indians eventually lost to Kansas City by a score of 2-1 in 14 innings.

Courtesy of Keith Allison

Corey Kluber's brilliant pitching helped lead the Indians to their first World Series appearance in nearly two decades in 2016

Kluber followed that up with another brilliant effort, surrendering just three hits and recording eight strikeouts during a 2-0 complete-game victory over the Seattle Mariners on July 30, 2014.

Kluber dominated the St. Louis lineup on May 13, 2015, surrendering just a seventh-inning single to shortstop Jhonny Peralta and recording a career-high 18 strikeouts over the first eight innings of a 2-0 victory over the Cardinals. Kluber's 18 strikeouts tied Bob Feller's 77-year-old franchise record for the most punch-outs in a nine-inning game.

Kluber hurled another gem on August 9, 2015, recording 10 strikeouts and yielding just three hits and one walk during an 8-1 complete-game victory over the Minnesota Twins.

Kluber proved to be even more dominant in his next start, fanning seven batters and surrendering only a fourth-inning home run by Joe Mauer, in recording a 6-1, one-hit victory over the Minnesota Twins on August 14, 2015.

Kluber cruised to a 10-1 win over the Detroit Tigers on April 23, 2016, recording 10 strikeouts and allowing just two hits and one run over the first eight innings, before turning the game over to the Cleveland bullpen.

Kluber tossed a three-hit shutout against Tampa Bay on June 21, 2016, recording nine strikeouts and allowing just three harmless singles and two walks during a 6-0 Tribe win.

Kluber continued his magnificent pitching in the 2016 postseason, nearly leading the Indians to their first world championship in 68 years by compiling a record of 4-1 and an ERA of 1.83, while striking out 35 batters in 34⅓ total innings of work. Particularly impressive during Cleveland's 6-0 victory over Boston in Game Two of the ALDS, Kluber worked seven strong innings, fanning seven Red Sox batters and yielding just three hits and three walks. He also defeated the Cubs twice in the World Series, performing especially well in Game One, when he recorded nine strikeouts and surrendered just four hits over six shutout innings.

After sitting out the previous month with a strained lower back, Kluber made a triumphant return to the Cleveland starting rotation on June 1, 2017, tossing six shutout innings, recording 10 strikeouts, and surrendering just two hits and one walk to Oakland, in a game the Indians went on to win by a score of 8-0.

Kluber earned his first complete-game victory of the year on June 19, 2017, when he struck out 11 batters and yielded just three hits during a 12-0 shutout of the Baltimore Orioles.

Kluber extended his record for the month to a perfect 4-0 on June 29, 2017, when he recorded 12 strikeouts and allowed just three hits, one walk, and one run in eight innings of work, in earning a 5-1 victory over the Texas Rangers.

Although Kluber ended up suffering a 1-0 defeat at the hands of the San Diego Padres on July 4, 2017, he continued to excel on the mound, fanning 10 batters and surrendering just five hits and one walk in his eight innings of work. By recording at least 10 strikeouts for the fifth straight time, Kluber established a new franchise record.

Kluber turned in another dominant performance on July 23, 2017, when, over the first 7⅔ innings of an 8-1 win over the Toronto Blue Jays, he struck out 14 batters and yielded just five hits, two walks, and one run.

Kluber continued his extraordinary pitching on August 3, 2017, when he earned a 5-1 complete-game victory over the Yankees by surrendering just three hits and recording 11 strikeouts, becoming in the process just the fourth pitcher ever to fan at least eight batters in 12 consecutive starts.

Kluber followed that up with another exceptional effort, once again striking out 11 batters and yielding just three hits during a 4-1 victory over the Colorado Rockies on August 8 that the Indians won in walk-off fashion in the bottom of the ninth inning on a two-out, three-run homer by Yan Gomes.

Kluber hurled his third shutout of the 2017 campaign against Detroit on September 12, when he allowed just five hits and recorded eight strikeouts during a 2-0 win over the Tigers that gave the Indians their 20th consecutive victory.

Notable Achievements:

- Has won 18 games three times.
- Has posted winning percentage in excess of .600 four times, topping the .800-mark once (.818 in 2017).
- Has compiled ERA under 3.00 twice.
- Has posted WHIP under 1.000 once (0.869 in 2017).
- Has struck out more than 200 batters four times, topping 250 strikeouts twice.
- Has thrown more than 200 innings four times.
- Has led AL pitchers in: wins twice, winning percentage once, ERA once, WHIP once, shutouts twice, complete games twice, and starts once.
- Has finished second in AL in: strikeouts twice, innings pitched once, complete games once, and strikeouts-to-walks ratio twice.
- Has finished third in AL in: wins once, ERA once, WHIP once, strikeouts once, innings pitched once, and complete games once.
- Holds Indians single-season record for most strikeouts per nine innings pitched (12.070 in 2017).
- Holds Indians career record for best strikeouts-to-walks ratio (4.942).

- Ranks among Indians career leaders in: WHIP (2nd), strikeouts (7th), most strikeouts per nine innings pitched (2nd), and fewest bases on balls allowed per nine innings pitched (10th).
- Five-time AL Pitcher of the Month.
- Two-time AL Cy Young Award winner (2014 and 2017).
- Finished third in 2016 AL Cy Young voting.
- Two-time Sporting News AL Pitcher of the Year (2016 and 2017).
- Two-time AL All-Star (2016 and 2017).
- 2016 AL champion.

44

GEORGE BURNS
1920 – 1921, 1924 – 1928

One of the forgotten men of baseball, George Burns proved to be an outstanding hitter over the course of his 16-year Major League career that included stints with five different teams, including two tours of duty with the Indians. Playing some of his best ball for the Tribe, Burns batted over .300 in five of his seven seasons in Cleveland, en route to compiling an overall mark of .327 that ranks as the fifth-highest in franchise history. Burns also topped 40 doubles three times and 200 hits once as a member of the Indians, leading the league in both categories in 1926, when he became the first Cleveland player to be named AL MVP. The hard-hitting first baseman perhaps made his greatest contribution to the Indians, though, when he delivered the game-winning hit in Game Six of the 1920 World Series, helping them capture their first world championship in the process.

Born in Niles, Ohio on January 31, 1893, George Henry Burns spent much of his youth living in Tioga, Pennsylvania, before moving with his family to Philadelphia as a teenager. After dropping out of Central High School at the age of 16 to pursue a career in baseball, Burns spent the next few years playing semi-pro ball, before signing his first professional contract with Quincy (IL) of the Central Association in 1913. He subsequently split the 1913 campaign between four different teams, performing well enough at each stop that the Detroit Tigers acquired him prior to the start of the 1914 season.

Burns had a solid rookie year for the Tigers, hitting five homers, driving in 57 runs, stealing 23 bases, and batting .291 under the tutelage of Ty Cobb, who took the youngster under his wing. In fact, Burns learned a great deal from Cobb, stating years later, "The little tricks and details of batting that Cobb taught me enabled me to get hits that I otherwise wouldn't have made all the way through my career. For a while, I even

George Burns earned AL MVP honors in 1926
when he amassed a franchise-record 64 doubles

used Cobb's type of bat. Later, I switched to a longer and heavier bat." However, plagued by injuries and illnesses that included bouts with malaria, typhoid fever, and appendicitis, Burns struggled somewhat the next three seasons, driving in more than 50 runs and batting higher than .260 just once between 1915 and 1917.

After being dealt to the Philadelphia Athletics prior to the start of the war-shorted 1918 campaign, a healthy Burns had a breakout year, finishing second in the league with 70 RBIs and a batting average of .352, while topping the circuit with 178 hits and 236 total bases. But, when he failed to compile similarly impressive numbers over the course of the next season-and-a-half, Burns found himself on the move once again on May 29, 1920, when Philadelphia sold him to the Indians for $10,000.

Serving the Indians primarily as a backup to starting first baseman Doc Johnston and a right-handed bat off the bench, Burns batted .268 and knocked in 13 runs, in only 44 games and 56 official at-bats in 1920. But he came up big for the Tribe in Game Six of that year's World Series, giving the Indians a 1-0 victory over Brooklyn by driving in Tris Speaker all the way from first base with an RBI double in the sixth inning. Although Burns assumed a similar role the following year, appearing in only 84 games and accumulating just 244 official at-bats, he gave the Indians outstanding production at the plate, knocking in 49 runs and batting a robust .361.

Subsequently included in a four-player trade the Indians completed with Boston that netted them veteran first baseman Stuffy McInnis, Burns performed extremely well for the Red Sox the next two seasons, batting .306 and hitting a career-high 12 homers in 1922, before driving in 82 runs, scoring 91 times, collecting 181 hits, and batting .328 the following year.

Reacquired by the Indians prior to the start of the 1924 campaign, Burns spent the next 4½ years starting at first base for the Tribe, batting well over .300 and ranking among the league leaders in doubles four straight times. After batting .310, driving in 68 runs, and amassing 37 doubles in 1924, Burns hit .336, knocked in 79 runs, and collected 41 two-baggers in 1925. He then reached the apex of his career in 1926, finishing the year with 115 RBIs, 97 runs scored, a batting average of .358, and a league-leading 216 hits and 64 doubles, with the last figure setting a new single-season major-league record (since broken). With the Indians finishing second in the AL, just three games behind the pennant-winning Yankees, Burns's exceptional play earned him league MVP honors. He followed that up with another solid year, batting .319, driving in 78 runs, and finishing second in the league with 51 two-baggers in 1927.

Certainly, the dimensions of League Park contributed greatly to the inordinate amount of doubles that Burns compiled during his peak seasons. An excellent line-drive hitter who had the ability to hit the ball to all fields, the 6'1", 180-pound Burns took dead aim at his home ball park's short right-field wall, which stood only 290 feet from home plate down the line and 317 feet from the batter's box towards right-center. Employing an unusual batting stance in which he stood very straight at the plate, with his feet close together and his bat resting on his shoulder, Burns very much resembled a soldier standing at attention.

In addition to establishing himself as one of the league's better hitters during his second tour of duty with the Indians, Burns gradually developed a reputation for being one of the dirtiest players of his time. While he remained a gentleman off the field, Burns played angry, displaying little regard for his opponent and a win-at-all-cost mentality, much like his good friend and mentor, Ty Cobb.

Failing to reach the same level of production in 1928, Burns found himself headed to New York during the latter stages of the campaign when the Yankees purchased him from the Indians in mid-September. After making only 13 pinch-hit appearances for them during his time in New York, the Yankees sold Burns to the Philadelphia Athletics on June 19, 1929. He spent the remainder of the year serving as Jimmie Foxx's back-up, before being released by the A's, marking the end of his big-league career. Over the course of 16 seasons, Burns amassed 72 home runs, 954 RBIs, 901 runs scored, 2,018 hits, 444 doubles, 72 triples, and 154 stolen bases, batted .307, compiled an on-base percentage of .354, and posted a slugging percentage of .429. During his time in Cleveland, Burns hit 22 homers, knocked in 432 runs, scored 402 times, accumulated 853 hits, 230 doubles, 20 triples, and 62 stolen bases, batted .327, compiled a .375 on-base percentage, and posted a .455 slugging percentage. At the time of his retirement, Burns's 2,018 hits represented the third-highest total of any right-handed batter in American League history.

Following his major league career, Burns played for five seasons in the Pacific Coast League, before spending another five years managing in that same circuit. His playing days long behind him, Burns settled in the Seattle area, taking a job as a sheriff's deputy in King's County in 1947. He continued to serve in that capacity until he announced his retirement in 1968. Unfortunately, Burns spent his final years living alone in a small, dingy apartment in Bremerton, Washington, where he passed away less than one-month shy of his 85th birthday, on January 7, 1978, after losing an eight-year battle with cancer.

Indians Career Highlights:

Best Season: Although Burns also performed well for the Indians in 1925 and 1927, he clearly played his best ball for them during his MVP campaign of 1926. In addition to ranking among the league leaders in batting average (.358), RBIs (115), runs scored (97), slugging percentage (.494), and total bases (298), Burns topped the circuit with 216 hits and 64 doubles, establishing in the process a new major league record for most two-baggers in a season. Aside from earning him AL MVP honors, Burns's exceptional play gained him recognition as Cleveland Man of the Year.

Memorable Moments/Greatest Performances: Burns had a big day at the plate for the Indians on May 8, 1921, going 5-for-6, with a pair of doubles, two RBIs, and three runs scored during a 17-3 rout of the Chicago White Sox.

Burns tripled twice in the same game for the only time as a member of the Indians on August 20, 1921, when he helped lead them to a 7-3 win over the Red Sox by going 3-for-3, with a walk and three runs scored.

Burns had the only 6-for-6 day of his career on June 19, 1924, collecting a triple, three doubles, and two singles during a 16-5 pasting of the Detroit Tigers.

Although the Indians lost their July 23, 1924 meeting with the Boston Red Sox by a score of 16-12, Burns had a huge game, going 4-for-5, with two homers, a pair of doubles, four RBIs, and three runs scored.

Burns had an extremely productive day at the plate on June 4, 1925, contributing to an 11-10 win over the St. Louis Browns by going 3-for-4, with four RBIs and three runs scored.

Burns helped lead the Indians to a lopsided 13-2 victory over the Boston Red Sox on July 12, 1925 by going 3-for-4, with five RBIs and two runs scored.

Burns delivered the decisive blow of a 10-inning, 8-6 win over the Detroit Tigers on September 13, 1925, driving in the winning runs with a bases-loaded single in the top of the 10th. He finished the game with three hits, four RBIs, and one run scored.

Continuing to be a thorn in the side of Detroit's pitching staff, Burns homered, doubled, and singled, knocked in four runs, and scored three times during a 13-1 blowout of the Tigers on June 2, 1926.

Once again tormenting Tigers pitchers, Burns led the Indians to a 9-5 win over Detroit on August 29, 1928 by driving in five runs with two homers and two singles.

Yet, Burns experienced his most memorable moment as a member of the Indians in Game Six of the 1920 World Series, when his sixth-inning double drove home Tris Speaker with the game's only run. The victory gave the Indians a 4-2 lead in the Fall Classic, which they closed out with another win the very next day. Following the Game Six win, Cleveland player-manager Tris Speaker praised Burns, stating, "George Burns has played first base in very few games this season, being used mostly as a pinch-hitter. As such, he has won a few games for us this year, but has he ever risen to the occasion any more successfully than he did today when he rapped one of Sherrod Smith's best offerings to the center-field bleachers for two bases and scored me all the way from first? The best of it was he told me he was going to do it."

Notable Achievements:

- Batted over .300 five times, topping the .330-mark on three occasions.
- Knocked in more than 100 runs once (115 in 1926).
- Surpassed 200 hits once (216 in 1926).
- Surpassed 30 doubles four times, topping 50 two-baggers twice.
- Led AL with 216 hits and 64 doubles in 1926.
- Finished second in AL with 51 doubles in 1927.
- Finished third in AL with 115 RBIs in 1926.
- Ranks fifth in Indians history with .327 career batting average.
- Holds Indians single-season record for most doubles (64 in 1926).
- 1926 AL MVP.
- 1926 *Sporting News* All-Star selection.
- 1920 AL champion.
- 1920 world champion.

45

CLIFF LEE
2002 – 2009

In arguably the greatest single-season turnaround in franchise history, Cliff Lee went from being one of the American League's least effective starting pitchers in 2007 to earning Cy Young honors the following year, when he put together one of the finest seasons turned in by any Tribe hurler in recent memory. In addition to posting a league-leading 22 victories in 2008 that made him the first Indians pitcher in more than three decades to win as many as 20 games in a season, Lee lost only three times, giving him a winning percentage of .880 that ranks as the second-highest single-season mark ever compiled by a member of the team's starting rotation. Yet, while Lee's extraordinary 2008 campaign represented easily his best as a member of the Indians, the left-handed hurler proved to be much more than just a one-year wonder during his time in Cleveland. Posting 18 victories another time and 14 wins on two other occasions, Lee compiled an overall record of 83-48 over parts of eight seasons with the Indians that gives him the fifth-highest winning percentage in team annals. Meanwhile, in addition to topping the junior circuit in wins in 2008, Lee led the league in winning percentage twice, ERA once, and shutouts once, earning in the process one All-Star selection, two top-five finishes in the Cy Young voting, and one top-12 finish in the MVP balloting.

Born in the Little Rock suburb of Benton, Arkansas on August 30, 1978, Clifton Phifer Lee attended Benton High School, where he developed a reputation as an extremely confident pitcher who enjoyed showing up his opponent. After being selected by the Florida Marlins in the eighth round of the 1997 MLB Draft following his senior year at Benton High, Lee elected to delay the start of his professional career and enroll instead at Meridian Community College in Mississippi, where he spent the next two years refining his skills, before accepting a scholarship offer from the

University of Arkansas. After spending his junior year at Arkansas further sharpening his game, Lee decided to turn pro when the Montreal Expos selected him in the fourth round of the 2000 MLB Draft.

Lee remained in Montreal's farm system until the Expos included him in a six-player trade they completed with the Indians on June 27, 2002, that sent him, fellow minor leaguers Grady Sizemore and Brandon Phillips, and veteran first baseman Lee Stevens to Cleveland, in exchange for right-handed pitchers Bartolo Colon and Tim Drew. Lee then spent most of the next year-and-a-half with Cleveland's Triple-A farm team in Buffalo, although he also made brief appearances with the parent club in both 2002 and 2003, compiling an overall record of 3-4 and an ERA of 3.30 in a total of 11 starts, while recording 50 strikeouts and surrendering 47 hits in 62⅔ innings of work.

Earning a regular spot in the Cleveland starting rotation in 2004, Lee got off to a tremendous start, winning 10 of his first 11 decisions. However, he slumped during the season's second half, going just 4-7 the rest of the way, to finish the year with a record of 14-8 and an ERA of 5.43, although he still managed to tie Jake Westbrook for the team lead in wins and finish first on the club with 161 strikeouts. Returning to his first-half form the following year, Lee established himself as the ace of the Tribe's pitching staff, earning a fourth-place finish in the AL Cy Young voting by posting a record of 18-5 that gave him the league's best winning percentage (.783). He also compiled an ERA of 3.79 and a WHIP of 1.218, threw 202 innings, and recorded 143 strikeouts. Meanwhile, with Lee putting together a nine-game winning streak following the All-Star break, the Indians compiled an overall record of 23-9 in his 32 starts.

Although Lee subsequently finished second on the team with 14 wins in 2006, he pitched less effectively, going 14-11, with a 4.40 ERA, a WHIP of 1.405, and 129 strikeouts, in just over 200 total innings of work. Lee then suffered through a horrendous 2007 campaign that he began on the disabled list after straining an abdominal muscle during spring training. Upon returning to the team, Lee never found his rhythm, struggled with his control, and became far more predictable, with his inability to locate his fastball forcing him to rely heavily on his off-speed stuff. Growing increasingly frustrated with himself over time, Lee threw his glove 20 rows into the stands after being removed from a contest by manager Eric Wedge on one occasion. Things eventually got so bad that the Indians finally demoted Lee to the minors for five weeks, before summoning him

Courtesy of Alan Turkus

En route to earning AL Cy Young honors in 2008, Cliff Lee led all league hurlers with 22 victories and an .880 winning percentage

back to Cleveland during the latter stages of the campaign. However, they subsequently left him off their postseason roster, with Lee finishing the season with a record of just 5-8 and an unseemly ERA of 6.29.

The difficulties Lee encountered over the course of that 2007 campaign still remain fresh in his mind to this day, with the former pitcher revealing that his most memorable game as a member of the Indians proved to be one that he sat in the dugout watching late that year: "It was the postseason in 2007, when we were up on Boston, three to one [in the ALCS], and I didn't pitch in any of the games. I would have liked to have had a shot at one of those last three games, but we lost them all, and I didn't pitch in any of them. I'm not saying we would have won it if I had pitched in one of those games, but that was definitely motivation for me to get my career turned around."

Determined to reclaim his regular spot in the starting rotation, Lee worked extensively with pitching coach Carl Willis during the subsequent off-season and got himself into the best shape of his young career. Lee also altered his approach on the mound somewhat, becoming more adept at mixing up his pitches and working the corners of the plate. Far more focused and relaxed than ever before, Lee emerged as the AL's best pitcher, leading the league with a record of 22-3, a 2.54 ERA, and two shutouts, while also ranking among the leaders with a WHIP of 1.110, 223⅓ innings pitched, four complete games, and 170 strikeouts. Commenting years later on the incredible improvement in his performance, Lee recalled, "It was the low point and the high point of my career, from one year to the next. I went from being really bad to being really good, real quick."

Certainly, the 6'3", 205-pound Lee owed much of his success to his improved control and development into more of a complete pitcher. Better able to locate his 90-93 mph four-seam and two-seam fastballs, his 85-88 mph cut fastball, and his slider, curveball, and circle change-up, Lee mastered every pitch in his repertoire. In describing his approach to pitching, Lee suggested, "You've got to be able to pitch with your fastball. If you can't do that, if you can't locate your fastball and put it where you want to, the other pitches, what good are they?" He then added, "Working ahead, mixing speeds, and staying out of the heart of the plate—that's what you need to do to be a successful pitcher."

However, sportswriter Sheldon Ocker also credited Lee's fabulous performance to his newfound calm, noting, "Whether he is on the mound or in the clubhouse, Cliff Lee is the picture of serenity. Unfazed, unhurried, unflappable, unexcitable."

Indeed, Lee's mound presence proved to be one of his greatest weapons. Thriving under pressure, Lee unnerved his opponents with his stoic nature and tremendous self-confidence that eventually helped make him one of the finest postseason pitchers of his generation.

Unfortunately, Lee reached the aforementioned status as a member of the Philadelphia Phillies, to whom the Indians traded him on July 29, 2009, in what is generally considered to be one of the worst trades in franchise history. With Lee having compiled a record of 7-9 through the season's first four months and scheduled to become a free agent following the conclusion of the 2010 campaign, the Indians decided to minimize their losses by dealing him and outfielder Ben Francisco to the Phillies for four minor leaguers—pitchers Carlos Carrasco and Jason Knapp, infielder Jason Donald, and catcher Lou Marson. Commenting on the trade years later, Lee stated, "I was somewhat surprised by the trade, but there were rumors floating around, and I knew that they traded C.C. [Sabathia] the year before, so, knowing all that, it wasn't that much of a surprise." In addition to posting an overall record of 83-48 during his time in Cleveland, Lee compiled an ERA of 4.01 and a WHIP of 1.312, threw 10 complete games and three shutouts, and struck out 826 batters in 1,117 innings of work.

Lee performed extremely well for the Phillies the rest of the year, going 7-4 with a 3.39 ERA over the final two months of the regular season, before compiling a perfect 4-0 record and a brilliant 1.56 ERA in the postseason, although Philadelphia ended up losing the World Series to the Yankees in six games. Nevertheless, the Phillies elected to trade Lee to the Seattle Mariners for three players at season's end, with the veteran left-hander subsequently splitting the 2010 campaign between the Mariners and Texas Rangers, compiling an overall record of 12-9 and a 3.18 ERA during the regular season, en route to earning the second of his four All-Star nominations. He then helped lead the Rangers to their first American League pennant by winning all three of his playoff starts, before dropping both his decisions against San Francisco in the World Series.

Choosing to return to Philadelphia when he became a free agent at season's end, Lee spent the next four years with the Phillies, earning two more All-Star selections and a third-place finish in the NL Cy Young voting in 2011, when he went 17-8 with a 2.40 ERA, finished second in the league with a career-high 238 strikeouts, and topped the circuit with six shutouts. However, after missing the entire 2015 campaign due to a left common flexor tendon tear, Lee elected to announce his retirement, ending his career with a record of 143-91, an ERA of 3.52, a WHIP of 1.196, 29 complete games, 12 shutouts, and 1,824 strikeouts in 2,156⅔ total innings of work. After leaving the game, Lee returned to his home state of Arkansas, where he now lives with his family.

Indians Career Highlights:

Best Season: Lee's Cy Young campaign of 2008 proved to be easily his best as a member of the Indians. In addition to leading all AL hurlers in wins (22), winning percentage (.880), ERA (2.54), and shutouts (2), he finished second in the league in WHIP (1.110), innings pitched (223⅓), and complete games (4), en route to also earning *Sporting News* AL Pitcher of the Year honors and a 12th-place finish in the league MVP voting. Particularly effective during the month of April, Lee earned Pitcher of the Month honors for the first of two times by going 5-0 with a 0.96 ERA. Meanwhile, Lee's .880 winning percentage ranks as the fourth-best ever by a pitcher with more than 30 starts, with only Lefty Grove, Ron Guidry, and Randy Johnson posting higher marks. It also ranks as the second-best single-season winning percentage ever compiled by an Indians' pitcher, trailing only the mark of .938 that Johnny Allen (15-1) posted for the Tribe in 1937.

Memorable Moments/Greatest Performances: Lee turned in a dominant performance against Anaheim on May 8 2007, surrendering just three hits and two walks during a 5-1, complete-game victory over the Angels.

Lee threw 28 consecutive scoreless innings from April 13 to April 30, 2008, with the highlight of the streak being his three-hit, nine-strikeout effort against Kansas City on April 24 that earned him a 2-0 victory and his first career shutout.

Lee worked eight strong innings against San Francisco on June 26, 2008, allowing just four hits and one run, while recording 11 strikeouts during a 4-1 win over the Giants.

Lee yielded just five hits during a 5-0 complete-game shutout of the Chicago White Sox on September 1, 2008 that earned him his 20th victory of the season, making him the first Indians pitcher to reach that mark since Gaylord Perry posted 21 victories for the Tribe in 1974.

Lee turned in one of his most dominant performances for the Indians on June 14, 2009, when he surrendered just three hits and two walks during a 3-0 complete-game shutout of the St. Louis Cardinals. After walking two of the first three batters he faced, Lee did not allow another man to reach base until Yadier Molina led off the top of the eighth inning with an opposite-field double.

Notable Achievements:

- Won more than 20 games once, posting 18 victories one other time.
- Posted winning percentage in excess of .600 three times, topping the .700-mark twice and the .800-mark once (.880 in 2008).
- Compiled ERA under 3.00 once (2.54 in 2008).
- Threw more than 200 innings three times.
- Led AL pitchers in: wins once, winning percentage twice, ERA once, and shutouts once.
- Finished second in AL in: wins once, WHIP once, innings pitched once, and complete games once.

- Ranks among Indians career leaders in winning percentage (5th) and strikeouts-to-walks ratio (8th).
- Two-time AL Pitcher of the Month.
- Finished fourth in 2005 AL Cy Young voting.
- 2008 AL Cy Young Award winner.
- 2008 *Sporting News* AL Pitcher of the Year.
- 2008 AL Comeback Player of the Year.
- 2008 AL All-Star.

46

GAYLORD PERRY
1972 – 1975

Already an extremely accomplished pitcher by the time he arrived in Cleveland in 1972, Gaylord Perry previously won 134 games as a member of the San Francisco Giants, topping 20 victories twice and 15 wins four other times, en route to earning two All-Star selections and one runner-up finish in the NL Cy Young voting. Although Perry ended up spending just 3½ years with the Indians, he continued to add to his legacy of excellence by surpassing 20 wins another two times, earning in the process two more All-Star nominations and a pair of top-five finishes in the AL Cy Young balloting, claiming the award in 1972, when he put together arguably the most dominant season turned in by any Indians pitcher in the last 50 years. Although Perry celebrated his 37th birthday before he left Cleveland midway through the 1975 campaign, he remained an effective pitcher for several more years, posting another 110 victories for six other teams, and becoming in 1978 the first pitcher in baseball history to win the Cy Young Award in both leagues. Yet, in spite of his many accomplishments, Perry is perhaps remembered more than anything else for his purported used of the spitball, or grease-ball, which embarrassed batters, confounded umpires, and infuriated opposing managers for two decades.

Born in Williamston, North Carolina on September 15, 1938, Gaylord Jackson Perry grew up on a farm, where he and his older brother, Jim, helped their parents raise animals and grow tobacco, corn, and peanuts. Both Perry brothers attended local Williamston High School, with Gaylord starring in football, basketball, and baseball. After starting out as a third baseman on the diamond, the younger Perry gradually transitioned to the pitcher's mound, where he ended up winning 33 of 38 decisions. Despite being offered dozens of college scholarships in both baseball and

Courtesy of Mears Online Auctions

Gaylord Perry surpassed 20 victories in two
of his three full seasons with the Indians

basketball, Perry elected to sign with the Giants as an amateur free agent in 1958 for a bonus of $60,000.

Perry subsequently spent most of the next six years advancing through San Francisco's vast farm system, receiving brief trials with the parent club in both 1962 and 1963, before arriving in the big leagues to stay in 1964. Serving the Giants as a spot starter/long reliever in his first full season, Perry performed well as a rookie, compiling a record of 12-11 and an ERA of 2.75. Although the 6'4", 210-pound right-hander took a step backwards the following year, he emerged as a top-flight starter in 1966, after getting himself into the best shape of his young career, learning how to throw the spitball from teammate Bob Shaw, and working with pitching coach Larry Jansen on developing a slider that he incorporated into his repertoire of pitches that also included a curveball, change of pace, and excellent fastball. En route to earning All-Star honors for the first of five times, Perry posted 21 victories, compiled an ERA of 2.99, recorded 201 strikeouts, and threw 255⅔ innings.

Even though Perry spent most of the next five seasons pitching in the shadow of the great Juan Marichal, he remained one of the senior circuit's top hurlers, annually ranking among the league leaders in wins, ERA, strikeouts, complete games, and innings pitched. Performing particularly well in 1970, Perry earned his second All-Star selection and a runner-up finish in the NL Cy Young voting by leading the league with 23 wins, five shutouts, and 328⅔ innings pitched, while also ranking among the leaders with a 3.20 ERA, 214 strikeouts, and 23 complete games.

After posting 16 victories for San Francisco in 1971, Perry found himself headed for Cleveland when the Giants and Indians completed a trade on November 29, 1971, that sent the veteran right-hander and shortstop Frank Duffy to the Tribe, in exchange for hard-throwing southpaw Sam McDowell. Commenting on the trade years later, Mike Paul, who roomed with McDowell in Cleveland, said, "What the Giants told the writers was that Gaylord was thirty-three and Sam was twenty-nine, so they were getting a younger pitcher. What I said was that Gaylord would still be pitching long after Sam had retired. Perry had a much younger body than Sam, and I told the writers that, but most didn't believe me."

Not only did Perry end up pitching many more years than McDowell, but he also performed much better over the course of the next few seasons. Taking the American League by storm following his arrival in Cleveland, Perry earned AL Cy Young honors and a sixth-place finish in the MVP balloting his first year with the Tribe by compiling a record of 24-16 for a team that finished the regular season with a mark of just 72-84. In addition to winning more games than any other AL hurler, Perry topped the circuit with 29 complete games, placed second in the league with a 1.92 ERA and 342⅔ innings pitched, and finished third in strikeouts (234) and WHIP (0.978). Although Perry proved to be less dominant in 1973, concluding the campaign with a record of 19-19 and an ERA of 3.38, he still managed to lead the league with 29 complete games and establish career-high marks in strikeouts (238), shutouts (7), and innings pitched (344), also placing among the leaders in each of those categories. Returning to top form in 1974, Perry earned All-Star honors and a fourth-place finish in the Cy Young voting by going 21-13, with a 2.51 ERA, 216 strikeouts, 28 complete games, and 322⅓ innings pitched.

Looking back at Perry's performance for the Indians over the course of those three seasons, former team President Gabe Paul stated, "Gaylord was fantastic, simply fantastic. His contributions were even better than the records show, and they show plenty. He was such a great influence on the younger players. Perry was far and away the best pitcher in the American League."

As Perry took his place among the American League's elite pitchers, he continued to build on his reputation for doctoring baseballs that he established during his earlier days with the Giants. Frequently accused of using foreign substances, such as spit, jelly, and grease, to make his pitches move in an atypical manner, Perry became the subject of controversy throughout the league, resulting in numerous accusations and strip-searches on the mound. Perry, though, seemed to revel in the attention, using it to his advantage as a means of creating doubt in the hitter's mind. Fidgeting with his glove and touching his face, uniform, cap, belt, or pockets repeatedly while awaiting the signs from his catcher, Perry toyed with opposing batters, making them believe that he intended to deceive them with every pitch.

Although Perry spent most of his career dodging questions related to his purported use of the spitball, he later provided an account of the way he believed his reputation gave him an edge over opposing hitters, revealing: "Cincinnati had a great team in the late '60s, early '70s, and one day I was watching them take batting practice. I said to myself, 'I have to do something different today.' I went out and I shook Rose's hand, Morgan's hand, Perez, and Griffey Sr. with a handful of Vaseline. They thought about that all the rest of the day. I was pitching against them tomorrow, so, what do you think they were looking for? Maybe I used it, maybe I didn't."

For his part, umpire Bill Haller suggested that he never caught Perry doing anything illegal on the mound, stating, "I watched Gaylord like a hawk. I've never found anything. I'll tell you what he's got: a good curve, a fine fastball, a good change, and a fine sinker. I'll tell you what Perry is: He's one helluva pitcher, and a fine competitor."

Years later, Perry discussed more openly his somewhat devious reputation in his autobiography, which he entitled, *Me and the Spitter*. Although he contended that he rarely threw the spitball, Perry admitted, "I'd always have it [grease] in at least two places, in case the umpires would ask me to wipe one off. I never wanted to be caught out there with anything though...

it wouldn't be professional." Perry's methods worked since, despite being under constant surveillance, he didn't suffer his first ejection for using an illegal substance until 1982—his 21st big-league season.

After serving as the ace of Cleveland's pitching staff the previous three seasons, Perry got off to a slow start in 1975, compiling a record of just 6-9 through mid-June, as his relationship with second-year manager Frank Robinson grew increasingly hostile. With both men harboring feelings of resentment towards each other from their National League days, Perry quietly undermined Robinson's authority, often choosing not to abide by his rules for conditioning, and frequently questioning his handling of veterans and younger players alike. Left with no other recourse, the Indians finally decided to trade away their best player, dealing Perry to the Texas Rangers on June 13 for three young pitchers—Jim Bibby, Rick Waits, and Jackie Brown. Perry left Cleveland having compiled an overall record of 70-57, along with an ERA of 2.71, a WHIP of 1.104, 17 shutouts, 96 complete games, and 773 strikeouts in 1,130⅔ innings pitched. During his time with the Indians, he accounted for 39 percent of the team's wins.

Perry remained in Texas for 2½ years, winning 15 games for the Rangers in each of his two full seasons there, before returning to the National League in 1978, where he had a big year for the San Diego Padres, leading all NL hurlers with 21 wins and a .778 winning percentage, en route to becoming the first pitcher to earn Cy Young honors in both leagues. However, he failed to experience the same level of success in any of his five remaining big-league seasons, posting no more than 12 victories in any single campaign while splitting his time between the Padres, Rangers, Yankees, Braves, Mariners, and Royals. After winning his 300th game with the Mariners in 1982, Perry retired one year later, ending his career with an overall record of 314-265, an ERA of 3.11, a WHIP of 1.181, 53 shutouts, 303 complete games, and 3,534 strikeouts in 5,350 innings of work. In addition to compiling the 17th-most wins of any pitcher in MLB history, Perry ranks among the all-time leaders in strikeouts (8th), innings pitched (6th), and starts (9th).

Following his playing career, Perry retired to his 500-acre farm in Martin County, North Carolina, where he grew tobacco and peanuts. After going bankrupt a few years later, he briefly worked for Fiesta Foods as a sales manager, before accepting the position of head baseball coach at the University of South Carolina. Perry remained in that post until 1991, when he retired to private life.

Indians Career Highlights:

Best Season: Perry had a huge year for the Indians in 1974, earning a fourth-place finish in the AL Cy Young voting by compiling a record of 21-13, finishing second in the league with a 2.51 ERA and 28 complete games, and also ranking among the leaders with a WHIP of 1.021, 216 strikeouts, and 322⅓ innings pitched. However, he performed even better in 1972, when he earned AL Cy Young honors and a sixth-place finish in the MVP voting by topping the circuit with 24 victories and 29 complete games, while also placing in the league's top three in ERA (1.92), WHIP (0.978), strikeouts (234), and innings pitched (342.7). Perry proved to be so dominant over the course of the campaign that, despite pitching for an Indians team that finished 12 games under .500, he posted 15 straight wins at one point during the season.

Memorable Moments/Greatest Performances: Perry hit one of his six career home runs, and the only one he ever hit as a member of the Indians, on June 9, 1972, during a 7-1 win over the Minnesota Twins in which he surrendered six hits and recorded 11 strikeouts.

Although Perry failed to earn the win, he pitched brilliantly against the Texas Rangers on July 14, 1972, striking out nine batters and yielding nine hits over the first 13 innings of a contest the Indians won by a score of 2-0 in 14 innings.

Perry hurled a gem against Baltimore on August 1, 1972, surrendering just two hits and two walks during a 2-0 win over the Orioles.

Perry out-dueled New York left-hander Fritz Peterson on October 1, 1972, recording 11 strikeouts and yielding just four hits and one run during a 2-1, 11-inning win over the Yankees.

Perry dominated the Detroit lineup on April 15, 1973, striking out nine batters and allowing just two hits and one walk during a 7-0 shutout of the Tigers.

Perry turned in another extremely impressive performance on June 21, 1973, yielding seven hits and recording 14 strikeouts during a lopsided 9-1 victory over the Milwaukee Brewers.

Perry worked all 12 innings of a 1-0 win over the Chicago White Sox on August 22, 1973, striking out eight batters and allowing six hits and five walks during the contest.

Although the Indians ended up losing their April 17, 1974 meeting with the Brewers by a score of 5-4 in the bottom of the 16th on a solo home run by Milwaukee center-fielder Rob Coluccio, Perry performed heroically for the Tribe, surrendering eight hits, four runs, and recording 14 strikeouts over the first 15 innings.

Perry won a 2-1 pitcher's duel with Detroit's Joe Coleman on May 19, 1974, recording 11 strikeouts and yielding just two hits and four walks during the contest.

Notable Achievements:

* Won more than 20 games twice, posting 19 victories another time.
* Posted winning percentage in excess of .600 twice.
* Compiled ERA under 3.00 twice, finishing with mark under 2.00 once (1.92 in 1972).
* Posted WHIP under 1.000 once (0.978 in 1972).
* Struck out more than 200 batters three times.
* Threw more than 300 innings three times.
* Threw more than 25 complete games three times.
* Led AL pitchers in wins once and complete games twice.
* Finished second in AL in: ERA twice, shutouts once, innings pitched twice, and complete games once.
* Finished third in AL in: WHIP twice, strikeouts once, and innings pitched once.
* Ranks among Indians career leaders in WHIP (4th) and fewest hits allowed per nine innings pitched (6th).
* June 1974 AL Player of the Month.
* 1972 AL Cy Young Award winner.
* Finished fourth in 1974 AL Cy Young voting.
* Finished sixth in 1972 AL MVP voting.
* 1972 *Sporting News* All-Star selection.
* Two-time AL All-Star (1972 and 1974).
* Number 97 on *The Sporting News'* 1999 list of Baseball's 100 Greatest Players.
* Elected to Baseball Hall of Fame by members of BBWAA in 1991.

47

JOE GORDON
1947 – 1950

Arguably the finest all-around second baseman of his time, Joe Gordon became known for his acrobatic defense, ability to produce the long ball, and outstanding run production over the course of his 11-year major-league career, which he split between the New York Yankees and Cleveland Indians. Earning one MVP trophy, five top-10 finishes in the MVP voting, six *Sporting News* All-Star selections, and nine AL All-Star nominations, Gordon knocked in more than 100 runs four times and surpassed 20 homers seven times, topping 30 round trippers twice. Possessing outstanding range and athleticism, Gordon also led all players at his position in assists four times, putouts once, and double plays three times. Although Gordon achieved much of his success while wearing a Yankee uniform, he proved to be a tremendous asset to the Indians during his four years in Cleveland, topping 20 homers three times and 100 RBIs once, en route to earning a pair of top-10 finishes in the AL MVP balloting, two *Sporting News* All-Star selections, and his final three AL All-Star nominations.

Born in Los Angeles, California on February 18, 1915, Joseph Lowell Gordon moved with his mother and older brother to Portland, Oregon shortly after he lost his father at the age of four. Developing into an outstanding all-around athlete as a teenager, Gordon played right halfback for Jefferson High School's football team, while also starring in center field for the varsity baseball team as a junior, before moving to shortstop the following year, when he earned All-Portland honors. Continuing to excel in multiple sports after enrolling at the University of Oregon following his graduation from Jefferson High, Gordon served as a member of the men's gymnastics team and played football for one season, before choosing to focus exclusively on baseball. Establishing himself as a top prospect while in college, Gordon earned All-Conference honors as a sophomore by batting .380, before leading Oregon to its second consecutive Northwest Conference championship the following year by posting a mark of .415.

Signed by New York Yankees scout Bill Essick in the spring of 1936, Gordon spent his first season in pro ball manning shortstop for the Oakland Oaks in the Pacific Coast League, before sliding over to play second base the following year for the International League's Newark Bears. Summoned to New York in 1938, Gordon ended up having an outstanding rookie season for the Yankees after replacing Hall of Famer Tony Lazzeri at second, earning a 12th-place finish in the AL MVP voting by hitting 25 homers, driving in 97 runs, scoring 83 times, and batting .255. Improving upon those numbers in each of the next three seasons, the right-handed hitting Gordon averaged 27 homers, 100 RBIs, and 103 runs scored from 1939 to 1941, while also compiling batting averages of .284, .281, and .276. Gordon reached the apex of his career, though, in 1942, when he claimed AL MVP honors by hitting 18 homers, knocking in 103 runs, and batting a career-high .322, which placed him fourth in the league rankings. More than just an outstanding hitter, Gordon annually ranked among the top players at his position in putouts, assists, and double plays, with his exceptional range and athleticism gaining him widespread acclaim as one of the finest defensive second basemen in all of baseball. Yankee skipper Joe McCarthy, who also managed all-time greats Lou Gehrig and Joe DiMaggio during his time in New York, once expressed his admiration for Gordon by proclaiming, "The greatest all-around player I ever saw, and I don't bar any of them, is Joe Gordon."

After earning his fifth straight All-Star selection in 1943, Gordon entered the United States Air Force to serve his country during World War II. He spent most of the next two years stationed in Hawaii and San Diego, where he played for the Seventh Air Force team. Following his release in November 1945, Gordon returned to the Yankees, for whom he struggled terribly in 1946, when, limited to 112 games by a series of injuries, he batted just .210, with only 11 homers and 47 RBIs.

With the Indians seeking to upgrade their offense and the Yankees looking to add pitching, the two teams completed a deal on October 11, 1946, that sent Gordon to Cleveland, in exchange for 29-year-old right-hander Allie Reynolds, who had compiled an overall record of 51-47 over parts of five seasons with the Tribe. Upon making the deal, Indians owner Bill Veeck stated, "I don't believe Gordon is through, despite a bad season, and I don't think Reynolds will ever be a consistently good pitcher."

Courtesy of Mears Online Auctions

Joe Gordon earned All-Star honors in
three of his four years with the Indians

Veeck proved to be only half right because, while Gordon still had some good years left in him, Reynolds emerged as an elite hurler with the Yankees, making significant contributions to six world championship teams during his eight-year stay in New York. Nevertheless, the Indians never regretted making the move, with batting instructor Rogers Hornsby expressing the sentiments of the team during 1947 spring training, when he said the Tribe would have the greatest double play duo in the game. Meanwhile, Boston's Bobby Doerr, who rivaled Gordon as the American League's top second baseman throughout the 1940s, suggested, "There ought to be a law against having two guys like Gordon and Lou Boudreau on the same team."

Gordon ended up having an outstanding first season in Cleveland, earning his seventh All-Star selection and a seventh-place finish in the AL MVP voting by batting .272, scoring 89 runs, finishing second in the league with 29 homers and 279 total bases, ranking among the leaders with 93 RBIs, a .496 slugging percentage, and an OPS of .842, and leading all players at his position with 466 assists, which represented the third-highest total of his career. Commenting years later on the impression the 5'10", 180-pound Gordon made on him, teammate Bob Feller offered, "He was a wild swinger at the plate, a free swinger with power. He was an acrobat around the bag, he was all over the place in the field."

Gordon also contributed greatly to the sense of unity on the ball club by welcoming with open arms Larry Doby, the American League's first black player, who joined the team in early July 1947. Recalling years later how Gordon relieved some of the anxiety he felt the first time he donned an Indians uniform, Doby recounted, "I couldn't believe how this was. I put on my uniform, and I went out on the field to warm up, but nobody wanted to warm up with me. I had never been so alone in my life. I stood there alone in front of the dugout for five minutes. Then Joe Gordon, the second baseman who would become my friend, came up to me and asked, 'Hey, rookie, you gonna just stand there or do you want to throw a little?' I will never forget that man." With Gordon's Indians teammates holding him in extremely high esteem due to the level of success he previously experienced in New York, even those who initially balked at the idea of accepting Doby as one of their own subsequently found themselves compelled to treat him with respect.

Gordon compiled outstanding numbers again in 1948, helping the Indians capture their first pennant in 28 years by leading the team with 32 homers and 124 RBIs, batting .280, and scoring 96 runs, earning in the process his eighth All-Star nomination and a sixth-place finish in the league MVP balloting. Gordon subsequently made the All-Star team for the last time in 1949, concluding the campaign with 20 homers, 84 RBIs, 74 runs scored, and a .251 batting average, before hitting 19 homers, driving in only 57 runs, and batting just .236 in somewhat limited action the following year, as he gradually gave way at second to future AL batting champion Bobby Avila. Displaying his level of professionalism, Gordon spent a considerable amount of time working with Avila, saying of his pupil, "That kid knows more about pitchers and batters after two years on the bench than most of the ten-year men in the game." Responding in kind, Avila said of his mentor, "I pattern myself after Number Four, Joe Gordon. I watch him all the time. He teaches me everything. There was never anybody like Joe Gordon. He helps me all the time."

Released by the Indians following the conclusion of the 1950 campaign, the 35-year-old Gordon chose not to field offers from any other teams, ending his big-league career with 253 home runs, 975 RBIs, 914 runs scored, 1,530 hits, 264 doubles, 52 triples, 89 stolen bases, a .268 batting average, a .357 on-base percentage, and a .466 slugging percentage. In his four seasons with the Indians, Gordon hit 100 homers, knocked in 358 runs, scored 318 times, collected 530 hits, 78 doubles, 14 triples, and 21 stolen bases, batted .262, compiled a .354 on-base percentage, and posted a .463 slugging percentage.

After leaving Cleveland, Gordon began a lengthy career in managing and scouting, spending the next two years serving as player-manager of the Sacramento Solons of the Pacific Coast League, a Chicago White Sox affiliate, before landing a job as supervisor of West Coast scouting for the Detroit Tigers. After a few years in that role, Gordon became manager of the Indians in 1958—a position he held until August 3, 1960, when Cleveland GM "Trader" Frank Lane dealt him to the Detroit Tigers for their skipper, Jimmy Dykes. After resigning as Detroit manager at season's end, Gordon briefly managed the Kansas City Athletics, before serving the Los Angeles Angels as a scout and batting instructor from 1962 to 1968. He then spent his last three years in baseball working for the expansion Kansas City Royals, serving them first as manager and, then, as a scout. Retiring from the game in 1972, Gordon spent his remaining years selling real estate, hunting, and fishing, before passing away from a heart ailment at 63 years of age, on April 14, 1978. The Baseball Hall of Fame opened its doors to him 31 years later, when the members of the Veteran's Committee elected him in 2009.

Although some people have since questioned the legitimacy of Gordon's induction, those who played against him feel he clearly earned his place in Cooperstown, with Bobby Doerr saying of his former rival, "He was a great hitter . . . probably lost thirty points on his average being a right-handed hitter at Yankee Stadium, yet he could drive the ball out of that park."

Hall of Fame broadcaster Jerry Coleman, who became the Yankees' starting second baseman two years after Gordon left New York, stated, "He [Gordon] was one of the greats of the game—a truly brilliant defensive player. To me, he was the perfect second baseman, with his ability to turn the double play and hit for power in such a difficult hitter's park as Yankee Stadium. He made Phil Rizzuto and Lou Boudreau better. He wasn't just good, he was great."

Indians Career Highlights:

Best Season: Although Gordon also posted excellent numbers for the Indians in 1947, concluding the campaign with 29 homers, 93 RBIs, 89 runs scored, and a .272 batting average, he had his finest season as a member of the team the following year, when he helped lead the Tribe to the pennant by batting .280, scoring 96 runs, finishing second in the league with 32 home runs, and placing fourth in the circuit with a career-high 124 RBIs.

Memorable Moments/Greatest Performances: Gordon had his first big game for the Indians on May 3, 1947, when he helped lead them to a 9-3 win over the Boston Red Sox by driving in five runs with a pair of homers, including a fourth-inning grand slam.

Gordon again reached the seats twice just eight days later, going 3-for-4, with two homers, four RBIs, and four runs scored, during a 16-1 pasting of the St. Louis Browns on May 11, 1947.

Gordon provided much of the offensive firepower during a 5-4 win over the Philadelphia Athletics on June 13, 1947, driving in three runs with a pair of homers, including a two-run shot in the top of the eighth inning that provided the margin of victory.

Gordon helped the Indians celebrate Independence Day in 1947 by going 3-for-5, with two homers, a double, three RBIs, and three runs scored, during a 13-6 win over the Tigers.

Gordon delivered the game-winning blow of a 10-8 victory over Boston on September 11, 1947, when his three-run homer in the top of the eighth inning put the Indians ahead to stay. He finished the contest with three hits, three runs scored, and a career-high six runs batted in.

Gordon proved to be the difference in a 5-3 win over Philadelphia just five days later, going 3-for-4, with a pair of homers and four RBIs

Gordon came back to haunt his former team on June 12, 1948, when he collected three hits, four RBIs, and three runs scored during a 9-4 win over the Yankees.

Gordon led the Indians to a 6-4 victory over Detroit on September 30, 1949, by going 3-for-3, with two homers, a double, four RBIs, and three runs scored, with his two-run blast off Hall of Fame southpaw Hal Newhouser in the top of the seventh inning providing the winning margin.

Gordon had the only 5-for-5 day of his career on July 17, 1950, leading the Indians to an 11-6 win over the Red Sox by homering once, collecting four singles, and driving in four runs.

Notable Achievements:

- Hit more than 20 home runs three times, topping 30 homers once (32 in 1948).
- Knocked in more than 100 runs once (124 in 1948).
- Posted slugging percentage in excess of .500 once (.507 in 1948).
- Finished second in AL in home runs twice and total bases once.
- Led AL second basemen in assists once.
- Finished in top 10 of AL MVP voting twice.
- Two-time *Sporting News* All-Star selection (1947 and 1948).
- Three-time AL All-Star (1947, 1948, and 1949).
- 1948 AL champion.
- 1948 world champion.
- Elected to Baseball Hall of Fame by members of Veteran's Committee in 2009.

48

GRADY SIZEMORE
2004 – 2011

    One of the finest all-around players in the game before a series of debilitating injuries caused him to experience a precipitous fall from grace, Grady Sizemore performed brilliantly for the Indians his first few years in Cleveland. After establishing himself as the Tribe's starting centerfielder in 2005, Sizemore hit more than 20 homers, scored more than 100 runs, stole more than 20 bases, and accumulated more than 30 doubles in each of the next four seasons, leading the AL in runs scored and doubles once each during that time. An exceptional defender as well, Sizemore annually ranked among the league leaders in outfield putouts, earning Gold Glove honors in both 2007 and 2008, with his varied skill-set also enabling him to earn three All-Star selections and three top-12 finishes in the league MVP voting. However, beset by injuries that placed severe limitations on him the rest of his career, Sizemore found himself unable to sustain the same level of excellence in subsequent seasons, forcing us all to wonder what might have been.

    Born in Seattle, Washington on August 2, 1982, Grady Sizemore grew up some 30 miles north, in the city of Everett, where he attended Cascade High School. An outstanding all-around athlete, Sizemore starred in basketball, baseball, and football at Cascade High, excelling as a guard on the hardwood, an outfielder on the diamond, and as both a running back and a quarterback on the gridiron. After being recruited by some of the top West Coast football programs, including Arizona State and the University of California, Sizemore signed a letter of intent to play football and baseball at the University of Washington. However, he changed his plans after the Montreal Expos selected him in the third round of the 2000 MLB Draft and subsequently offered him a $2 million signing bonus.

Grady Sizemore surpassed 20 homers, 20 steals,
and 100 runs scored four straight times for the Indians

Sizemore spent the next two-and-a-half years advancing through Montreal's farm system, before switching organizations on June 27, 2002, when the Expos traded him and fellow minor leaguers Cliff Lee and Brandon Phillips to the Cleveland Indians for ace right-hander Bartolo Colon. After developing into more of a power threat at the plate under the tutelage of Kinston manager Ted Kubiak during the second half of the 2002 campaign, Sizemore earned Rookie of the Year honors as a member of the Akron Aeros of the Class AA Eastern League the following year, prompting the Indians to promote him to their farm team in Buffalo. Continuing to perform well at Buffalo in 2004, Sizemore earned his first call-up to the big leagues in mid-July, making his major-league debut with the Indians on July 21, 2004. Spending the season's final 10 weeks serving the Tribe as a part-time outfielder, Sizemore acquitted himself well, displaying excellent instincts in centerfield, while also holding his own on offense, batting .246, hitting four homers, and driving in 24 runs, in only 138 official at-bats.

After being named the Indians' starting centerfielder prior to the start of the ensuing campaign, Sizemore emerged as one of the league's best players at that position, hitting 22 homers, driving in 81 runs, scoring 111 times, batting .289, accumulating 185 hits, 37 doubles, and 11 triples, and stealing 22 bases out of the leadoff spot in the batting order, while also making several spectacular diving catches in center. Sizemore's hustle and all-out style of play brought new energy and enthusiasm to an Indians team that went on to win 93 games, making him an immediate favorite of the hometown fans. Meanwhile, the young outfielder's exceptional play in just his first full season prompted several notable baseball men to sing his praises, with Cubs manager Lou Piniella stating, "Grady is a very good all-around player. He's on his way to stardom."

Former Indians centerfielder Rick Manning noted, "The way he carries himself, he acts like he has been here for ten years."

Indians GM Mark Shapiro added, "His approach is what separates him from other players. We knew Grady had talent, but what we couldn't know is the maturity, focus, and poise he would bring so soon."

Continuing his ascent to stardom in 2006, Sizemore hit 28 homers, knocked in 76 runs, stole 22 bases, batted .290, posted an OPS of .907, ranked among the league leaders with 190 hits, 11 triples, and 349 total bases, topped the circuit with 53 doubles and 134 runs scored, and led all AL outfielders with 409 putouts, with his tremendous all-around play earning him All-Star honors for the first of three straight times and an 11th-place finish in the league MVP voting. He followed that up with a similarly impressive performance in 2007, when, in addition to winning the first of his two Gold Gloves, he hit 24 homers, knocked in 78 runs, batted .277, compiled a .390 on-base percentage, and placed near the top of the league rankings in runs scored (118), stolen bases (33), and walks (101). With Sizemore leading the Indians to their first division title in six years, he finished 12th in the AL MVP balloting.

Fast becoming an icon in the city of Cleveland, Sizemore emerged as the Tribe's most popular player, with his good looks making him particularly appealing to fans of the female persuasion. Yet, Sizemore remained mostly unaffected by his early success, with GM Mark Shapiro telling *Sports Illustrated* in May 2007, "There is a superstar on our team, but if you walked into our clubhouse, you'd have no idea who it is. To watch him [Sizemore] play day in and day out is a rare treat. All of us, from the front office, to the players, to the batboys, are fortunate to see him every day. He is without a doubt one of the greatest players of our generation."

Indians coach Derek Shelton also expressed his admiration for Sizemore by stating, "Grady is what every boy in America should grow up to be."

Meanwhile, former All-Star Robby Thompson praised Sizemore for his old-school approach to the game, noting, "Whether he hits a shot to the gap or a ground ball to second, he runs full speed…you don't have to remind him how the game is supposed to be played."

Indians manager Eric Wedge added, "What matters to me is the consistency he brings to the ballpark every day, and how he handles things."

Blessed with an extremely athletic physique, the 6'2", 205-pound Sizemore proved to be a rarity of sorts in that he possessed more speed than most sluggers and more power than most speedsters. Capable of driving the ball with power to all fields with his smooth, left-handed swing, Sizemore also used his speed and hustle to often turn singles into doubles and doubles into triples. He also gradually developed a keen knowledge of the strike zone, drawing a total of 199 bases on balls from 2007 to 2008, with his only true weakness as a hitter being his high strikeout totals (he fanned more than 130 times four straight times, from 2005 to 2008).

Sizemore continued to perform at an elite level in 2008, earning a 10th-place finish in the AL MVP voting and his lone Silver Slugger by hitting 33 homers, driving in 90 runs, scoring 101 times, amassing 39 doubles, stealing 38 bases, batting .268, and compiling an OPS of .876. Sadly, though, the 2008 campaign proved to be Sizemore's last truly productive season, since he subsequently suffered a string of injuries that made him just a shell of his former self. After hurting his left groin during 2009 spring training, Sizemore sustained an injury to his left elbow shortly thereafter that forced him to spend most of the year playing in pain. Limited to only 106 games, Sizemore finished the season with just 18 homers, 64 RBIs, 73 runs scored, and a batting average of .248. Sizemore's bad luck continued in each of the next two seasons, as he missed all but 33 games in 2010 after undergoing microfracture surgery on his left knee, and more than half of the ensuing campaign with a right knee contusion and a sports hernia.

Although Sizemore's injury woes prompted the Indians to decline the 2012 option on his contract, the two sides eventually reached an agreement that allowed the 29-year-old centerfielder to return to Cleveland at a reduced rate. However, another string of injuries followed, preventing Sizemore from ever again appearing in a game as a member of team. After surgery on his back and microfracture surgery on his right knee kept him off the field for all of 2012 and 2013, Sizemore left the Indians when he became a free agent again, finishing his time in Cleveland with 139 home runs, 458 RBIs, 601 runs scored, 948 hits, 216 doubles, 43 triples, 134 stolen bases, a .269 batting average, a .357 on-base percentage, and a .473 slugging percentage.

After signing with Boston prior to the start of the 2014 campaign, Sizemore split his final two seasons between the Red Sox, Phillies, and Tampa Bay Rays, failing to regain his earlier form while serving all three teams as a part-time outfielder. A free agent again at the end of 2015, Sizemore chose to announce his retirement, ending his career at only 33 years of age, with 150 home runs, 518 RBIs, 660 runs scored, 1,098 hits, 252 doubles, 47 triples, 143 stolen bases, a .265 batting average, a .349 on-base percentage, and a .457 slugging percentage. Sizemore subsequently spent one year away from the game, before returning to the Indians in February 2017 as an advisor to the team's player development department.

Indians Career Highlights:

Best Season: Sizemore had an exceptional year for the Indians in 2008, becoming just the second player in franchise history to surpass 30 homers and 30 steals in the same season by hitting 33 homers and swiping 38 bases, while also driving in a career-high 90 runs, scoring 101 times, accumulating 39 doubles and 318 total bases, batting .268, and posting an OPS of .876. However, he compiled better overall numbers in 2006, concluding the campaign with 28 home runs, 76 RBIs, 190 hits, 22 stolen bases, a .290 batting average, and a career-high OPS of .907, while also finishing second in the league with 11 triples and 349 total bases and topping the circuit with 134 runs scored, 53 doubles, and 92 extra-base hits. By surpassing 25 homers, 10 triples, 50 doubles, and 20 stolen bases in the same season, Sizemore became just the second player in MLB history to do so, joining Chuck Klein, who accomplished the feat for the Philadelphia Phillies in 1932.

Memorable Moments/Greatest Performances: Sizemore proved to be the difference in a 6-1 victory over the Kansas City Royals on August 10, 2005, driving in five of the Indians' six runs with grand slam homer and a pair of singles.

Sizemore had another big day against Kansas City on September 22, 2005, leading the Indians to an 11-6 win over the Royals by going 5-for-6, with a pair of doubles, two RBIs, and two runs scored.

Sizemore came through in the clutch for the Indians on May 21, 2006, when, after striking out in four of his five previous plate appearances, he gave them a 3-2 victory over the Pittsburgh Pirates by driving in the winning run from third base with a two-out RBI single in the bottom of the 10th inning.

Sizemore led the Indians to an 11-6 win over the Texas Rangers on September 24, 2006, by hitting a pair of two-run homers.

Sizemore proved to be too much for the Cincinnati Reds to handle on May 18, 2007, leading the Tribe to 9-4 victory over the Reds by going 4-for-5, with a homer, three RBIs, and three runs scored.

Sizemore led the Indians to a 12-0 rout of the Toronto Blues on May 10, 2008, by scoring three times and driving in five runs with a double and a pair of homers.

Sizemore turned in a tremendous all-around effort against Kansas City on August 21, 2008, going 4-for-5, with a homer, triple, stolen base, and career-high seven RBIs during a 10-3 win over the Royals.

Notable Achievements:

- Hit more than 20 home runs four times, topping 30 homers once (33 in 2008).
- Scored more than 100 runs four times, topping 130 runs scored once (134 in 2006).
- Finished in double digits in triples twice.
- Surpassed 30 doubles four times, topping 50 two-baggers once (53 in 2006).
- Stole more than 20 bases four times, topping 30 thefts twice.
- Surpassed 30 home runs and 30 stolen bases in same season once (2008).
- Drew more than 100 bases on balls once (101 in 2007).
- Posted slugging percentage in excess of .500 twice.
- Led AL in: runs scored once, doubles once, games played twice, and plate appearances once.
- Finished second in AL in triples once and total bases once.
- Finished third in AL in triples once and bases on balls once.
- Led AL outfielders with 409 putouts in 2006.
- Holds Indians single-season record for most plate appearances (751 in 2006).

- 2008 Silver Slugger winner.
- Two-time Gold Glove winner (2007 and 2008).
- Finished 10th in 2008 AL MVP voting.
- 2008 *Sporting News* All-Star selection.
- Three-time AL All-Star (2006, 2007, and 2008).

49

VEAN GREGG
1911 – 1914

The only twentieth-century pitcher to win at least 20 games in each of his first three big-league seasons, Vean Gregg experienced a meteoric rise to stardom following his arrival in Cleveland in 1911, before experiencing an equally swift fall from grace just three years later after developing arm problems. A lanky southpaw with a wicked curveball, Gregg gained widespread acclaim as one of the finest pitchers in the game his first few years in the league, with both Ty Cobb and Eddie Collins calling him the best left-hander in the American League, and Hall of Fame umpire Billy Evans saying Gregg was "one of the greatest southpaws I ever called balls and strikes for." In addition to surpassing 20 victories three straight times, Gregg led all AL hurlers in ERA and WHIP once each, tossed more than 250 innings twice, and threw more than 20 complete games three times. Unfortunately, Gregg's period of dominance proved to be all short-lived, since the aforementioned arm problems limited his effectiveness throughout the remainder of his career.

Born in Chehalis, Washington on April 13, 1885, Sylveanus Augustus Gregg spent much of his youth assisting his father in his plastering business, later crediting years of "trowel wielding" for developing the strong hands that enabled him to snap off his sharp-breaking curve ball. After moving with his family to Clarkston, Washington at the age of 12, Gregg ended up earning a bookkeeping diploma from the Clarkston Commercial School, before choosing to follow in his father's footsteps and make his living as a plasterer. However, while working in that capacity during the week, Gregg supplemented his income on weekends by starring on the mound for several amateur, semi-pro, and college teams in the Palouse region of eastern Washington, typically earning $25 per game. In discussing his decision not to pursue a career in pro ball at the time, Gregg explained years later, "I did not go into professional baseball any sooner because I could make more money outside than I could inside. In my semi-pro days, I played baseball all over Washington, Montana, and Idaho. On these barnstorming tours, a player can often make more money than he could as a member of a regular league."

Nevertheless, Gregg eventually elected to turn pro, spending the final three months of the 1908 campaign pitching for the Baker City Nuggets in the short-lived Class D Inland Empire League. After struggling somewhat at Spokane the following year, Gregg joined Portland, where he had a breakout season in 1910, winning 32 games, tossing 14 shutouts, and striking out 379 batters in 387 innings of work. Impressed with Gregg's performance, Cleveland scout Jim "Deacon" Maguire purchased him for the Naps, who he joined in 1911 at the rather advanced age of 26.

After beginning his rookie season in the bullpen, Gregg gradually worked his way into the starting rotation, performing so well that, after posting his 10th consecutive victory on July 27, his record stood at an eye-popping 18-3. Following a particularly strong outing against the New York Highlanders in July, Gregg drew praise from New York first baseman Hal Chase, who called him "the leading pitcher of the league, and, in my opinion, the most marvelous southpaw I have ever looked at." Bothered by a sore arm during the latter stages of the campaign, Gregg pitched somewhat less effectively towards season's end, winning just five of his last nine decisions, before sitting out the rest of the year after recording a 9-2 victory over Chicago on September 4. Nevertheless, Gregg finished the season with a sparkling record of 23-7, 22 complete games, five shutouts, and a league-leading 1.80 ERA and 1.054 WHIP. In addition to being named a member of *The Sporting News* "All-American League" team at season's end, Gregg received accolades from the *Chicago Tribune*, which wrote, "Unless something unexpected happens, he promises to take a place among the great left-handers of baseball history."

Standing close to 6'2" tall and weighing somewhere between 180 and 185 pounds, Gregg presented a long and lean figure on the mound to the opposition. Employing a pitching motion described as "a free and easy delivery" and a wind-up depicted as "a graceful sweep above the head that bothers the batters not a little," Gregg had the ability to come at opposing hitters from various angles, occasionally using either a submarine-style or sidearm delivery, although he more commonly threw straight overhand. While he had a good fastball, Gregg relied primarily on his exceptional curve, which one writer described thusly: "It sweeps to the plate, and, just as the batter sets to take a swing at the pill, the ball shoots toward him like lightning." In discussing Gregg's signature pitch, another writer claimed, "It drops between three and four feet in a space of eight or 10 feet, possibly less." An extremely intelligent pitcher, Gregg drew praise from umpire Billy Evans, who stated, "I never saw a young pitcher grasp the finer points of the game or the weakness of batters more quickly than the Western Wonder."

Although Gregg continued to experience occasional soreness in his pitching arm his second year in the league, he followed up his spectacular rookie season with an exceptional sophomore campaign, compiling a record of 20-13 and an ERA of 2.59, completing 26 of his 34 starts, throwing 271⅓ innings, and finishing fourth in the league with 184 strikeouts. Naps manager Harry Davis, who tired of a bickering, faction-torn team and resigned a month before the end of the season, claimed, "That fellow Gregg is an exact duplicate of Waddell when the Rube was at his best." Gregg again pitched extremely well in 1913, going 20-13 with a 2.24 ERA, and placing among the league leaders with 23 complete games, 285⅔ innings pitched, and 166 strikeouts.

Unfortunately, Gregg's arm troubles grew increasingly worse the following year, allowing him to start only 12 games over the course of the season's first four months, although he pitched well whenever he found himself able to take the mound, winning nine of his 12 decisions and compiling an ERA of 3.07. But, as his availability became more and more problematic to a Cleveland team that won just 30 of its first 91 games, Naps owner Charles Somers decided to trade his star pitcher to the Boston Red Sox for three players on July 28, 1914. Gregg left Cleveland having compiled an overall record of 72-36, a 2.31 ERA, and a WHIP of 1.233. He also recorded 531 strikeouts and threw 10 shutouts, 77 complete games, and 898⅓ innings as a member of the Naps.

Gregg ended up spending the next 2½ years in Boston, during which time his sore arm limited him to only 25 starts and an overall record of just 9-11. After Gregg failed to make a single appearance for the Red Sox in either the 1915 or 1916 World Series, Boston optioned him to Providence, where he experienced a rebirth in 1917, winning 21 games and leading the International League in ERA and strikeouts. Dealt to the Philadelphia Athletics at season's end, a healthy Gregg compiled a record of 9-14 and an ERA of 3.12 for the last-place A's in 1918, before retiring to his ranch in

Alberta, Canada when World War I brought the season to a premature end. However, after spending the next three years away from the game, Gregg decided to mount a comeback when crop prices hit rock bottom in 1921. Starring on the mound for the Pacific Coast League's Seattle Indians the next three seasons, Gregg won 19 games in 1922, led the league in ERA in 1923, and posted another 25 victories in 1924, earning in the process a return trip to the Major Leagues as a member of the Washington Senators. Working primarily out of the Washington bullpen in 1925, the 40-year-old Gregg appeared in 26 games, compiling a record of 2-2 and an ERA of 4.12, before being optioned to the New Orleans Pelicans of the Southern Association during the latter stages of the campaign and subsequently announcing his retirement. Gregg ended his major league career with a record of 92-63, an ERA of 2.70, a WHIP of 1.286, 14 shutouts, 105 complete games, and 720 strikeouts in 1,393 innings pitched. But, factoring into the equation the seven years he spent pitching in the minor leagues, Gregg won a total of 224 games in 15 seasons of pro ball.

Following his retirement, Gregg moved to Hoquiam, Washington, where, for 37 years, he owned and operated The Home Plate, a multipurpose establishment that featured sporting goods, cigars, and a lunch counter. Gregg spent his final days suffering from prostate cancer, which claimed his life on July 29, 1964, at the age of 79. Five years later, a poll of Cleveland Indians fans named him the greatest left-handed pitcher in franchise history.

Indians (Naps) Career Highlights:

Best Season: Although Gregg won 20 games in each of the next two seasons, his rookie campaign of 1911 proved to be the finest of his career. In addition to compiling a record of 23-7 that gave him the league's second-best winning percentage (.767), he threw 22 complete games, tossed five shutouts, and led all AL pitchers with a 1.80 ERA and a WHIP of 1.054, establishing career-best marks in both categories. Gregg's brilliant pitching earned him a 10th-place finish in the league MVP voting, even though the Naps finished well out of contention, 22 games behind the pennant-winning Philadelphia Athletics.

Memorable Moments/Greatest Performances: Gregg turned in the first dominant performance of his career on June 25, 1911, when he allowed just four hits, one walk, and recorded seven strikeouts during a 2-0 victory over the St. Louis Browns.

Courtesy of the Bain News Service Collection at the Library of Congress

Vean Gregg surpassed 20 victories in each of his first three big-league seasons

Gregg compiled nearly identical numbers less than two weeks later, surrendering only four hits and one walk, while striking out four, during a 4-0 win over the Philadelphia A's on July 6.

Gregg pitched equally well on August 27, 1911, when he defeated the Washington Senators by a score of 1-0, surrendering just four hits and two walks, while striking out five during the contest.

Gregg tossed back-to-back three-hitters in June 1912, allowing just three safeties during a 3-1 win over Detroit on the 19th of the month, before duplicating that effort with a 2-1 victory over Chicago four days later.

Gregg hurled another gem later in 1912, allowing just four hits and recording six strikeouts, en route to defeating the Boston Red Sox by a score of 1-0 on July 25.

Gregg threw 32 consecutive scoreless innings from June 11, 1913 to June 22, 1913, defeating Boston, Philadelphia, Washington, and Detroit along the way. The highlight of the streak came on June 14, when he surrendered just four harmless singles during a 3-0 win over the Athletics.

However, Gregg turned in the most dominant performance of his career in a game that didn't even count in the standings. With the Naps facing the Pittsburgh Pirates in a best-of-seven postseason series in the fall of 1913, Gregg tied the series at three games apiece by scattering five singles and striking out 19 batters, including Honus Wagner twice, in winning a 13-inning, 1-0 pitcher's duel with Pittsburgh's Claude Hendrix. Cleveland manager Joe Birmingham and Napoleon Lajoie both called Gregg's outing the greatest game a Cleveland pitcher had ever thrown, including Addie Joss's perfect game and Bob Rhoads's no-hitter. Meanwhile, home plate umpire Bob Emslie said, "I have seen all of the great ones; [Amos] Rusie, [Charles] Radbourne, [Christy] Mathewson; but I am confident that I never saw any pitcher show the stuff that Gregg had." Pirates first baseman Dots Miller added, "I can't understand how anyone ever hits that fellow."

Notable Achievements:

- Won at least 20 games three times.
- Posted winning percentage in excess of .600 four times, finishing with mark above .700 twice.
- Compiled ERA under 2.00 once, finishing with mark under 3.00 two other times.
- Threw more than 250 innings twice.
- Threw more than 20 complete games three times.
- Led AL pitchers in ERA once and WHIP once.
- Finished second in AL in winning percentage once and strikeouts once.
- Ranks among Indians career leaders in ERA (3rd) and winning percentage (2nd).
- Finished 10th in 1911 AL MVP voting.

50

MICHAEL BRANTLEY
2009 – Present

A solid line-drive hitter whose understated manner often causes him to go unnoticed, Michael Brantley has been one of the American League's most overlooked and underappreciated players since he first became a member of the Indians' starting outfield in 2011. En route to compiling a lifetime batting average of .292, Brantley has batted over .300 three times, finishing third in the junior circuit with a career-high mark of .327 in 2014. The left-handed hitting outfielder has also surpassed 20 homers once, 200 hits once, and 40 doubles twice, earning in the process two All-Star selections, one Silver Slugger, and one top-five finish in the AL MVP voting. An excellent defender as well, Brantley holds the Indians' franchise record for most consecutive games without an error by an outfielder, once going an entire season without committing a defensive miscue. Meanwhile, Brantley's career success rate of just under 80 percent on stolen base attempts places him fourth in team annals.

Born in Bellevue, Washington on May 15, 1987, Michael Charles Brantley Jr. grew up around baseball, being the son of former major leaguer Mickey Brantley, who spent four years with the Seattle Mariners during the late 1980s, before playing, coaching, and managing in the minor leagues for several years. Raised in Port St. Lucie, Florida, Brantley Jr. attended Central High School in nearby Fort Pierce, where he starred on the diamond, earning an athletic scholarship from Coastal Carolina University by batting .595, scoring 22 runs, and stealing 32 bases as a high school senior. However, after signing a letter of intent to play baseball for the Chanticleers following his graduation, Brantley decided to turn pro when the Milwaukee Brewers selected him in the seventh round of the 2005 MLB Draft, with the 205th overall pick.

Brantley subsequently spent most of the next four years competing at various levels in Milwaukee's farm system, before being dealt to the Indians on October 3, 2008, as the player to be named later in a trade completed three months earlier that also sent Matt LaPorta, Zach Jackson, and Rob Bryson to Cleveland, in exchange for star hurler C.C. Sabathia. Brantley then spent most of the 2009 campaign with Cleveland's Triple-A farm team in Columbus, Ohio, before joining the Indians when rosters expanded on September 1. Performing well during the season's final month after replacing an injured Grady Sizemore in center field, Brantley batted .313 and knocked in 11 runs, in 28 games and 112 official at-bats. Splitting the following season between Cleveland and Columbus, Brantley appeared in a total of 72 games with the Indians, batting .246, hitting three homers, driving in 22 runs, and scoring 38 others, in just under 300 official at-bats, while once again spending most of his time in center.

Earning a starting job in the Cleveland outfield in 2011, Brantley appeared in 114 games, before missing the final two months of the campaign after undergoing surgery to repair the hamate bone in his right hand. Garnering 451 official at-bats, Brantley hit seven homers, knocked in 46 runs, scored 63 times, stole 13 bases, and batted .266, while splitting his time between left field and center. After laying claim to the starting center field job in 2012, Brantley began the season hitting leadoff for the Tribe, before eventually assuming the cleanup spot in the batting order. Gradually establishing himself as the team's most reliable hitter over the course of the campaign, Brantley batted .288, hit six homers, knocked in 60 runs, scored 63 others, and amassed 37 doubles. He followed that up by hitting 10 homers, driving in 73 runs, scoring 66 times, stealing 17 bases, and batting .284 in 2013. Meanwhile, after being moved back to his more natural position of left field, Brantley went the entire season without committing an error, breaking in the process Rocky Colavito's previous franchise record of 212 straight errorless games by an outfielder (by season's end, Brantley's streak had reached 245 games).

Having already established himself as arguably the Tribe's best all-around player, Brantley emerged as a full-fledged star in 2014, earning his first All-Star selection and a third-place finish in the AL MVP voting by hitting 20 homers, driving in 97 runs, stealing 23 bases in 24 attempts, and ranking among the league leaders with 94 runs scored, 200 hits, 45 doubles, 309 total bases, a batting average of .327, and an OPS of .890. Brantley's 200 safeties made him the first Indians player in 18 years to

Courtesy of Keith Allison

Michael Brantley finished third in the AL MVP in 2014
when he surpassed 20 homers, 20 steals, and 200 hits

reach that milestone, with Kenny Lofton last accomplishing the feat for
the Tribe in 1996.

A hard worker who conducts himself in an extremely professional
manner, Brantley eventually had the nickname "Dr. Smooth" assigned to
him by Cleveland sports writer Dennis Manoloff for his smooth swing
and patient approach at the plate. Rarely offering at the first pitch, Brantley does so only if he has guessed the right location and type of pitch.
Meanwhile, even though the 6'2", 200-pound Brantley has good power, he
employs a short, compact swing that makes him more of a line-drive hitter
who tends to drive the ball to the outfield gaps.

Despite missing the latter stages of the 2015 campaign after injuring his shoulder while making a diving catch, Brantley had another solid
year, finishing the season with 15 home runs, 84 RBIs, 68 runs scored, a
.310 batting average, and a league-leading 45 doubles. After undergoing
surgery during the subsequent off-season, Brantley returned to the Indians
in April 2016. But it soon became apparent that his injury had not healed

properly, forcing him to undergo a second surgery that limited him to only 11 games the entire year.

With Brantley working extremely hard to mount a comeback in 2017, he drew praise from Houston Astros manager A. J. Hinch, who said, "He's such an unheralded player. After missing most of last year, getting Brantley back is like signing a middle-of-the-order bat as a free agent. Just an all-around good hitter."

Indians manager Terry Francona also expressed his admiration for Brantley, stating, "I knew if he didn't come back that it wouldn't be for a lack of trying. He worked so hard last year, and it was tough to see all that effort not pay off for him. I know how hard it was for him to have to sit and watch. Typical of Mikey, he never got down and was a great teammate for the rest of the guys. He's such a competitor, though, that I know it had to hurt."

Francona then added, "Getting him back in name is one thing, but getting him back as the player he was, that's pretty impressive on his part. It's great to have him back because you just write his name on the lineup card and he takes care of the rest."

Although Brantley ended up missing two months this past season due to an assortment of injuries, he performed well whenever he found himself able to take the field, earning his second All-Star selection by hitting nine homers, driving in 52 runs, scoring 47 times, collecting 20 doubles, and batting .299. He will enter the 2018 campaign with career totals of 70 home runs; 452 RBIs; 454 runs scored; 1,019 hits; 212 doubles; 17 triples; and 106 stolen bases; a .292 batting average; a .349 on-base percentage; and a .423 slugging percentage.

Indians Career Highlights:

Best Season: Brantley had easily his finest season in 2014, when he earned his lone Silver Slugger and a third-place finish in the AL MVP voting by establishing career-high marks in virtually every offensive category. In addition to hitting 20 homers, driving in 97 runs, scoring 94 times, amassing 309 total bases, swiping 23 bags, compiling a slugging percentage of .506, and posting an OPS of .890, Brantley placed second in the league with 200 hits, finished third with 45 doubles and a .327 batting average, and ranked fourth with an on-base percentage of .385.

Memorable Moments/Greatest Performances: Brantley led the Indians to a 9-6 win over Detroit on July 7, 3013, by going 3-for-4, with a pair of homers, three runs scored, and a career-high 5 RBIs, with his two-run shot in the bottom of the eighth inning proving to be the game's decisive blow.

Brantley helped pace the Tribe to a resounding 17-7 victory over the Texas Rangers on June 9, 2014, by going 3-for-3, with a homer, a pair of walks, and a career-high five runs scored.

Brantley proved to be the difference in a 7-5 win over the Milwaukee Brewers on July 22, 2015, going 4-for-5, with a homer, double, four RBIs, and two runs scored.

Brantley put an end to a 16-inning marathon with the Yankees on August 11, 2015, giving the Indians a 5-4 win with a walk-off RBI single off New York reliever Branden Pinder.

Brantley had a big day at the plate exactly two weeks later, leading the Indians to an 11-6 win over the Milwaukee Brewers on August 25, 2015, by going 3-for-4, with a pair of homers, four RBIs, and three runs scored.

Brantley again homered twice during a 7-5 win over the Detroit Tigers on September 10, 2015, with his two-run blast in the bottom of the eighth inning providing the margin of victory.

Brantley delivered another game-winning hit on April 11, 2017, when his RBI single in the bottom of the 10th inning gave the Indians a 2-1 walk-off win over the Chicago White Sox.

Notable Achievements:

- Has hit more than 20 home runs once (20 in 2014).
- Has batted over .300 three times, topping the .320-mark once (.327 in 2014).
- Has surpassed 200 hits once (200 in 2014).
- Has surpassed 30 doubles three times, topping 40 two-baggers twice.
- Has stolen more than 20 bases once (23 in 2014).
- Has posted slugging percentage in excess of .500 once (.506 in 2014).
- Led AL with 45 doubles and at-bat-to-strikeout ratio of 10.4 in 2015.

- Finished second in AL with 200 hits in 2014.
- Has finished third in AL in: batting average once, on-base percentage once, and doubles once.
- Led AL outfielders with 1.000 fielding percentage in 2013.
- Ranks fourth in Indians history with career stolen base percentage of 79.70.
- 2014 Silver Slugger winner.
- Finished third in 2014 AL MVP voting.
- Two-time AL All-Star (2014 and 2017).
- 2016 AL champion.

SUMMARY AND HONORABLE MENTIONS

(The Next 25)

Having identified the 50 greatest players in Cleveland Indians history, the time has come to select the best of the best. Based on the rankings contained in this book, the members of the Indians all-time team are listed below. Our squad includes the top player at each position, along with a pitching staff that features a five-man starting rotation, a set-up man, and a closer, whose name I took from the list of honorable mentions that will soon follow. I have listed a second team as well.

Indians First-Team Starting Lineup:

Player:	Position:
Tris Speaker	CF
Napoleon Lajoie	2B
Shoeless Joe Jackson	RF
Manny Ramirez	DH
Earl Averill	LF
Al Rosen	3B
Jim Thome	1B
Lou Boudreau	SS
Sandy Alomar Jr.	C

Indians First-Team Pitching Staff:

Bob Feller	SP
Bob Lemon	SP
Addie Joss	SP
Stan Coveleski	SP
Early Wynn	SP
George Uhle	SU
Cody Allen	CL

Indians Second-Team Starting Lineup:

Player:	Position:
Kenny Lofton	CF
Joe Sewell	SS
Roberto Alomar	2B
Hal Trosky	1B
Albert Belle	DH
Larry Doby	LF
Rocky Colavito	RF
Victor Martinez	C
Ken Keltner	3B

Indians Second-Team Pitching Staff:

Mel Harder	SP
Mike Garcia	SP
Wes Ferrell	SP
Sam McDowell	SP
C.C. Sabathia	SP
Jim Bagby	SU
Doug Jones	CL

Although I limited my earlier rankings to the top 50 players in Indians history, many other fine players have performed for the Tribe over the years, some of whom narrowly missed making the final cut. Following is a list of those players deserving of an honorable mention. These are the men I deemed worthy of being slotted into positions 51 to 75 in the overall rankings. The statistics they compiled during their time in Cleveland and their most notable achievements as a member of the team are also included.

51—Ray Chapman (SS, 1912-1920)

Career Numbers: 17 HR; 364 RBIs; 671 Runs Scored; 1,053 Hits; 162 Doubles; 81 Triples; 238 Stolen Bases; .278 AVG; .358 OBP; .377 SLG PCT; .735 OPS

Notable Achievements:

- Batted over .300 four times.
- Scored more than 100 runs once (101 in 1915).
- Finished in double digits in triples four times.
- Stole more than 20 bases six times, topping 30 thefts three times and 50 thefts once (52 in 1917).
- Led AL in: runs scored once, bases on balls once, sacrifice hits three times, and plate appearances once.
- Finished third in AL in: runs scored once, triples once, and stolen bases once.
- Led AL shortstops in assists once and putouts three times.
- Holds MLB single-season record for most sacrifice hits (67 in 1917).
- Ranks sixth in MLB history with 334 sacrifice hits.
- Holds Indians career record for most sacrifice hits (334).
- Ranks among Indians career leaders in triples (6th) and stolen bases (5th).

52—Luis Tiant (P, 1964-69)

Indians Numbers: 75-64 Record; .540 Win Pct; 2.84 ERA; 63 CG; 21 Shutouts; 12 Saves; 1,200 IP; 1,041 Strikeouts; 1.143 WHIP

Notable Achievements:

- Won 21 games in 1968.
- Posted winning percentage in excess of .700 twice.
- Compiled ERA under 3.00 four times, posting mark under 2.00 once (1.60 in 1968).
- Posted WHIP under 1.000 once (0.871 in 1968).
- Threw nine shutouts in 1968.
- Struck out more than 200 batters twice.
- Threw more than 200 innings three times, tossing more than 250 innings once (258⅓ in 1968).
- Led AL pitchers in ERA once and shutouts twice.
- Finished second in AL in WHIP once and complete games once.
- Finished third in AL in: wins once, winning percentage once, and strikeouts once.
- Holds Indians single-game record for most strikeouts (19 vs. Minnesota Twins on July 3, 1968 for 10 innings).

- Holds Indians single-season record for fewest hits allowed per nine innings pitched (5.295 in 1968).
- Ranks among Indians career leaders in: WHIP (8th), shutouts (9th), and fewest hits allowed per nine innings pitched (4th).
- Threw 42 consecutive scoreless innings in 1968.
- Finished fifth in 1968 AL MVP voting.
- 1968 AL All-Star.

53—Bill Bradley (3B, 1901-1910)

Indians (Naps) Numbers: 27 HR; 473 RBIs; 649 Runs Scored; 1,265 Hits; 238 Doubles; 74 Triples; 157 Stolen Bases; .272 AVG; .317 OBP; .373 SLG PCT; .690 OPS

Notable Achievements:

- Batted over .300 three times, posting mark of .340 in 1902.
- Scored more than 100 runs twice.
- Finished in double digits in home runs once (11 in 1902).
- Finished in double digits in triples three times, topping 20-three baggers once (22 in 1903).
- Surpassed 30 doubles four times.
- Stole more than 20 bases four times.
- Posted slugging percentage in excess of .500 once (.515 in 1902).
- Led AL in sacrifice hits twice.
- Finished second in AL in: home runs once, runs scored once, triples once, total bases once, and slugging percentage once.
- Finished third in AL in: RBIs once, runs scored once, hits twice, doubles twice, and total bases twice.
- Led AL third basemen in: assists once, putouts twice, double plays three times, and fielding percentage four times.
- Ranks among Indians career leaders in: triples (tied-10th), stolen bases (9th), and sacrifice hits (4th).
- Hit home runs in four straight games in 1902.
- Hit for the cycle vs. Washington Senators on September 24, 1903.

54—Herb Score (P, 1955-59)

Indians Numbers: 49-34 Record; .590 Win Pct; 3.17 ERA; 41 CG; 10 Shutouts; 714⅓ IP; 742 Strikeouts; 1.327 WHIP

Notable Achievements:

- Won 20 games in 1956.
- Posted winning percentage in excess of .600 twice.
- Compiled ERA under 3.00 twice.
- Struck out more than 200 batters twice.
- Threw more than 200 innings twice.
- Led AL pitchers in strikeouts twice and shutouts once.
- Finished second in AL in: wins once, winning percentage once, and ERA once.
- Finished third in AL in WHIP once.
- Holds Indians career record for fewest hits allowed per nine innings pitched (6.174).
- Ranks third in Indians history for most strikeouts recorded per nine innings pitched (9.349).
- 1955 AL Rookie of the Year.
- Two-time AL All-Star (1955 and 1956).

55—Jason Kipnis (2B, 2011-Present)

Career Numbers: 88 HR; 389 RBIs; 477 Runs Scored; 886 Hits; 201 Doubles; 21 Triples; 121 Stolen Bases; .268 AVG; .340 OBP; .422 SLG PCT; .762 OPS

Notable Achievements:

- Has hit more than 20 home runs once (23 in 2016).
- Has batted over .300 once (.303 in 2015).
- Has surpassed 40 doubles twice.
- Has stolen more than 30 bases twice.
- Has posted slugging percentage in excess of .500 once (.507 in 2011).
- Has finished second in AL in doubles once and sacrifice flies once.
- Has led AL second basemen in assists once.
- Holds Indians record for most hits in one month (51 in May 2015).
- Two-time AL Player of the Month.
- 2012 AL Wilson Defensive Player of the Year.
- Two-time AL All-Star (2013 and 2015).
- 2016 AL champion.

56—Cody Allen (P, 2012-Present)

Career Numbers: 20-23 Record; .465 Win Pct; 2.67 ERA; 122 Saves; 373⅔ IP; 484 Strikeouts; 1.159 WHIP

Notable Achievements:

- Has surpassed 30 saves three times.
- Has posted winning percentage in excess of .600 twice.
- Has compiled ERA under 3.00 five times.
- Has recorded more strikeouts than innings pitched five times.
- Ranks fourth in Indians history with 122 career saves.
- 2016 AL champion.

57—Charles Nagy (P, 1990-2002)

Indians Numbers: 129-103 Record; .556 Win Pct; 4.51 ERA; 31 CG; 6 Shutouts; 1,942⅓ IP; 1,235 Strikeouts; 1.419 WHIP

Notable Achievements:

- Won 17 games three times and at least 15 games three other times.
- Posted winning percentage in excess of .600 five times.
- Compiled ERA under 3.00 once (2.96 in 1992).
- Threw more than 200 innings six times, tossing more than 250 innings once (252 in 1992).
- Led AL pitchers in assists once and fielding percentage twice.
- Finished second in AL with .773 winning percentage in 1996.
- Finished third in AL in winning percentage once and ERA once.
- Ranks among Indians career leaders in: wins (10th), strikeouts (6th), and starts (6th).
- Two-time AL Pitcher of the Month.
- Finished fourth in 1996 AL Cy Young voting.
- Three-time AL All-Star (1992, 1996, and 1999).
- Two-time AL champion (1995 and 1997).

58—Larry Gardner (3B, 1919-1924)

Indians Numbers: 10 HR; 401 RBIs; 321 Runs Scored; 693 Hits; 128 Doubles; 36 Triples; 22 Stolen Bases; .301 AVG; .365 OBP; .400 SLG PCT; .765 OPS

Notable Achievements:

- Batted over .300 three times.
- Knocked in more than 100 runs twice.
- Scored more than 100 runs once (101 in 1921).
- Finished in double digits in triples twice.
- Surpassed 30 doubles three times.
- Led AL with 154 games played in 1920.
- Led AL third basemen in: assists twice, putouts once, double plays three times; and fielding percentage once.
- 1920 AL champion.
- 1920 world champion.

59—Willis Hudlin (P, 1926-1940)

Indians Numbers: 157-151 Record; .510 Win Pct; 4.34 ERA; 154 CG; 11 Shutouts; 31 Saves; 2,557⅔ IP; 662 Strikeouts; 1.471 WHIP

Notable Achievements:

- Surpassed 17 victories twice and 15 wins three other times.
- Posted winning percentage of .600 three times.
- Threw more than 200 innings six times, tossing more than 250 innings on three occasions.
- Threw 22 complete games in 1929.
- Led AL pitchers in assists twice and putouts once.
- Finished second in AL in innings pitched once and saves twice.
- Finished third in AL in innings pitched once and complete games once.
- Ranks among Indians career leaders in: wins (7th), innings pitched (4th), complete games (7th), and starts (4th).
- Threw 15-inning shutout vs. Philadelphia Athletics on 8/24/35.

60—Carlos Santana (C, 1B, DH, 2010-Present)

Career Numbers: 174 HR; 587 RBIs; 573 Runs Scored; 995 Hits; 236 Doubles; 13 Triples; 40 Stolen Bases; .249 AVG; .365 OBP; .445 SLG PCT; .810 OPS

Notable Achievements:

- Has hit more than 20 home runs five times, topping 30 homers once (34 in 2016).
- Has surpassed 30 doubles four times.

- Has walked more than 100 times twice.
- Has compiled on-base percentage in excess of .400 once (.401 in 2010).
- Led AL with 113 bases on balls in 2013.
- Has finished second in AL in bases on balls twice.
- Has finished third in AL in bases on balls three times.
- Has led AL first basemen in assists once and fielding percentage once.
- Ranks fourth in Indians history with 726 bases on balls.
- 2016 AL champion.

61—Brook Jacoby (3B, 1B, 1984-1991)

Indians Numbers: 120 HR, 524 RBIs, 521 Runs Scored, 1,178 Hits, 192 Doubles, 24 Triples, 14 SB, .273 AVG, .338 OBP, .412 SLG PCT, .750 OPS

Notable Achievements:

- Hit more than 20 home runs twice, topping 30 homers once (32 in 1987).
- Batted over .300 once (.300 in 1987).
- Surpassed 30 doubles once (30 in 1986).
- Posted slugging percentage in excess of .500 once (.541 in 1987).
- Led AL third basemen in putouts once.
- Hit three home runs in one game vs. Chicago White Sox on 7/3/87.
- June 1990 AL Player of the Month.
- Two-time AL All-Star (1986 and 1990).

62—Steve O'Neill (C, 1911-1923)

Indians Numbers: 11 HR; 458 RBIs; 394 Runs Scored; 1,109 Hits; 220 Doubles; 33 Triples; 30 Stolen Bases; .265 AVG; .348 OBP; .341 SLG PCT; .689 OPS

Notable Achievements:

- Batted over .300 three times.
- Surpassed 30 doubles twice.
- Compiled on-base percentage in excess of .400 three times.

- Led AL catchers in: assists twice, double plays five times, and fielding percentage once.
- Finished sixth in 1922 AL MVP voting.
- 1920 AL champion.
- 1920 world champion.

63—Francisco Lindor (SS, 2015-Present)

Career Numbers: 60 HR; 218 RBIs; 248 Runs Scored; 482 Hits; 96 Doubles; 11 Triples; 46 Stolen Bases; .293 AVG; .349 OBP; .474 SLG PCT; .823 OPS

Notable Achievements:

- Has hit more than 30 home runs once (33 in 2017).
- Has batted over .300 twice.
- Has surpassed 30 doubles twice, topping 40 two-baggers once (44 in 2017).
- Has posted slugging percentage in excess of .500 once (.505 in 2017).
- Has led AL in: sacrifice hits once, sacrifice flies once, and at-bats once.
- Finished third in AL with 81 extra-base hits in 2017.
- Has led AL shortstops in double plays once.
- Holds Indians single-season record for most home runs by a shortstop (33 in 2017).
- September 2015 AL Rookie of the Month.
- Finished second in 2015 AL Rookie of the Year voting.
- Finished ninth in 2016 AL MVP voting.
- 2016 Gold Glove winner.
- 2016 AL Platinum Glove winner.
- 2017 Silver Slugger winner.
- Two-time AL All-Star (2016 and 2017).
- 2016 AL champion.

64—Bartolo Colon (P, 1997-2002)

Indians Numbers: Record: 75-45; .625 Win Pct; 3.92 ERA; 15 CG; 6 Shutouts; 1,029⅔ IP; 873 Strikeouts; 1.363 WHIP

Notable Achievements:

- Won 18 games once and at least 14 games three other times.
- Posted winning percentage in excess of .600 four times.

- Compiled ERA under 3.00 once (2.55 in 2002).
- Struck out more than 200 batters twice.
- Threw more than 200 innings three times.
- Finished second in AL in: wins once, winning percentage once, strikeouts once, and shutouts once.
- Ranks among Indians career leaders in winning percentage (7th) and strikeouts per nine innings pitched (10th).
- Two-time AL Pitcher of the Month.
- Finished fourth in 1999 AL Cy Young voting. 1998 AL All-Star.
- 1997 AL champion.

65—Luke Easter (1B, 1949-1954)

Career Numbers: 93 HR; 340 RBIs; 256 Runs Scored; 472 Hits; 54 Doubles; 12 Triples; .274 AVG; .350 OBP; .481 SLG PCT; .830 OPS

Notable Achievements:

- Hit more than 25 home runs three times, topping 30 homers once (31 in 1952).
- Knocked in more than 100 runs twice.
- Batted over .300 once (.303 in 1953).
- Posted slugging percentage in excess of .500 once (.513 in 1952).
- Finished second in AL with 31 home runs in 1952.
- 1952 *Sporting News* AL Player of the Year.

66—Mike Hargrove (1B, OF, 1979-1985)

Indians Numbers: 33 HR, 383 RBIs, 388 Runs Scored, 860 Hits, 139 Doubles, 14 Triples, 14 SB, .292 AVG, .396 OBP, .382 SLG PCT, .778 OPS

Notable Achievements:

- Batted over .300 three times.
- Drew more than 100 bases on balls twice.
- Compiled on-base percentage in excess of .400 three times.
- Posted slugging percentage in excess of .500 once (.500 in 1979).
- Led AL with .424 on-base percentage in 1981.
- Finished third in AL with 111 bases on balls in 1980.

- Led AL first basemen in assists once and putouts once.
- Ranks ninth in Indians history with .396 career on-base percentage.

67—Doug Jones (P, 1986-1991, 1998)

Indians Numbers: 27-34 Record; .443 Win Pct; 3.06 ERA; 129 Saves; 452⅓ IP; 367 Strikeouts; 1.227 WHIP

Notable Achievements:

- Saved more than 30 games three times, topping 40 saves once (43 in 1990).
- Compiled ERA under 3.00 three times, finishing with mark under 2.50 twice.
- Finished third in AL in saves twice.
- Ranks second in Indians history with 129 career saves.
- Three-time AL All-Star (1988, 1989, and 1990).

68—Buddy Bell (3B, OF, 1972-78)

Indians Numbers: 64 HR, 386 RBIs, 462 Runs Scored, 1,016 Hits, 155 Doubles, 27 Triples, 24 SB, .274 AVG, .328 OBP, .382 SLG PCT, .710 OPS

Notable Achievements:

- Finished second in AL with 631 at-bats in 1973.
- Led AL third basemen in: assists once, putouts twice, and double plays twice.
- 1973 AL All-Star.

69—Johnny Allen (P, 1936-1940)

Indians Numbers: 67-34 Record; .663 Win Pct; 3.65 ERA; 60 CG; 9 Shutouts; 6 Saves; 929⅔ IP; 505 Strikeouts; 1.341 WHIP

Notable Achievements:

- Won 20 games once (1936) and at least 14 games two other times.
- Posted winning percentage in excess of .600 three times.
- Compiled ERA under 3.00 once (2.55 in 1937).
- Threw 19 complete games in 1936.
- Threw more than 200 innings twice.

- Led AL pitchers with .938 winning percentage in 1937.
- Finished second in AL in ERA once and strikeouts once.
- Finished third in AL in: wins once, ERA once, and shutouts once.
- Holds Indians single-season record for highest winning percentage (.938 in 1937).
- Ranks third in Indians history with .663 career winning percentage.
  1937 *Sporting News* Major League Player of the Year.
- 1938 AL All-Star.

70—Terry Turner (SS, 3B, 2B, 1904-1918)

Indians (Naps) Numbers: 8 HR; 521 RBIs; 692 Runs Scored; 1,472 Hits; 204 Doubles; 77 Triples; 254 Stolen Bases; .254 AVG; .310 OBP; .320 SLG PCT; .630 OPS

Notable Achievements:

- Batted over .300 once (.308 in 1912).
- Finished in double digits in triples once (14 in 1905).
- Stole more than 25 bases four times, topping 30 thefts once (31 in 1910).
- Led AL with 38 sacrifice hits in 1914.
- Finished second in AL in sacrifice hits once and games played once.
- Finished third in AL with 14 triples in 1905.
- Led AL shortstops in: assists once, double plays twice, and fielding percentage twice.
- Led AL third basemen in double plays once and fielding percentage twice.
- Holds Indians career record for most games played (1,619).
- Ranks among Indians career leaders in: hits (10th), triples (9th), stolen bases (3rd), plate appearances (7th), and at-bats (3rd).

71—Jhonny Peralta (SS, 3B, 2003-2010)

Indians Numbers: 103 HR, 456 RBIs, 477 Runs Scored, 906 Hits, 201 Doubles, 16 Triples, 9 SB, .264 AVG, .329 OBP, .422 SLG PCT, .751 OPS

Notable Achievements:

- Hit more than 20 home runs three times.

- Scored more than 100 runs once (104 in 2008).
- Surpassed 30 doubles three times, topping 40 two-baggers once (42 in 2008).
- Posted slugging percentage in excess of .500 once (.520 in 2005).
- Finished fifth in AL with 104 runs scored in 2008.
- Led AL shortstops in assists once and putouts once.
- Holds Indians career record for most home runs by a shortstop (103).

72—Sonny Siebert (P, 1964-69)

Indians Numbers: 61-48 Record; .560 Win Pct; 2.76 ERA; 33 CG; 8 Shutouts; 9 Saves; 991 IP; 786 Strikeouts; 1.090 WHIP

Notable Achievements:

- Won 16 games twice.
- Posted winning percentage in excess of .600 twice.
- Compiled ERA under 3.00 four times, finishing with mark under 2.50 twice.
- Posted WHIP under 1.000 once (0.981 in 1965).
- Threw more than 200 innings twice.
- Led AL with strikeouts-to-walks ratio of 4.152 in 1965.
- Finished second in AL in WHIP twice.
- Finished third in AL in: winning percentage once, ERA twice, and WHIP once.
- Ranks among Indians career leaders in WHIP (3rd) and fewest hits allowed per nine innings pitched (3rd).
- Threw no-hitter vs. Washington Senators on June 10, 1966.
- 1966 AL All-Star.

73—Shin-Soo Choo (OF, 2006-2012)

Indians Numbers: 83 HR, 372 RBIs, 389 Runs Scored, 736 Hits, 162 Doubles, 19 Triples, 85 SB, .292 AVG, .383 OBP, .469 SLG PCT, .853 OPS

Notable Achievements:

- Hit more than 20 home runs twice.
- Batted over .300 three times.

- Surpassed 30 doubles three times, topping 40 two-baggers once (43 in 2012).
- Stole more than 20 bases three times.
- Compiled on-base percentage in excess of .400 once (.401 in 2010).
- Posted slugging percentage in excess of .500 once (.549 in 2008).
- Led AL outfielders with 14 assists in 2010.
- Hit three home runs in one game vs. Kansas City Royals on 9/17/10.
- September 2008 AL Player of the Month.

74— Jose Mesa (P, 1992-98)

Indians Numbers: 33-36 Record; .478 Win Pct; 3.88 ERA; 104 Saves; 4 CG; 1 Shutout; 647⅓ IP; 447 Strikeouts; 1.361 WHIP

Notable Achievements:

- Saved more than 30 games twice, topping 40 saves once (46 in 1995).
- Posted winning percentage of 1.000 in 1995.
- Compiled ERA under 3.00 twice, posting mark under 2.00 once (1.13 in 1995).
- Threw more than 200 innings once (208⅔ in 1993).
- Led AL with 46 saves and 57 games finished in 1995.
- Finished second in AL with 39 saves in 1996.
- Holds Indians single-season record for most saves (46 in 1995).
- Ranks fifth in Indians history with 104 saves.
- Set major-league record (since broken) by successfully converting 38 consecutive save opportunities in 1995.
- 1995 *Sporting News* AL Fireman of the Year.
- 1995 Rolaids AL Relief Man of the Year.
- Finished fourth in 1995 AL MVP voting.
- Finished second in 1995 AL Cy Young voting.
- Two-time AL All-Star (1995 and 1996).
- Two-time AL champion (1995 and 1997).

75—Jim Hegan (C, 1941-42, 1946-1957)

Indians Numbers: 90 HR; 499 RBIs; 526 Runs Scored; 1,026 Hits; 171 Doubles; 45 Triples; 15 Stolen Bases; .230 AVG; .299 OBP; .349 SLG PCT; .648 OPS

Notable Achievements:

- Led AL catchers in: putouts three times, assists three times, double plays three times, fielding percentage twice, and caught stealing percentage three times.
- Five-time AL All-Star (1947, 1949, 1950, 1951, and 1952).
- Ranks fourth in Indians history in games played (1,526).
- Holds Indians record for most games played as a catcher (1,491).
- Two-time AL champion (1948 and 1954).
- 1948 world champion.

GLOSSARY

Abbreviations and Statistical Terms

AVG. Batting average. The number of hits divided by the number of at-bats.

CG. Complete games pitched.

CL. Closer.

ERA. Earned run average. The number of earned runs a pitcher gives up, per nine innings. This does not include runs that scored as a result of errors made in the field and is calculated by dividing the number of runs given up, by the number of innings pitched, and multiplying the result by 9.

HITS. Base hits. Awarded when a runner safely reaches at least first base upon a batted ball, if no error is recorded.

HR. Home runs. Fair ball hit over the fence, or one hit to a spot that allows the batter to circle the bases before the ball is returned to home plate.

IP. Innings pitched.

OBP. On-base percentage. Hits plus walks plus hit-by-pitches, divided by plate appearance.

RBI. Runs batted in. Awarded to the batter when a runner scores upon a safely batted ball, a sacrifice or a walk.

RUNS. Runs scored by a player.

SB. Stolen bases.

SLG PCT. Slugging percentage. The number of total bases earned by all singles, doubles, triples and home runs, divided by the total number of at-bats.

SO. Strikeouts.

SP. Starting pitcher.

SU. Set-up reliever.

WIN PCT. Winning percentage. A pitcher's number of wins divided by his number of total decisions (i.e. wins plus losses).

BIBLIOGRAPHY

Books:

DeMarco, Tony, et al. *The Sporting News Selects 50 Greatest Sluggers.* St. Louis: The Sporting News, a division of Times Mirror Magazines, Inc., 2000.

Linkugel, Wil A. *They Tasted Glory: Among the Missing at the Baseball Hall of Fame.* McFarland, and Company, Jefferson, NC, 1998.

Shalin, Mike, and Neil Shalin. *Out by a Step: The 100 Best Players Not in the Baseball Hall of Fame.* Lanham, MD: Diamond Communications, Inc., 2002.

Thorn, John, and Pete Palmer, eds. *Total Baseball.* New York: Harper-Collins Pub., Inc., 1993.

Williams, Ted. *Ted Williams' Hit List.* Indianapolis, IN: Masters Press, 1996.

Videos:

Ritter, Lawrence and Bud Greenspan. *The Glory of their Times.* Cappy Productions, Inc., 1985.

The Sporting News' 100 Greatest Baseball Players. National Broadcasting Co., 1999.

Internet Websites:

Baseball Almanac, Inc. "The Ballplayers: A Baseball Player Encyclopedia." Last modified 2005. http://www.baseball-almanac.com/players/baseball_biographies.shtml.

BaseballChronology.com. "TSN-ALL-Stars." Last modified 2005. http://www.baseballchronology.com/Baseball/Awards/TSN-AllStars.asp.

BaseballLibrary.com. *The Ballplayers.* http://www.baseballlibrary.com/baseballlibrary/ballplayers.

MLB Advanced Media. "Historical Stats." Last modified January 20, 2016. http://www.mlb.com/stats.historical/individual_stats/player.

Retrosheet.org. "The Players." http://www.retrosheet.org/boxesetc/index.
    html#Players.

Society for American Baseball Research. "SABR Baseball Biography
    Project." Last modified November 12/2016. .

Sports Reference, LLC. "Players." Last modified October 9, 2017. http://
    www.baseball-reference.com/players.

Sports Reference, LLC. "Teams." Last modified October 9, 2017. http://
    www.baseball-reference.com/teams.